NEWCOMER'S HANDBOOK®

FOR MOVING TO AND LIVING IN

New York City

Including Manhattan,
Brooklyn, The Bronx,
Queens, Staten Island,
and Northern New Jersey

20th Edition

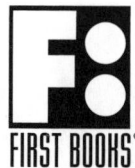

FIRST BOOKS®

6750 SW Franklin
Portland, OR 97223
503-968-6777
www.firstbooks.com

20th edition

Newcomer's Handbook® and First Books® are registered trademarks of First Books.

Editor: Bernadette Duperron
Publisher: Jeremy Solomon
Contributors: Belden Merims, Jennifer Cecil, Chris Hornsby
Cover and interior design, composition: Erin Johnson Design
Transit map courtesy of the MTA. Used with permission.

Published by First Books®, 6750 SW Franklin Street, Portland, OR 97223-2542, 503-968-6777, www.firstbooks.com.

ISBN 0-912301-56-2
ISSN 1535-4415

Printed in the USA on recycled paper.

What readers are saying about Newcomer's Handbooks:

I recently got a copy of your Newcomer's Handbook for Chicago, and wanted to let you know how invaluable it was for my move. I must have consulted it a dozen times a day preparing for my move. It helped me find my way around town, find a place to live, and so many other things. Thanks.

—Mike L.
Chicago, Illinois

Excellent reading (Newcomer's Handbook for San Francisco and the Bay Area) ... balanced and trustworthy. One of the very best guides if you are considering moving/relocation. Way above the usual tourist crap.

—Gunnar E.
Stockholm, Sweden

I was very impressed with the latest edition of the Newcomer's Handbook for Los Angeles. It is well organized, concise and up-to-date. I would recommend this book to anyone considering a move to Los Angeles.

—Jannette L.
Attorney Recruiting Administrator for a large Los Angeles law firm

I recently moved to Atlanta from San Francisco, and LOVE the Newcomer's Handbook for Atlanta. It has been an invaluable resource—it's helped me find everything from a neighborhood in which to live to the local hardware store. I look something up in it everyday, and know I will continue to use it to find things long after I'm no longer a newcomer. And if I ever decide to move again, your book will be the first thing I buy for my next destination.

—Courtney R.
Atlanta, Georgia

In looking to move to the Boston area, a potential employer in that area gave me a copy of the Newcomer's Handbook for Boston. It's a great book that's very comprehensive, outlining good and bad points about each neighborhood in the Boston area. Very helpful in helping me decide where to move.

—no name given (online submit form)

TABLE OF CONTENTS

CONTENTS

INTRODUCTION

THIS BOOK IS DEDICATED TO THE PROPOSITION THAT LIVING IN New York City is something extraordinary and wonderful. However, the transition from newcomer to New Yorker isn't necessarily achieved without some discomfort. To minimize the difficulties involved in moving to the Big Apple, we have written the Newcomer's Handbook® for Moving to and Living in New York City, which has been continually updated since its 1980 inception, in order to keep up with change in this fastest-paced of cities.

This is the second edition of this book since the tragedy of September 11th, 2001 shook the city and the world. For many months after the devastating attack on the World Trade Center in lower Manhattan, New Yorkers remained in a state of disbelief. While the city will continue to bear the emotional scars of 9/11, today, New York City is once again flourishing. So, whether you are looking for the right neighborhood, the right health club, the right synagogue or simply a quiet, green oasis, these chapters will guide you in your search.

The 1990s brought a boom in two pillars of the New York economy: the stock market and tourism. These resurgent industries, plus a lower crime rate and an upbeat feeling created a tight real estate market, especially in the more desirable neighborhoods. While a softened economy in 2001 brought an easing of rents, the rental market has tightened, and the quest for a good, affordable apartment is once again difficult, though not impossible. Use this handbook as a tool in that quest and in making your life in New York more rewarding once you've landed.

In addition to regular updating, this 20th edition includes new information on renting or buying a home in the **Finding a Place to Live** chapter, as well as a survey of services for seniors and information for immigrant newcomers in **Helpful Services**, and a guide to moving in the **Moving and Storage** chapter. Throughout the book, wherever available, we've included web sites for institutions and establishments that are mentioned. There is information on getting around the city by subway, bus, bike, and by car in the **Transportation** chapter. For the outdoorsy and nature loving, you'll find the **Greenspaces** chapter helpful, and for the active and athletic, check the **Sports and Recreation** chapter.

As usual, we welcome readers' suggestions and comments on the tear-out page at the back of the book.

We hope that the information presented on the following pages will help you establish a New York City residence smoothly and speedily. We also hope that once you select your neighborhood and settle in, the book will help you get on with the pleasure part: enjoyment of the city's myriad and unrivaled resources. Should you have any city specific queries, from questions about parking, trash pick-up, or upcoming neighborhood festivals, dial the city's call center at 311 (outside New York City, 212-639-9675). Operators are on 24/7 and work to answer your questions or will direct you to the appropriate New York City agency. Or go to www.nyc.gov.

F ROM THE WIND-WHIPPED CORNER OF EAST END AVENUE ON AN ICY January evening, Greenwich Village seems as accessible as Alaska. So, you cancel plans to meet a Village acquaintance downtown, call a friend on East 67th and get together at an uptown bistro instead. Clearly, the neighborhood in which you live affects what you do and whom you see in New York City. The cachet of shared space in the Upper East Side (or another of Manhattan's established communities) usually has more allure for the neophyte than space of one's own in the boroughs or a recently gentrified enclave. It takes time, familiarity with the city, and a certain street-honed sophistication to be totally at ease in distant or just-emerging districts. Still, unless money is no object, today's rental market often requires compromises, not only in the way you live but also in the neighborhood you choose. But wherever you settle, once established, you're likely to become rooted in your own special area.

New Yorkers are indeed neighborhood proud. More than just an address or a source of necessary services, neighborhoods provide residents with identification and a sense of belonging, which in turn provides sufficient sustenance and heart for daily confrontations with the city's size and pace. Most New Yorkers feel fairly chauvinistic about their area and delight in extolling its virtues—and its faults. As large as New York City is, individual neighborhoods are often as tight-knit as small towns.

In the following profiles, Manhattan neighborhoods are listed clockwise (picture an exceedingly elongated clock) starting with Yorkville, continuing south along the East River downtown around the tip of the island and then uptown along the Hudson ending with Washington Heights/Inwood. Descriptions of communities in The Bronx, Brooklyn, Queens, and Staten Island, as well as five in New Jersey follow Manhattan. No description, however, can substitute for your own experience. You are strongly encouraged to visit the neighborhoods that interest you and talk to residents before signing a lease. (Among other things, it is an excellent way to get leads on apartments that might otherwise escape your attention.) Resources and city services within each neighborhood are included in order to facilitate orientation once you're settled.

For newcomers who might wish to look further afield, to the suburbs for example, we have listed additional communities worth investigating in Brooklyn, Queens, and Staten Island, as well as suburban towns in New Jersey, Connecticut, Westchester County, NY, and Long Island, none more than an hour's commute from Manhattan. Your choice of location will depend largely on where you will be working, your life situation (single, married, family, gay, etc.), your economic situation, what you enjoy doing, and what neighborhood ambiance appeals to you. Suggestions on how to go about finding an apartment or house and how best to enjoy the city come after **Neighborhoods** in **Finding a Place to Live** and in other sections.

FORMULAS FOR FINDING STREET AND AVENUE ADDRESSES ABOVE 14th Street are described below. Crosstown street numbers follow a more-or-less set pattern; not so, avenue street numbers. In a town where 950 Amsterdam Avenue is at 107th Street, 950 Broadway at 23rd, 950 Fifth at 76th, and 950 Third at 57th, the somewhat elaborate system used to discover the location of an avenue address is worth knowing.

EAST AND WEST SIDE AVENUES

To determine the cross street for an address on an avenue, proceed as follows: first, take off the last digit of the building number; second, divide the remainder by two; third, add or subtract the number given in the column below.*

Avenues A,B,C,D	+ 3
1st Ave.	+3
2nd Ave.	+3
3rd Ave.	+10
4th Ave.	+8
5th Ave.	
Up to 200	+13
Up to 400	+16
Up to 600	+18
Up to 775	+20
From 775 to 1286	
(cancel last figure)	−18
6th Ave.	
(Ave. of the Americas)	−12
7th Ave.	
Below 110th St.	+12
Above 110th St.	+20
8th Ave.	+10
9th Ave.	+13
10th Ave.	+14
Amsterdam Ave.	+60
Broadway	
Above 23rd St.	−30
Columbus Ave.	+60
Convent Ave.	+127
Lenox Ave.	+110
Lexington Ave.	+22
Madison Ave.	+26
Manhattan Ave.	+100
Park Ave.	+35
West End Ave.	+60

EAST SIDE CROSSTOWN STREETS

5th to Madison & Park	1-99
Park to Lexington	100-139
Lexington to 3rd	140-199
3rd to 2nd	200-299
2nd to 1st	300-399
1st to York	400-499

WEST SIDE CROSSTOWN BELOW 58TH

5th to Ave. of Americas	1-99
Ave. of Americas to 7th	100-199
7th to 8th	200-299
8th to 9th	300-399
9th to 10th	400-499
10th to 11th	500-599

WEST SIDE CROSSTOWN ABOVE 58TH

Central Park West to Columbus	100-199
Columbus to Amsterdam	200-299
Amsterdam to West End	300-399
West End to Riverside	400-499

*Central Park West and Riverside Drive do not fit into this formula. Divide the house number by 10 and add 60 to find the cross street on Central Park West; for Riverside Drive, divide the house number by 10 and add 72.

MANHATTAN
Left: North Manhattan
Right: South Manhattan

MANHATTAN

"New York, New York, it's a wonderful town, The Bronx is up and the Battery's down," goes the song. That'll do for a start. Like the rest of the world, when New Yorkers say New York they generally mean Manhattan. And from Manhattan, The Bronx is up (north), and the Battery is the southern-most tip of this long, skinny island. To navigate Manhattan you need to know that the island is plotted out in a grid, with crosstown streets running east and west, and avenues stretching north and south, except below 14th Street, where much of the street pattern becomes irregular. Fifth Avenue bisects most of this grid, with cross streets designated east or west. For example, West 25th Street runs west of Fifth Avenue, East 25th stretches east from Fifth. Building numbers begin at Fifth, so 15 West 25th Street is on the first block west of Fifth Avenue and 15 East 25th Street is the block east of Fifth Avenue. North to south there are 20 city blocks to a mile; cross town blocks are longer, but not uniformly. The longest avenue in Manhattan, and the oldest, Broadway follows an old Indian trail from the Battery up north through the top of the island into The Bronx. Unlike the other avenues, it crosses from the east side to the west side as it winds its way along.

YORKVILLE

Boundaries and Contiguous Areas: **North**: East 96th Street and East Harlem; **East**: East River; **South**: East 79th Street and Upper East Side; **West**: Lexington Avenue and Upper East Side

What distinguished Yorkville from its Upper East Side surroundings until recently was the character imbued by immigrants from Germany and Eastern Europe. Now, however, you'll find more co-op signs and health clubs than residents of Hungarian or Czechoslovakian ancestry. In the 1980s, a co-op, condo, and rental apartment boom finished off what World War II started: the erosion of Yorkville's old-world ethnicity. Although you will still find some old walkups on cross streets in the east 80's, most of these pre-war buildings were leveled, beginning in the late 1940s, to make way for new apartment buildings attractive to professionals who, once drawn to the neighborhood, began replacing the immigrants in the remaining railroad flats. Only traces of Yorkville's European heritage remain, and while Yorkville is still the most accessible part of the Upper East Side, what began as a scattering of stolid brick apartment buildings in mid-century is now an area chockablock with a range of high-rises.

Eighty-sixth Street, from Lexington to First avenues, has been attempting to redefine itself into a pricier shopping strip. However, the hoped for stability has not entirely materialized. Most of the shopping choices along the well-traveled 86th Street are currently of the chain store variety, including well-known fast food eateries and popular electronics retailers. Several multi-plex cinemas also have sprung up and draw the younger set for the latest hit films.

Yorkville was a pleasant rural community when the first wave of German and Irish immigrants arrived on these shores in the 1850s. Tranquil pastures surrounded river estates owned by wealthy merchants, many of whom were of German origin. In the 1880s the completion of the Second and Third Avenue elevated lines opened the area to settlement, and German immigrants, many attracted by jobs in the developing breweries, moved north from the Lower East Side. Irish immigrants followed and then, as they grew more prosperous, Hungarians, Czechs, and Slovaks. Today, the second and third generations are more likely to be found in Queens and Westchester than in Yorkville, and it is a dwindling, elderly Middle European population that patronizes the few remaining ethnic bakeries, butcher shops, and restaurants. Not that these stores are empty; customer ranks have been swelled by appreciative young professionals who now dominate the area.

The inviting mix of buildings, old and new, that characterizes Yorkville, as well as the community's relatively low crime rate, upper middle class status, and good public schools, makes it an attractive destination for the determined apartment seeker. After a slow-down in the early 1990s, housing construction is again active, with luxury rentals rising between East 86th and 96th streets. Variations in pricing for housing will be determined by proximity to the only Upper East Side subway that runs up and down Lexington Avenue; the closer you are the more your rent will be. According to a recent article from the *New York Times*, good deals on housing can be found on First, Second, and York avenues, perhaps because of the many bars lining those streets, especially First and Second.

For a refreshing pause, explore Carl Schurz Park bordering the East River at 86th Street and East End Avenue, where you can also spy the mayor's residence, graceful Gracie Mansion built in 1799. Jutting over F.D.R. Drive, this relatively green oasis recalls Yorkville of yore and affords a spectacular view of the East River, its islands, boats, and barges. The charm of this park is that other than neighborhood residents, most New Yorkers don't know it's there, allowing for more elbowroom in an often-crowded city. Astors, Rhinelanders, and Schermerhorns once had their estates here, and this quiet neighborhood is still Yorkville's most coveted roost and home to two of the city's best private girls' schools, not to mention the Asphalt Green sports/community center and adjacent AquaCenter.

While the upscale new apartment towers continue to attract a tide of young professionals to the upper northeast reaches of Yorkville, many of the older, six story redbrick buildings and the more affordable tall towers are now also attracting many families. It's not uncommon to see parents or nannies pushing strollers and kids pointing to the child-inspired goods displayed in store windows. The gentrification of so many other parts of the city combined with the vast number of buildings that have been built here over the past twenty years has made it considerably easier to find apartments in Yorkville and the adjacent Upper East Side.

Web Sites: www.nyc.gov, www.newyorkmetro.com/realestate
Area Codes: 212, 646
Post Offices: Yorkville Station, 1617 Third Avenue (at 91st Street), NYC 10128; Gracie Station, 229 East 85th Street, NYC 10028, 800-275-8777
Zip Codes: 10128, 10028, 10021
Police Precinct: Nineteenth, 153 East 67th Street, NYC 10021, 212-452-0600
Emergency Hospitals: Mt. Sinai Hospital, Fifth Avenue at 100th Street, NYC 10029, 212-241-6500; Metropolitan Hospital Center, 1901 First Avenue, NYC 10029, 212-423-6262; Beth Israel Medical Center—North Division, 170 East End Avenue, NYC 10128, 212-870-9197
Libraries: 96th Street Branch, 112 East 96th Street, NYC 10128, 212-289-0908, Yorkville Branch, 222 East 79th Street, NYC 10021, 212-744-5824; www.nypl.org
Public School Education: School District #2 in region 9 (see **Chelsea**).
Community Resources: 92nd Street Y (Young Men's and Young Women's Hebrew Association), 1395 Lexington Avenue, NYC 10128, 212-427-6000, www.92y.org (also see **Upper East Side**).
Transportation—Subway: #4, #5, #6 Lexington Avenue at 96th Street, 86th Street (Exp.), 77th Street, 68th Street, 59th Street (Exp.)
Transportation—Bus: Crosstown 96th Street (#96); Crosstown 86th Street (#86); Crosstown 79th Street (#79); Uptown First Avenue - Downtown Second Avenue (#15); Uptown Third Avenue - Downtown Lexington Avenue (#98, #101, #102)

UPPER EAST SIDE

Boundaries and Contiguous Areas: North: East 96th Street; **East**: the East River; **South**: 59th Street; **West**: Fifth Avenue

The affluent heart of the Upper East Side—that quadrant caught between Fifth, 79th, Lexington, and 59th Street and the panhandle stretching from 79th along Fifth to 96th Street—has landmark status. But this does not mean that Manhattan's most popular neighborhood for the wealthy and the upwardly mobile is completely homogeneous. Each avenue that traverses the area, from Fifth east to York, has a distinctive character all its own. Fifth Avenue, flanking Central Park, glitters with some of the city's most magnificent museums, most exclusive cooperatives, and some of its most glamorous relics, those wonderfully ornate mansions that so clearly reflect the tastes and fortunes of our turn-of-the-century millionaires. Fricks, Dukes, Carnegies, Whitneys—their versions of palaces, chateaux, and Gothic castles established the avenue as highly fashionable. Dominating Fifth physically and artistically in the East 80s, the Metropolitan Museum is also the site of one of the liveliest street scenes in town. Its sprawling stone steps, while providing access to the museum, offer seats and a meeting place from which to watch the mimes, musicians, and street vendors who use the sidewalk around the entrance as performing space.

Madison Avenue between 60th and 86th streets is a veritable gauntlet of classy international boutiques and fine arts galleries. This solid wall of chic includes The Limited, Ralph Lauren, Timberland, and Barneys. Around 81st Street and P.S. 6 (Public School #6), the premier elementary school on the Upper East Side, a number of trendy designers have set up shop. Above 86th Street, where Andrew Carnegie built the elaborate mansion that now houses the Cooper-Hewitt Museum, most of the other palatial beaux-arts residences constructed in the early 1900s have been acquired by schools, consulates, and cultural institutions. Today these grand buildings, interspersed with bow-fronted, brick Georgian homes and solid pre-World War II apartment buildings, form an exceedingly harmonious neighborhood.

On Park, the handsome center strip of year-round greenery and seasonal plantings make the stately square cooperative buildings that proceed shoulder to elegant shoulder up the avenue more gracious still.

Lexington Avenue has largely taken over from Madison as purveyor of quality produce to Upper East Siders. Immaculate, and imaginative, shops harboring fishmongers and florists, greengrocers and bakers are crowded into the ruddy, rustic brick buildings that line the street.

The area from Third Avenue east to the river, once the province of the "el" train and tenements, has been "Trumped up." Today, sleek glass and granite shafts intersperse postwar brick apartment blocks that loom over the once characteristic, and now disappearing, five-story walkups. Popular eateries featuring ethnic fare—Chinese, Thai, Greek, Italian, Indian—line the avenues, and turn-of-century buildings once aimed at young professional singles are now home to many young professional parents. The multitude of strollers and busy youngsters cramming into St. Catherine's Park (playground) between 67th and 68th streets on First Avenue, is testimony to the baby boom that is in full swing on the Upper East Side. The proliferation of apartments, and gentrification of other neighborhoods, plus an increase in what are considered "safe" parts of town, has made living in this area more accessible than in previous years. As realtors explain it, the Upper East Side is still a terrific neighborhood and has not changed much in the past two decades. However, unlike 20 years ago, there are now other excellent neighborhoods to be found throughout Manhattan, so the waiting lists to get into apartments in the Upper East Side have lessened. That said, however, the Upper East Side's luxury co-ops and condominiums are some of the most expensive in the city, and with the recent upward turn in the economy, prices are now reaching the price peaks of 1999. According to the *New York Times*, in 2004 the average prices for a high-end apartment in the Upper East Side was $7.2 million, $7.7 for a townhouse.

Web Sites: www.uppereast.com, www.uppereastside.about.com, www.decny.com/cb8, www.nyc.gov

Area Codes: 212, 646

Post Offices: Lenox Hill Station, 217 East 70th Street, NYC 10021; nearby, Gracie Station, 229 East 85th Street, NYC 10028; 800-275-8777

Zip Codes: 10128, 10028, 10021, 10022

Police Precinct: Nineteenth, 153 East 67th Street, NYC 10021, 212-452-0600

Emergency Hospitals: Lenox Hill Hospital, 100 East 77th Street, NYC 10021, 212-434-2000; New York Presbyterian Hospital-Cornell Medical Center, 525 East 68th Street, NYC 10021, 212-746-5454; Manhattan Eye, Ear and Throat Hospital, 210 East 64th Street, NYC 10021, 212-838-9200; nearby: Mt. Sinai Hospital, Fifth Avenue at 100th Street, NYC 10029, 212-241-6500

Libraries: 96th Street Branch, 112 East 96th Street, NYC 10128, 212-289-0908; Webster Branch, 1465 York Avenue between 77th and 78th streets, NYC 10021, 212-288-5049; 67th Street Branch, 321 East 67th Street, 212-734-1717; www.nypl.org; The New York Society Library, 212-288-6900, www.nysoclib.org, a private institution, with membership dues of $175 per year and 250,000 volumes, it is an outstanding resource; located at 53 East 79th Street, NYC 10021.

Public School Education: School District #2 in region 9 (see **Chelsea**).

Adult Education: Marymount Manhattan College, 221 East 71st Street, NYC 10021, 212-517-0400; Hunter College, 695 Park Avenue at 68th Street, NYC 10021, 212-772-4000

Community Resources: 92nd Street Y (Young Men's and Women's Hebrew Association) 1395 Lexington Avenue, NYC 10128, 212-415-5500, www.92y.org; the Cooper-Hewitt Museum, 2 East 91st Street, 212-849-8400, www.ndm.si.edu; the Jewish Museum, 1109 Fifth Avenue at 92nd Street, 212-423-3200, www.jewishmuseum.org; the

Solomon Guggenheim Museum, 1071 Fifth Avenue at 89th Street, 212-423-3500, www.guggenheim.org; the Whitney Museum of American Art, 945 Madison Avenue at 75th Street, 212-570-3676, www.whitney.org; the Metropolitan Museum of Art, Fifth Avenue at 82nd Street, 212-535-7710 for recorded information, 212-879-5500 for assistance, www.metmuseum.org; the Frick Collection, 1 East 70th Street, 212-288-0700, www.frick.org; The Asia Society, 725 Park Avenue (at 70th Street) 212-517-ASIA, www.asiasociety.org; the China Institute, 125 East 65th Street, 212-744-8181, www.chinainstitute.org; Society of Illustrators, 128 East 63rd Street, 212-838-2560, www.society illustrators.org, and numerous other societies, museums, galleries and auction houses.

Transportation—Subway: #4, #5, #6 Lexington Avenue at 96th Street, 86th Street (Exp.), 77th Street, 68th Street, 59th Street (Exp. and transfer to the R & N trains) Lexington Avenue at 63 rd Street to Queens (F) to Roosevelt Island (B,Q)

Transportation—Bus: Crosstown 96th Street (#96); Crosstown 86th Street (#86); Crosstown 79th Street (#79); Crosstown 72nd Street (#72); Crosstown 66th/67th Street (#66); Crosstown 57th Street (#28); Crosstown 57th & 72nd (#30); Crosstown 57th & Uptown/Downtown on York Avenue (#31), Uptown Madison Avenue - Downtown Fifth Avenue (#1, #2, #3, #4)

ROOSEVELT ISLAND

Located off of 59th Street in the East River

Roosevelt Islanders have always had an unusual commute: a silent aerial ride to and from 59th Street and Second Avenue in Manhattan (every 5 to 15 minutes for $1.50) up and over the East River with the city's skyline first at eye level and then, incredibly, beneath your feet. Small wonder that the tram finds favor with tourists and day-trippers. Residents used to be reduced to taking cabs or a roundabout bus ride through Queens to Manhattan when the tram occasionally faltered. Now, however, the city's Transit Authority has a subway line (the Q train) connecting the island with Queens (at 21st Street and 41st Avenue) and Manhattan (at 63rd and Lexington Avenue).

An appealing small-town quality pervades this island community of modern apartment buildings. It's quiet. Automobile access is limited, and a red minibus (25¢) provides regular service between the tram terminal and high rises lining relatively spotless streets where strolls with baby carriages and street corner chats are ritual—a sort of time zip back to the 1940s.

Several spacious parks, six historical landmarks, a waterfront Promenade and unparalleled views of the Manhattan skyline highlight life on this 147-acre island. Roosevelt Island has extensive recreational facilities and shops that supply the basic needs, if not the exotic or ethnic ones. Built by early farmers in 1796, the Manor House is preserved at the foot of Main Street. The Octagon Lighthouse is now restored. Schools go up to the eighth grade and are part of District #2 (information in the **Chelsea** section).

Inauguration of the long-awaited subway line in 1989 was accompanied by **Manhattan Park's** five-building development on an eight-acre site, which added 1,100 units to the housing stock and some 2,500 inhabitants to the island's population, which is now 8,000 people. Manhattan Park attracts upper middle class families (no studios) with stunning views and concierge service at prices about 25% below comparable Manhattan rents. Northtown, Island House, Westview, Eastwood, and Rivercross are all housing developments providing a wide array of apartments for middle- to upper-income families. **Southtown** is the newest series of high-rises, with two buildings completed and five more planned. Contact the Roosevelt Island Development Corporation for more information: 212-832-4540, www.rioc.com. While residents enjoy the peaceful, low-crime character of this narrow two-and-a-half-mile island, some are concerned that the island is beginning to get too crowded. Drawbacks? Despite the marvelous views of Manhattan, which sits just a stone's throw away, there is still limited access when commuting back and forth.

Manhattan Park buildings are managed by Grenadier Realty Corporation, 212-759-8660, www.manhattanpark.com. The Roosevelt Island Housing Management Corporation, 212-838-4747, at 552 Main Street manages the rental units and subsidized apartments (for which there are specified income limits) in Westview, Eastwood, and Island House; Rivercross Tenants Corporation, the island's only co-ops, can be reached at 212-308-7271.

Note: If you own a dog, Roosevelt Island isn't for you; dogs are *verboten* on the island.

Web Sites: www.rooseveltisland.us, www.rioc.com, www.decny.com/cb8, www.nyc.gov

Area Codes: 212, 646

Post Office: Island Post Office, 694 Main Street, Post Office Information, 800-275-8777

Zip Code: 10044

Police Precinct: One Hundred and Fourteenth, 34-16 Astoria Boulevard, Astoria 11103, 718-626-9311

Emergency Hospital: Goldwater Memorial Hospital, Roosevelt Island, 212-318-4315, www.nychac.org

Library: Roosevelt Island Community Library, 524 Main Street, NYC 10044, 212-308-6243, www.nypl.org

Public School Education: School District #2 in region 9 (see **Chelsea**).

Community Resources: The Chapel of the Good Shepherd Community Center, 543 Main Street, Roosevelt Island 11103, 212-832-6778, built in 1888, this old chapel now serves the island as an active community center; Youth Programs Inc., 506 Main Street, Roosevelt Island 10044, 212-935-3645, offers various classes for children; Main Street Theatre & Dance Alliance, 548 Main Street, Roosevelt Island 10044, 212-371-4449, features performances and offers classes in theater, dance, yoga and aerobics for kids and adults.

Transportation—Tramway (59th Street and Second Avenue); **Bus**: Queens (Q32); **Subway**: Manhattan 63rd Street & Lexington Avenue (B, Q)

EAST FORTIES AND FIFTIES

Boundaries and Contiguous Areas: **North**: 59th Street and the Upper East Side; **East**: East River; **South**: 42nd Street and Murray Hill; **West**: Lexington Avenue

In 1763, when James Beekman built a summer home called Mount Pleasant on the rural landscape that is now the bustling corner of 51st Street and First Avenue, it's unlikely he could have imagined the value this property would eventually command. With steady growth and development, by the late 18th century this urbane neighborhood was known as Turtle Bay Farm. The mid-19th century brought industrialization and the "el" or elevated subway trains, rumbling over tenements built along the East River. A construction boom in the 1920s left the heart of **Turtle Bay** much as you see it today: handsome, tree-shaded blocks of carefully maintained brownstones interspersed with relatively small apartment buildings. But not until the 1940s, when the squalid slaughterhouses that had replaced the riverside slums were razed to make room for the United Nations, and the 1950s, when the "el" came tumbling down, did Turtle Bay become eminently respectable from Lexington Avenue clear to the East River. Today the neighborhood is one of the most prestigious—and one of the safest—in town; a self-assured place with charming cul-de-sacs such as Amster Yard on 49th Street, Greenacre Park on 51st and the private, somewhat secret, garden enclosed by twenty Italianate townhouses in which Katharine Hepburn and E.B. White once lived.

Apartment prices, as befits a neighborhood embracing exclusive Sutton Place, Beekman Place, the two glass towers at United Nations Plaza, and the latest and tallest Trump tower, are among the highest around. For the least rarefied rates look along First and Second avenues and the side streets in between.

Tudor City lies southwest of Sutton Place. Bounded by 40th and 43rd streets, this huge complex of Tudor-style buildings between First and Second avenues includes a hotel, church, and private parking area. Unfortunately for would-be tenants, eleven of the twelve buildings completed in 1930 have been converted to cooperatives.

The opening, in 1999, of the long awaited Bridgemarket in the extraordinary Gustavino-tile-vaulted hall beneath the Queensborough Bridge at 59th Street, between First and York avenues, is probably the most exciting development in this otherwise sedate neighborhood since the building of the UN. Designed originally in 1914 as an open-sided marketplace, but left dormant for many years, the 24 to 44 foot-high domed ceilings house a market-style food emporium, two restaurants, and a high-end Conran home furnishings store. Predictably, the completion of this project has stimulated new residential development in the neighborhood. A half-mile to the south, Donald Trump's 72-story Trump World Tower is making its own waves—not to mention casting a long shadow—throughout the area.

Web Sites: www.nyc.gov, www.tudorcity.com
Area Codes: 212, 646
Post Office: Tudor City Station, 5 Tudor City Place, NYC 10017; 800-275-8777
Zip Codes: 10022, 10017, 10016
Police Precinct: Seventeenth, 167 East 51st Street, NYC 10022, 212-826-3211
Emergency Hospitals (nearest): New York Presbyterian Hospital-Cornell Medical Center, 525 East 68th Street, NYC 10021, 212-746-5454; New York University Hospital and Medical Center, 550 First Avenue, Between 30th and 33rd streets, NYC 10016, 212-263-7300
Libraries (nearest): 58th Street Branch, 127 East 58th Street, NYC 10022, 212-759-7358; Mid-Manhattan, 455 Fifth Avenue, NYC 10016, 212-340-0833; www.nypl.org
Public School Education: School District #2 in region 9 (see **Chelsea**).
Adult Education: Turtle Bay Music School, 244 East 52nd Street, NYC 10022, 212-753-8811
Community Resources: Young Men's Christian Association of Greater New York, Vanderbilt Branch, 224 East 47th Street, NYC 10017, 212-756-9600; YWCA of the City of New York, 610 Lexington Avenue, NYC 10022, 212-755-2700, www.ywcanyc.org; Japan Society, 333 East 47th Street, NYC 10017, 212-752-3015, www.japansociety.org; Phillip Morris branch of the Whitney Museum of American Art at Altria, 120 Park Avenue, NYC 10017, 917-663-2453, www.whitney.org

Transportation—Subway: Crosstown 42nd Street Shuttle (S), Lexington Avenue; Crosstown (#7) Lexington/Third Avenues; Uptown/Downtown #4, #5, #6 Lexington Avenue at 59th Street (Exp.), 51st Street, 42nd Street (Exp.), Downtown/Queens at Lexington & 53rd Street (V)

Transportation—Bus: Crosstown 49th/50th streets (#27, #50); Crosstown 42nd Street (#42); Uptown Madison Avenue - Downtown 5th Avenue (#1, #2, #3, #4); Uptown Third Avenue - Downtown Lexington Avenue (#101, #102, #103); Uptown First Avenue - Downtown Second Avenue (#15)

MURRAY HILL

Boundaries and Contiguous Areas: North: 42nd Street and the East Forties and Fifties; **East**: East River; **South**: 34th Street and the Gramercy Park Area; **West**: Fifth Avenue

Murray Hill is the kind of neighborhood where you can walk into a compact, ground-floor apartment, open a back door and have access to a garden larger than the flat. Time was when the great mansions of Fifth and Madison avenues—lastingly elegant buildings such as J.P. Morgan's magnificent McKim, Mead, and White-designed library—conferred social status on the houses highest on the hill. Below these were the stables and carriage houses serving them, and in the shadow of the old Third Avenue "el," tenements. The tenements are gone now, and as Fifth Avenue became more commercial, residential Murray Hill shifted east and the carriage houses proved to be fashionable—indeed, charming—homes. The streets are a mix of tranquil landmarks such as Sniffen Court, a private mews at 150-158 East 36th Street, nondescript brick apartment buildings, postmodern fantasies such as the undulating, 57-story Corinthian, and brownstones: solid and unpretentious turn-of-the-century buildings that are nonetheless elegant and lend a particularly substantial quality to city life.

The neighborhood takes its name from a Quaker merchant, Robert Murray, who built a farmhouse at what is now the corner of 37th Street and Park Avenue. Grand Central Station stands on what was his cornfield. Murray's wife and daughters played a minor role in the Revolutionary War by detaining General Howe and his officers at tea while Washington and his troops escaped their pursuit. Among the historic buildings in the area is the slender brownstone at 125 East 36th Street where Franklin and Eleanor Roosevelt first lived. An active neighborhood association guards the quiet residential character of Murray Hill.

University and Bellevue Hospitals and related New York University medical facilities are a major presence just to the south, and the casual, inviting shops and restaurants crowding Second and Third avenues play to a youthful audience. Housing possibilities include proliferating high rises on the flatlands east of Third as well as brownstones and carriage houses on Murray Hill itself.

Web Sites: www.murrayhill.org, www.nyc.gov

Area Codes: 212, 646

Post Office: Murray Hill Station, 115 East 34th Street, NYC 10016, 800-275-8777

Zip Code: 10016

Police Precinct: Seventeenth, 167 East 51st Street, NYC 10022, 212-826-3211

Emergency Hospitals (nearest): New York University Hospital & Medical Center, 550 First Avenue (Between 30th and 33rd streets), NYC 10016, 212-263-7300; Bellevue Hospital Center, 462 First Avenue (at 27th Street), NYC 10016, 212-562-4141

Libraries: Kips Bay Branch, 446 Third Avenue, NYC 10016, 212-683-2520, www.nypl.org; New York Public Library's Science, Industry, and Business Library (SIBL), 188 Madison Avenue at 34th Street, NYC 10017, 212-592-7000; Pierpont Morgan Library, 29 East 36th Street, NYC 10016, 212-685-0008, www.morganlibrary.org, an exquisite edifice housing an extraordinary collection of rare books, including three Gutenberg Bibles, manuscripts, and works of art.

Public School Education: School District #2 in region 9 (see **Chelsea**).

Adult Education: American Academy of Dramatic Arts, 120 Madison Avenue, NYC 10016, 212-686-9244, www.aada.ny.org; Stern College, Yeshiva University, 245 Lexington Avenue at 35th Street, NYC l0016, 212-340-7700, www.yu.edu

Community Resources: Murray Hill Neighborhood Association, 36 East 36th Street, NYC 10016, 212-886-5867, www.murrayhill.org

Transportation—Subway: Crosstown 42nd Street Shuttle (S), Lexington Avenue; Crosstown & Queens (#7), Lexington/Third Avenues; Uptown/Downtown #4, #5, #6 Lexington Avenue at 42nd Street (Exp.), 33rd Street

Transportation—Bus: Crosstown 34th Street (#16, #34); Uptown Madison Avenue - Downtown Fifth Avenue (#1, #2, #3, #4); Uptown Third Avenue - Downtown Lexington Avenue (#101, #102); Uptown First Avenue - Downtown Second Avenue (#15)

GRAMERCY PARK AREA

Boundaries and Contiguous Areas: North: 34th Street and Murray Hill; **East**: First Avenue and Stuyvesant Area; **South**: East 14th Street; **West**: Park Avenue South/Chelsea and the Flatiron District

The actual park, and namesake of the neighborhood, Gramercy Park, is a verdant, block-square, fenced and locked enclave to which only residents of the surrounding buildings hold keys. With its lovely old trees, squirrels, flowering spring plantings and the occasional nanny, the park is reminiscent of a quiet London square. But it wasn't the work of a homesick Brit; a real estate developer wanting to increase the value of his 66 lots laid out the private park in 1831. That this strategy was successful is evidenced by the quality of the ornate later-19th century buildings that still surround the square—elaborate structures such as The Players Club (Edwin Booth's former home) and the National Arts Club (designed in a Gothic Revival style by Calvert Vaux).

The air of dignified elegance which permeates Gramercy Park and sets such a pleasant tone for the neighborhood as a whole is reinforced by historic Stuyvesant Square (located four blocks to the southeast at 15th Street) with its lovely brick Friends Meeting House and brownstone St. George's Church, where J.P. Morgan worshipped. In general, this is an enclave of small townhouses and rows of trim brickfronts interspersed with renovated tenements, modest apartment houses and an occasional high-rise.

North of the park, the **Kips Bay** neighborhood, stretching from Lexington Avenue to the East River, houses a fairly middle-class populace, including medical personnel from the hospitals along First Avenue, in corner high-rises and side-street brownstones. Subsidized rental complexes include the highly desirable **Waterside** between 23rd and 28th streets, overlooking the East River, and **Henry Phipps Plaza** along Second Avenue in the 20s.

To the west, Lexington Avenue in the 20s, redolent with the spices of the Indian restaurant strip known locally as "Curry Hill" (a play on adjacent Murray Hill), is recently gentrified. Apartment buildings there have been upgraded, making the area worth a look. Convenient take-out is a bonus.

Renovation of the once-again handsome Madison Square Park and Union Square Park has coincided with the resurgence of Park Avenue South as a commercial market and a dining destination, attracting residents, many from the fashion and publishing fields, to newly available housing. On Second Avenue, and in the 20s and low 30s, new condos have sprouted like field mushrooms after a fall rain. The newly renovated Union Square Park is filled with business types lunching on warm days.

As this area increases in popularity, available apartments become scarcer. The most desirable, overlooking Gramercy Park, are expensive and vacancies are rare. You will have a better chance in one of the newer high rises in the east 20s. In any event, the Gramercy area is neighborly, although busy, with a healthy community presence. Area safety is assisted by the presence of young police cadets in training, and by the police station on 21st Street. As is the case throughout the city, it's a good idea to walk through the community talking with doormen, building superintendents, and, if possible, residents when searching for an apartment here.

Web Site: www.nyc.gov

Area Codes: 212, 646

Post Offices: Murray Hill Station, 115 East 34th Street, NYC 10016; Madison Square Station, 149 East 23rd Street, NYC 10010; 800-275-8777

Zip Codes: 10016, 10010, 10003

Police Precincts: Seventeenth (above 30th Street), 167 East 51st Street, NYC 10022, 212-826-3211; Thirteenth, 230 East 21st Street, NYC 10010, 212-477-7411

Emergency Hospitals (nearest): New York University Hospital Medical Center, 560 First Avenue (between 30th and 33rd streets), NYC 10016, 212-263-7300; Bellevue Hospital Center, First Avenue at 27th Street, NYC 10016, 212-562-4141; Cabrini Medical Center, 227 East 19th Street, NYC 10003, 212-995-6000, www.cabrininy.org; Beth Israel Medical Center, 16th Street at First Avenue, NYC 10003, 212-420-2000

Libraries: Kips Bay Branch, 446 Third Avenue, NYC 10016, 212-683-2520; Epiphany Branch, 228 East 23rd Street, NYC 10010, 212-679-2645; www.nypl.org

Public School Education: School District #2 in region 9 (see **Chelsea**).

Adult Education: School of Visual Arts, 209 East 23rd Street, NYC 10010, 212-592-2000, www.schoolofvisualarts.edu; Baruch College of Adult and Continuing and Professional Studies, 17 Lexington Avenue, Registration Room 910, NYC 10010, 212-802-5600, www.baruch.cuny.edu

Community Resources: Theodore Roosevelt House, 28 East 20th Street, NYC 10003, between Broadway and Park Avenue South, 212-260-1616, www.trthegreatnewyorker.com; Roosevelt's exuberantly Victorian birthplace contains letters, books and objects collected from his many trips contained in this two house gallery and museum.

Transportation—Subway: Crosstown 14th Street/Brooklyn (L) at Union Square, Brooklyn/Uptown-West Side/Queens (R, N, W) at Union Square, Third Avenue; #4, #5, #6 Uptown/Downtown, Lexington Avenue at 33rd Street, 28th Street, 23rd Street, 14th Street/Union Square (Exp.)

Transportation—Bus: Crosstown 34th Street (#16, #34); Crosstown 23rd Street (#23); Crosstown 14th Street (#14); Uptown Madison Avenue - Downtown Fifth Avenue (#1, #2, #3, #4); Uptown Third Avenue - Downtown Lexington Avenue (#101, #102); Uptown First Avenue - Downtown Second Avenue (#15)

STUYVESANT TOWN AND PETER COOPER VILLAGE

Boundaries and Contiguous Areas: **North**: 23rd Street; **East**: FDR Drive; **South**: 14th Street and the East Village; **West**: First Avenue and Gramercy Park Area

Today, two of the oldest and best known properties in New York City, **Stuyvesant Town**, 14th to 20th streets, and its upscale (larger apartments and rents) little brother, **Peter Cooper Village**, 20th to 23rd streets, are easier to penetrate. Major renovation of many formerly rent-regulated apartments has opened the door to new tenants. While, with over 11,000 apartments in the two enclaves, the process of complete deregulation is expected to take a couple of decades, market-rate apartments are now available for those who meet the income requirements. What makes these developments so desirable is their resolutely middle-class, family-oriented population, complete with 15 playgrounds and grassy areas tucked away within. Both developments, with their full-time security force, remain safe, and—after 50 years' growth of trees, flowers, ivy and climbing hydrangea against the red brick walls—they are unpretentious and attractive. Apply at the renting office for both developments at the Peter Cooper Management Office, at 332 First Avenue (between 19th and 20th Streets), NYC 10009, 212-780-1100, or visit www.pcvst.com.

The community surrounding Peter Cooper and Stuyvesant includes luxury buildings as well as owner-occupied brownstones and upgraded tenements. When scouting the area (First Avenue west to Lexington), try the side streets. The neighborhood is a comparison shopper's dream, with major supermarkets and many ethnic food stores (especially south on First Avenue), clothing shops and decorating showrooms along First and Second avenues vying for your dollars. The nearby 14th Street and Union Square area covers you for electronics, books (Barnes & Noble) and toys (Toys R Us). There are large, quiet, tree-shaded parks for breaks between apartment visits, and in warm weather the renovated public swimming pool at 23rd Street and Asser Levy Place is available for a cooling few laps. (In fact, look for this turn-of-the-century stone, Roman bath, even if you can't swim; it's a beauty.) And if you are, like so many people, concerned about available health care, this neighborhood, with five top hospitals within walking distance, merits serious consideration.

Web Sites: www.nyc.gov, www.pcvst.com
Area Codes: 212, 646
Post Offices: Peter Stuyvesant Station, 432 East 14th Street, NYC 10009; Madison Square Station, 149 East 23rd Street, NYC 10010; 800-275-8777
Zip Codes: 10010, 10009
Police Precinct: Thirteenth, 230 East 21st Street, NYC 10010, 212-477-7411
Emergency Hospitals: New York University Hospital Medical Center, 560 First Avenue (Between 30th and 33rd Streets), NYC 10016, 212-263-7300; Bellevue Hospital Center, First Avenue at 27th Street, NYC 10016, 212-562-4141; Cabrini Medical Center, 227 East 19th Street, NYC 10003, 212-995-6000, www.cabrininy.org; Beth Israel Hospital Medical Center, 16th Street and First Avenue, NYC 10009, 212-420-2000
Libraries: Epiphany Branch, 228 East 23rd Street, NYC 10010, 212-679-2645; Kips Bay Branch, 446 Third Avenue, NYC 10016, 212-683-2520; www.nypl.org
Public School Education: School District #2 in region 9 (see **Chelsea**).
Adult Education: School of Visual Arts, 209 East 23rd Street, NYC 10010, 212-592-2000, www.schoolofvisualarts.edu; Baruch College of Continuing & Professional Education, 17 Lexington Avenue, Registration, Room 910, NYC 10010, 212-802-5600, www.baruch.cuny.edu
Transportation—Subway: Crosstown 14th Street (L) at Lexington Avenue, Third Avenue, First Avenue; #4, #5, #6 Lexington Avenue at 23rd Street, 14th Street/Union Square (Express and local service)
Transportation—Bus: Crosstown 34th Street (#16) goes across 34th Street and down Second Avenue, then east across 23rd Street and uptown to 34th Street along F.D.R. Drive; Crosstown 23rd Street (#26); Crosstown 14th Street (#14); Uptown First Avenue - Downtown Second Avenue (#15)

EAST VILLAGE

Boundaries and Contiguous Areas: **North**: 14th Street and the Stuyvesant Area; **East**: East River; **South**: Houston Street and the Lower East Side; **West**: Broadway and Greenwich Village

Once again, this colorful neighborhood is in the process of reinventing itself. Time was when it was best described as the upper Lower East Side, both geographically and socio-economically. But sometime in the 1960s, perhaps in an attempt to bestow a bit of cachet, this largely immigrant neighborhood with an emerging avant-garde colony was dubbed the East Village. Attracted by low rents, a lively arts scene and street life, boutiques, and a burgeoning restaurant and club life, college students flocked east, followed by young professionals. In the 1980s, it became one of the most desirable alternative neighborhoods in town. An ethnic population, which includes Italians, Poles, Ukrainians and Latinos, along with the bakeries, butcher shops, restaurants, and cultural institutions they nurtured, adds diversity as well as depth to the neighborhood.

The retaking of **Alphabet City**— avenues A, B, and C east of First Avenue (D is still a little shaky)—from the control of drug dealers and junkies has been a major factor in the further gentrification of the East Village. "There are still some rough blocks," says one realtor, "but it has changed from a low-income neighborhood to a trendy, hip area for young people." Rents have escalated as tenements are upgraded, and new buildings have shot up, condos and co-ops included, to attract a wider range of populace. In the middle of it all, a nicely restored Tompkins Square remains the East Village's leafy back yard. You'll still find a bevy of characters in the East Village, some are throwbacks to the spiked, leather-clad scene that characterized the late 1980s and early '90s, and others sport the latest in piercings and tattoos. Although the area still remains thick with a variety of artists and thespian types, there are more families in the area. Some innovative public schools have recently evolved to serve the influx of children into the neighborhood. The focus at P.S. 363, on East 3rd Street, is on learning in a non-competitive environment, and P.S. 364 on East 6th Street, known as the Earth School, offers studies with an ecological bent and innovative teaching/learning opportunities.

To the west, the Astor Place area bubbles with student life centered around Cooper Union and nearby NYU, the ever-lively Joseph Papp Public Theater, and good buys in books, booze, and youthful clothing along Broadway. Connecting Astor Place with the Second Avenue heart of the East Village is St. Mark's Place, actually part of 8th Street, where hippies and flower children once frolicked, and W.H. Auden lived. Today St. Mark's runs to the tawdry side, with cheap hat and t-shirt stands, and plenty of tourists and teenagers filling the streets. Old and worn brownstone apartments have been torn down to make way for bland apartment complexes. Nearby however, on East Seventh, Ninth, and Stuyvesant streets, clusters of Japanese restaurants, shops, and saki bar/cafes offer variety, catering to the area's young Japanese ex-pats. A small ethnic enclave, sometimes referred to as Little India, runs along Sixth Street, between First and Second avenues.

To the south, the area between the Bowery and Broadway, where Vanderbilts and Astors once lived, has re-acquired a bit of its old chic—if not its elegance—and the tag **NoHo** (for **No**rth of **Ho**uston Street). Clubs, cafes, and restaurants abound, attracting upscale singles and the hip, and while there's a rapid turnover of conventional rentals and walk-ups, they don't come cheap. Plan to walk for groceries; there's nary a supermarket. Spacious lofts in the brick and cast-iron industrial buildings fetch lofty prices, but much of NoHo is legally reserved for certified artists. Prospective residents should check with the City Loft Board, 212-788-7610, to determine their eligibility and to be sure the particular building is in compliance with city loft laws.

Perhaps the next happening neighborhood in the area will be the new self-contained development called Cooper Square. The NYC Department of Housing Preservation & Development (HPD), in conjunction with community leaders, elected officials, and city agencies, has worked hard to solidify a plan since 2000 to build mixed income housing between East Houston Street and East Fourth Street, along Second Avenue. Finally, after much debate, in November 2003 construction began on the 712-unit development that will include 150,000 square feet of commercial retail space.

Although condo conversions are increasing in the East Village, be prepared for walk-ups, as most of the housing stock consists of improved tenements. Start your apartment search by studying ads in *The Village Voice*, check Cooper Union and NYU bulletin boards, or walk the streets and talk to people who live there.

Web Site: www.nyc.gov

Area Codes: 212, 646

Post Offices: Cooper Station, 93 Fourth Avenue, NYC 10003; Peter Stuyvesant Station, 432 East 14th Street, NYC 10009; Tompkins Square Station, 244 East Third Street, NYC 10009; 800-275-8777

Zip Codes: 10003, 10009

Police Precinct: Ninth, 321 East Fifth Street, NYC 10003, 212-477-7811

Emergency Hospitals: Beth Israel Hospital Medical Center, 16th Street and First Avenue, NYC 10009, 212-420-2000; New York Eye and Ear Infirmary, 310 East 14th Street, NYC 10003, 212-979-4000

Libraries: Ottendorfer Branch, 135 Second Avenue, NYC 10003, 212-674-0947 (Between St. Marx and Ninth streets); Tompkins Square Branch, 331 East 10th Street, NYC 10009, 212-228-4747; www.nypl.org

Public School Education: School District #1 in region 9, 333 7th Avenue, NYC 10001, 212-356-7500, www.nycenet.edu

Adult Education: Third Street Music School Settlement, 235 East 11th Street, NYC 10003, 212-777-3240

Community Resources: La Mama Experimental Theater Club, 74A East Fourth Street, 212-475-7710, www.lamama.org, on the cutting edge of avant-garde theater for over two decades; PS (Performing Space) 122, 150 First Avenue, 212-477-5288, www.ps122.org, is a reclaimed public school featuring an array of performers; Joseph Papp Public Theater, 425 Lafayette Street, 212-260-2400, www.publictheater.org, founded in 1954 and home to plays, musicals, and Shakespeare; the Classic Stage Company has been successfully producing classics for more than 35 years at 136 East 13th Street, 212-677-4210, www.classic stage.org; Third Street Music School (see above) offers concerts and recitals; Cooper Union, 51 Astor Place, 212-353-4195, has frequent exhibits, concerts and lectures; theater and opera thrive even on the Bowery: classics at the Jean Cocteau Repertory at 330 Bowery, 212-677-0060, and Italian opera at The Amato Opera Theater at 319 Bowery, 212-228-8200.

Transportation—Subway: Crosstown & Brooklyn 14th Street (L) at Union Square, Third Avenue, First Avenue; Uptown/Downtown at 14th Street/Union Squar (#6 Exp.), Astor Place and Bleecker Street; Broadway/Lafayette Street and Houston Street/Second Avenue (F); Uptown, Brooklyn, and Queens at 14th Street/Union Square and 8th Street/Broadway (R, N)

Transportation—Bus: Crosstown 14th Street (#14); Crosstown East-West 8th/9th Streets (#8) Uptown Third Avenue/Lexington - Downtown Lexington/Third Avenue (#101, #102); Uptown First Avenue - Downtown Second Avenue (#15); Crosstown East-West Houston Street (#M21)

LOWER EAST SIDE, LITTLE ITALY AND CHINATOWN

Boundaries and Contiguous Areas: **North**: Houston Street and the East Village; **East**: East River; **South**: Downtown; **West**: Broadway and SoHo

"Give me your tired, your poor..." wrote Emma Lazarus, and when they arrived, many of them settled on the Lower East Side. Between 1870 and 1920, wave upon wave of immigrants from Italy, China, and the ghettos of Eastern Europe poured into the warren of then fetid tenements on Mulberry, Elizabeth, Hester, and Division streets. Here many lived and worked until able to move up and out to the suburbs or more spacious quarters in other boroughs, leaving room for the next wave. Others remained, and many generations have grown up in this neighborhood that defined what coming to America was all about.

Public housing, especially along the easternmost strip of the Lower East Side, alleviated some of the crowding and let in some light and air, and along Grand Street, from Essex to the river, 28 co-op buildings provided affordable housing for the middle class. The Grand Street co-ops now sell at market rates their previous owners could not have imagined. Renewal began along the fringes, where the young and impecunious—artists, students and the like—established beachheads. Formerly vacant tenements have been renovated, attracting a more affluent crowd. Along East Houston (pronounced how-ston) and grungy Ludlow Street, clubs, trendy restaurants, and boutiques are unmistakable signs of gentrification. Nonetheless, an old-fashioned community spirit pervades the Lower East Side, and many long-time tenants still pay much lower rents then newcomers to this area.

There are actually three Lower East Side neighborhoods, each very distinctive and all crowded with shops and restaurants lining narrow streets and scarce parking. To the east is the old Jewish **Lower East Side**, now largely Latino and Chinese; **Chinatown** is in the southwest portion, which continues to expand inexorably northward into the third area, **Little Italy**. Colorful Orchard Street is still chockablock with little stores and Yiddish-speaking shopkeepers, many of them Hasidim, although much of the once vibrant Jewish community is gone, and forlorn old synagogues have been converted into churches or are used for other purposes. Some of the buildings above the shops, formerly vacant, now house young professionals in $3,000-a-month studios, and antique shops and young designer boutiques have crept in among the dusty menswear shops.

A wave of recent arrivals has burst **Chinatown's** traditional seams past East Broadway into the old Jewish enclave and north over Canal Street into Little Italy, which is now two-thirds Asian. Housing is impossibly crowded, and sweatshops can still be found. But walking the almost impassable sidewalks of Chinatown on a Saturday, one would think this area existed solely to satisfy the city's insatiable appetite for Chinese food.

Little Italy, between Canal and Houston streets, has a vanishing Italian population but an expanding selection of Italian restaurants and cafes. Along Mulberry Street on a warm spring evening, the combined hisses of uncountable cappuccino machines sound like a locomotive gathering steam. The neighborhood seems destined to become a restaurant district. And although frozen dim sum take the place of frozen ravioli in innumerable small stores, a bit of the old Southern Italian character remains, as does the community's reputation as a don't-mess-with-us, low-crime neighborhood with strong ethnic ties around the old, original St. Patrick's on Mulberry Street. On the northern edge of Little Italy, galleries, boutiques, and cafes are filling the once-vacant storefronts, and the neighborhood has acquired the name **Nolita** (for **No**rth of **Li**ttle **Ita**ly).

Infiltration of the Lower East Side by the middle class is no longer news. In 1984, intrepid souls brave enough to sign leases on The Bowery, Rivington, or Pitt streets were featured in the *New York Times*. Most notably, the refurbished Police Building at 240 Centre Street, a granite Renaissance Revival palazzo built in 1909, reopened with crystal chandeliers and 54 luxury condos behind a statuary-cluttered facade in the heart of Little Italy. Rents in the neighborhood move ever upward and apartment listings are sparse. Those considering a rental here would do best to talk to someone who lives in the neighborhood and to walk around, looking, block by block, as one can be quite different from the next in tone and character.

Web Site: www.nyc.gov

Area Codes: 212, 646

Post Offices: Knickerbocker Station, 128 East Broadway, NYC 10002; Chinatown Station, 6 Doyers Street, NYC 10013; 800-275-8777

Zip Codes: 10012, 10013, 10002

Police Precincts: Fifth, 19 Elizabeth Street, NYC 10013, 212-334-0711; Seventh, 19 1/2 Pitt Street, NYC 10002, 212-477-7311

Emergency Hospital (nearest): New York Downtown Hospital, 170 William Street, NYC 10038, 212-312-5000

Libraries: Hamilton Fish Park Branch, 415 East Houston Street, NYC 10002, 212-673-2290; Seward Park Branch, 192 East Broadway, NYC 10002, 212-477-6770; www.nypl.org

Public School Education: School District #1 and #2 in region 9, 333 7th Avenue, NYC 10001, 212-356-7500, www.nycenet.edu

Community Resources: The Henry Street Settlement offers a variety of resources, including its Abrons Arts Center and Settlement Playhouse at 466 Grand Street, NYC 10002, 212-598-0400, www.henrystreet.org. The New Federal Theatre, at 292 Henry Street, NYC 10002, 212 353-1176, www.newfederaltheatre.org, specializes in minority dramas and has been a staple of the neighborhood for nearly 35 years. The Lower East Side Tenement Museum, 90 Orchard Street, NYC 10002, 212-431-0233, www.tenement.org, includes exhibits in three buildings (one of which has been "unrestored" to illustrate life as it was) as well as neighborhood walking tours. The Museum of Chinese in the Americas, 70 Mulberry Street, NYC 10013, 212-619-4785, www.moca-nyuc.org, offers historical walking tours as well as exhibits and video documentaries.

Transportation—Subway: Uptown/downtown #6 Lafayette Street at Spring Street, Canal Street (Exp.); Brooklyn, Uptown & Queens (F and V at Houston/Second Avenue, Delancey Street; Brooklyn, Uptown, Queens (N, R, W) at Broadway and Canal; Brooklyn & Downtown J, M, Z at Canal, Bowery and Essex Street

Transportation—Bus: Crosstown Houston Street (#21); Uptown First Avenue - Downtown Second Avenue (#15); Uptown Bowery/Third Avenue - Downtown Third Avenue/Bowery (#101, #102)

DOWNTOWN

Boundaries and Contiguous Areas: North: Chambers Street and Tribeca; **East:** East River; **South:** Upper New York Bay; **West:** Hudson River

The downtown section of Manhattan Island, also known as lower Manhattan, was the scene of the worst terrorist attacks ever on American soil. The destruction of the World Trade Center on September 11, 2001 left its mark on the nation and the world. Needless to say, this area remains a shell of its former self with a vast "construction site" sitting on the grounds that once held New York's tallest skyscraper. An eerie calm has replaced the once bustling financial structures that were home to thousands of businesses and a must see stop for millions of tourists annually. Visitors still come to pay homage to the victims of 9/11 at the old Trinity Church, which somehow remained standing.

While plans for the redevelopment of the World Trade Center site are being finalized (go to www.lowermanhattan.info for the latest), and include a stunning memorial by architects Michael Arad and Peter Walker that will encompass the foot prints of the original Twin Towers, the area north of the site has made significant strides toward recovery. Shops and businesses are finally reporting increased customer volume, and apartment occupancy is now back to normal, indicating that people are either returning or settling into the area for the first time. Housing here includes old warehouses, offices, and bank buildings, some of which have been converted for residential use, along with modern residential structures going up. Supermarkets and food specialty shops along the western edge continue to serve the neighborhood, although residents of the **Wall Street** area are still under-served, especially at night and on weekends. An Amish Market on Cedar Street brings some relief. The downtown area as a residential and business district is still in the throes of rebuilding, both physically and in spirit. Area amenities and services include several hotels, a branch library, and the weekly *Downtown Express*.

Recent expansion in lower Manhattan includes the opening of the Ritz-Carlton Downtown Hotel and Skyscraper Museum, plus additions to the Museum of Jewish Heritage and Holocaust Memorial. On the east side of the island, you'll see the masts of old time sailing vessels docked at the bustling South Street Seaport Museum alongside the Fulton Fish Market and the Rouse Development Corporation's South Street Seaport renewal. Consisting of renovated Schermerhorn Row, museum shops, the Fulton Market, and a shopping mecca on Pier 17, the Seaport edges the East River at Fulton Street and, like sister developments in Boston and Baltimore, is a pleaser. Crowds browse craft stands and upscale boutiques, stroll and nosh their way through a tantalizing assortment of ethnic snack bars, queue for the multimedia show at the Trans-Lux Theater, and dine in the glamorous, glass-enclosed pavilion shimmering over East River waters.

The most distinguished housing in lower Manhattan remains **Battery Park City**, built between West Street and the Hudson River on landfill excavated from the original construction of the World Trade Center. It is the largest development ever constructed in Manhattan. With a third of its 92 acres reserved for parks, plazas, and esplanades, the development comprises a collection of architecturally diverse residential and financial complexes managed by the Battery Park City Authority. The World Financial Center—four stunning, copper-topped buildings fastidiously designed by Cesar Pelli (which saw significant damage from the terrorist attacks)—sits in between the large housing complex and the former site of the World Trade Center. At the center of Battery Park City, like an imperial gateway to the city, the soaring glass and polished-steel Winter Garden with sixteen California palms set in gleaming marble provides an elegant site for free concerts edging the North Cove Yacht Harbor. Surrounding the Winter Garden throughout the ground floor of the World Financial Center, upscale shops and restaurants beckon. The beautifully landscaped Esplanade—connecting the Winter Garden with South Cove and Rockefeller Park—constitutes the spine of the development as it stretches over a mile along the Hudson River. Battery Park City is a work in progress nearing completion. About 9,000 people, mostly young professionals who work in Lower Manhattan, are currently living in its 6,000 mixed high- and low-rise condos and upscale rental apartments. Construction of another 2,000 units, including three-bedroom apartments to attract families, have recently been completed. In addition, as part of the new "green building movement" the apartment complex is proud to unveil The Solaire at 20 River Terrace, a unique environmentally-friendly apartment building designed to be more energy-efficient, conserve water and provide cleaner air for residents. The 27-story building is the first of a planned eight green buildings in Battery Park City. The size and splendor of this mega-project should not, however, obscure the presence in Lower Manhattan of other residential possibilities. For example, small, architecturally distinguished condominiums such as Greenwich Court have sprung up on the West Side below Chambers Street.

Web Sites: www.downtownny.com, www.worldfinancialcenter.com, www.cb1.org, www.batteryparkcity.org, www.nyc.gov

Area Codes: 212, 646

Post Offices: Peck Slip Station, 1-19 Peck Slip, NYC 10038; Bowling Green Station, 25 Broadway, NYC 10004; 275-8777

Zip Codes: 10007, 10038, 10006, 10004, 10005, 10041, 10280, 10281, 10282

Police Precinct: First, 16 Ericsson Place, NYC 10013, 212-334-0611
Emergency Hospital: New York Downtown Hospital, 170 William Street, NYC 10038, 212-312-5000
Library: New Amsterdam Branch, 9 Murray Street, NYC 10007, 212-732-8186; www.nypl.org
Public School Education: School District #2 in region 9 (see **Chelsea**).
Adult Education: Pace University, 1 Pace Plaza, NYC 10038, 212-346-1200, www.pace.edu
Community Resources: South Street Seaport Museum, Fulton and Water streets, NYC 10038, 212-SEA-PORT, www.southstreetseaport.com; American Numismatic Society (display on the history of money) at the Federal Reserve Bank at 32 Liberty Street (by appointment only), 212-720-6130; National Museum of the American Indian, Alexander Hamilton US Customs House, 1 Bowling Green, NYC 10004, 212-514-3700, www.conexus.si.edu; the Museum of Jewish Heritage, 18 First Place, Battery Park City, NYC 10004-1484, 212-968-1800, www.mjhnyc.org; Trinity Church, Broadway at Trinity Place, 10006, 212-602-0800, www.trinitywallstreet.org, houses a museum and offers mid-day concerts on weekdays, as does St. Paul's Chapel up Broadway at Fulton (concert information is available at 212-602-0874, www.trinitywallstreet.org). (Also see **Tribeca**.)
Transportation—Subway: Uptown, Downtown, and Brooklyn #2, #3 Varick/Greenwich streets at Chambers (Exp.), Cortlandt, Rector, South Ferry/Battery Park, Park Place/Broadway, Fulton (Exp.), Wall Street; Uptown, Downtown #1, #9, Chambers, South Ferry last stop. Uptown, Downtown & Brooklyn #4, #5 at Brooklyn Bridge, Fulton (Exp.), Wall (Exp.), Bowling (Exp.); J, M Fulton (Exp.); Broad (Exp.), #6 same stops but does not go to Brooklyn, last stop Brooklyn Bridge.
Transportation—Bus: Crosstown Chambers/West/Vesey/Park Row to Madison Street (#22); Uptown Church/Hudson/Eighth Avenue - Downtown Seventh Avenue/Varick/West Broadway (#10); Uptown Church/Sixth Avenue - Downtown Broadway (#6); Uptown and Downtown Grand Central Terminal - Wall Street Express (#X25) weekdays only, Uptown Lincoln Center, Downtown Battery Park City (#20)

TRIBECA

Boundaries and Contiguous Areas: North: Canal Street and SoHo; **East**: Broadway; **South**: Chambers Street and Downtown; **West**: Hudson River

South of Canal Street, where the island of Manhattan narrows toward its tip, Greenwich Street angles toward West Broadway, leaving in its wake not only the loft district dubbed Tribeca (**tri**angle **be**low **Ca**nal) but triangular blocks and crossroad parks unique in the city. Felicitous little Duane Park, the most charming of the lot, breathes into an area composed of 19th century brick and cast iron structures, sprawling warehouses, and commercial space, an air of peace and tranquility that is rare in the Big Apple.

Before becoming "Tribeca-ized," the area consisted of a warren of scruffy walkups that housed the city's wholesale fruit, vegetable, and flower district, the Washington Market, as well as the butter and egg district. Most of the market was razed and sent packing to The Bronx in the late 1960s, to be replaced in part by the ponderous brick Independence Plaza project at 40 Harrison Street, but a few vestiges of the produce district remain, including a row of Federal houses tucked under Independence Plaza's angular wing, and the two-block Staple Street—an alley actually. There are no staples there.

Tribeca is also home to a number of elegantly sculptural cast-iron buildings—the first built not far from Duane Park by James Bogardus in 1849. The noticeably cleaner of the arched and colonnaded facades front residential lofts and cooperatives skillfully adapted from commercial space, as well as the galleries and offices of the avant-garde establishment (the pioneering fringe has moved to the Lower East Side and across the East River into Queens and Brooklyn). Loft living with amenities is now an accepted urban lifestyle, and Tribeca has changed radically from the quiet backwater it remained throughout the 1970s. It is a prime destination for those who like their buildings wide and their spaces open. Catering to such tastes, antique and design stores cluster along Franklin and Duane streets.

The vaunted, often vaulted warehouses just south of the Holland Tunnel housed the clubs responsible for Tribeca's once-famous nightlife scene. Restaurants that the area's early disco devotees haunted now feed a more staid clientele. Tribeca hosts a kaleidoscopic range of dining—including some of the best three- and four-star restaurants in Manhattan—frequented by the hip, the chic, and the up-and-coming; midday these eateries nourish Wall Street suits and rumpled denizens of city hall.

Competing pressures—southbound from booming SoHo, from 10,000 students at Manhattan Community College in its midst, and most insistently from the ever-expanding Battery Park City—have transformed Tribeca into a thriving, cohesive, mixed-use community. The conversion of former warehouses and factories to handsome, upscale residential lofts continues, many now selling at seven-digit prices hitherto associated with the Upper East Side. A growing population of children where once there were none, an attractive neighborhood school (P.S. 234), and now a small-town newspaper, *The Tribeca Trib*, along with unimpeded bike riding on weekends, the architecture and night life, are among the attractions of living in Tribeca. Drawbacks? Few grocery stores.

Web Sites: www.cb1.org, www.nyc.gov

Area Codes: 212, 646

Post Office: Canal Street Station, 350 Canal Street, NYC 10013, 800-275-8777

Zip Code: 10013

Police Precinct: First, 16 Ericsson Place, NYC 10013, 212-334-0611

Emergency Hospitals (nearest): New York Downtown Hospital, 170 William Street, NYC 10038, 212-312-5000; St. Vincent's Hospital and Medical Center, 153 West 11th Street (at Seventh Avenue), NYC 10011, 212-604-7000

Library (nearest): New Amsterdam Branch, 9 Murray Street, NYC 10007, 212-732-8186; www.nypl.org

Public School Education: School District #2 in region 9 (see **Chelsea**).

Adult Education: Borough of Manhattan Community College, Office of Continuing Education, Room S763, 199 Chambers Street, NYC 10007, 212-346-8000, www.www.bmcc.cuny.edu, offers a variety of inexpensive evening and weekend courses ranging from computer to business to self-improvement. Concerts and theater are also presented regularly in the College's Triplex Theater.

Community Resources: Tribeca houses alternative spaces displaying works for and by the avant-garde, much as upper Madison Avenue houses deluxe galleries catering to the establishment; one such gallery is the Artists Space at 38 Greene Street, 3rd Floor, NYC 10013, 212-226-3970, www.artistsspace.org. Others include: Studio 18 Gallery at 18 Warren Street, NYC 10007, 212-385-6734; Art Initiatives at 148 Duane Street, NYC 10013, 212-406-4073, and the Watts Gallery at 123 Watts Street, NYC 10013, 212-219-1482. Also in Tribeca is the Tribeca Film Center at 375 Greenwich Street, NYC 10013, 212-941-4000, host of the Tribeca Film Festival, www.tribecafilmfestival.com.

Transportation—Subway: A, C, E at Canal Street (Exp.), Chambers Street (Exp.); #1, #9, #2, #3 Varick Street at Canal Street, Franklin Street, Chambers Street (Exp.)

Transportation—Bus: Crosstown Madison & Chambers Street/West Street & Grand Street (#22); Uptown Hudson Street/Eighth Avenue - Downtown Seventh Avenue/Varick Street (#10); Uptown Sixth Avenue - Downtown Seventh Avenue/Broadway (#6); Uptown and Downtown Grand Central Terminal - Wall Street Express (X25) weekdays only

SOHO

Boundaries and Contiguous Areas: **North**: West Houston Street and Greenwich Village; **East**: Broadway and Lower East Side; **South**: Canal Street and Tribeca; **West**: Sixth Avenue

SoHo's cast iron buildings are justifiably famous and a visual delight. Look up to appreciate the beauty of the patterns—columnar shapes, Greek Revival capitals, and other architectural embellishments—pressed into the cast iron facades. Windowsill house plants, paintings, and some of the city's most colorful walls reveal the loft residences, which now occupy most of what was manufacturing space. Behind these slightly grimy fronts live some of New York's trendiest trendsetters, often in 4,000-square-foot spreads. The structures are based on a technique perfected by James Bogardus around 1850. Forerunners of today's "curtain wall" skyscrapers, these cast iron buildings are supported by interior columns, obviating the need for thick walls and allowing the use of much more glass than was previously possible. As a result, the graceful windows, many of them arched, nicely complement the strong, solid buildings, and the whole is extremely harmonious. The buildings are also exceedingly attractive to the city's artists, ever on the lookout for good light and space. In the early 1960s they began to move into the area, just as industry had previously moved into what had been the city's red light district a century before; loft living became legal in 1971. With the subsequent discovery of SoHo by the affluent, high prices have driven many of the original artists to less costly neighborhoods. But art galleries and audacious boutiques remain to prosper and proliferate.

The popularity of SoHo has in no way diminished. On the contrary, monied arrivistes commingle with painters and sculptors on the upper floors of the converted cast iron structures while at street level, hard-edged, minimalist (whatever the fashion-of-the-moment) showrooms spread their plate glass windows far and wide. "An international marketplace for style and design," the *New York Times* calls it, attracting shoppers from Jersey to Germany. "This feels like the world's greatest shopping mall," exclaims a merchant of upscale linens. Just so. You can buy the latest in wearable art, Japanese designer clothes, French prêt-à-porter, exquisite antique blouses and accessories, antique or art deco furniture, and more. Take a shopping break in a chic eatery along West Broadway's restaurant row. Bring money. And if you live here, don't venture out on the weekend. It's packed.

What has changed in recent years is the eastern edge of SoHo. Galleries, clothing shops, and even offices have spread east from West Broadway past Wooster, Greene, and Mercer to Broadway and beyond. Once drab and lifeless, Broadway has undergone a personality change as faux marble and hand-grained surfaces replace the tatty showrooms of fabric wholesalers. The relocation of Dean and DeLuca's extraordinary food emporium to a vast, white space resembling an edible art gallery was a sure sign of the Broadway revival. Recent renovations to the former Canal Jeans store, also on Broadway, by Bloomingdale's, and the establishment of the very chic Prada store in the former SoHo Guggenheim space make this strip a shopper's dream. As SoHo crawls ever eastward, the boundary between SoHo and Little Italy is blurring.

While loft living is legal in many buildings, and you need not necessarily qualify as an artist to rent or sublet SoHo space, caution is advised in taking over a lease or paying key money for a loft or apartment. Check with the New York City Loft Board for the status of legal rents and living situations (see **Lofts** in **Finding a Place to Live**). Many artists sublet when they go on sabbatical or receive grants that take them out of town. If you're not in the market for a condo, the best line on housing availability down here is by word-of-mouth (and conversation is lively at the local art galleries and show openings, which anyone can attend) and by browsing community bulletin boards.

Web Sites: www.artseensoho.com, www.nyc.gov
Area Codes: 212, 646
Post Office: Prince Street Station, 103 Prince Street, NYC 10012, 800-275-8777
Zip Codes: 10012, 10013
Police Precinct: First, 16 Ericsson Place, NYC 10013, 212-334-0611
Emergency Hospitals (nearest): St. Vincent's Hospital and Medical Center, Seventh Avenue and 11th Street, NYC 10011, 212-604-7000; New York Downtown Hospital, 170 William Street, NYC 10038, 212-312-5000
Libraries (nearest): Jefferson Market Branch, 425 Avenue of the Americas, NYC 10011, 212-243-4334; Hudson Park Branch, 66 Leroy Street, NYC 10014, 212-243-6876, has an excellent film program for children; www.nypl.org.
Public School Education: School District #2 in region 9 (see **Chelsea**).
Adult Education: The French Culinary Institute, 462 Broadway, 7th Floor, NYC 10013, 212-219-8890, www.frenchculinary.com; offers a variety of professional and non-professional cooking courses (lunch and dinner too at their restaurant, L'Ecole: dial 212-219-3300 for reservations).
Community Resources: New Museum of Contemporary Art, 583 Broadway, NYC 10012, 212-219-1222, www.newmuseum.org; the Fire Museum, 278 Spring Street, NYC 10012, 212-691-1303, www.nycfiremuseum.org. The district is crammed with great and small gallery spaces—investigate them at leisure. Most are closed Sunday and Monday. A scan of *Art Now's Gallery Guide*, available in gal-

leries throughout the city, gives a total picture of the area's resources and current shows. For weekly guides to arts events in SoHo see *The Village Voice*, the "Weekend" section on Friday, the "Arts and Leisure" section of the Sunday *New York Times*, *Time Out New York*, and *The New Yorker's* "Goings on About Town" section or *New York Magazine's* "Cue" section. Nearby Tribeca also offers opportunities to explore the more avant-garde side of the arts, as does the East Village, from which, amoeba-like, galleries have spread throughout the Lower East Side.

Transportation—Subway: Uptown, Downtown, A, C, E Sixth Avenue at Spring Street, Canal Street (Exp.); B, D, F, Q at Broadway/Lafayette; Uptown, Brooklyn & Queens (N, R & W) at Prince Street, Canal Street; #4, #6 at Bleecker Street, Spring Street, Canal Street, Uptown & Brooklyn, #1, #9 at West Houston

Transportation—Bus: Crosstown Houston Street (#21); Downtown Fifth Avenue - Uptown Sixth Avenue (#5); Downtown Seventh Avenue/ Broadway (#10); Uptown Sixth Avenue - Downtown Seventh Avenue/ Broadway (#6)

GREENWICH VILLAGE

Boundaries and Contiguous Areas: North: 14th Street, Chelsea and Flatiron District; **East**: Broadway and the East Village; **South**: West Houston Street and SoHo; **West**: Hudson River

Greenwich Village is the kind of community where neighbors look after each other's plants and pets and where people do call the police or fire department if they notice something amiss. Residents still tend to be arts-oriented, and more liberal and politically active than most, particularly when it comes to incursions, real or threatened, on the free-wheeling life style adopted by some or on the neighborhood's cherished landmarks and signature style. It was the Village's great good fortune to have its 18th century farm lane streets in place before city planners superimposed the grid pattern on most of Manhattan. The crooked streets that intersect major arteries at skew angles are a refreshing change although navigating the streets may take time and determination.

Since the 19th century, the brick, Federal-style structures along these crooked streets have housed more than their share of the city's talented and creative. Writers came first: Edgar Allan Poe in 1837, later Mark Twain, Henry James, and Walt Whitman. Artists and intellectuals followed. A handful of people and institutions played key roles in the evolution of the Village as a magnet for those in the vanguard of the arts and letters. Gertrude Vanderbilt Whitney opened her first studio here, exhibiting and encouraging the artists who subsequently became the nucleus of the "Ashcan school" of social realist painters. Mabel Dodge's famed literary salon was on Washington Square, and the Provincetown Players established an early experimental theater on Macdougal Street in 1916. New York University was founded on Washington Square in the 1830s, the New School on West 12th Street in the 1920s. By then the local populace included John Dos Passos, e.e. cummings, Willa Cather, Henry Miller, and Edna St. Vincent Millay, making Greenwich Village the avant-garde capital of the nation.

After WW II, abstract expressionists, method actors, controversial novelists, and muckraking journalists all coexisted, bringing creative vitality to the area. The written word was set to music in the fifties and sixties as folk legends performed anti-war hymns in small coffee houses. Hippies, yippies, and the latest in fashionable cultural trends and lifestyles have always been part of the Village's attraction. Only as recently as the early 1970s and the advent of spiraling rents has this neighborhood's appeal lessened as a haven for artists and writers. These days there are probably more art appreciators around than artists, but the charm of the Village, with its pleasing proportions and special kind of peacefulness, remains. An annual art show on the streets around Washington Square Park and the city's foremost (and most outrageous) Halloween Parade are among the festivities that make this neighborhood special.

Greenwich Village contains a balanced mix of high-rise elevator buildings, older, rent-stabilized apartments, lofts, renovated tenements, and brownstones (a harmonious ensemble threatened, in the West Village at least, by the emergence of several buildings above the prescribed height limit to obtain Hudson River views). New, pricey rental apartments and condos in the handsome conversions in the wholesale antiques district bordering University Place and in the now-fashionable converted warehouses lining West and Washington streets are widely advertised.

The meatpacking district in the far-West Village, south of 14th Street, is experiencing a complete makeover, with film studios, trendy restaurants, galleries, and upscale-clothing stores, and now luxury housing. Recent additions to Village housing stock can be found on lower Hudson Street and along the river on West Street, where new rentals and condos continue to rise, offering upscale living options outside the landmarked district.

Because the area is essentially an assembly of small communities—the predominantly Italian **South Village**, the central **Washington Square** neighborhood, and the **West Village**, bounded by Seventh Avenue and the Hudson River—searching for rentals is best done on foot and through reliable real estate agents.

Web Sites: www.greenwich-village.com, www.nyc.gov
Area Codes: 212, 646

Post Offices: Patchin Station, 70 West 10th Street, NYC 10011; West Village Station, 527 Hudson Street, NYC 10014; Cooper Station, 93 Fourth Avenue, NYC 10003; Village Station, 201 Varick Street, NYC 10014; 800-275-8777

Zip Codes: 10014, 10011, 10012, 10003

Police Precinct: Sixth, 233 West 10th Street, NYC 10014, 212-741-4811

Emergency Hospital: St. Vincent's Hospital and Medical Center, Seventh Avenue and 11th Street, NYC 10011, 212-604-7000

Libraries: Jefferson Market Branch, 425 Avenue of the Americas, NYC 10011, 212-243-4334; Hudson Park Branch, 66 Leroy Street, NYC 10014, 212-243-6876, has an excellent film program for children; www.nypl.org.

Public School Education: School District #2 in region 9 (see **Chelsea**). Greenwich Village has two elementary schools. Public School 41 offers "traditional" public school education, while P.S. 3 with an "open corridor" program is more experimental. Go to www.nycenet.edu for more information.

Adult Education: Parsons School of Design (Part of the New School University), 66 Fifth Avenue, NYC 10011, 212-229-8900, www.parsons.edu; New School University, 66 West 12th Street, NYC 10011, 212-229-5600, www.newschool.edu; The Cooper Union for the Advancement of Science and Art, Third Avenue and 7th Street, NYC 10003, 212-353-4195, www.cooper.edu; Greenwich House Music School, 46 Barrow Street, NYC 10014, 212-242-4770, www.gharts.org; Greenwich House Pottery, 16 Jones Street, 212-242-4106, www.greenwichhousepottery.org; New York University, 50 West 4th Street, NYC 10003, 212-998-1212, www.nyu.edu; Pratt Manhattan, the local branch of Brooklyn's Pratt Institute, 144 West 14th Street, NYC 10011, 212-647-7775, www.pratt.edu, has extensive evening and weekend course offerings in the arts and professional areas.

Community Resources: Yeshiva University Museum, 15 West 16th Street, NYC 10011, 212-294-8330, www.yumuseum.org; Cherry Lane Theater, 38 Commerce Street 212-989-2020; Actor's Playhouse, 100 Seventh Avenue, 212-463-0060; Minetta Lane Theater, 18 Minetta Lane, 212-420-8000; You'll also find a variety of galleries and historic buildings as you explore the village.

Transportation—Subway: Crosstown & Brooklyn, L at Eighth Avenue, Sixth Avenue, Broadway/Union Square; A, C, E at Eighth Avenue and 14th Street (Exp.), West 4th/8th Street (Exp.); #1/9, #2, #3 at Seventh Avenue and 14th Street (Exp.), Christopher Street/Sheridan Square, Houston Street; F, D, B, Q at 14th Street, West 4th/8th Street (Exp.); Uptown, Downtown, #4, #5, #6 at 14th Street/Union Square (Exp.), Astor Place, Bleecker Street at Lafayette; Uptown, Downtown, Brooklyn & Queens, N, R & W at 14th Street/Union Square (Exp.), 8th Street/NYU;

PATH (between New Jersey and 33rd Street) Christopher Street at Hudson, 9th and 14th Streets at Sixth Avenue

Transportation—Bus: Crosstown 14th Street (#14); Crosstown 8th/9th Streets (#8); Crosstown Houston to Avenue C (#21), Uptown Greenwich Street/Tenth Avenue - Downtown Ninth Avenue/Hudson Street (#11); Uptown Hudson Street/Eighth Avenue - Downtown Seventh Avenue (#10); Uptown Sixth Avenue - Downtown Fifth Avenue (#5) Uptown Sixth Avenue - Downtown Seventh Avenue (#6), Uptown University Place/Madison Avenue - Downtown Fifth Avenue (#2, #3)

FLATIRON DISTRICT

Boundaries and Contiguous Areas: North: 23rd Street and Madison Square; **East**: Park Avenue South and Gramercy Park Area; **South**: 14th Street; **West**: Sixth Avenue and Chelsea

Thanks to the famous wintry photograph by Edward Steichen, the thrusting nose of the Flatiron Building is familiar, even to out-of-towners. The triangular structure at the convergence of Broadway and Fifth Avenue at 23rd Street was a wonder, a skyscraper, when completed in 1902. The 21-story steel-frame edifice was also at the apex of the Ladies' Mile, New York's elegant shopping district. Macy's, Tiffany, Lord & Taylor, and other luxurious emporiums now forgotten cut a fashionable swath down Broadway, Fifth, and Sixth avenues in the late 19th century.

But just as the rumbling Sixth Avenue elevated subway had stimulated the development of the Ladies' Mile, so the city's booming economy caused the great stores to move uptown. The elegant buildings with rhythmic cast iron fronts, elaborate mansard roofs, Byzantine columns, and Gothic finials were abandoned to a dim and sooty half-life as manufacturing lofts and warehouses. The 1990s saw a reawakening south of 23rd Street, and the wedge-shaped Flatiron Building has lent its name to the neighborhood. Andy Warhol was, perhaps, among the first to make a mark in the Flatiron District when he established his notorious Factory on **Union Square**. Professional photographers began moving bed-and-tripod into the neighborhood's vast manufacturing lofts in the 1970s. Photo supply houses and model agencies came next, followed by publishing houses, advertising agencies and, most recently, internet and media startups. Lower Fifth Avenue is experiencing a retail renaissance, led by such fashion heavyweights as Armani, Paul Smith, and Matsuda. The abandoned palaces of the Ladies Mile on Sixth Avenue have re-opened as mega-stores selling books, housewares, office supplies, and clothes. On Broadway, home furnishing stores cluster around the feet of ABC Carpet and Home.

Young cyber whizzes working in hi-tech computer studios earned a new name for the area: "Silicon Alley" at the turn of the latest century, but many of the new hi-tech companies have now fallen by the way side, victims of the dotcom meltdown of 2001. Nonetheless, some of the city's trendiest and most popular eateries and increased shopping options, including popular favorites like Barnes & Noble, 33 East 17th Street, have attracted a growing number of young professionals into the area. On and off the avenues, trendy restaurants proliferate like chanterelles after a rain, as have fitness clubs of every persuasion.

There are rare rentals in the handsome Zeckendorf Towers, set back from Union Square with airy, teal pyramid points atop the brick towers and a 24-hour supermarket downstairs. Madison Green, overlooking restful **Madison Square Park**, is among the notable modern condominiums. And a sleek apartment tower, 1 Union Square South, rises above the new Circuit City. Building and renovation along the 14th Street corridor between Third and Seventh avenues is adding housing stock to the area, much of it for NYU, as well as a much improved streetscape. More typical of the Flatiron District, however, are the elegant, converted living lofts hidden away in the stolid manufacturing buildings that darken the side streets. Consult a real estate broker for the occasional sublet that comes on the market. Besides a prime location with good public transportation, you'll have the graceful, green breathing space that is now the completely refurbished Union Square for a front yard. The park itself, once a haven for drug trafficking, has become a lunching spot for those working on nearby Lexington Avenue or Park Avenue.

The four-day-a-week greenmarket (see **Greenmarkets** in the **Shopping for the Home** chapter) is the Square's *pièce de résistance*. Manhattanites trek year round to the northwest corner at East 16th and Broadway for fresh produce, fish, sausages, cheese, pretzels, breads, honey—oh, endless edibles—and colorful armloads of cut flowers.

Web Sites: www.cb1.org, www.unionsquaresouth.com, www.nyc.gov
Area Codes: 212, 646
Post Offices (nearest): Cooper Station, 93 Fourth Avenue, NYC 10003, Madison Square Station, 149 East 23rd Street, NYC 10010, Post Office Information, 800-275-8777
Zip Codes: 10003, 10010, 10011
Police Precinct: Thirteenth, 230 East 21st Street, NYC 10010
Emergency Hospitals (nearest): Cabrini Medical Center, 227 East 19th Street, NYC 10003, 212-995-6000, www.cabrininy.org; St. Vincent's Hospital and Medical Center, 153 West 11th Street at Seventh Avenue, NYC 10011, 212-604-7000
Libraries (nearest): Muhlenberg Library, 209 West 23rd Street, NYC

10011, 212-924-1585; Epiphany Branch, 228 East 23rd Street, NYC 10010, 212-679-2645; www.nypl.org

Public School Education: School District #2 in region 9 (see **Chelsea**).

Adult Education: School of Visual Arts, 209 East 23rd Street, NYC 10010, 212-592-2000, www.schoolofvisualarts.edu; Baruch College of Continuing and Professional Studies, 17 Lexington Avenue, Room 910, NYC 10010, 212-802-5600

Community Resources: Tibet House, 22 West 15th Street, NYC 10011, www.tibethouse.org, 212-807-0563; Theodore Roosevelt Birthplace and Museum, 28 East 20th Street, NYC 10003, 212-260-1616; birthplace of the 26th US President and his home for 14 years, now contains two museum galleries and a bookstore. (Also, see **Chelsea**.)

Transportation—Subway: Crosstown & Brooklyn, L on 14th Street at Sixth Avenue, Uptown, Downtown & Brooklyn (Except the #6) Union Square; #4, #5, #6 at 23rd Street, 14th Street/Union Square (Exp.); Uptown, Downtown, Brooklyn & Queens, N, R & W at 14th Street/Union Square (Exp.); PATH (between New Jersey and 33rd Street) at 14th and 23rd Streets at Sixth Avenue, Uptown, Downtown (#2 & #3 also to Brooklyn) #1, #2, #3 & #9 at 18th and 23rd at Seventh Avenue

Transportation—Bus: Crosstown 23rd Street (#23); Crosstown 14th Street (#14); Uptown Madison Avenue - Downtown Fifth Avenue South (#1, #2, #3), Uptown Sixth Avenue - Downtown Fifth Avenue (#5), Uptown Sixth Avenue - Downtown Broadway (#6), Uptown Sixth Avenue - Downtown Seventh Avenue (#7)

CHELSEA

Boundaries and Contiguous Areas: **North**: 34th Street and Clinton; **East**: Sixth Avenue and Flatiron District; **South**: 14th Street and Greenwich Village; **West**: Hudson River

Residential Chelsea is a sunny community renowned for peace, quiet, and four- and five-story brownstone row houses, but its origins date back to 1750, when Capt. Thomas Clarke's farm encompassed the area. In the 1830s, Clarke's grandson, Clement Clarke Moore, began developing Chelsea as a highly desirable suburb. Moore donated land for the block-square General Theological Seminary just down the street from the Gothic Revival style St. Peter's Episcopal Church, where he read his "A Visit from Saint Nicholas" to family and parishioners. The tree-shaded Seminary Close is still a neighborhood oasis.

To the west, the Hudson River Railroad attracted slaughterhouses, breweries and shanties, and in 1871, Chelsea was darkened by the city's first elevated railroad, on Ninth Avenue. Successive decades saw the brief emergence of West 23rd Street as the city's theater district; the raising of vast cast iron structures on Sixth Avenue to house fashionable emporiums such as the original B. Altman's; and in the 1920s and 1930s a thriving vice district; the beginning of the nation's movie industry; and the opening of one of the city's first cooperative apartment houses, now the Hotel Chelsea, home over the years to artists and writers. Urban renewal in the 1950s and 1960s spurred the restoration of many fine townhouses and made way for two low-income housing projects and the middle-income International Ladies Garment Workers cooperative between Eighth and Ninth avenues.

Sharing the side streets with restored one- and two-family houses are the occasional apartment house and tenement, not to mention formidable **London Terrace**, 405 West 23rd Street, with 14 buildings. The lofts in the photography, flower, fur, and fashion districts (roughly 15th to 30th streets between Fifth and Eighth avenues, which includes the Flatiron District) were discovered by artists in the 1950s and some now attract young families and professionals.

In 1982 the down-at-the-heels Elgin, a 1930s movie house on Eighth Avenue, was transformed into the exuberantly art deco Joyce Theater, the first theater in the dance capital of the world to be specifically designed for small and medium-sized dance troupes. Since then, Chelsea has become something of a dance and performance district. Way west, nightclubs offer do-it-yourself dance in between auto-repair shops and factories.

Eighth Avenue, between 14th and 23rd streets, is Main Street, Chelsea. With a lively restaurant scene and boutiques punctuating the relatively unobtrusive condos and co-ops, Eighth Avenue caters to a youthful and predominately gay population. Chelseaites and Villagers shop Chelsea Market for quality foods in the imaginatively recycled Nabisco factories on Ninth Avenue and 15th Street. The new block-long Whole Foods Market on 24th Street and Seventh Avenue is a magnificent addition to the area, featuring 30,000 square feet of organic foods, fine cheeses, and free range meats. Along with great food shopping, the other recent wave to hit Chelsea is the art scene: more than 100 trendy galleries cluster near the pioneering Dia Center for the Arts on 22nd Street and along the western corridor between 17th and 27th streets. Ninth and Tenth Avenue eateries feed the gallery crowd.

Simultaneously anchoring the western edge of Chelsea is the extraordinary 1.7 million square-foot Chelsea Piers Sports and Entertainment complex in four piers over the Hudson River, stretching between 17th and 23rd streets. The movie industry returned to Chelsea in the new film and television studios housed in the pier-head, through which once streamed passengers from some of the world's great ocean liners. In fact, in 1912, this was to be the destination of the ill-fated Titanic. In the handsome complex stretched out behind the studios, workout devotees strain and sweat on state-of-the-art equipment while others (especially youngsters from all over the city) run, ice skate, in-line pirouette, play league hockey, soccer, lacrosse, and basketball, scale a climbing wall, bowl, refine gymnastic skills or drive balls to target greens on a 200-foot Astroturf fairway under nightlights. Others watch and hang out at one of several restaurants. For those who enjoy watching sports, you can take in the professionals at Madison Square Garden, which draws crowds to the west 30s to see the Knicks, Rangers, and Liberty, along with the circus and other events.

North of the piers and looming over the Hudson, the vast industrial Starrett-Lehigh Building, long semi-vacant, attracts high-profile tenants now, including art galleries, film studios, and new media groups. And much of that industrial neighborhood is becoming luxury lofts. It's the new SoHo.

Chelsea's hot now; housing here is much in demand, expensive, and living spaces are often small. The new frontier, less attractive but accessible, is Sixth, Seventh, and Eighth avenues, from 23rd to 31st streets, where a zoning change now allows construction of apartment buildings in a previously industrial zone. Currently, there is limited residential space; what is there is tucked between numerous businesses crowding the side streets—during weekdays trucks abound. On weekends, every parking lot in the west 20s transforms itself into a flea market and crowds abound. At night, however, except for the area around the Fashion Institute of Technology where the "designers of tomorrow" reside, the streets are somewhat deserted.

Web Site: www.nyc.gov

Area Codes: 212, 646

Post Offices: General Post Office, Eighth Avenue at 33rd Street, NYC 10001, open 24 hours; London Terrace Station, 232 Tenth Avenue, near 24th Street, NYC 10011, Old Chelsea Station, 217 West 18th Street, NYC 10011; Port Authority Station, 76 Ninth Avenue, NYC 10011; 800-275-8777

Zip Codes: 10001, 10011

Police Precincts: Midtown South, 357 West 35th Street, NYC 10001, 212-239-9811; Tenth, 230 West 20th Street, NYC 10011, 212-741-8211

Emergency Hospitals (nearest): St. Clare's Hospital and Health Center, 415 West 51st Street, NYC 10019, 212-586-1500; St. Vincent's Hospital and Medical Center, Seventh Avenue and 11th Street, NYC 10011, 212-604-7000

Libraries: Muhlenberg Branch, 209 West 23rd Street, NYC 10011, 212-924-1585, www.nypl.org; Andrew Heiskell Library for the Blind and

Physically Handicapped, 40 West 20th Street, NYC 10011, 212-206-5400

Public School Education: Chelsea is in School District #2 in region 9, 333 7th Avenue, NYC 10001, 212-356-7500; Committee on the Handicapped, District Manager, P.S. 33, 281 Ninth Avenue, NYC 10011, 212-244-6426. Bayard Rustin High School for the Humanities, 351 West 18th Street, 212-675-5350, is the city's newest college preparatory high school. www.nycenet.edu

Adult Education: Fashion Institute of Technology, 227 West 27th Street, NYC 10001, 212-217-7999, classes plus art gallery open to the public, www.fitnyc.suny.edu

Community Resources: McBurney YMCA, 125 West 14th Street, NYC 10011, 212-741-9210; the Joyce Theater, 175 Eighth Avenue at 19th Street, NYC 10011, 212-691-9740, www.joyce.org; Dance Theatre Workshop, 219 West 19th Street, NYC 10011, 212-924-0077, www.dtw.org; The Kitchen, 512 West 19th Street, NYC 10011, 212-255-5793, www.thekitchen.org; Dia Center for the Arts, 548 West 22nd Street, NYC 10011, 212-989-5566, www.diaart.org; Atlantic Theater Company, 336 West 20th Street, NYC 10011, 212-645-1242, www.atlantictheater.com; Chelsea Art Museum, 556 West 22nd Street, 212-255-0719, www.chelseaartmuseum.org; and galleries galore.

Transportation—Subway: Crosstown & Brooklyn (L) at Eighth Avenue and 14th Street (crosses 14th Street and continues into Brooklyn); #1, #2, #3 at 34th Street/Penn Station (Exp.), 28th Street, 23rd Street, 18th Street, 14th Street (Exp.); A, C, E at Sixth Avenue and 34th Street (Exp.), 23rd Street, 14th Street (Exp.); PATH (between New Jersey and 33rd Street) 14th, 23rd, and 33rd streets on Sixth Avenue

Transportation—Bus: Crosstown 34th Street/Ninth Avenue (#16); Crosstown 23rd Street (#23); Crosstown 14th Street (#14) also down Avenue A and Avenue D; Uptown Tenth Avenue - Downtown Ninth Avenue (#11); Uptown Eighth Avenue - Downtown Seventh Avenue (#10)

MIDTOWN

Boundaries and Contiguous Areas: North: 59th Street (Central Park South) and Central Park; **East**: Lexington Avenue and East 40s and 50s, Fifth Avenue (south of 42nd Street) and Murray Hill; **South**: 34th Street and Chelsea; **West**: Eighth Avenue and Clinton

For all that it contains within its bounds, Midtown is not a neighborhood. Some 700,000 people work here, but few call it home. Not since the mansions of the mighty—the Rockefellers, the Havemeyers, the Vanderbilts— were left to the wrecker's ball and commercial development around the turn of the 20th century has Midtown felt like a neighborhood. This core of the core of the city throbs and bustles daily with industry in the garment district, commerce between Lexington and Sixth Avenue (or Avenue of the Americas, its official name rarely used by New Yorkers), with shoppers from Macy's to Bergdorf Goodman to Bloomingdale's, and tourists everywhere. Except for the theater district, the 40s and 50s west of Sixth Avenue, Midtown is quiet at night, all but deserted in some areas.

There are no supermarkets here, no children's playgrounds, and only one city park, the elegantly renovated Bryant Park, one block square and a little bit of Europe, behind the New York Public Library at 42nd Street. What is here is almost all of the city's legitimate theater, ballet at City Center Theater, music at Carnegie Hall, and smaller venues, museums, restaurants of every conceivable persuasion, Rockefeller Center, major art galleries along 57th Street, and shopping until you're dropping. Not to mention that perhaps your job is here.

You *can* live in Midtown. On the high side in Trump and other glassy towers along Fifth and Park avenues and Central Park South, in some fine pre-war (WW II, that is) apartment buildings between Sixth and Eighth avenues in the 50s, and just a bit more modestly in modern doorman buildings. The occasional brownstone is a side-street surprise west of Fifth. Affordable apartments may be found in the 40s between Broadway and Eighth Avenue; explore the area first and talk to residents in order to be sure about location.

The ongoing transformation of Times Square and West 42nd Street has attracted major law firms, publishing houses, investment firms, and family friendly entertainment to the glassy new towers and renovated theaters in this throbbing, neon-lit "crossroads of the world." Tourists and New Yorkers use a comprehensive array of services at the Times Square Visitor's Center and at the city's official Visitor Information Center. This transformation is driving the development of a formerly shabby Eighth Avenue in the 50s as a new frontier of upscale modern apartment living. Where once the peep shows and XXX theaters huddled, gleaming apartment towers rise, offering marble baths and health clubs at East Side prices. Between these towering newcomers, housing will continue to be spotty but increasingly less shabby as the area continues to transform. Keep in mind, this is a busy, often noisy area and no place for a car. If you're working in the area, enjoy nightlife, theater, and dining out, this may be for you. If you like a more neighborhood feel or particularly if you're moving with kids in tow, look elsewhere.

The search here is best made with the help of reliable real estate agents. Watch the ads in the *Sunday Times* and *The Village Voice* to find agents handling properties in the area. You may also find the list of brokers in the **Finding a Place to Live** chapter helpful.

Web Sites: www.nyc.gov, www.timessquare.org
Area Codes: 212, 646
Post Offices: Grand Central Station, 450 Lexington Avenue, NYC 10017, Midtown Station, 221 and 223 West 38th Street, NYC 10018; Rockefeller Center Station, 610 Fifth Avenue, NYC 10020; Bryant Station, 23 West 43rd Street, NYC 10036; Murray Hill Station, 115 East 34th Street, NYC 10016; Station #138 Macy's, 151 West 34th Street, NYC 10001; 800-275-8777
Zip Codes: 10001,10016,10017,10018, 10019, 10020, 10022, 10036
Police Precincts: Midtown North, 306 West 54th Street, NYC 10019, 212-767-8400; Midtown South, 357 West 35th Street, NYC 10001, 212-239-9811
Emergency Hospital (nearest): St. Luke's-Roosevelt Hospital Center, 1000 Tenth Avenue (at 58th Street), NYC 10023, 212-523-4000
Libraries: The Mercantile Library, 17 East 47th Street, NYC 10017, 212-755-6710, a membership library; General Society Library, 20 West 44th Street, NYC 10036, 212-921-1767, a membership library; Donnell Library Center, New York Public Library, 20 West 53rd Street, NYC 10019, 212-621-0618; Fifty-Eighth Street Branch, 127 East 58th Street, NYC 10022, 212-759-7358; Mid-Manhattan Branch, 455 Fifth Avenue, NYC 10016, 212-340-0833; New York Public Library, Fifth Avenue and 42nd Street, NYC 10018, 212-869-8089; www.nypl.org; the Science, Industry and Business Branch (SIBL) in the former B. Altman building, 188 Madison Avenue at 34th Street, NYC 10016, 212-592-7000
Public School Education: School District #2 in region 9 (see **Chelsea**).
Adult Education: Graduate School and University Center, City University of New York (CUNY), 365 Fifth 10016, 212-817-7000, www.gc.cuny.edu
Community Resources: International Center of Photography (ICP) Midtown, 1133 Avenue of the Americas at 43rd Street, NYC 10036, 212-857-0000, www.icp.org; American Folk Art Museum, 45 West 53rd Street, New York 10019, 212-265-1040, www.folkartmuseum.org; NY Museum of Modern Art, 11 West 53rd Street, NYC 10019, 212-708-9400, www.moma.org; Museum of Television and Radio, 25 West 52nd Street, NYC 10019, 212-621-6600, www.mtr.org; Museum of Arts & Design, 40 West 53rd, NYC 10019, 212-956-3535; City Center Theater, 130 West 55th Street, NYC 10019, 212-581-1212, www.city center.org; Carnegie Hall and Weill Recital Hall, 154 West 57th Street, NYC 10019, 212-247-7800, www.carnegiehall.org; NYC's Official Visitor Information Center, 810 Seventh Avenue, 212-484-1200, www.nycvisit.com; Times Square Visitors Center, 1560 Broadway between 46th and 47th streets, NYC 10036, www.timessquarebid.org
Transportation—Subway: Crosstown S train (shuttle), 42nd Street from Times Square to Grand Central; #7, 42nd Street at Times Square,

Fifth Avenue, Grand Central; A, C, E, Eighth Avenue at 34th Street (Exp.), 42nd Street (Exp.), 50th Street, 59th Street (A, C), 50th Street at Seventh, Fifth Avenue and Lexington Avenue (E); #1/#9, #2, #3, Seventh Avenue at 34th Street (Exp.), 42nd Street (Exp.), 50th Street and Broadway, 59th Street and Broadway; B, D, F, Q, Sixth Avenue at 34th Street (Exp.), 42nd Street (Exp.), 47-50th Street (Exp.), 57th Street (B, Q), 53rd Street at Fifth Avenue and Lexington Avenue (F); #4, #5, #6, Lexington at 42nd Street (Exp.), 51st Street, 59th Street; R, N, W, Seventh Avenue & 49th, Seventh Avenue & 57th Street, Lexington Avenue & 59th Street.

Transportation—Bus: Crosstown 34th Street (#34); Crosstown 42nd Street (#42) Downtown Broadway - Crosstown 42nd Street, (#104); Crosstown 49/50th streets (#50); Crosstown 57th Street (#31, #57) Crosstown 57th Street - Uptown York Avenue (#30); Uptown Eighth Avenue - Downtown Seventh Avenue (#10); Uptown Sixth Avenue - Downtown Fifth Avenue (#5); Uptown Sixth Avenue - Downtown/ Seventh Avenue and Broadway (#6, #7); Uptown Madison Avenue - Downtown Fifth Avenue (#1, #2, #3, #4); Uptown Lexington Avenue - Downtown Third Avenue (#101, #102, #103)

CLINTON

Boundaries and Contiguous Areas: North: 59th Street and Lincoln Center; **East**: Eighth Avenue and the Theater District; **South**: 34th Street and Chelsea; **West**: Hudson River

Not so long ago Clinton was "Hell's Kitchen," the neighborhood—and it is a real neighborhood— which produced gangster Owney Madden and inspired *West Side Story*. Traditionally a poor workingman's district with often-squalid tenements and rooming houses, Clinton is still home to some street gangs and has some raunchy blocks catering to transients. Reason enough to explain why this area, so close to midtown that developers are calling it "Midtown West," remained something of a backwater until the incursion of desirable living space brought some respectability.

Upgrading began in the 1970s when Manhattan Plaza, 400 West 43rd Street, with its two towers, pool and tennis courts, was built. People with enough money to pay the high rents originally charged for the apartments were disinclined to live here because of the neighborhood, so the buildings were converted to subsidized housing for the long-time residents that were displaced by the complex and for people in the performing arts. This new population helped found and now supports the thriving off-Broadway Theater Row on the south side of 42nd Street, a bonanza for

New York's theater-going public, not to mention the theater world. The new respectability is firmly anchored on far-west 42nd Street by 1 River Place, a vast luxury rental building zigzagging across a whole block on the city's western edge. Now in an area once characterized by sleaze and depression, there are good restaurants, theaters featuring more "cutting edge" off-Broadway shows, blocks of spiffed-up townhouses, and handsome co-op renovations such as the Piano Factory. Clinton's new frontier is Tenth Avenue, where The Foundry, a 222-apartment mixed-income rental complex rose over a parking lot and taxi garage in 2000. The transformation of **West 42nd Street** from the tawdry "Deuce" that it once was to a safer, family-oriented entertainment/business center continues, especially apparent with a Disney Store and Disney-owned theaters in the midst of the hustle and bustle.

One Worldwide Plaza, a 49-story tower capped by a nouveau mansard roof, is both a symbol and a powerful instrument of change in Clinton. Prestigious law firms and ad agencies now occupy space at Eighth Avenue and 50th Street, where the shabby, old Madison Square Garden once squatted, and winos, hookers, and drug pushers roamed. A plaza separates the office spire in the mixed-use Zeckendorf development from the residential area, which is located to the west in the block-square complex. There sit a 39-story high rise and a series of attractive brick low rise condominiums containing some 650 units. Eighth and Ninth avenues and the adjoining side streets are starting to move up as well. While much of the neighborhood around 42nd street and Time Square has been revamped, remnants of the old remain in the form of run down theaters and several adult video stores—and yes, there is still a shady element found on some of the streets after dark. Perhaps the biggest concern when considering this neighborhood is congestion—too many buildings, too many residents, and too many visitors, not to mention traffic. However, for the young trendsetter, theatergoer, or thespian, this may be the "hottest" place to settle. For a family with kids or those seeking a quiet refuge, Clinton would be an unlikely option.

One mammoth presence that has profoundly affected Clinton is the Jacob K. Javits Convention Center, 655 West 34th Street. Now, where there had been a nondescript patch of garages, warehouses, and parking lots, a mini-neighborhood springs forth, dubbed **TunJav** (for Lincoln Tunnel, which empties here, and Javits Center, which it adjoins) by the *New York Times*. A few artists, designers, architects, and others have carved homes out of these industrial buildings. The ethnic food shops and tantalizing fruits and vegetables along Ninth Avenue feed them. Talk of expanding the center has sparked both interest and opposition from the neighborhood. Additional talk of a New York Jets Stadium in the area has garnered great protest from numerous West Side neighborhood groups that would be affected by such a project. Concerns about the stadium focus particularly on the traffic bottleneck such a project would cause in an already traffic heavy area. Further development in this area is a foregone conclusion. The question remains as to what form such development will take, commercial or residential. Because the neighborhood is in the midst of radical transformation, any apartment hunting here should be done block by block, on foot, and at different hours of the day. Besides the possibility of lucking into a reasonable rental, it will give you a good idea about the feel of an area and if it changes at night. Consult the weekly *Chelsea Clinton News* as an informative neighborhood reference, 212-268-2552.

Web Sites: www.hellskitchen.net, www.clintoncommunitygarden.org, www.nyc.gov

Area Codes: 212, 646

Post Offices: Midtown Station, 223 West 38th Street, NYC 10018, Times Square Station, 340 West 42nd Street, NYC 10036; 800-275-8777

Zip Codes: 10019, 10036, 10018

Police Precincts: Midtown North, 306 West 54th Street, NYC 10019, 212-767-8400; Midtown South, 357 West 35th Street, NYC 10001, 212-239-9811

Emergency Hospitals: St. Luke's Roosevelt Hospital Center: The Roosevelt Hospital at 1000 Tenth Avenue at West 59th Street, NYC 10019, 212-523-4000; St. Clare's Hospital and Health Care Center, 415 West 51st Street, NYC 10019, 212-586-1500

Libraries: Columbus Branch, 742 10th Avenue, NYC 10036, 212-586-5098, www.nypl.org

Public School Education: Clinton falls within School District #2 in region 9 (see **Chelsea**).

Adult Education: John Jay College of Criminal Justice, 899 10th Avenue, NYC 10019, 212-237-8000, www.jjay.cuny.edu

Community Resources: St. Clement's Episcopal Church, 423 West 46th Street, NYC 10036, 212-246-7277, has a special mission to the arts community, and its services are as likely to consist of theatrical performances as liturgy. The Intrepid Sea-Air-Space Museum, Pier 86 at West 46th Street and 12th Avenue, 212-245-0072, www.intrepidmuseum.org, is housed in and around the aircraft carrier Intrepid and contains, among other permanent and changing exhibits, the USS Growler submarine and the USS Edson destroyer.

Transportation—Subway: #1/#9, #2, #3 Broadway at 59th Street, 50th Street, 42nd Street (Exp.), 34th Street (Exp.); A, C, E at 59th Street (Exp.), 50th Street, 42nd Street (Exp.), 34th Street (Exp.), R, N, W, Seventh Avenue & 49th, Seventh Avenue & 57th Street, Lexington Avenue & 59th Street.

Transportation—Bus: Crosstown 57th Street (#57); Crosstown 49th/50th streets (#27, #50); Crosstown 42nd Street (#42); Crosstown 34th Street (#16, #34); Uptown Tenth Avenue - Downtown Ninth Avenue (#11); Uptown Eighth Avenue - Downtown Seventh Avenue (#10); Downtown Broadway (#104) to 42nd Street and then crossing to the East Side along 42nd Street.

LINCOLN CENTER AREA

Boundaries and Contiguous Areas: North: 72nd Street and the Upper West Side; **East**: Central Park West; **South**: 59th Street and Clinton; **West**: Hudson River

This neighborhood, dubbed **Lincoln Square**, is a prime example of how a major cultural facility can improve a marginal New York location. Construction in 1960 of the glass and travertine Lincoln Center complex with theaters, opera and ballet houses, concert halls, library, and the Juilliard School transformed a dreary stretch of rundown tenements and warehouses. Limousines now queue up where once trucks double-parked, and it seems as if every other pedestrian carries a musical instrument or moves with the marked grace of a ballet dancer. In 2000, the design for the Columbus Centre development was unveiled, a 2.1 million square foot mixed-use facility. Now complete, it includes AOL/Time Warner World Headquarters, the luxury Mandarin Oriental Hotel at 60th Street, office and retail space, fine dining, as well as the Jazz at Lincoln Center concert hall.

Columnar apartment and office buildings rise above the cafes, restaurants, and boutiques lining Broadway, Columbus, and Amsterdam avenues. Fordham University's West Side Campus and ABC are also firmly planted in the neighborhood, adding a boost to the renaissance of Columbus and Amsterdam avenues, which cater to the food, drink, and clothing needs of West Side residents.

Condo spires and columns have shot up south and west of the culture complex, even on barren Tenth Avenue, which may be the new frontier of Lincoln Square. Tall white brick luxury buildings compose most of Lincoln's Square's housing. Breaking that mold, 35-story twin towers on a stone base, designed to appeal to families with dogs, opened to renters on West End Avenue between 64th and 65th streets in 2000. The builder was quoted in the *Times* as saying he chose that neighborhood because "it's young, vibrant, and cultural, blends the old New York with the new ... and appeals to a broad range of people."

And now we have the beginnings of **Trump Place**, the much-heralded riverfront project known in the planning stages as Trump City. When

Donald Trump (New Yorkers know him as "The Donald") purchased the site of the now-defunct railroad yards fronting the Hudson River between 59th and 72nd streets, plans for the development of an enormous housing, shopping, and business complex to the west of Lincoln Center received a boost. But resistance to the "Trumping of Lincoln Square" solidified among residents and community planners, and future development is likely to be less dense and less grandiose than the original Trump model. For now, three structures housing condos and luxury rentals tower alone over the Hudson River, not to mention (and the ads don't) the noisy West Side Highway. Nonetheless, the area surrounding Lincoln Center remains a vibrant location, wonderful for walking, or sitting outside in warm weather at one of the many cafes. A wide range of popular stores including a Barnes & Noble superstore can be found, and best of all, it's near Central Park and of course, Lincoln Center.

Web Sites: www.nyc.gov, www.trumpplace.com

Area Codes: 212, 646

Post Office: Columbus Circle Station, 27 West 60th Street, NYC 10023, 800-275-8777

Zip Codes: 10023, 10019

Police Precinct: Midtown North, 306 West 54th Street, NYC 10019, 212-767-8400

Emergency Hospital (nearest): St. Luke's-Roosevelt Hospital Center: The Roosevelt Hospital at 1000 Tenth Avenue, at 59th Street, NYC 10019, 212-523-4000

Library: Library of the Performing Arts at Lincoln Center, 111 Amsterdam Avenue, NYC 10023, 212-870-1630; marvelous for researching the arts.

Public School Education: Region 10, 4360 Broadway, NYC 10033, 917-521-3700; School District #3, remote location office, 154 West 93rd Street, NYC, 212-678-2880; Committee on Special Education, 122 Amsterdam Avenue, NYC 10025, 917-441-3600; www.nycenet.edu

Adult Education: Fordham University, 113 West 60th Street, NYC 10023, 212-636-6000, www.fordham.edu; The Juilliard School, Lincoln Center Plaza, NYC 10023, 212-799-5000, www.lincoln center.org; Art Students League of New York, 215 West 57th Street, NYC 10019, 212-247-4510, www.theartstudenteleague.org; The Elaine Kaufman Cultural Arts Center at the Goodman House, 129 West 67th Street, 212-362-8060, www.elainekaufmancenter.org, offers courses in music, dance, art and the theater.

Community Resources: for the plethora of cultural events, theaters, library, shops, restaurants, exhibits, and tours at Lincoln Center call their customer service department at 212-875-5456 or go to www.lincolncenter.org. Merkin Concert Hall at the Elaine Kaufman Cultural Arts Center, 129 West 67th Street, 212-362-8060, www.elainekaufmancenter.org, presents a variety of concerts, primarily ethnic and chamber music; American Folk Art Museum, 2 Lincoln Square, NYC 10023, 212-595-9533, www.folkartmuseum.org.

Transportation—Subway: #1/9 Broadway at 66th Street, 59th Street; #1/9, #2, #3 Broadway at 72nd Street (Exp.); A, B, C, D at 59th Street (Exp.)

Transportation—Bus: Crosstown 72nd Street (#72); Crosstown 66th/67th streets (#66); Crosstown 57th Street (#57, #31); Crosstown 57th/72nd streets (#30), Uptown Tenth/Amsterdam Avenue - Downtown Ninth/Columbus Avenue (#11); Uptown Eighth Avenue - Downtown Central Park West/Seventh Avenue (#10)

THE UPPER WEST SIDE

Boundaries and Contiguous Areas: North: 110th Street and Morningside Heights; **East**: Central Park West; **South**: 72nd Street and Lincoln Center; **West**: Hudson River

For decades, large sprawling apartments and an active community life have been luring writers, musicians, intellectuals—in general, those seeking an alternative to the Upper East Side's more constrained life-style—to the West Side. Indeed, the city's first large apartment buildings, with lofty ceilings, thick walls and space to waste, were built here around the turn of the century. Grand structures rose first along Central Park West (note the famed Dakota at 72nd Street), claimed by some aficionados to be the most architecturally elegant avenue in New York; next on Broadway (the neoclassical Ansonia between 73rd and 74th streets and the block-square Apthorp between 78th and 79th are particularly grand), which was to be Park Avenue West but isn't; and then on West End Avenue and Riverside Drive.

Most buildings along the apartment-lined avenues—with the notable exception of **Columbus** and **Amsterdam**, which have only recently emerged from the Dickensian 19th to enter the trendiest century—managed to remain sufficiently attractive to hold the middle class. But the rows of brick, limestone, and brownstone townhouses built for the newly affluent on the cross streets during the early 1900s declined into squalid tenements and SRO (single room occupancy) rooming houses. Not until the late 1960s, when an ambitious urban renewal plan spurred building and renovation, did this veritable architectural museum again become an address for affluent achievers. Today, the typical brownstone houses the owner's family on the garden or parlor floors and tenants on the original bedroom floors above. Ranks of condo towers have shot up along Columbus and, more recently, Amsterdam between 87th and 97th streets—just outside the boundaries of the Central Park West Historic District. These svelte and pricey (though less expensive than Lincoln Square) condominiums provide residents with plenty of play space: health clubs, pools, rooftop gardens, party rooms, and in-house parking are standard. Meanwhile, **Upper Broadway** is being transformed as high rises are slotted among the wearier old-timers between 97th Street and Columbia University. A short-term rental in one of these buildings offers the undecided newcomer an opportunity to try out the neighborhood before making a long-term commitment.

Most of the handsome pre-war stone buildings fronting Central Park—the San Remo, the Beresford, the Majestic, etc—are cooperatives now, and as sought after and as pricey as those on Fifth Avenue across the park. Just south of 96th Street, a few condos and rentals are to be found, and north of 96th to 110th, in the area known as **Manhattan Valley**, a mix of condos, co-ops and rentals makes Central Park West more accessible for those with slimmer pocketbooks. The vast apartment co-ops lining West End Avenue and curving along Riverside Drive have enduring appeal. Pioneers stake their claims in Manhattan Valley east of Broadway in the upper 90s and 100s, and west of Broadway between 96th and 110th streets. For the less adventurous and thicker of purse, existing rental apartments are well worth pursuing, if only to live between Manhattan's greenest playgrounds, Central and Riverside parks, and near one of its cultural stalwarts, the massive Museum of Natural History, which devotes almost 25 acres of floor space to some of the finest scientific collections in the world.

Residents of the Upper West Side are privy to Central Park, the city's premiere playground, and Riverside Drive, which stretches quietly from 72nd Street to 165th Street, looking west over Riverside Park, the Hudson River, and stunning sunsets over the Jersey Palisades. Market rate rental apartments are mostly between 92nd and 96th streets, the rest being largely co-ops whose boards tend to be less snobbish than in some other neighborhoods. Broadway is two blocks away, with its addictive gourmet food markets. But, it is Riverside Park that gives the neighborhood its sense of community. Residents raise their children there, walk their dogs, play, and dream there. Says one, "With its many levels it is a wonderful place to walk and stroll, sit and read, and have a sandwich—even in the colder months."

Web Site: www.nyc.gov
Area Codes: 212, 646
Post Offices: Cathedral Station, 215 West 104th Street, NYC 10025;

Planetarium Station, 131 West 83rd Street, NYC 10024, 212-873-3701; Ansonia Station, 178 Columbus Avenue, NYC 10023; 800-275-8777

Zip Codes: 10025, 10024, 10023

Police Precincts: Twenty-fourth, 151 West 100th Street, NYC 10025, 212-678-1811; Twentieth, 120 West 82nd Street, NYC 10024, 212-580-6411

Emergency Hospitals (nearest): Both branches of the St. Luke's-Roosevelt Hospital Center: The Roosevelt Hospital at 1000 Tenth Avenue at 59th Street, NYC 10019, and St. Luke's Hospital at 1111 Amsterdam Avenue, NYC 10025, at 114th street, both 212-523-4000

Libraries: Bloomingdale Branch, 150 West 100th Street, NYC 10025, 212-222-8030; St. Agnes Branch, 444 Amsterdam Avenue, NYC 10024, 212-877-4380; Riverside Branch, 127 Amsterdam Avenue, NYC 10023, 212-870-1810; www.nypl.org

Public School Education: School District #3 in region 10 (see **Lincoln Center Area**).

Adult Education: Bank Street College of Education, 610 West 112th Street, NYC 10025, 212-875-4400, www.bankstreet.edu

Community Resources: Central Park, stretching from 59th Street over 840 acres up to 110th Street is the city's playground, rich with athletic activities, playgrounds, sunbathing sections, a zoo, restaurants and food vendors, street entertainers, a skating rink, summer concert series, and more. The Beacon Theater, 2124 Broadway, between 74th and 75th streets, 212-496-7070; American Museum of Natural History and the Rose Center for Earth and Space, Central Park West from 79th Street to 81st Street, museum information: 212-769-5100, www.amnh.orj; the Bard Graduate Center for Studies in the Decorative Arts, 18 West 86th Street, NYC 10024, 212-501-3000, www.bgc.bard.edu; Children's Museum of Manhattan, 212 West 83rd Street, 212-721-1234, www.cmom.org; Nicholas Roerich Museum, 319 West 107th Street, NYC 10025, 212-864-7752, www.roerich.org

Transportation—Subway: #1/9, Broadway at 110th Street, 103rd Street; #1/9, #2, #3, 96th Street (Exp.); #1/9, 86th Street, 79th Street; #1/9, #2, #3, 72nd Street (Exp.); B, C at Central Park West and 110th Street, 103rd Street, 96th Street, 86th Street, 81st Street, 72nd Street

Transportation—Bus: Crosstown 96th Street (#96); Crosstown 96th/106th streets (#106) Crosstown 86th Street (#86); Crosstown 79th Street (#79); Crosstown 72nd Street (#72); Crosstown 66th/67th streets (#66) ending at Central Park West and 72nd Street; Uptown Riverside Drive - Downtown Riverside Drive (#5); Uptown Amsterdam (Ninth) Avenue - Downtown Columbus (Tenth) Avenue (#7, #11); Uptown Amsterdam - Downtown Broadway (#100), Uptown Broadway - Downtown Broadway (#104)

MORNINGSIDE HEIGHTS

Boundaries and Contiguous Areas: North: 125th Street and Harlem; **East:** Morningside Drive; **South:** 110th Street and Upper West Side; **West:** Hudson River

Academia amidst a gritty urban-scape, this lively community occupying the formerly rocky slopes of northern Manhattan is dominated—physically, economically, and socially—by Columbia University, one of the nation's oldest, richest, and largest educational institutions. In addition, Barnard College as well as two important religious seminaries, the Manhattan School of Music, a large teaching hospital, and two major churches share the Heights with a mixture of students, professors, professionals, and urban poor. Up here next to the granite bulk of Ulysses S. Grant's pompous tomb, Upper West Side gray is relieved by Riverside Park, used extensively by residents as a front yard, and by Morningside Park, until recently avoided as unsafe. Spearheaded by the Morningside Area Alliance, efforts to clean up the park have involved the Parks Department, Columbia students, and the "Friends of Morningside Park." Daytime strollers, dog-walkers, and joggers now use the park. Safe at night? Maybe not.

Work on its massive towers remains halted indefinitely, but if they are ever completed, the Episcopal Cathedral Church of St. John the Divine will literally tower over the community; now spireless, the world's largest Gothic cathedral just looms. (The tall Gothic church tower you do see rising northwest of Columbia belongs to Riverside Church, the Rockefellers' non-denominational gift to the city.) Part of St. John's was destroyed by a five-alarm fire in late 2001, but the church reopened within a week and continues to serve the community with little remaining visible damage. St. John's caters to cultural as well as spiritual needs, sponsoring a particularly rich and wide-ranging series of concerts from chamber music through liturgical works to jazz and other events including poetry readings, craft fairs, and dance programs.

Broadway, Morningside Heights' main street, showcases bookstores, coffee shops, all-night fruit stands, student bars/jazz joints, boutiques, and restaurants ranging from fast food to ethnic and elegant. In recent years Columbia has actively promoted the transformation of the ten blocks south of the campus between Broadway and Amsterdam, and this once-desolate area now appeals to a more sophisticated crowd than heretofore. The lively street life that continues late at night makes the neighborhood relatively safer than in the past and certainly interesting.

As owners of one-third of the community's housing stock, over half of which is occupied by tenants affiliated with the college, Columbia

University is the Heights' biggest landlord. However, an occasional rental does hit the open market, and sometimes space becomes available when Columbia-connected roommates separate (graduate, marry, or move) leaving behind an empty room and half the monthly rent bill. Co-ops, keenly sought now, escalated steeply in price during the 1990s, but still represent good value, if not a bargain, when compared to Upper West Side prices.

Web Sites: www.morningsideheights.net, www.nyc.gov

Area Codes: 212, 646

Post Office: Columbia University Station, 534 West 112th Street, NYC 10025, 800-275-8777

Zip Codes: 10027, 10026, 10025

Police Precinct: Twenty-sixth, 520 West 126th Street, NYC 10027, 212-678-1311

Emergency Hospital: St. Luke's-Roosevelt Hospital Center: St. Luke's Hospital, 1111 Amsterdam Avenue, NYC 10025, at 114th street, 212-523-4000

Libraries: 115th Street Branch, 203 West 115th Street, NYC 10026, 212-666-9393 (temporarily at 2011 Adam Clayton Powell Jr. Boulevard); Morningside Heights Library, 2900 Broadway, NYC 10025, 212-864-2530; www.nypl.org

Public School Education: School District #3 in region 10 (see **Lincoln Center Area**).

Adult Education: Barnard College, 3009 Broadway, NYC 10027, 212-854-5262, www.barnard.edu; Columbia University, Broadway and 114th Street to 120th Street, NYC 10027, 212-854-1754, www.columbia.edu; Union Theological Seminary, 3041 Broadway at 120th Street, NYC 10027, 212-662-7100, www.uts.columbia.edu; Bank Street College of Education, 610 West 112th Street, NYC 10025, 212-875-4400, www.bankstreet.edu; Jewish Theological Seminary, 3080 Broadway, NYC 10027, 212-678-8000, www.jtsa.edu; Manhattan School of Music, 120 Claremont Avenue, NYC 10027, 212-749-2802, www.msnnyc.edu

Community Resources: Cathedral Church of St. John the Divine, West 112th Street, NYC 10025, 212-316-7540, www.stjohndivine.org, also has on its large grounds a Biblical Garden with plantings inspired by the Old Testament. Riverside Church, 400 Riverside Drive (at West 120th Street), NYC 10027, 212-870-6700, www.theriver sidechurchny.org, offers educational and cultural programs in addition to religious services.

Transportation—Subway: A, B, C, D at 125th Street (Exp.), 116th Street, 110th Street, 1,9, Broadway at 110th, 116th & 125th

Transportation—Bus: Crosstown 116th Street (#116); Uptown Amsterdam Avenue - Downtown Columbus Avenue (#11); Uptown Broadway - Downtown Broadway (#104) Uptown Amsterdam - Crosstown 125th Street - Downtown Broadway (#100); La Guardia Airport via 125th Street (#60)

THE HARLEMS

Boundaries and Contiguous Areas: *East Harlem*: **North** and **East**: Harlem River; **South**: 96th Street, Upper East Side and Yorkville; **West**: Central Park; *Harlem*: **North**: 155th Street and Washington Heights; **East**: Harlem River; **West**: Hudson River; **South**: 125th Street and Morningside Heights

This neighborhood, rich in culture, remains the spiritual focus of black America. Although Harlem pockets some of the worst poverty and crime in New York City, many of its high-stooped, row-house-lined streets are perfectly safe. A strong economy in the 1990s into the new millennium stimulated renovation of Harlem's brownstones and abandoned apartment buildings, increased national chain retailers in its business district, and ignited the rebirth of restaurants and nightlife. The result has been an influx of middle-class professionals, black and white.

Originally settled in 1636 by Dutch tobacco farmers, Harlem blossomed into a prosperous suburb in the 1800s. Around 1900, black New Yorkers began settling into an abundance of apartment buildings left empty when real estate developers' plans for a white middle-class neighborhood failed to materialize. In addition to brand new housing stock, Harlem offered its first black residents a less racially hostile environment than other parts of the city.

Harlem of the 1920s, home to the largest black community in the US, is synonymous with the Harlem Renaissance. Musicians, playwrights, and novelists flocked to the neighborhood bursting with jazz clubs and casinos. For several decades beginning in the 1940s, the area fell on hard times, and by the 1960s, the racial tension and overall poor economy of the city caused Harlem to decline further. A revitalized Harlem greets visitors and newcomers today.

Since the 1930s, prominent African-American Harlemites have lived on Striver's Row, on West 138th and 139th streets, between Seventh and Eighth avenues. Dominated by brownstones now part of the **St. Nicholas Historic District**, Abyssinian Baptist Church, New York's oldest black church, is located at 132 West 138th Street. Equally appealing to professionals, and to City College professors, is the **Hamilton Heights** area just north of the college, in particular Hamilton Terrace, with its handsome landmarked brownstones. The central area around the **Mount Morris Park Historic District**, between 116th and 125th streets, has become a highly desirable location. The western strip along the water continues to be the site of forthcoming redevelopment with a waterside plaza, shopping, a hotel, and housing in the planning stages.

To the south, just above Central Park, in the area known as **West Central Harlem** or **Manhattanville**, between 110th and 116th streets, are rentals and co-ops in a redeveloped and now popular area. Some rentals here, particularly those north of 116th Street to 125th are priced below market. City-sponsored renovation of abandoned apartment buildings has recently created affordable condos across from Morningside Park. Thorough exploration and the help of a good realtor are essential here. Further north, **Sugar Hill**, with its mixture of high rise and pleasing brownstone apartments in the 140s and 150s between St. Nicholas and Edgecombe avenues, has an enduring appeal, as does **Riverside Drive**, a racially mixed area housing professionals, middle- and low-income residents.

Cultural and educational institutions and welcoming green spaces abound in Harlem. In its heart, at Lenox Avenue (Malcolm X Boulevard) and West 135th Street, is the Schomburg Center for Research in Black Culture, which houses the world's largest collection of black history. On West 135th Street is the facility's outdoor sculpture garden; the outdoor amphitheater is on West 136th. Another neighborhood treasure is the splendid Riverbank State Park—28 acres of landscaped greenery with spectacular sunset views over the Hudson at 145th Street. Completed in 1993 atop a waste treatment plant, the recreational complex comprises indoor and outdoor swimming pools, a gym and fitness room, softball fields, basketball, tennis and handball courts outdoors, an indoor theater and an amphitheater, and an ice and roller skating rink. Admission is free, open daily from 6 a.m. to 11 p.m., with a fee for the use of tennis courts and a nominal fee for the pool (see **Sports and Recreation**).

Harlem's east side is known as **Spanish Harlem** or **El Barrio**. Here you'll find mostly tenements and housing projects. Above 100th Street, newcomers should take care and know where they're going. La Marqueta, a Latino produce, meat, and housewares market keeps things bustling along El Barrio's busiest street, East 116th to Park Avenue. Some of the tenements in Spanish Harlem are being renovated, but the area has not seen great progress yet. A small section of El Barrio is benefiting from some new apartments and townhouses, a result of $605 million designated to the area by the New York City Housing Authority. The revamped housing has brought in trendy cafes and art galleries. The Boricua Gallery and El Museo del Barrio are poised to be the epicenter for future development that is expected around East 106th Street.

Class and racial tensions have kept Harlem somewhat isolated from the rest of Manhattan but many say it is entering a second Renaissance. Indeed, with new families restoring many of Harlem's brownstone buildings and a thriving cultural scene (see **Community Resources** below), this neighborhood is pumping with life around the clock now. Tourism has increased, restaurants and jazz clubs have proliferated, and if the good life is defined by jazz clubs, all night dancing, authentic soul food, urban poetry, and the return of the Apollo Theater, then Harlem is indeed providing all the necessary elements. The highly touted Dance Theater of Harlem, productions by the award-winning Classical Theater of Harlem, the annual Harlem Book Fair, the Urban World Film Festival, numerous jazz venues, and the home purchases by African-American celebrities including Maya Angelou and Roberta Flack have generated great interest here. Visitors, who for years did not venture past 96th street, are now beating down a path to check out this revitalized neighborhood. Even former president Bill Clinton has set up shop with an office on 125th Street. Over the next few years condominium projects are expected to emerge throughout Harlem. The recently built, and already filled, Sugar Hill Condominiums at 146th street are a prime example of what's to come. A converted six-story building, Sugar Hill Condos feature two- and three-bedroom units at slightly lower rates than Chelsea. Also new in the area are the Rosa Parks Condominiums at 118th Street and St. Nicholas Avenue, the recently completed Washington Irving Condominiums on 112th street, and the 1400 Fifth Avenue Co-ops at 125th Street.

Start your search for Harlem housing in the *Amsterdam News*, 212-932-7400, real estate section.

Web Sites: www.hometoharlem.com, www.east-harlem.com, www. nyc.gov

Area Codes: 212, 646

Post Offices: Hamilton Grange Station, 521 West 146th Street, NYC 10031; Manhattanville Station, 365 West 125th Street, NYC 10027; Hell Gate Station, 153 East 110 Street, NYC 10029; Triborough Station, 167 East 124th Street, NYC 10035; College Station, 217 West 140th Street, NYC 10030; 800-275-8777

Zip Codes: 10026, 10027, 10029, 10030, 10031, 10032, 10035, 10039

Police Precincts: Twenty-third, 164 East 102nd Street, NYC 10029, 212-860-6411; Twenty-fourth, 151 West 100th Street, NYC 10025, 212-678-1811; Twenty-fifth, 120 East 119th Street, NYC 10035, 212-860-6511; Twenty-eighth, 2271 Eighth Avenue, NYC 10027, 212-678-1611; Thirtieth, 451 West 151st Street, NYC 10032, 212-690-8811; Thirty-second, 250 West 135th Street, NYC 10030, 212-690-6311

Emergency Hospitals: Harlem Hospital Center, 506 Lenox Avenue at

135th Street, NYC 10037, 212-939-1000, includes a crisis intervention center for battered wives, children and rape victims; Mount Sinai Hospital, 101st Street and Madison Avenue, NYC 10029, 212-241-6500. **Libraries**: a regional branch of the New York City Public Library, Countee Cullen, is located at 104 West 136th Street, NYC 10037, 212-491-2070; Hamilton Grange Branch, 704 St. Nicholas Avenue, NYC 10031, 212-926-2147; www.nypl.org; The Schomburg Center for Research In Black Culture, 515 Malcolm X Boulevard (135th Street at Lenox Avenue), NYC 10037, 212-491-2200, houses the city's African-American archives and presents local artists' works. **Public School Education**: East Harlem schools fall in region 9, 333 7th Avenue, NYC 10001, 212-356-7500, www.nycenet.edu; high schools include the Manhattan Center for Science and Mathematics, 208 Pleasant Avenue, NYC 10029, at the FDR Drive and 116th Street, 212-876-4639; and A. Phillip Randolph Campus, Convent Avenue and 135th Street (on City College campus), NYC 10031, 212-926-0113. **Adult Education**: City College, City University of New York (CUNY) 138th Street and Convent Avenue, NYC 10031, 212-650-7000, www.ccny.cuny.edu; Boricua College, a private Hispanic liberal arts college, 3755 Broadway at 155th Street, NYC 10032, 212-694-1000, www.boricuacollege.edu **Community Resources**: Harlem celebrates its past and present history each August by hosting a one-week African-American and Hispanic festival, call the Manhattan Chamber of Commerce, 212-479-7772, for details. Also here: the Apollo Theater, 253 West 125th Street, NYC 10027, 212-749-5838, an institution and the hub for Harlem based entertainment since 1914, www.apollotheater.com; Studio Museum in Harlem, 144 West 125th Street, NYC 10027, 212-864-4500, www.studiomuseum.org; The Museum of the City of New York, 1220 Fifth Avenue at 103rd Street, NYC 10029, 212-534-1672, www.mcny.org; El Museo del Barrio, 1230 Fifth Avenue and 104th Street, NYC 10029, 212-831-7272, www.elmuseo.org (art, culture, heritage of Puerto Rico and Latin America); Dance Theater of Harlem, 466 West 152nd Street, NYC 10031, 212-690-2800, www.dancetheaterofharlem.com; Harlem School of the Arts, 645 St. Nicholas Avenue between 141st and 145th streets, NYC 10030, 212-926-4100, www.harlemschoolofarts.org; The Classical Theater of Harlem, 645 Nicholas Avenue, NYC 10029, 212-868-4444, www.ctharlem.org. **Transportation—Subway**: #4, #5, #6, Lexington Avenue at 125th (Exp.), 116th, 110th, 103rd Street and 96th Streets; #1/#9 at 157th, 145th, 137th, 125th, 116th, 110th, 103rd Street and 96th Street (Exp.), all on Broadway; #2, #3, Lenox Avenue Terminal (Exp.), Lenox Avenue at 145th Street (Exp.), 135th (Exp.), 125th (Exp.), 116th and 110th

Street (Exp.), Central Park West at 103rd Street, Broadway at 96th Street (Exp.); A (as in the song "Take the A Train"), B, C, D, St. Nicholas/8th avenues at 155th, 145th (Exp.), 135th, 125th (Exp.), and 116th, Central Park West at 110th, 103rd, and 96th Street

Transportation—Bus: Crosstown 96th Street (#96); Crosstown 116th Street (#116); Uptown Riverside Drive - Downtown Columbus Avenue (#11); Uptown/Downtown Broadway (#7, #100, #104); Uptown/Downtown Powell Avenue (#2) Uptown/Downtown St. Nicholas Avenue (#3); Uptown/Downtown Third, Lexington, Amsterdam Avenue (#101); Third, Lexington, Lennox Avenue (#102)

WASHINGTON HEIGHTS–INWOOD

Boundaries and Contiguous Areas: North: Harlem River and Riverdale; **East**: Harlem River; **South**: 155th Street and Harlem; **West**: Hudson River

Up here, where outcroppings from the Hudson riverbed rise to form Manhattan's highest ground, the tawny stone arches rhythmically lining the central courtyard at The Cloisters are echoed by the exceptionally graceful curve of the steel suspension cables of the silvery two-level George Washington Bridge. Long before John D. Rockefeller, Jr. gave the city the magnificent medieval Cloisters Museum as well as Fort Tryon Park, George Washington headquartered Revolutionary forces on the strategic terrain now called Washington Heights.

Six hundred acres of parkland, almost all of it in Fort Tryon Park and rocky, wooded Inwood Hill Park, refresh and beautify one of the most densely populated, and narrowest, sections of New York. On the map, the top of Manhattan looks like a knobby finger pointing across the Harlem River at The Bronx from the elongated fist of Manhattan. Washington Heights and Inwood are all "West Side" on both sides of the island as the Harlem River lops off the "East Side" at 138th Street.

Narrow as it is, this finger of Manhattan contains many neighborhoods, only two of which, along the western edge, we describe here. Commercial Broadway cuts through the area on a north-south bias, dividing the almost solidly Hispanic, mostly low-income Harlem River (eastern) half from the more middle-income (western) half overlooking the Hudson River. The western section contains the most coveted housing—solidly constructed pre-WW II one- and two-bedroom apartments, many with marvelous pleasing river views—situated in square, five- to ten-story buildings. The clusters of yellow, buff, and occasionally red brick art deco buildings clumped along a rocky spine above the river in the Hudson Heights section of Washington Heights have special appeal. Half-timbered Hudson View Gardens, between 183rd and 185th streets, and Castle Village with its gardens and panoramic Hudson River views nearby, two of the most desirable complexes are cooperatives, as are many of the neighborhood buildings. Sublets, where you can get them, are still priced well below rentals further downtown, as are the co-ops.

In previous years, a violent drug trade made parts of **Washington Heights**, the West 150s and 160s in particular, a dicey neighborhood despite its solidly middle class population and the presence of prestigious New York Presbyterian Hospital. Most recently, however, crime is way down, and though rentals and co-op prices are up, they are significantly less than what comparable properties cost further downtown. There are brownstones and large apartments in pre-war buildings, well worth a look, especially along Riverside Drive West, Fort Washington Avenue, and the connecting streets.

For another dimension, travel up to **Inwood** and stroll the grassy fields of Inwood Hill Park near 218th Street and Indian Road. Ahead of you, to the north, the Harlem River sweeps under the Henry Hudson Bridge, beyond which you can see the Jersey Palisades. To your immediate right are Columbia University's Baker Field, the only college stadium in Manhattan, and the college boathouse and tennis bubble. Straight ahead is one of the city's loveliest and least-known parks, Inwood Hill Park, with wetlands, rolling greens and six miles of footpaths rising into rocky woods where there are Indian caves to be seen. It's quiet, except for an astonishing variety of birds. The man jogging past is as likely to be an opera singer or an artist as he is to be a broker or a police officer.

If you find the friendly unassuming neighborhood attractive, plan to search, and search hard, on foot, questioning supers and building managers. Inwood is a small neighborhood of pleasing pre-war brick apartment buildings located between the park and Broadway, north of 207th Street, which are the two main streets. There are no trendy restaurants, lively after-hours clubs, or art film houses here. But the cost of a sunny one-bedroom (or two or three) on the park, if you can find one to rent, will make you giggle if you've been looking downtown, although prices are on the rise. Consult a reputable local real estate agent when pursuing housing here.

Web Site: www.nyc.gov
Area Codes: 212, 646
Post Offices: Audubon Station, 511 West 165th Street, NYC 10032; Washington Bridge Station, 555 West 180th Street, NYC 10033; Fort George Station, 4558 Broadway, NYC 10040; Inwood Station, 90 Vermilyea Avenue, NYC 10034; 800-275-8777
Zip Codes: 10034, 10040, 10033, 10032

Police Precincts: Thirty-fourth, 4295 Broadway, NYC 10033, 212-927-9711; Thirty-third, 2120 Amsterdam Avenue, NYC 10032, 212-927-3200

Emergency Hospital: Columbia-Presbyterian Medical Center, 622 West 168th Street, NYC 10032, 212-305-2500

Libraries: Fort Washington Branch, 535 West 179th Street, NYC 10033, 212-927-3533; Washington Heights Branch, 1000 St. Nicholas Avenue, NYC 10040, 212-923-6054; Inwood Branch, 4790 Broadway, NYC 10034, 212-942-2445; www.nypl.org

Public School Education: School District #6 in region 10, 4360 Broadway, NYC 10033, 917-521-3700, www.nycenet.edu

Adult Education: Yeshiva University, 500 West 185th Street, NYC 10033, 212-960-5400, www.yu.edu; Inwood Community Services, 651 Academy Street (just north of Dyckman Street), NYC 10034, 212-942-0043

Community Resources: The Cloisters, division of the Metropolitan Museum of Art, Fort Tryon Park (193rd Street and Fort Washington Avenue), NYC 10034, 212-923-3700, www.metmuseum.org, devoted to the art and architecture of Medieval Europe; Audubon Terrace Museum complex, Broadway between West 155th and 156th streets, including the American Academy of Arts and Letters, 633 West 155th Street, NYC 212-368-5900; The Hispanic Society of America, 613 West 155th Street, 212-926-2234, www.hispanicsociety.org, includes a library and museum; Morris-Jumel Mansion and Museum, 65 Jumel Terrace, NYC 10032, 212-923-8008, www.morrisjumel.org, a colonial home in garden surroundings used by Washington during the Revolution and later redecorated by Eliza Jumel; Dyckman Farmhouse Museum, 4881 Broadway at 204th Street, NYC 10034, 212-304-9422, www.dyckman.org, is a restored 18th century Dutch farmhouse-museum belonging to the city and well worth a visit; with children's crafts on selected Saturdays.

Transportation—Subway: A, 207th, Dyckman, 190th, 181st, 175th, 168th (all Exp.) 163rd streets: stops along Fort Washington Avenue, Broadway; B, C at 168th, 163rd, 155th streets on Amsterdam Avenue; #1/#9 at 215th, 207th, Dyckman, 191st, 181st, 168th and 157th streets: all stops along St. Nicholas Avenue

Transportation—Bus: Crosstown 181st Street (#3, #11, #13, #36); Uptown/Downtown Fort Washington Avenue to Broadway (#4); Uptown/Downtown Broadway (#7, #100); Uptown/Downtown St. Nicholas Avenue (#3); Uptown/Downtown Eighth Avenue, Central Park West, Douglass Blvd. to 159th Street ($10); Uptown/Downtown Lexington Avenue to 193rd Street (#101); Uptown/Downtown Third Avenue, Adam Clayton Powell Blvd. (#102); Washington Heights/Midtown - limited Service Between Cabrini Avenue and 34th Street (# 98)

THE BRONX

Poor "The Bronx," a borough that's seldom mentioned without its article. The northernmost and smallest, though not by much, of New York City's five parts is more often celebrated for a rude cheer and for Fort Apache, the south central section that has begun to struggle back from dilapidation and worse, than for large verdant parks, colleges, and top-flight high schools or for some singularly attractive neighborhoods. To set the record straight, then, you should know that The Bronx boasts all of these, not to mention being home to Edgar Allan Poe and Mark Twain, and current home of the single most successful professional sports franchise in American history, the beloved New York Yankees.

Four of the city's finest high schools are situated in The Bronx: the prestigious public Bronx High School of Science, from which many Intel (formerly Westinghouse) Science Award winners graduate, as well as the private Fieldston, Horace Mann, and Riverdale Country Day schools. Eight universities and colleges enhance the borough's scholastic character.

A wealth of public land is probably The Bronx's greatest asset; parkland accounts for almost a quarter of the 43 square mile borough. Partially forested Van Cortlandt Park, a mecca for cross country skiers in the winter, is the spot for soccer, rugby, and football in the summer, along with the city's oldest public golf course. Even larger Pelham Bay Park, from which little City Island dangles, harbors Orchard Beach along its sandy shore. But the star is Bronx Park with 500 acres about equally divided between two of the city's most enjoyable institutions: the Bronx Zoo (officially the New York Zoological Society's International Wildlife Conservation Park) and the New York Botanical Garden. The Haupt Conservatory, a sparkling crystal greenhouse complex, displays thousands of plant varieties in natural micro-climates and must be seen. Kids of all ages, naturalists and explorers too, frequent the zoo, using the tramlike Skyfari for an overview of the African exhibit as well as to commute between pavilions that include the World of Darkness and World of Birds.

Just south of Westchester County, City Island floats rather quaintly in placid Long Island Sound, providing a delightful, New Englandesque escape from city life, not to mention the finest seafood around. And over on the Hudson shore, Riverdale shelters some estates and sylvan lanes worthy of suburban Scarsdale, although more densely packed. In between these two neighborhoods, apartment buildings embellished with art deco motifs line the once-elegant Grand Concourse.

While chunks of The Bronx do flourish, the majority of residential sections continue to struggle toward economic recovery with low- to middle-income housing in pre-war buildings. Cooperatives and condominiums continue to slowly replace rental apartments, but The Bronx has few

THE BRONX

0   1 Mile

0   1 Kms

NEW JERSEY / NEW YORK

TUCKAHOE

BRONXVILLE

NEW ROCHELLE

IONA COLLEGE

TWIN LAKES CO. PK

Cross County Pkwy

YONKERS

CROSS COUNTY SHOPPING CTR.

PELHAM

COLLEGE OF NEW ROCHELLE

YONKERS RACEWAY

MOUNT VERNON

PELHAM MANOR

WAVE HILL

VAN CORTLANDT PK

233rd St

ST. PAUL'S CHURCH NAT'L HIST. SITE

GLEN ISLAND PK

RIVERDALE PK

VAN CORTLAND HOUSE

WOODLAWN CEMETERY

RIVERDALE

KINGSBRIDGE

SPUYTEN DUYVIL

Jerome Park Res.

BRONX HIST. MUS.

CO-OP CITY

BARTOW-PELL MANSION

INWOOD HILL PK

LEHMAN COLLEGE C.U.N.Y

NYC BOTANICAL GARDEN

PELHAM PARKWAY

PELHAM BAY PARK

WASHINGTON HEIGHTS

FORDHAM UNIV.

Pelham Pkwy

PARKCHESTER

NORTH WIND UNDERSEA INSTITUTE

CITY ISLAND

Bronx

Cross Bronx Expwy

Tremont Av

HIGHBRIDGE

TREMONT

BRONX ZOO/ WILDLIFE CONSERVATION PARK

Eastchester Bay

BRONX MUSEUM FOR THE ARTS

FORD-HAM

161st St

YANKEE STADIUM

Bruckner Expwy

THROGS NECK

MOTT HAVEN

SOUND VIEW PK

FERRY POINT PK

FT. SCHUYLER

ST. ANN'S CHURCH

HUNTS POINT

East River

WHITESTONE

Wards Island

Rikers Island

COLLEGE POINT

14th Av

QUEENS

Hell Gate

LA GUARDIA AIRPORT

14th Av

LONG ISLAND CITY

ASTORIA

Astoria Bl

FLUSHING

neighborhoods that attract the younger set in the fashion of Brooklyn and Hoboken, and families still await the return to the heyday of this once vibrant part of New York City. Bronx realtors are listed under **Apartment Hunting** in the **Finding a Place to Live** chapter.

RIVERDALE

Boundaries and Contiguous Areas: **North**: 263rd Street and Yonkers; **East**: Broadway and Van Cortlandt Park; **South**: West 239th Street and West 242nd Street, Spuyten Duyvil and Kingsbridge; **West**: Hudson River

Riverdale seems more like Westchester than New York and is certainly a departure from the rest of The Bronx. Call it a suburb in the city. It was mostly farmland, in fact, until the mid-nineteenth century, when a few wealthy souls moved out of smelly Manhattan with its occasional cholera epidemics, and carved estates overlooking the river. Among these was Wave Hill (see below). In 1853, with the completion of a railroad bridge across Spuyten Duyvil Creek (now known as the Harlem River), Riverdale soon became a prosperous suburb, desirable for possessing the best of both rural and urban life. When Riverdale was appended to New York City in 1874, it took the objections of Frederick Law Olmstead, co-designer of Central Park, to prevent the re-mapping of the winding, wooded roads that make Riverdale so beguiling today. But no one could prevent Robert Moses from bisecting both Riverdale and Spuyten Duyvil with a clean slash of the Henry Hudson Parkway in the 1930s. Many of the original mansions survive along the winding roads, often invisible behind ivy-crusted stone fences. One can buy a part of one, as many have been "condoed." Posh private schools attract kids who drive in from New Jersey and the suburbs as well as those who arrive by subway and bus from the boroughs. Shops are discreetly confined to a few zones of mom and pop businesses. Supermarket complexes are built elsewhere. Riverdale's low, tree-shaded profile appeals to both affluent New York professionals and resident foreigners.

Tall, red-brick apartment towers cluster in clumps along the potholed lanes in south Riverdale, built mostly in the 1960s and '70s, and now almost all co-ops and condos. Spacious apartments, many with enviable views, can occasionally be had at prices slightly below Manhattan standards, but are increasingly harder to find as the area has become dense with ex-Manhattanites.

In north Riverdale, along the Yonkers border, brick and stucco houses on smallish lots can be had in a quiet neighborhood, but again the prices are rising. There are plenty of mini-mansions in Riverdale, too, although perhaps the single largest concentration of elegant single-family residences is located in adjoining **Fieldston**, a somewhat exclusive community with private streets. The urban grid and bustle so typical of New York is found on the flats below in **Kingsbridge**. If you're looking here, pick up a copy of the *Riverdale Review*, published by Mondo Times, www.mondo times.com, available in stores, lobbies, and libraries.

For a great day in this neighborhood, visit Wave Hill, West 249th Street and Independence Avenue (call 718-549-3200 or go to www. wavehill.org for directions; express buses run by Liberty Lines, 718-652-8400, provide direct service to West 252nd Street). The Hudson-side complex at 249th Street and Independence Avenue consists of two stone manor houses offering occasional chamber music, a café, a greenhouse and 28 acres of perfectly gorgeous gardens, wherein summer outdoor sculpture exhibits compete for your attention with lovely river views.

Web Sites: www.ilovethebronx.com, www.nyc.gov

Area Codes: 718, 347

Post Offices: Riverdale Station, 5951 Riverdale Avenue, Bronx 10471, 718-549-7519; Kingsbridge Station, 5517 Broadway, Bronx 10463; 800-275-8777

Zip Codes: 10463, 10471

Police Precinct: Fiftieth, 3450 Kingsbridge Avenue, Bronx 10463, 718-543-5700

Emergency Hospital (nearest): Montefiore Medical Center, 210th Street and Bainbridge Avenue, Bronx 10467, 718-920-4321, the medical center has several leading hospital facilities throughout the Bronx including the University Hospital for Albert Einstein Medical University.

Library: Riverdale Public Library, 5540 Mosholu Avenue at 256th Street, Bronx 10471, 718-549-1212, www.nypl.org

Public School Education: School District #10 in region 1, 1 Fordham Plaza, Bronx, NY 10458, 718-741-7090, www.nycenet.edu

Adult Education: Manhattan College, Manhattan College Parkway and West 242nd Street, Bronx 10471, 718-862-8000, www.manhattan.edu; College of Mt. St. Vincent, 6301 Riverdale Avenue and West 263rd Street, Bronx 10471, 718-405-3267, www.cmsv.edu

Community Resources: Wave Hill, 675 West 252nd Street, Bronx 10471, 718-549-3200, www.wavehill.org; Riverdale YM-YWHA, 5625 Arlington Avenue, Bronx 10471, 718-548-8200

Transportation—Subway: #1/#9 at 242nd and 238th streets (in Kingsbridge)

Transportation—Bus: commuters in Fieldston and Riverdale tend to use Liberty Line, 718-652-8400, express buses to mid-Manhattan and Wall Street, 45 minutes, $3 one way. Local buses include the BX7 or BX10. Get a Bronx bus map for local MTA routes or go to www.mta.info

Transportation—Train: Metro-North Hudson line, 212-532-4900, station at West 254th Street by the Hudson River, 25 minutes from Grand Central. Note: tickets cost significantly more if you buy them on the train. Purchase tickets at station ticket windows or online at www.mta.info.

SPUYTEN DUYVIL

Boundaries and Contiguous Areas: **North**: 239th Street and 242nd Street and Riverdale; **East**: Waldo and Johnson avenues and Kingsbridge; **South**: Harlem River and Washington Heights-Inwood; **West**: Hudson River

Henry Hudson gazes off at his river from atop a 100-foot Doric column in Henry Hudson Memorial Park. Spuyten Duyvil (pronounced SPY ten DIE vul) has a southward pitch, so it seems to look back at Manhattan, but if you live here you're sure to look west to the spectacular sunsets, which blaze and bleed over the river.

There's little to distinguish Spuyten Duyvil from Riverdale, which abuts it to the north. Both are bisected by the Henry Hudson Parkway and they share a rocky perch high over the Hudson River. But little Spuyten Duyvil, which has its own zip code and post office, feels like a village, despite being sliced and dotted with co-ops and condos. Perhaps it's charming little Edgehill Church, a country church, or the 19th century wood frame houses on a winding street below in the shadow of the Henry Hudson Bridge. The narrow streets are all jammed and tangled down here, wiggling around Spuyten Duyvil Shorefront Park, where strollers meander a gravel path that wanders down to the railroad station. Back up the hill joggers run along scenic Palisade Avenue above Riverdale Park and the Metro-North tracks.

Housing here is mostly in apartments, though there are houses occasionally on the market, especially east of the parkway. Both rentals and co-ops are considerably below Manhattan price levels, with the most expensive being those west of the highway with river views. Shopping is available along Johnson Avenue, east of the parkway, from 235th to 236th streets, and along Riverdale Avenue between 235th and 238th streets. There's also a shopping area conveniently located around the 231st Street subway stop. In any of these places you can pick up a copy of the *Riverdale Review* to get a sense of the community.

You'll have fun living in Spuyten Duyvil, if for no other reason than listening to your friends trying to pronounce it.

Web Site: www.nyc.gov
Area Codes: 718, 347

Post Office: Spuyten Duyvil Station, 562 Kapock Street, Bronx 10463, 800-275-8777
Zip Code: 10463
Police Precinct: Fiftieth, 3450 Kingsbridge Avenue, Bronx 10463, 718-543-5700
Emergency Hospital (nearest): Montefiore, 210th Street and Bainbridge Avenue, Bronx 10467, 718-920-4321
Library (nearest): Riverdale Public Library, 5540 Mosholu Avenue, Bronx 10471, 718-549-1212, www.nypl.org
Public School Education: see **Riverdale**.
Adult Education: see **Riverdale**.
Community Resources: see **Riverdale**.
Transportation—Subway: #l/#9 at 238th, 231st and 225th streets (all in Kingsbridge)
Transportation—Bus: commuters tend to use Liberty Line, 718-652-8400, www.libertylines.com, for express bus service to mid-Manhattan and Wall Street. For local bus routes, use an MTA map or look at www.mta.info.
Transportation—Train: Metro-North Hudson Line, 212-532-4900, same pricing as Riverdale (see above).

You might also want to consider...

- **City Island**; no, it's not Nantucket, but this unselfconscious little island dangling off Pelham Bay Park provides boat fanciers and aquaphiles with salty air, technicolor sunsets, and the scruffy charm of this watery small town ... not to mention fresh seafood. It's fairly cheap though not altogether convenient living here, but you can park your sailboat out back. Housing on this tiny island is limited. www.cityisland.com
- **Pelham Parkway**; straddling the leafy parkway which stretches between Bronx Park and Pelham Bay Park in the central Bronx, this affordable neighborhood houses an ethnically and economically diverse populace in art deco and tudor style apartment buildings and detached houses along shady side streets convenient to the subway. "If you can't afford Riverdale, then you buy here," says one realtor.

BROOKLYN

It was home to Ralph Kramden and "The Honeymooners" at Brooklyn Studios, the Dodgers at Ebbets Field, and remains home to the popular Cyclone (a roller coaster) and the famous Nathan's at Coney Island. Rich with history and a head count that makes it one of the nation's ten most populous communities, Brooklyn remains a very viable option for anyone

BROOKLYN

looking to move to New York City.

"For safety and real rental value, Brooklyn beats Manhattan hands down." The chauvinistic local real estate broker might have added a qualifying "certain neighborhoods in Brooklyn." But it is true that by crossing the East River to Long Island's westernmost purchase you can pay less for housing than you might in Manhattan. Even rents in lovely old Brooklyn Heights are a bit cheaper than equally prestigious Manhattan locations, but as the popularity grows, the prices follow. Relative bargains can be found in the four- and five-story row houses, more often than not lovingly restored, that line the streets in less securely established communities such as Boerum Hill or Fort Greene/Clinton Hill. Among the salient features of these neighborhoods are the brick, clapboard, and brownstone row houses representing a virtual catalog of architectural styles from 1820s Federal through 1910s late Victorian.

Other pluses? Brooklyn boosters boast about excellent subway transportation, the quality of the public schools in District 15, and the lively cultural climate engendered by the culture scene's "big three": the Brooklyn Museum, Brooklyn Botanic Garden, and Brooklyn Academy of Music (BAM). Brooklyn, it is said, is a state of mind. To explore that state of mind visit a site called *1010 President's Street* at www.brooklyn.net, which has links to other Brooklyn sites worth meandering. For more about the history of the area check with the Brooklyn Historical Society, online at www.brooklynhistory.org.

The city's most populous borough is experiencing a renaissance of sorts, a transformation surely. Immigrants, most recently from the countries of the former Soviet Union and from Asia, have added to the population, especially in Sunset Park and in some of the further reaches of the borough. The year 1987 marked the beginning of the long-overdue commercial revitalization of downtown Brooklyn. Part of Metrotech Center, a 7.6 million square-foot commercial and academic complex in the heart of downtown Brooklyn, 1 Pierrepont Plaza opened first, housing Morgan Stanley operations. Metrotech Center serves as headquarters to KeySpan Energy and houses offices for Bear Stearns and Co., Goldman Sachs, and JP Morgan Chase, among others. Just across Jay Street, Renaissance Plaza houses corporate offices in a 32-story tower, which includes a luxury Marriott Hotel, the first new hotel in Brooklyn in 50 years. A suburban-type mall with megastores along Flatbush Avenue at Atlantic marks the completion of the first phase of the Atlantic Center; housing and office buildings to come. Rebuilding of the combination subway station and Long Island Railroad station there, long overdue, is underway. Tying it all together is the development of the Brooklyn Bridge Park. This 67-acre project will begin at the Manhattan Bridge and run south past Brooklyn Bridge along the East River to Pier 6 and Atlantic Avenue, transforming the waterfront area into a multi-million dollar gateway to Brooklyn from the East River. In addition to open green spaces, features of the park will include playing fields and playgrounds, an amphitheater, fishing piers, recreation facilities, as well as a hotel and conference center. Besides drastically changing the face of downtown Brooklyn, these developments represent the most significant changes in Brooklyn since the completion of the Brooklyn Bridge.

Young artists, musicians, and writers, many from Manhattan, come here to find affordable and larger spaces in areas such as Park Slope, Fort Greene, Williamsburg, and, lately, in Brooklyn's newest neighborhood, DUMBO (see under **Brooklyn Heights**). While some neighborhoods are still in need of revitalization, many sections of Brooklyn are indeed family friendly and affordable.

Names of Brooklyn realtors can be found under **Apartment Hunting** in the **Finding a Place to Live** chapter.

BROOKLYN HEIGHTS

Boundaries and Contiguous Areas: **North**: Fulton Ferry Landing and Cadman Plaza West; **East**: Cadman Plaza and Court Street; **South**: Atlantic Avenue and Cobble Hill; **West**: The Esplanade overlooking the East River and Brooklyn-Queens Expressway (BQE)

A *New York Times* article described two young lawyers walking home along Henry Street in the Heights one summer evening discussing cooperative apartments they had just bought. Not only did they estimate the purchase prices to be about 20% lower than comparable real estate in Manhattan, but they also believed the location couldn't be topped professionally. And as generalizations go, that is a fair one. A large percentage of Heights residents have arrived, are established, and will continue to lead the good life in carefully restored 19th and early 20th century townhouses built by earlier generations of successful Manhattan professionals.

Robert Fulton's steamboat ferry service, inaugurated in 1814, spurred the development of the rural Brooklyn settlement. Newly accessible to lower Manhattan, and cooled by East River breezes, the Heights attracted merchants and lawyers, who built the substantial homes and noteworthy churches which characterize the community today. Brooklyn Heights boasts 684 pre-Civil War era houses alone, and more than a dozen mostly-Gothic Revival churches.

The opening of the Brooklyn Bridge in 1883 brought the Heights that much closer to Wall Street and provided its most spectacular landmark, the gossamer span flung from Gothic tower to Gothic tower over the busy

East River. Wealth crossed the bridge to Brooklyn Heights and created one of the richest communities in the nation by the turn of the century. But the Depression wiped out many residents, the bankers and businessmen who worked on Wall Street, and blight came to the Heights.

In the 1950s and early 1960s, Brooklyn's first "brownstoners," attracted by the innate quality of the rundown housing stock, discovered Brooklyn Heights. These pioneers began a wave of renovation that, in the ensuing decades, has swept over row upon row of dilapidated Brooklyn townhouses. Today, the Heights' relatively cohesive population resides in stolid prewar apartment buildings and lovingly restored brownstones, as well as in striking warehouse conversions down at Fulton Ferry Landing. Besides the obvious, a five-minute subway zip to Manhattan; other commuting modes include the feet. Hearty residents stride briskly along the soaring raised center walkway of the Brooklyn Bridge to their jobs in Lower Manhattan.

From the start, accessibility to Wall Street attracted residents to the Heights, and the exceptional view of Manhattan and the harbor kept them there. The magnificent panorama of the sweeping East River beneath the soaring bridges and lower Manhattan beyond brings a steady stream of day-trippers. Strolling the wide and gracious Esplanade and visiting the quiet, historic district with its informal restaurants and pleasant shops are popular pastimes.

From the north end of the Esplanade, continue down the hill past the pristine Watchtower complex to the foot of the hill and the great stone base of the Brooklyn Bridge. There along the water to the underbelly of the Manhattan Bridge, you are in Brooklyn's newest neighborhood, **DUMBO** (for **D**own **U**nder **M**anhattan **B**ridge **O**verpass). Some prefer to call it "Down Under," but the first moniker seems to have stuck as evidenced by the DUMBO Neighborhood Association now in existence. Artists, ever in search of affordable space, started moving into this somewhat spooky industrial area in the 1970s, despite the lack of services or other people. It's not exactly SoHo, and many of the pioneers there hope it won't ever be. Make no mistake about it, this is an area in transition. In 1992, with the announcement of the creation of Brooklyn Bridge Park, of which DUMBO sits at the northern point, the neighborhood has segued from an obscure locale to up and coming, no question about it. In addition to the creation of open green spaces, development in DUMBO is expected to include restaurants, retail shops, an art gallery, and performance space in an area now occupied by an old warehouse. Expected completion is 2007. Recently completed projects include the mixed-use community by Two Trees Development, with residential, retail, industrial, and recreational space, including high-end condos in the converted Clock Building, and rental lofts and apartments. Also, check the Two Trees project that is currently underway at the corner of Court and Atlantic, a 300+ unit apartment building. Expected opening is 2005.

Web Sites: www.brooklynheights-ny.com, www.southbrooklyn.net, www.brooklyn.org, www.brooklyn.net, www.nyc.gov

Area Codes: 718, 347

Post Offices: General Post Office, 271 Cadman Plaza East, Brooklyn 11201; Municipal Building Station, Municipal Building, 210 Joralemon Street, Brooklyn 11201; 800-275-8777

Zip Code: 11201

Police Precinct: Eighty-fourth, 301 Gold Street between Tillary and Johnson Streets, Brooklyn 11201, 718-875-6811

Emergency Hospital (nearest): Long Island College Hospital, 340 Henry Street at Amity Street, Brooklyn 11201, 718-780-1000

Libraries: The Business Library, 718-623-7000, and Brooklyn Heights Branch of the Brooklyn Public Library, 718-230-2100, share the same address: 280 Cadman Plaza West, Brooklyn 11201.

Public School Education: School Districts #13 and #15 in region 8, 131 Livingston Street, Brooklyn, NY 11201, 718-935-3900, www.nycenet.edu

Adult Education: Long Island University, 1 University Plaza, Brooklyn 11201, 718-488-1000 www.lie.edu; New York City Technical College, 300 Jay Street, Brooklyn 11201, 718-260-5000, www.nyctc.cuny.edu; St. Francis College, 180 Remsen Street, Brooklyn 11201, 718-522-2300, www.stfranciscollege.edu

Community Resources: Arts at St. Ann's, formerly housed in St. Ann's Church, now at St. Ann's Warehouse, 38 Water Street, Brooklyn 11201, 718-834-8794, www.artsatstanns.org, sponsors numerous concerts and other cultural events as well. The Brooklyn Arts & Culture Association, Inc. (BACA), 195 Cadman Plaza West, Brooklyn, 11201, 718-625-0080, coordinates and supports the efforts of a wide range of cultural programs within the borough; call or go to the web site to receive BACA's monthly Calendar of Cultural Events, www.brooklynartscouncil.org; New York Transit Museum (located in a former subway station), Boerum Place and Schermerhorn Street, Brooklyn, 718-694-1600, www.mta.info; DUMBO Neighborhood Association, 39 Pearl Street, Brooklyn 11201, membership@dumbo-dna.org.

Transportation—Subway: #2, #3, Clark Street, Borough Hall; #4, #5, Borough Hall; A, C High Street/Brooklyn Bridge; N, M, R at Court Street

Transportation—Bus: for a bus map and schedule of Brooklyn: stop by Brooklyn Transit Headquarters Information Center, 370 Jay Street, call 718-330-1234, write to the Metropolitan Transit Authority, 347 Madison Avenue, NYC 10017, or go to www.mta.info.

COBBLE HILL

Boundaries and Contiguous Areas: **North**: Atlantic Avenue and Brooklyn Heights; **East**: Court Street and Boerum Hill; **South**: DeGraw Street and Carroll Gardens; **West**: Hicks Street

If it were possible to walk across the Mediterranean, a stroll starting at Atlantic Avenue down Court, Cobble Hill's main shopping street, to Carroll Gardens could be compared to a walk from the Middle East to Italy. Atlantic's famed Near East and Middle Eastern spice and grocery stores and restaurants filter along Court south for a couple of blocks before meeting up with the pizzerias, Neapolitan bakeries, and shops selling Italian housewares, near the heavily Italian Carroll Gardens on Cobble Hill's southern boundary. This intriguing ethnic mix results in top-notch food sources that attract shoppers from all over Brooklyn.

The row upon row of brownstones—less expensive and not quite as grand as those in Brooklyn Heights—shaded by large, leafy trees (note particularly the sycamore trees that completely cover Clinton Street as it crosses Baltic, Veranda, and Congress streets on the way to the Heights) attract a young professional crowd. Cobble Hill is probably the most homogeneous of all the Brooklyn brownstone communities, and award-winning Cobble Hill Park is a monument to neighborhood cohesiveness here. Apartment buildings and converted industrial properties have been established in Cobble Hill, notably The Henry Street Mews condos and One Tiffany Place, just west of the Brooklyn-Queens Expressway. Other conversions include Cobble Hill Towers, the city's first low-income housing project when it was built in 1878, and the P.S. 78 condominiums, lodged in a late-19th century public school on Pacific Street.

It is not necessary to leave the neighborhood to find a good movie, a chic new sweater, or a bistro meal. The Cobble Hill Cinema boasts five screens. And along Smith Street, where it moves down into Carroll Gardens, boutiques and restaurants cater to a young and prosperous clientele from the neighborhood and beyond.

Web Sites: www.southbrooklyn.net, www.brooklyncb6.org, www. brooklyn.org, www.nyc.gov
Area Codes: 718, 347
Post Office (nearest): Municipal Building Station, Municipal Building, 210 Joralemon Street, Brooklyn 11201, 800-275-8777
Zip Codes: 11201, 11231
Police Precinct: Seventy-sixth, 191 Union Street between Hicks and Henry Streets, Brooklyn 11231, 718-851-5611

Emergency Hospital: Long Island College Hospital, 339 Hicks Street, Brooklyn 11201, 718-780-1000, corner of Atlantic Avenue

Library (nearest): Carroll Gardens Branch of the Brooklyn Public Library, 396 Clinton Street at Union Street, Brooklyn 11231, 718-237-7996, www.nypl.org

Public School Education: School District #15 in region 8, 131 Livingston Street, Brooklyn, NY 11201, 718-935-3900, www.nycenet.edu

Adult Education: see **Brooklyn Heights** and **Boerum Hill**.

Community Resources: Cobble Hill Fine Art Gallery, 141 Union Street, Brooklyn 11231, 718-243-0718, www.cobblehillfineart.com; also see **Brooklyn Heights** and **Boerum Hill**.

Transportation—Subway: #2, #3, #4, #5, Borough Hall; F, G, Bergen Street

Transportation—Bus: for a bus map and schedule of Brooklyn: stop by Brooklyn Transit Headquarters Information Center, 370 Jay Street, call 718-330-1234, write to the Metropolitan Transit Authority, 347 Madison Avenue, NYC 10017, or go to www.mta.info.

CARROLL GARDENS

Boundaries and Contiguous Areas: **North**: DeGraw Street and Cobble Hill; **East**: Gowanus Canal; **South**: Hamilton Avenue; **West**: Brooklyn-Queens Expressway

In Carroll Gardens, singularly deep and lushly planted gardens front the four- and five-story row houses so characteristic of Brooklyn's brownstone neighborhoods. These splendid yards, with trees as tall as the high-stooped townhouses, form part of an eleven-block tract laid out in the 1850s. Verdant block fronts are, however, only part of the reason urban homesteaders began moving to Carroll Gardens in the 1970s. This predominantly Italian community has a lower crime rate than many other areas in Brooklyn. And furthermore, just like Cobble Hill, another "tight" neighborhood to the north, Carroll Gardens boasts better-than-average public elementary and secondary schools.

Other pluses? Great food shopping. You'll find plenty of vegetable stands lining Court Street, where bulbous pecorino cheeses, salamis, and whole prosciuttos hang from grocery store ceilings. Subway transportation to Manhattan by F Train is fast and direct.

Less expensive, and less gentrified than the Heights and Cobble Hill, Carroll Gardens has long had limited housing stock. But apartment conversions in industrial buildings on the southern edge of Carroll Gardens have accelerated recently. On the eastern edge, an area in revival, the former St. Agnes School has become the School House in Carroll Gardens, a

90-unit middle-income rental on DeGraw Street. The occasional low-rise condo appears.

Walk along Court and you'll still hear Italian spoken. Boccie is still the game of choice among the senior set in sweet little Carroll Park, where handsome brownstones on the park's north side and graceful old trees make it feel like Washington Square in Greenwich Village. Heading north along Smith Street you can buy designer clothes in chic boutiques and eat Vietnamese, French, or nouveau Italian in smart eateries. Use a real estate agent to find an apartment here, if, after a stroll on the park-like streets, you find it appealing.

Another area to consider is the more affordable **Columbia Street Waterfront District**, adjacent to but separated from Carroll Gardens and Cobble Hill by the Gowanus Expressway. Its modest brick row houses were once the homes of the longshoremen who worked the docks here, but the neighborhood declined when the expressway isolated it from its loftier neighbors. Revival began in the 1980s with the construction of the Columbia Terrace condominiums and the conversion of a former Tiffany lamp factory into condos on cobblestoned Tiffany Place. There are no subway stations, schools, banks, or supermarkets here, but on-street parking is easy and the view from its quiet streets across Buttermilk Channel to the Statue of Liberty and Lower Manhattan is stunning.

Web Sites: www.southbrooklyn.net, www.brooklyncb6.org, www. brooklyn.org, www.nyc.gov

Area Codes: 718, 347

Post Office: Red Hook Station, 615 Clinton Street, Brooklyn 11231, 800-275-8777

Zip Code: 11231

Police Precinct: Seventy-sixth, 191 Union Street, Brooklyn 11231, 718-834-3211

Emergency Hospital (nearest): Long Island College Hospital, 339 Hicks Street, Brooklyn 11201, 718-780-1000, corner of Atlantic Avenue

Library: Carroll Gardens Branch of the Brooklyn Public Library, 396 Clinton Street at Union Street, Brooklyn 11231, 718-237-7996, www.nypl.org

Public School Education: School District #15 in region 8, 131 Livingston Street, Brooklyn, NY 11201, 718-935-3900, www.nycenet.edu

Adult Education: see **Brooklyn Heights** and **Boerum Hill**.

Community Resources: see **Brooklyn Heights** and **Boerum Hill**.

Transportation—Subway: F, Carroll Street, Smith Street; G, Carroll Street, Smith Street

Transportation—Bus: for a bus map and schedule of Brooklyn: stop by Brooklyn Transit Headquarters Information Center, 370 Jay Street, call

718-330-1234, write to the Metropolitan Transit Authority, 347 Madison Avenue, NYC 10017, or go to www.mta.info.

BOERUM HILL

Boundaries and Contiguous Areas: North: State Street; **East**: Third Avenue; **South**: Degraw Street; West: Court

East and slightly downhill from sedate Cobble Hill and just south of bustling downtown Brooklyn, Boerum Hill seems lighter and more spacious along its blocks of three- and four-story brick and brownstone homes. Stately sycamores shade quiet streets such as Bergen, where children play untended on sidewalks that line the flowering yards fronting setback row houses. Ethnically more heterogeneous than its neighbors to the west, it is a community of families, who shop along commercial Smith and Court streets. Smith has also been dubbed the new "restaurant row" featuring French bistro-esque cafes. Nearby Atlantic Avenue is home to antique stores and Middle-Eastern restaurants.

The Boerum Hill Historic District, bounded roughly by Hoyt and Nevins, Pacific and Wyckoff streets, contains an outstanding assemblage of pre-Civil War Italianate and Greek Revival row houses, which constituted a fashionable district in the mid-19th century; the stretch of State Street between Hoyt and Smith has national landmark status. The neighborhood declined in later years, and today it is a monument to the efforts of new homeowners who, in the early 1960s, fought off a city effort to tear down the then-dispirited rooming houses to make way for urban renewal. Boerum Hill's turnaround—from near-slum to tight residential community—was achieved by a dedicated band of pioneers with enough foresight to see the area's potential. The neighborhood has a strong sense of community, and many keep close tabs on proposed development.

It was the construction of the Gowanus Canal and the draining of the swamps south of Warren Street beginning in 1845 that prompted the development of what are now Cobble Hill and Boerum Hill.

Rentals (when they can be found) in the handsome townhouses here are relatively affordable, by New York City standards. Co-ops and condos can also be found. House prices are approaching the cost of comparable homes in Brooklyn Heights.

Slicing across Boerum Hill from the waterfront, noisy Atlantic Avenue is somewhat blighted by the presence of the grim Brooklyn House of Detention and its surroundings, but from Hoyt Street eastward its concentration of inviting antique and Victorian bric-a-brac shops attracts shoppers from all over the city.

Web Sites: www.southbrooklyn.net, www.brooklyn.org, www.nyc.gov
Area Codes: 718, 347
Post Office: Times Plaza Station, 542 Atlantic Avenue, Brooklyn 11217, 800-275-8777
Zip Code: 11217
Police Precincts: Seventy-sixth, 191 Union Street between Hicks and Henry Streets, Brooklyn 11231, 718-851-5611; Seventy-eighth, 65 Sixth Avenue between 6th and Bergen streets, Brooklyn 11217, 718-636-6411
Emergency Hospital: Long Island College Hospital, 339 Hicks Street, Brooklyn 11201, 718-780-1000, corner of Atlantic Avenue
Library: Pacific Branch, 25 Fourth Avenue, Brooklyn 11217, 718-638-1531, www.nypl.org
Public School Education: School District #15 in region 8, 131 Livingston Street, Brooklyn, NY 11201, 718-935-3900, www.nycenet.edu
Adult Education: Brooklyn YWCA, 30 Third Avenue, Brooklyn 11217, 718-875-1190, offers a health program plus a variety of adult classes.
Transportation—Subway: #2, #3, Hoyt Street, Nevins Street; #4, #5 Nevins Street; F, Bergen Street; G, Bergen Street, Hoyt/Schermerhorn streets; A to Hoyt/Schermerhorn streets
Transportation—Bus: for a bus map and schedule of Brooklyn: stop by Brooklyn Transit Headquarters Information Center, 370 Jay Street, call 718-330-1234, write to the Metropolitan Transit Authority, 347 Madison Avenue, NYC 10017, or go to www.mta.info.

PARK SLOPE

Boundaries and Contiguous Areas: **North**: Flatbush Avenue; **East**: Prospect Park West; **South**: Windsor Place; **West**: Fifth Avenue

If Cobble Hill is the most homogeneous of Brooklyn's brownstone neighborhoods, Park Slope is the most heterogeneous, and proud of it. (It is also by far the largest of these communities.) The fact that the population is still economically and ethnically mixed appears, for a majority of residents, to be the neighborhood's most attractive attribute. Second place is probably a tie between the 526-acre Prospect Park, designed by Central Park architects Frederick Law Olmstead and Calvert Vaux, and Park Slope's proximity to three of Brooklyn's cultural bastions: the Brooklyn Museum, the Central Library at Grand Army Plaza, and the Brooklyn Botanic Garden. A recent addition to Prospect Park is the re-opened Wildlife Conservation Center, a state-of-the-art children's zoo with a restored 1912 carousel.

Park Slope's development paralleled that of Prospect Park in the 1880s. Sites with a park view were most highly prized, and small Victorian mansions line Prospect Park West. Proximity to the park and Grand Army Plaza determined the quality of the Victorian bow-fronted townhouses that march row upon stolid row down the west-sloping streets. North Slope, nearest Prospect Park West and the Plaza, is considered the classiest part of the neighborhood. South Slope, below 9th Street, is the less expensive, still-developing section. Old industrial properties, such as the Ansonia Clock factory complex on 12th Street, once the country's largest clock works and now deluxe condominiums, have been converted to apartments and co-ops. Seventh Avenue, the principal shopping street and scene of a hugely successful fair each spring, reflects neighborhood needs: the boutiques, card shops, and unisex hair cutters once found exclusively at the North Slope end of Seventh have infiltrated blocks in South Slope as well. With the arrival of a Barnes & Noble, the neighborhood is officially literate and upscale. Eateries abound along Fifth Avenue, and for those who enjoy shopping in a community setting, the Park Slope Food Co-op, 782 Union Street, Brooklyn, NY 11215, 718-622-0560, www.foodcoop.com, provides fresh organic foods and household supplies. Since members do not have to be residents of Park Slope to join, folks come from all over Brooklyn.

Without qualification Park Slope, together with Brooklyn Heights, has arrived as a suitable address for middle-class professionals, especially those with families. P.S. 321, District 15's progressive, well-regarded elementary school, has served as an additional attraction to young families. But don't go looking for bargains; in real estate parlance, the neighborhood is "hot" (and has been for a while), especially along the park. Prices are lower down the slope and in adjoining **Windsor Terrace** and **Prospect Heights**, two revitalizing communities nicely situated near Prospect Park. (For more on these see below.) Down the slope west of Fifth Avenue around the Gowanus Canal, artists and crafters have established homes and studios in a neighborhood known now simply as **Gowanus**. Cleaned up, if not yet pristine, the canal twists through a somewhat gritty area, which may yet become the Venice of Brooklyn. Also, investigate the **Sunset Park/Green-Wood Cemetery** area, bounded by 65th Street on the south and Prospect Expressway on the north. This ethnically mixed community offers inexpensive rentals and fun neighborhood shopping and dining along Fifth Avenue. In the northeast corner is the hilly and inviting Green-Wood Cemetery (see **Greenspace and Beaches**). As you search, pick up a copy of the *Park Slope Courier*, 718-769-4400, to get a feel for the neighborhood.

Web Sites: www.southbrooklyn.net, www.brooklyncb6.org, www. brooklyn.org, www.nyc.gov
Area Codes: 718, 347

Post Office: Van Brunt Station, 275 9th Street, Brooklyn 11215, 800-275-8777

Zip Codes: 11215, 11217

Police Precincts: Seventy-second, 830 Fourth Avenue between 29th and 30th streets, Brooklyn 11230, 718-965-6311; Seventy-eighth, 65 Sixth Avenue between 6th and Bergen streets, Brooklyn 11217, 718-636-6411

Emergency Hospital: Methodist Hospital, 506 Sixth Street between Seventh and Eighth avenues, Brooklyn 11215, 718-780-3000

Library: Brooklyn Central Library, Grand Army Plaza at Flatbush Avenue, Brooklyn 11238, 718-230-2100, www.nypl.org

Public School Education: School Districts #13 and #15 in region 8, 131 Livingston Street, Brooklyn, NY 11201, 718-935-3900, www.nycenet.edu

Adult Education: Brooklyn Museum Art School, 200 Eastern Parkway, Brooklyn 11238, 718-638-5000, www.brooklynmuseum.org; Brooklyn Botanic Garden, 1000 Washington Avenue, Brooklyn 11225, 718-623-7200, www.bbg.org, holds classes for plant enthusiasts. Brooklyn Conservatory of Music, 58 Seventh Avenue, Brooklyn 11217, 718-622-3300. www.brooklynconservatory.com

Community Resources: Brooklyn Museum, 200 Eastern Parkway at Washington Avenue, Brooklyn 11238, 718-638-5000; www.brooklyn museum.org, behind the six Ionic columns of McKim, Mead and White's famed building are housed a number of exemplary collections as well as facilities for the cultural and educational programs sponsored daily by the museum. Also offered are lectures and special programs; Brooklyn Arts Exchange, 421 Fifth Avenue at Eighth Street, 718-832-0018, St. John's Recreation Center, 1251 Prospect Place, 718-771-2787.

Transportation—Subway: with the exception of the A and C trains, subways stop near one part of Park Slope or the other. #2, #3, #4, #5 trains stop at Grand Army Plaza; F stops at Fourth Avenue, Seventh Avenue and 15th Street; D stops at Seventh Avenue and Atlantic Avenue; B, M, N, R stop along Fourth Avenue at Pacific Street, Union Street, 9th Street and Prospect Avenue.

Transportation—Bus: for a bus map and schedule of Brooklyn: stop by Brooklyn Transit Headquarters Information Center, 370 Jay Street, call 718-330-1234, write to the Metropolitan Transit Authority, 347 Madison Avenue, NYC 10017, or go to www.mta.info.

FORT GREENE/CLINTON HILL

Boundaries and Contiguous Areas: **North**: Myrtle Avenue; **East**: Classon Avenue; **South**: Atlantic Avenue; **West**: Flatbush Avenue and Boerum Hill

"... Brooklyn's other fine residential district, the Hill ... abounded in churches and middle-class houses, the majority of whose owners worked in New York." So wrote a Brooklyn historian of late 19th century Fort Greene and Clinton Hill. Despite a decline in the intervening years, that description is valid once again, except for the fringe areas to the north and east. What occasioned the turnabout? Historic designation and the brownstone revival, mainly.

Revival came late, in the 1970s, to **Fort Greene**. Even the once-elegant brownstones on the choice streets nearest Fort Greene Park had become dilapidated wino rows. But beneath the grime and neglect the original detailing remained, awaiting the attention of determined urban pioneers. Now, perfectly restored Anglo-Italianate brownstones line Washington Park, South Oxford Street, and South Portland Avenue. And sweeping 33-acre Fort Greene Park, the community's centerpiece designed by Olmsted and Vaux, has been restored to its rather English graciousness.

Fort Greene is integrated, both racially and socio-economically, and determined to stay that way. The throbbing cultural presence of the Brooklyn Academy of Music (BAM) helped stimulate the growth of a substantial community of African-American artists in Fort Greene. The area around BAM continues to grow as a cultural enclave with dance troupes and artists moving into the neighborhood.

Clinton Hill, like Fort Greene, which it borders and from which it is barely distinguishable, contains an astonishing treasury of late 19th century urban architecture. The key name in this neighborhood is Pratt. Kerosene magnate Charles Pratt built several handsome mansions on Clinton Avenue including the present residence of the Bishop of Brooklyn, and also founded, built, and, until his death in 1891, ran Pratt Institute, the focal point and cultural center of the community. Now the students, grads, and faculty of Pratt (art, design, architecture, engineering, computers, and library sciences) fill the streets and much of the local housing.

Clinton Hill has a few high rises and therefore greater variety of housing than Fort Greene. But Clinton Hill has only one subway line, the sporadic G train, which requires a transfer to reach Manhattan. Many find the five-minute bus ride to downtown Brooklyn with a free transfer to a variety of trains more convenient. Fort Greene, on the other hand, is well tended by the subway system (see below). Both neighborhoods offer easy on-street parking.

Both the Metrotech commercial development to the west on Flatbush Avenue and the Atlantic Center mixed-use development on the southeast edge of Fort Greene have boosted the value and the cost of housing on the hill. Apartment hunting here is best done through a knowledgeable real estate agent.

Web Sites: www.brooklyn.org, www.nyc.gov

Area Codes: 718, 347

Post Offices: Pratt Station, 524 Myrtle Avenue, Brooklyn 11205; General Post Office, 271 Cadman Plaza East, Brooklyn 11201; Times Plaza Station, 542 Atlantic Avenue, Brooklyn 11217; 800-275-8777

Zip Codes: 11201, 11205, 11217, 11238

Police Precinct: Eighty-eighth, 298 Classon Avenue, Brooklyn 11205, 718-636-6511

Emergency Hospital: Brooklyn Hospital, 121 DeKalb Avenue, Brooklyn 11201, 718-250-8000

Libraries: Brooklyn Public Library, Clinton Hill Branch, 380 Washington Avenue, Brooklyn 11238, 718-398-8713; Walt Whitman Branch, 93 St. Edwards Street at Auburn Plaza, Brooklyn 11205, 718-935-0244; www.nypl.org

Public School Education: School District #13 in region 8, 131 Livingston Street, Brooklyn, NY 11201, 718-935-3900, www.nycenet.edu

Adult Education: Pratt Institute, Continuing Education, 200 Willoughby Avenue, Brooklyn 11205, 718-636-3453, www.pratt.edu; Medgar Evers Community College, 1150 Carroll Street, Brooklyn 11225, 718-270-6400, www.mec.cuny.edu; St. Joseph's College, 245 Clinton Avenue, Brooklyn 11205, 718-636-6800, www.sjcny.edu; nearby: Long Island University, 1 University Plaza, Flatbush at DeKalb avenues, Brooklyn 11201, 718-488-1011, www.brooklyn.liu.edu

Community Resources: Brooklyn Academy of Music (BAM), 30 Lafayette Avenue, Brooklyn 11217, 718-636-4100, www.bam.org; the borough's premier cultural resource, founded in 1859, BAM contains four theaters of differing sizes presenting a spectrum of performances by artists from all disciplines and hosting the annual Next Wave Festival; and the Brooklyn Children's Museum, splendidly renovated, at 145 Brooklyn Avenue (Crown Heights), Brooklyn 11213, 718-735-4400.

Transportation—Subway: A, C, Lafayette Avenue; B, D at DeKalb Avenue; M, N, Q, R, DeKalb Avenue; #2, #3, #4, #5 at Nevins Street; G at Fulton Street, Clinton/Washington avenues

Transportation—Bus: for a bus map and schedule of Brooklyn: stop by Brooklyn Transit Headquarters Information Center, 370 Jay Street, call 718-330-1234, write to the Metropolitan Transit Authority, 347 Madison Avenue, NYC 10017, or go to www.mta.info.

GREENPOINT/NORTHSIDE, WILLIAMSBURG

Boundaries and Contiguous Areas: North: Newtown Creek and Queens; **East**: Newtown Creek and the Brooklyn-Queens Expressway (BQE); **South**: Grand Street; **West**: the East River

This northernmost portion of Brooklyn, protruding into the underbelly of Queens and just 20 minutes by subway from Manhattan, is one of Brooklyn's best-kept secrets, and that's just fine with Greenpoint—or "Greenpernt," as they pronounced it in the gangster movies of the 1930s. Just across the East River from 23rd Street in Manhattan, it might as well be another country. Modest two-, three-, and four-story houses, colorfully sided and impeccably tidy, line quiet streets. The feel is 1940-something small town. Housewives chat on front steps, and they are as likely to be speaking Polish as English.

Along Manhattan Avenue, Greenpoint's Main Street, *kielbasi* drape the butcher shops, restaurants offer *pierogi* and *golumpki*, and the travel agencies advertise flights to Poland. Italian restaurants, bodegas along Franklin Street, and the occasional shamrock define the ethnic composition of this largely blue-collar community. In the Greenpoint Historic District just west of Manhattan Avenue, Java and India streets with their handsome brownstones and churches recall the coffee and spice trade that once flourished along the docks here. And in the rather British-feeling Monsignor McGolrick Park a monument to the Civil War battleship Monitor, which was built here, memorializes Greenpoint's shipbuilding past as well.

Just to the south beyond McCarren Park and the stunning, copper-domed Russian Orthodox Cathedral of the Transfiguration lie **Northside** and **Williamsburg**, with nothing to mark the boundary between them and Greenpoint, so similar are the three communities. Numbered streets—declining from North 15th to Grand—cross Bedford Avenue, Northside's tidy, quiet main street. To the east traffic roars along the elevated Brooklyn-Queens Expressway. From the undeveloped waterfront area to the west comes the occasional scent of molasses from the Domino sugar plant and now and then of garbage from the processing concerns there. No sign now of the fashionable resorts that flourished here near the ferry landings until the Williamsburg Bridge and trolley service in 1905 brought immi-grants streaming from the Lower East Side. By 1920, this influx made Williamsburg the most populous neighborhood in Brooklyn.

The upscale cafes, galleries, and an underground movie house with a candle-lit reflecting pool where a factory truck bay once stood are signs of continued change here. Williamsburg, described by one New Yorker as the hippest neighborhood in all Brooklyn, has had its own movie festival since 1998. Young artists and musicians who discovered the peace, quiet, and relatively low cost of living in Greenpoint began carving lofts out of former manufacturing space here in the 1980s and in Northside in the 1990s. Much to the dismay of long time residents, many of them Hasidim, who fear being priced out of their neighborhood, young professionals and recent grads are following. Near the waterfront, tucked away in shabby industrial exteriors are a bevy of restaurants serving sushi and other favorites along with the bright yellow Brooklyn Brewery, complete with tours and a space for catering a party. There's talk of developing the waterfront, with its spectacular view of lower Manhattan, into parkland, although a recent article in *New York* magazine also mentioned the possibility of using the land for a garbage processing plant. While you probably won't find a doorman in Greenpoint, Northside, or Williamsburg, or a health club, new housing in the form of condos can be found in the 200 block of South 2nd Street, and the 100 block of South 1st Street, and the Gretsch Building on Broadway, formerly a musical instrument factory, is being transformed into luxury condos. After a $4.8 million restoration highlighting its rather Andalusian glory, the Metropolitan Pool and Bathhouse at Bedford and Metropolitan avenues is a fabulous neighborhood amenity. Accessible to the disabled, the pool and recreation center are operated by the parks department. A few blocks north, the 35 acres of McCarren Park includes ball-fields, tennis courts, a running track, and a fitness course.

Available housing, whether apartments or lofts in newly converted industrial space, is sparse. Though occasionally appearing among the rental listings in *The Village Voice*, available space is best found through local real estate agents. Expect few amenities and rents generally below the Manhattan rate for a small one- or two-bedroom. Allow six weeks to two months to find a suitable spot in this tight little community. Walk around to get a feel of the neighborhood, check the bulletin board outside the health food store on Bedford for a sublet or a share, pick up a copy of the weekly *Greenpoint Gazette*, 718-389-6067, for the apartment ads, and drop in on a real estate office. Note the absence of fast food chains in favor of privately owned eateries, and good ones too.

Web Sites: www.brooklyn.org, www.nyc.gov
Area Codes: 718, 347
Post Office: Greenpoint Station, 66 Meserole Avenue, Brooklyn 11222, Williamsburg Station, 256 South 4th Street, Brooklyn 11211; 800-275-8777
Zip Codes: 11222, 11211
Police Precinct: Ninety-fourth, 100 Meserole Avenue, Brooklyn 11222, 718-383-3879

Emergency Hospital (nearest): Woodhull Medical Center, 760 Broadway, Brooklyn 11206, 718-963-8000

Library: Brooklyn Public Library, Greenpoint Branch, 107 Norman Avenue, Brooklyn 11222, 718-349-8504, www.nypl.org

Public School Education: School District #14 in region 8, 131 Livingston Street, Brooklyn, NY 11201, 718-935-3900, www.nycenet.edu

Transportation—Subway: L, Bedford Avenue; G, Greenpoint Avenue, Nassau Avenue

Transportation—Bus: for a bus map and schedule of Brooklyn: stop by Brooklyn Transit Headquarters Information Center, 370 Jay Street, call 718-330-1234, write to the Metropolitan Transit Authority, 347 Madison Avenue, NYC 10017, or go to www.mta.info.

You might also want to consider...

- **Bay Ridge**, way out by the Verrazano Bridge and overlooking the Narrows, studded with parks and restaurants. This conservative community with a Scandinavian and Italian heritage is 50 minutes by subway from Manhattan. Community Board 10, 718-745-6827
- **Flatbush**, fairly vast and varied, geographically and psychologically the heart of Brooklyn. Its most appealing neighborhoods are Prospect Park South and Ditmas Park, both of which feature lovely old Victorian homes along stately, tree-lined streets, and strong community spirit. Community Board 14, 718-859-6357
- **Fort Hamilton**, just beyond Bay Ridge around the base of the Verrazano Bridge, has more co-ops and condos among their one-family houses, with a similar perch on the Narrows and about an hour by subway to Manhattan. Community Board 10, 718-745-6827
- **Prospect Heights**, located uphill, but downscale in price, from Park Slope, Prospect Park, Brooklyn's major cultural institutions and accessible transportation. Its handsome brownstones, greystones, and co-op apartments have attracted young, professional arrivals in recent years. Community Board 8, 718-467-5574.
- **Red Hook** south of the Columbia Street Waterfront District on Upper New York Bay is still for pioneers. But a cluster of crafters—glassmakers, theatrical set builders, artists, and artisans—have made homes and studios here, where rows of small houses intersperse the industrial landscape. Stunning views, a vast sky and water edged by historic stone warehouses are a draw. Community Board 8, 718-467-5574
- **Stuyvesant Heights**, 12 landmarked blocks of exceptional brownstones along stately, tree-lined streets on the southern edge of Bedford-Stuyvesant houses a largely African-American professional community.

Twenty-five subway minutes from Manhattan. Community Board 3, 718-622-6601
- **Windsor Terrace**, a safe, old-fashioned community of small, detached houses, row houses, and apartments nicely sandwiched between Prospect Park and beautiful, park-like Green-Wood Cemetery. Quiet, except for the birds. Community Board 7, 718-854-0003

QUEENS

"Queens is not New York!" exclaims a character in the film *Quiz Show*. Many Manhattanites would agree—but that is a Manhattan state of mind.

Among the five boroughs, Queens is the acknowledged bastion of New York's middle class. As skyscrapers identify Manhattan and brownstones Brooklyn, so solid brick buildings—free-standing, Tudor-inspired houses, semi-detached, two-, three-, and four-family dwellings, and six-story apartment blocks—define a good part of the largest borough (in terms of land) in the city.

Until 1909 and the completion of the Queensborough Bridge, semi-rural Queens was a backwater connected to Manhattan only by ferry boat across the East River. But the bridge, followed almost immediately by train and then by subway service through new tunnels under the East River, opened the way for commuters and commerce. Developers snapped up great parcels of land, and 1908 saw the beginning of a building spree that continued, with few pauses, until World War II. While some communities are architecturally noteworthy—Forest Hills Gardens, a carefully designed 1909 enclave planned down to its English rustic street signs, and Malba, a charming mélange of lawns, leafy lanes, and handsome, mostly 1920s homes nestled under the Whitestone Bridge—most of the housing is sturdy, unremarkable pre-World War II stock often laid out, suburban-style, in tracts.

While many Queens neighborhoods are identified with various ethnic groups—Greeks gravitate to Astoria, Latin Americans to Jackson Heights, Russians to Rego Park, Asians to Flushing—an international mix (over 125 languages are spoken by the borough's residents) of businessmen, engineers, and other professionals and their families continues to move into the area. Just across the river from Manhattan is Long Island City, which a few years ago *New York* magazine proclaimed "The New Hot Neighborhood." Some think this call premature, at least as far as newcomers are concerned, as gentrification here has been slow, yet it marches steadily along and with some pleasing results. Astoria, just to the north of Long Island City and Sunnyside to the southeast, both equally accessible to Manhattan, are moderately priced areas. Within subway reach, Rego Park, Forest Hills, and Kew Gardens are popular established communities where one- and even two-bedroom apartments rent for about the same as a Manhattan studio. Further

QUEENS

0 ___ 5 Miles

0 ___ 5 Kms

ATLANTIC OCEAN

N
W E
S

east, condominium units crowd every nook and cranny of Bayside with an endless sea of high rises. Bayside has great appeal for those who prefer its quiet congestion to Manhattan's noise and immensity and who don't find the trip to Manhattan by express bus or Long Island Railroad too daunting. Names of Queens real estate brokers will be found in **Finding a Place to Live**. The local publication, the *Queens Chronicle*, 718-205-8000, www.queenschronicle.com, will provide real estate tips plus some insight into the borough itself.

ASTORIA/LONG ISLAND CITY

Boundaries and Contiguous Areas: *Astoria*: **North**: Grand Central Parkway; **East**: Brooklyn-Queens Expressway; **South**: 35th Avenue and Sunnyside; **West**: Long Island City; *Long Island City*: **North**: Astoria; **East**: Steinway Street; **South**: Pulaski Bridge; **West**: East River

Astoria and Long Island City are technically separate, but with only a vague dividing line. Long Island City is the area immediately along the waterfront between just north of the Queensborough Bridge (also known as the 59th Street Bridge) and the Pulaski Bridge; Astoria is slightly inland, following the route of the N train to the north of the Queensborough Bridge. **Astoria,** with its many residents of Greek or Hispanic (or Italian or Yugoslavian or German) descent, offers a distinct old world feel. With and without belly dancers, the tavernas on Ditmars Boulevard and Broadway vibrate long and late to the keening of Greek dance music. Long a neighborhood of immigrant newcomers, the most recent wave has brought an infusion of Irish, South Americans, Slavs, and Asians. And more recently, a slew of urban professionals, many ex-Manhattanites, have discovered the apartments in the decently maintained two-story houses and small apartment buildings bordering Astoria's relatively safe streets. In particular, check the area between Crescent and 35th streets, which is within walking distance of the N line and a 20-minute commute from Midtown. (A caveat: presumably Astorians have no problem with the improbably numbered streets, drives, and avenues here; outsiders find them nearly incomprehensible.) New York City's largest pool (over one acre in size) in spacious Astoria Park, just beneath the Triborough Bridge on the East River, is free, as is the uncrowded running space around the park. Condo living, with a health club and unobstructed view of the Manhattan skyline, came to Astoria with the opening of the 405-unit Shore Towers in 1990 at the southern end of the park.

There is even a flurry of cultural activity in the area with the recent addition of a 750-seat public theater, the colonnaded Athens Square in little Hellenic Park. Astoria was the home of Paramount Studios from 1919 until the 1930s, when the business moved—lock, stock and W.C. Fields—to Hollywood. The movies are back, sharing with television the enormous, refurbished Kaufman Astoria Studios on 35th Avenue between 34th and 37th streets. The complex also houses the Museum of the Moving Image, a museum dedicated to movies, TV, and the interactive media. Several production facilities have sprouted nearby, as well as a 14-screen cinema near the Kaufman Astoria Studios.

Immediately across the river from Manhattan, and part and parcel of the film industry taking place in Astoria, new life is being breathed into **Long Island City**. Artists are coming, attracted by P.S. 1, a highly successful alternative art, dance, and theater space, as well as filmmakers, actors, and designers to the enormous film and television production facility Silver Cup Studios, the Eaves-Brooks Costume Company, and the gargantuan International Design Center, which contains more than 100 acres of showroom space. Also here is the renovated Isamu Noguchi Museum and Sculpture Garden located on Vernon Boulevard at 33rd Road, and sculptor Mark Di Suvero has organized the Socrates Sculpture Park, with its changing display of monumental abstract works in a previously vacant East River lot. Putting Long Island City ever more on the map was the marriage in 1999 between P.S. 1 and the prestigious Museum of Modern Art in Manhattan, creating MoMA QNS. Now that renovations of the Modern's old home are complete, the plan for MoMA QNS is to convert it into a storage and study center for the museum.

The 42-story, glass Citicorp spire, towering over these industrial surrounds like a giant among midgets, now dominates Long Island City. Just to the south, in Long Island City's Hunters Point section, Citylights, with 522 co-op apartments, opened in 1997, the beginning of a long-planned residential/commercial development rising along the East River there. And the new Avalon Riverview Towers (www.avalonriverview.com) stand alongside, containing another 372 rental units with separate housing for the elderly. When finished, this Queens West development, across from the United Nations, will comprise 6,385 tower and low-rise apartments and a hotel and office complex spread over a 74-acre waterfront site. Expected completion is 2010.

To get a further fix on life in Astoria and in greater Long Island City, go to www.licweb.com.

Web Sites: www.licweb.com, www.nyc.gov
Area Codes: 718, 347
Post Offices: Astoria Station, 27-40 21st Street, Astoria 11102, Steinway Station, 43-04 Broadway, Astoria 11103; Woolsey Station, 22-68 31st Street, Astoria 11105; Broadway Station, 21-17 Broadway, Astoria

11106; 800-275-8777

Zip Codes: 11102, 11103, 11105, 11106

Police Precinct: One Hundred Fourteenth, 34-16 Astoria Boulevard at 35th Street, Astoria 11102, 718-626-9311

Emergency Hospital: Elmhurst Hospital Center, 79-01 Broadway, Elmhurst 11373, 718-334-4000

Library: Astoria Branch, Queens Public Library, 14-01 Astor Boulevard, Astoria 11102, 718-278-2220; Steinway Branch, 21-45 31st Street, Long Island City 11105, 718-728-1965; www.nypl.org

Public School Education: School District #30 in region 4, 28-11 Queens Plaza North, Queens, NY 11101, 718-391-8300, www.nycenet.edu

Community Resources: Queens Chamber of Commerce, www.queens chamber.org; The Isamu Noguchi Museum and Sculpture Garden, 9-01 33rd Road, 718-204-7088, www.noguchi.org; Socrates Sculpture Park, Broadway at Vernon Boulevard, Long Island City 11106, 718-956-1819, www.socratessculpturepark.org; Museum of the Moving Image, 36-01 35th Avenue, 718-784-4520, Program Information, 718-784-0077, www.ammi.org; P.S. 1 Contemporary Art Center, 22-25 Jackson Avenue, Long Island City 11101, 718-784-2084, www.ps1.org

Transportation—Subway: N, Queensborough Plaza, 39th Avenue, 36th Avenue, Broadway, 30th Avenue, Astoria Boulevard-Hoyt Avenue, Ditmars Boulevard; E, F, V, 23rd Street, Queens Plaza; G, R, Queens Plaza, 36th Street, Steinway Street and 46th Street; B, Q, 21st Street/Queens Bridge

Transportation—Bus: for a bus map and schedule of Queens, stop by the Queens Transit Headquarters Information Center, 128-15 28th Avenue, Flushing, or call 718-330-1234, or go to www.mta.info. Queens Surface Corp. at 28th Avenue, 718-445-3100, www.qsbus. com, also offers express service on several routes to midtown Manhattan for $4.

SUNNYSIDE

Boundaries and Contiguous Areas: **North**: Barnett Avenue and the Sunnyside Conrail Yards; **East**: 52nd Street and New Calvary Cemetery; **South**: Long Island Expressway; **West**: 36th Street and Long Island City

This traditionally blue-collar community bounded by railroad yards, industrial tracts, cemeteries and the legendary LIE (the Long Island Expressway, also known as the world's longest parking lot) won't be the next "in" New York neighborhood. But, the sensible, mostly-brick homes and apartments lining Sunnyside's residential streets, ten minutes by train from Manhattan, do attract young professionals, as well as immigrants, offering more space for lower-than-Manhattan rents.

Newcomers are especially drawn to **Sunnyside Gardens**. "The Gardens," the first US development to be modeled on the English garden community occupies 55 leafy acres north of bustling Queens Boulevard. Towering London plane trees shade the 650 one-, two- and three-family brick townhouses, which enclose long communal gardens. The effect is English village, with shrub-lined walks penetrating the landmarked blocks. "Like Greenwich Village and far more than Brooklyn Heights, it was a mixed community, in which one might mingle without undue intimacy with one's neighbors," recalls urban critic/historian Lewis Mumford, who lived in The Gardens from their inception in 1924 until 1936. They seem little changed.

There are private homes and rentals in greater Sunnyside as well, but most of the brick apartment blocks are non-rentable co-ops. The three main shopping thoroughfares are small-town Skillman Avenue at The Gardens' southern edge, Queens Boulevard in the shadow of the elevated IRT Flushing Line, and running diagonally southwest from the Boulevard is Greenpoint Avenue, which leads directly into neighboring Brooklyn. There and on the side streets you can rent Korean movies, buy Irish imports, eat Italian, Middle European or Chinese, or lift a pint at Moriarty's Pub Restaurant. The city's longest established Spanish language theater, The Thalia on Greenpoint Avenue, plays to sellout crowds on weekends.

Thanks in large part to the efforts of the Sunnyside Foundation, whose staff works on planning and preservation issues, Sunnyside is an appealingly cohesive community, for all its ethnic diversity. Stop by the foundation's office at 41-13 47th Street, 718-392-9139, for information, advice, and a free copy of *The Sunnyside Herald* if you're thinking of moving here.

Web Site: www.nyc.gov
Area Codes: 718, 347
Post Office: Sunnyside Station, 45-15 44th Street, Sunnyside 11104, 800-275-8777
Zip Code: 11104
Police Precinct: One Hundred Eighth, 5-47 50th Avenue, Long Island City 11104, 718-784-5411
Emergency Hospital (nearest): Elmhurst Hospital Center, 79-01 Broadway, Elmhurst 11373, 718-334-4000
Library: Queens Public Library, Sunnyside Branch, 43-06 Greenpoint Avenue, Sunnyside 11104, 718-784-3033, www.nypl.org
Public School Education: School District #24 in region 4, 28-11 Queens Plaza North, Queens, NY 11101, 718-391-8300, www.nycenet.edu

Community Resources: Museum for African Art, 36-01 43rd Avenue at 36th Street, Long Island City, NY 11101, 718-784-7718, www.africanart. org; Sunnyside Chamber of Commerce, www.sunnysidechamber.org

Transportation—Subway: #7 to Manhattan, 40th Street, 46th Street, 52nd Street

Transportation—Bus: for a bus map and schedule of Queens, stop by the Queens Transit Headquarters Information Center, 128-15 28th Avenue, Flushing, or call 718-330-1234, or go to www.mta.info. Queens Surface Corp. at 28th Avenue, 718-445-3100, www.qsbus.com, also offers express service on several routes to midtown Manhattan for $4.

Transportation—LIRR: nearest station: Woodside, at Roosevelt Avenue and 61st Street

REGO PARK

Boundaries and Contiguous Areas: **North**: Queens Boulevard; **East**: Yellowstone Boulevard and Forest Hills; **Southwest**: Woodhaven Boulevard

What distinguishes Rego Park from neighboring Forest Hills and Kew Gardens, which it very much resembles, is the appreciably higher ratio of apartment buildings to private dwellings, slightly lower rents, somewhat older population and proportionately more recent immigrants. While the number of Asians, particularly from Southeast Asia, has been increasing throughout the three communities, Rego Park has also attracted a sizable Russian population, a large Israeli group, and a nucleus of Iranians.

One of the borough's largest malls, the Queens Center housing Macy's, among others, is quartered on the Rego Park shopping stretch of Queens Boulevard, while smaller neighborhood shops line 63rd Drive. One- and two-family homes are found tucked behind the red brick six-story buildings lining 63rd. Running parallel to Queens Boulevard, the Long Island Railroad creates a barrier between commercial and residential environs.

It should be noted that the imposition of a rigid grid pattern was foiled in this part of Queens. Wherever possible, each numbered thoroughfare has an Avenue, Road, and Drive to its credit. For example, 63rd Avenue, 63rd Road, 63rd Drive in that order. Rego Park was first developed in 1923 and named for the company that built it: the Rego (for Real Good) Construction Company. It is a nice alternative to the "just over the 59th Street Bridge" neighborhoods of Long Island City, Astoria, and Sunnyside, with ample shopping and accessibility to the city by express bus or the Q60 on Queens Boulevard.

Web Site: www.nyc.gov
Area Codes: 718, 347
Post Office: Rego Park Station, 92-24 Queens Boulevard, Rego Park, NY 11374, 800-275-8777
Zip Code: 11374
Police Precinct: One Hundred and Twelfth, 68-40 Austin Street, Forest Hills, NY 11375, 718-520-9311
Emergency Hospital: St. John's Hospital, 90-02 Queens Boulevard, Elmhurst, NY 11373, 718-558-1000
Library: Queens Public Library, Rego Park Branch, 91-41 63rd Drive, Rego Park, NY 11374, 718-459-5140, www.nypl.org
Public School Education: School District #28 in region 3 (see **Forest Hills**).
Adult Education: Queens College (see **Flushing**); St. John's University (see **Forest Hills**).
Community Resource: Queens Chamber of Commerce, www.queens chamber.org
Transportation—Subway: R and G at Rego Park Station, 67th Avenue
Transportation—Bus: for a bus map and schedule of Queens, stop by the Queens Transit Headquarters Information Center, 128-15 28th Avenue, Flushing, or call 718-330-1234, or go to www.mta.info. Queens Surface Corp. at 28th Avenue, 718-445-3100, www.qsbus.com, also offers express service on several routes to midtown Manhattan for $4.
Transportation—LIRR: Nearest station: Forest Hills

FOREST HILLS

Boundaries and Contiguous Areas: North: Long Island Expressway; **East**: Grand Central Parkway and Corona Park; **South**: Union Turnpike and Kew Gardens; **West**: Yellowstone Boulevard and Rego Park

Practical Queens Boulevard, a major shopping thoroughfare that sensibly separates curbside businesses from through traffic with narrow concrete dividers, belies the charm of Forest Hills as it cuts through the heart of the neighborhood. Bordering Corona Park northwest of the boulevard, the "Cord Meyer" district consists of gracious, white-trimmed brick homes begun in 1904 and large apartment buildings constructed later by the Cord Meyer Development Co., which is still the largest landlord in the area. South a block just off Austin, considered one of the most enticing shopping streets in Queens, lies "The Gardens." Forest Hills Gardens, designed in the eclectic tradition by an architect of the Beaux-Arts school and sponsored by the Russell Sage Foundation, has few peers in the half-timbered world of

Victorian Tudor. Brick-fronted Cotswoldian houses face curving drives and landscaped plots originally planned by Frederick Law Olmstead, Jr. The walled Gardens area is distinctively exclusive. Shopping and noshing opportunities also add allure to the somewhat crowded Forest Hills neighborhood. In addition to the attractive Austin Street spots, appealing cafes and craft and antique stores have cropped up on Metropolitan Avenue.

Old and established, Forest Hills is becoming increasingly cosmopolitan. (A local real estate agent reports a map of Forest Hills on sale in Tokyo bookstores.) And increasingly, its brick apartment buildings have gone co-op. The six- to ten-story, mostly red brick rental buildings congregating on either side of Queens Boulevard stretch across 108th Street and over to Forest Hills High School, standing prominently above the Grand Central Expressway, which borders the neighborhood from nearby Flushing Meadow Park. The IND/BMT subway lines, as well as major arteries like Ascan, Metropolitan, and 108th Street, are worth pursuing for their quality pre-war construction as well as convenience to public transportation and shopping. Semi-detached apartments and units in private homes may require a slightly longer walk but offer landscaped lots and winding streets as dividends. While a great number of Forest Hills' residents have been firmly entrenched for many years, rentals and co-ops occasionally do pop up; act quickly, they won't stay on the market long.

Web Sites: www.queensnewyork.com, www.nyc.gov
Area Codes: 718, 347
Post Office: Forest Hills Station, 106-28 Queens Boulevard, Forest Hills, NY 11375, 800-275-8777
Zip Code: 11375
Police Precinct: One Hundred and Twelfth, 68-40 Austin Street, Forest Hills, NY 11375, 718-520-9311
Emergency Hospitals: North Shore University Hospital, 102-01 66th Road, Forest Hills, NY 11375, 718-830-4000; Parkway Hospital, 70-35 113th Street, Forest Hills, NY 11375, 718-990-4100
Library: Queens Public Library, Forest Hills Branch, 108-19 71st Avenue, Forest Hills, NY 11375, 718-268-7934, www.nypl.org
Public School Education: School District #28 in region 3, 30-48 Linden Place, Queens, NY 11354, 718-281-7575, www.nycenet.edu
Adult Education (nearest): St. John's University, 8000 Utopia Parkways, Jamaica, NY 11439, 888-9ST-JOHNS, www.stjohns.edu; Forest Hills High School, 67-01 110th Street, Forest Hills 11375, 718-263-8066, offers adult education programs.
Community Resources: Queens Chamber of Commerce, www.queenschamber.org; West Side Tennis Club, 1 Tennis Place (bounded by Burns and Dartmouth streets and 69th and 70th avenues), 718-268-

2300; Forest Hills Jewish Center, 106-06 Queens Boulevard, 718-263-7000, www.fhjc.org, offers a pool, gym, programs, classes, etc.

Transportation—Subway: E, F, G, and R, all to 71st and Continental avenues, Forest Hills

Transportation—Bus: for a bus map and schedule of Queens, stop by the Queens Transit Headquarters Information Center, 128-15 28th Avenue, Flushing, or call 718-330-1234, or go to www.mta.info. Queens Surface Corp. at 28th Avenue, 718-445-3100, www.qsbus.com, also offers express service on several routes to midtown Manhattan for $4.

Transportation—LIRR: Forest Hills Station, Austin and 71st streets

KEW GARDENS

Boundaries and Contiguous Areas: Northeast: Queens Boulevard; **South**: Metropolitan Avenue and Forest Park; **West**: Union Turnpike and Forest Hills

Bracketed by LaGuardia Airport and John F. Kennedy International, Queens is home to thousands of airline employees. Kew Gardens, sitting nearly midway between the city's two prime airports, is particularly popular with flight crews, hence the nickname, "Crew Gardens." Real estate agents report more rentals available and more singles residing in Kew Gardens than in Forest Hills and Rego Park.

The neighborhood's oldest section dates to 1912, when the Kew Gardens Corporation was formed. The substantial Colonial and Tudor-accented private homes built on high, comparatively hilly ground between Maple Grove Cemetery and Forest Park have cachet even today. The blocks of red brick apartment buildings that ring Kew's center, the older ones especially, represent real value, though most are co-op. Austin Street and Metropolitan Avenue together with Lefferts and Queens boulevards make up Kew's main shopping area. There's a pleasingly small-town feel on Austin around the railroad station, and Forest Park (see **Greenspace and Beaches**), which provides rustic peace and quiet.

Nevertheless, with the infusion of recent immigrants Kew Gardens has become a cosmopolitan community. Along Lefferts Boulevard a new Irish bar and restaurant, a Russian grocer, an Uzbekistan Cultural Center and a Caribbean nightclub suggest just a few of the ethnic components of this neighborhood. Good schools and easy accessibility to nearly all of the borough's main roads and highways make this a viable alternative to Forest Hills.

At its southeastern-most tip, Kew Gardens hosts not only the borough's newest commercial skyscraper, a tall, rectangular gray block with cutout circles at the corners, but also Queens Borough Hall just across the Van Wyck Expressway, a long bureaucratic brick and limestone structure usually filled with politicians and, occasionally, useful publications about the borough.

Web Site: www.nyc.gov
Area Codes: 718, 347
Post Office: Kew Gardens Station, 83-30 Austin Street, Kew Gardens, NY 11415, 800-275-8777
Zip Codes: 11415, 11375, 11365
Police Precinct: One Hundred and Second, 87-34 118th Street, Richmond Hill, NY 11418, 718-805-3200
Emergency Hospital (nearest): North Shore University Hospital, 102-01 66th Road, Forest Hills, NY 11375, 718-830-4000
Libraries: Queens Public Library, Lefferts Branch, 103-34 Lefferts Boulevard, Richmond Hill, 718-843-5950; Glen Oaks Branch, 256-04 Union Turnpike, Forest Park, NY 11004, 718-831-8636; www.nypl.org
Public School Education: School District #28 in region 3 (see **Forest Hills**).
Adult Education (nearest): Queens College, 65-30 Kissena Boulevard, Flushing NY 11367, 718-997-5000, www.qc.edu
Community Resources: Queens Borough Hall, 120-55 Queens Boulevard, Kew Gardens, NY 11424, 718-520-3220; Queens Chamber of Commerce, www.queenschamber.org
Transportation—Subway: E, F, Kew Gardens/Union Turnpike
Transportation—Bus: for a bus map and schedule of Queens, stop by the Queens Transit Headquarters Information Center, 128-15 28th Avenue, Flushing, or call 718-330-1234, or go to www.mta.info. Queens Surface Corp. at 28th Avenue, 718-445-3100, www.qsbus.com, also offers express service on several routes to midtown Manhattan for $4.
Transportation—LIRR: Kew Gardens Station, Lefferts Boulevard, Austin Street

FLUSHING

Boundaries and Contiguous Areas: North: Cross Island Parkway and Whitestone; **East**: Utopia Parkway and Francis Lewis Boulevard and Bayside; **South**: Union Turnpike; **West**: Grand Central Parkway and Forest Hills

Middle class Flushing sprawls on either side of the Long Island Expressway, embraced by two great parks, at the center of thriving northern Queens. The nexus of multiple bus routes, rail lines and traffic arteries, downtown

Flushing looks like the crossroads of the world. In recent years a strong influx of Asians—primarily Chinese and Koreans—have reshaped the neighborhood, changing the face of the northern section, which now resembles Manhattan's Chinatown. On weekends, the colorful Chinese fish-fruit-and-vegetable vendors, Korean gift stores, Muslim butchers, and sari shops along Main Street draw people from outside the area, and religious observances are as likely to be in Korean, Hindi, or Mandarin as in English or Hebrew. Toward the Long Island Expressway and surrounding Queens College is a less ethnically diverse area, where English is predominant and residents have lived for many years, some in red brick developments like Pomonok or Elechester, which were built for members of the electrical union.

Away from commercial Main Street, Union Turnpike, and Northern Boulevard, the grid of shady residential streets has changed little, except perhaps to have become more presentable. The profusion of well-established trees, 2,000 varieties throughout Flushing, constitutes a treasure and a living remnant of the nursery industry that flourished here from pre-Revolutionary times until recently. Another survivor, its back turned to Northern Boulevard, the austere Friends' Meeting House has been a place of worship since 1694, except during the Revolutionary War, when it was a British hospital, prison, and stable. Bowne House, built nearby in 1661, was an earlier site of Quaker worship and of the struggle for religious freedom in what was then a Dutch settlement. Down Bowne Street from this museum of colonial life, in a modest residential neighborhood, is an extraordinary Hindu temple covered with stone statues. That's Flushing.

Great tracts of green breathing space surround and bisect the neighborhood. Flushing Meadows-Corona Park contains within its 1,200 acres remnants of the 1939 and 1964 New York World's Fairs, two lakes, a marina, the Queens Zoo, a botanical garden, the Queens Museum, Theatre in the Park, the New York Hall of Science, and an indoor ice-skating rink. Adjacent is Shea Stadium, home of the New York Mets, and the USTA National Tennis Center, site of the annual US Open Tennis Championships. Tucked away within Flushing's borders is the more intimate and landscaped Kissena Park, which sits around a lake and contains an appealing nature center.

As might be expected, the presence of Queens College and Flushing's rich ethnic mix support an unusually vibrant cultural life: music, art, literary pursuits, and theater flourish here. The Flushing Branch of the Queens Borough Public Library on Main Street, handsomely rebuilt in 1998, is the busiest branch of the busiest library system in the nation. Open daily, its holdings include books, periodicals, videos, and CDs in some 30 languages, computer WorldLinQ in Chinese, Korean, Russian, Spanish, and French, an Adult Learning Center, and a unique International Resource

Center. Renovation of the Main Street Flushing subway station nearby has been a boon to the 100,000 commuters who use it, many of them transferring from the web of bus routes which cross here.

Besides the convenience of transportation and the physical amenities, what Flushing has to offer is more space at less-than-Manhattan rents. For luxury condos look elsewhere, Bayside perhaps. High-rise apartments cluster near downtown Flushing. The rest is two-story brick apartment enclaves, one and two-family houses, detached and semi-attached, all with on-street parking. Ads to sell or rent these properties are often placed in *Newsday* and the *New York Times* by their owners; consult these same pages and the list of realtors in **Finding a Place to Live** to find brokers who handle other properties.

Web Site: www.nyc.gov
Area Codes: 718, 347
Post Offices: Flushing Main Station, 41-65 Main Street, Flushing 11355; Fresh Meadow Station, 192-20 Horace Harding Expressway, Flushing 11365; Station "B," 136-50 Roosevelt Avenue, Flushing 11368; Pomonok Station, 158-05 71st Avenue, Flushing 11366; Utopia Station, 182-04 Union Turnpike, Flushing 11366; Station "A," 40-03 164th Street, Flushing 11358; Station "C," 75-23 Main Street, Flushing 11367; Linden Hill Station, 29-50 Union Street, Flushing 11354; 800-275-8777
Zip Codes: 11354, 11355, 11358, 11365, 11366, 11367, 11368
Police Precincts: One Hundred and Ninth, 37-05 Union Street, Flushing 11354, 718-321-2250; One Hundred and Seventh, 71-01 Parsons Boulevard, Flushing 11365, 718-969-5100
Emergency Hospitals: New York Hospital Medical Center of Queens, Main Street at Booth Memorial Avenue, Flushing 11355, 718-670-1231; Flushing Hospital Medical Center, 45th Avenue at Parsons Boulevard, Flushing 11355, 718-670-5000
Libraries: Flushing Main Branch, Queens Public Library, 41-17 Main Street, Flushing 11355, 718-661-1200; Hillcrest Branch, 187-05 Union Turnpike, Flushing 11366, 718-454-2786; McGoldrick Branch, 155-06 Roosevelt Avenue, Flushing 11354, 718-461-1616; Mitchell-Linden Branch, 29-42 Union Street, Flushing 11354, 718-539-2330; Pomonok Branch, 158-21 Jewel Avenue, Flushing 11365, 718-591-4343; Queensborough Hill Branch, 60-05 Main Street, Flushing 11355, 718-359-8332; www.nypl.org; Benjamin S. Rosenthal Library, Queens College, 65-30 Kissena Boulevard, Flushing 11367, 718-997-5000
Public School Education: School Districts #25 and #26 in region 3 (see **Forest Hills**).

Adult Education: Queens College, 65-30 Kissena Boulevard, Flushing 11367, 718-997-5000, www.qc.edu

Community Resources: Queens Historical Society, Kingsland House, 143-35 37th Avenue, Flushing 11354, 718-939-0647, www. preserve.org/queens; Queens Chamber of Commerce, www.queens chamber.org; The Bowne House, 37-01 Bowne Street, Flushing 11354, 718-359-0528; www.preserve.org/queens/bowne; New York Hall of Science, 47-01 111th Street, Flushing Meadows-Corona Park, Flushing 11368, 718-699-0005, www.nyhallsci.org, includes over 200 hands-on exhibits plus a science playground for children; Queens Museum of Art, New York City Building, Flushing Meadows-Corona Park, Flushing 11368, 718-592-9700, www.queensmuse.org; Colden Center for the Performing Arts, Queens College, Long Island Expressway and Kissena Boulevard, Flushing 11367, 718-793-8080; www.coldencenter.org; Flushing Council on Culture and the Arts at Town Hall, 137-35 Northern Blvd., Flushing 11354, 718-463-7700, www.flushingtown-hall.org; Kissena Park Nature Center, Rose Avenue and Parsons Boulevard, 718-699-4202; Queens Botanical Garden, 43-50 Main Street, Flushing 11355, 718-886-3800; Queens Theatre in the Park, Flushing Meadows-Corona Park, Flushing 11368, 718-760-0064, www.queenstheatre.org

Transportation—Subway: #7, Willets Point-Shea Stadium, Main Street; E, F, Union Turnpike-Kew Gardens

Transportation—Bus: for a bus map and schedule of Queens, stop by the Queens Transit Headquarters Information Center, 128-15 28th Avenue, Flushing, or call 718-330-1234, or go to www.mta.info. Queens Surface Corp. at 28th Avenue, 718-445-3100, www.qsbus.com, also offers express service on several routes to midtown Manhattan for $4.

Transportation—LIRR: Main Street Station, Main Street & 41st Avenue

BAYSIDE

Boundaries and Contiguous Areas: North and **East**: Cross Island Parkway; **South**: Long Island Expressway; **West**: Francis Lewis Boulevard and Utopia Parkway

The bright barn-red Long Island Railroad station, white-trimmed and snappy, differentiates Bayside from other Queens stops. So does the concentration of pubs and restaurants—some dim and glitzy, others homey-comfortable with fireplaces—that surround the station. These places attract singles and have a bubbling atmosphere after work and on weekends. North of this Bell Boulevard and 41st Avenue junction, one- and two-family homes re-establish that urban/suburban quiet which typifies residential Queens, until you reach **Bay Terrace**. Here, newer condominiums and co-op garden apartment buildings break the mold.

While the older, free-standing homes contain rental apartments, condominium rentals in the pristine **Bay Club**, among other high rises, are probably the biggest draw. The enormous development consists of 1,036 condominiums in two three-pronged towers, a glass-domed swim club, a health club, and five tennis courts. The **Bay Bridge** condo development nearby, with some 2,000 luxury townhouses, is a shorefront village in itself. From the Bay Club windows, and from those in the older co-ops, you can see how the community got its name—Bayside is bounded on two sides by Little Bay and Little Neck Bay. The Whitestone, Triborough, and Throgs Neck bridges connect Queens to The Bronx. Tucked within the densely populated high rises that pack many a Bayside block, several town parks, plenty of shopping, excellent schools, and the relative regularity of the LIRR schedule have combined to make this a commuter favorite for decades. It's very much a family area with good schools.

Bayside has water views but no direct subway connection to Manhattan. Commuters have three public transportation choices: the Long Island Railroad, express buses, or Queens buses to Flushing's Main Street Station and the #7 Flushing Line subway to 42nd street in Manhattan. The LIRR is typically the fastest route.

Web Sites: www.baysidequeens.com, www.nyc.gov

Area Codes: 718, 347

Post Office: Bayside Station, 212-35 42nd Avenue, Bayside, NY 11361, 800-275-8777

Zip Codes: 11360, 11361, 11364, 11357

Police Precinct: One Hundred and Eleventh, 45-06 215th Street, Bayside, NY 11359, 718-279-5200

Emergency Hospital: St. Mary's Hospital for Children, 29-01 216th Street, Bayside, NY 11360, 718-281-8800

Library: Queens Public Library, Bayside Branch, 214-20 Northern Boulevard, Bayside, NY 11361, 718-229-1834, www.nypl.org

Public School Education: School District #26 in region 3 (see **Forest Hills**).

Adult Education: Queensborough Community College, 222-05 56th Avenue, Bayside, NY 11364, 718-631-6262, www.qcc.cuny.edu

Community Resources: Crocheron Park, 33rd Avenue and Little Neck Parkway, 718-762-5966, a 45-acre park; Queensborough Community College Gallery, 222-05 56th Avenue, Bayside, 718-631-6396, www.qcc.cuny.edu; Queens Chamber of Commerce, www.queens chamber.org

Transportation—Train: regular LIRR service

Transportation—Bus: for a bus map and schedule of Queens, stop by the Queens Transit Headquarters Information Center, 128-15 28th Avenue, Flushing, or call 718-330-1234, or go to www.mta.info. Queens Surface Corp. at 28th Avenue, 718-445-3100, www.qsbus.com, also offers express service on several routes to midtown Manhattan for $4.

Transportation—LIRR Station: 213th Street and 41st Street

You might also want to consider...

- **Douglaston**; an upper middle-class community at the northeastern end of Queens bordering on Long Island, having mostly one- and two-family houses and co-ops, relatively low real estate taxes and lower prices than upscale Great Neck (Long Island) to the east. A 25-minute commute to Manhattan on the Long Island Railroad (LIRR) Community Board 11, 718-225-1054
- **Jamaica Estates**, with its winding roads, shady streets, Tudor houses, and English street names, is 45 minutes by the E or F train to Manhattan. Expensive homes in a small, rather exclusive community tucked away in mid to north Queens. Community Board 8, 718-591-6000
- **Middle Village** is mid-Queens, middle class and relatively affordable, with tidy one- and two-family houses and a scattering of condos housing an old fashioned "close-knit" community of civic-minded people and plenty of mom and pop stores. Amenities include Juniper Valley Park, from which the Manhattan skyline is visible, good schools, Italian specialty stores and German bakeries. Community Board 5, 718-366-1834
- **Richmond Hill**; with Victorian houses, golf and tennis in Forest Park, and a variety of ethnic stores, but less expensive than neighboring Kew Gardens and Forest Hills, for the most part. An easy commute by train or subway. Community Board 9, 718-286-2686; Richmond Hill Historical Society, www.richmondhillhistory.org
- **Ridgewood**; a half-hour from Grand Central by subway, boasts a German heritage, still apparent in its shops and restaurants, solid row houses, some of them landmarked, and a strong neighborhood feeling. Especially prized are the harmonious yellow-brick houses along Stockholm Street and two blocks of 69th Avenue, between Fresh Pond Road and 60th Street. Community Board 5, 718-366-1834
- **Whitestone**; between the Whitestone and Throgs Neck Bridges in northern Queens and 30 minutes on the #7 from Times Square (45 minutes by express bus). Highly residential, quiet family neighborhood

featuring some private homes plus many co-ops and condos—few rentals. Includes exclusive Malba (see the introduction to the Queens profile above) and Francis Lewis Park along the riverfront. Community Board 7, 718-359-2800

STATEN ISLAND

New York's least-populated borough is, for many, simply the turn-around point for New York's most beloved, and cheapest, boat ride, the Staten Island Ferry. Area residents would just as soon keep their 61-square-mile island off the coast of New Jersey to themselves. In fact, November 2, 1993 marked a red-letter day when islanders voted overwhelmingly to secede from New York City. (Final word rests with Albany and this question is not likely to be settled soon.) Dreams of remaining far from the maddening New York frenzy were, in fact, conclusively shattered when the austerely beautiful Verrazano-Narrows Bridge connecting Staten Island with Brooklyn was opened in 1964. The island's semi-rural isolation ended once and for all as Brooklynites flocked across the longest single-span bridge in the world to take up residence in dozens of new tract developments. And its population growth continues today. According to the *Times*, Staten Island is the fastest growing borough in the city, growing 17% in the 1990s, and many of its newcomers are minorities, going far to diversify the island's heretofore mostly white status.

Giovanni da Verrazano discovered hillocky Staten Island in 1524 but, until the dedication of his namesake bridge 440 years later, the island remained something of a backwater. Henry Hudson claimed *Staaten Eylandt* for the Dutch East India Company in 1609; however, Britain acquired Staten Island when the British took over New Amsterdam in 1644. Farming, and then oystering, flourished. By the mid-1800s, a railroad, trolley cars, and ferry service made the island's seashore and salubrious air accessible to the gentry.

The fickle fashionables had moved on though by the time Staten Island became part of New York City in 1898. Too bad, because the city improved the new borough's ferry service immeasurably: by 1904 there were a number of sturdy seaworthy boats running on schedule for the first time since young Cornelius Vanderbilt instituted ferry service to Manhattan around 1810. Today, three sunset-yellow ferries ply the choppy waters of the Upper Bay between St. George and the Battery during the rush hours. Off-peak, two modernized 1,200-passenger boats handle the immensely scenic 25-minute crossing. Now, not only do tracts and shopping malls flourish south of the Staten Island Expressway, straining the island's over-taxed infrastructure, but a modest renaissance is also under-

STATEN ISLAND

way in communities within walking distance of the ferry landing. Wall Streeters cherish the office-to-ferry walk, as well as the uphill stroll home, almost as much as they cherish the fare: it's free.

Hills—precipitous slopes reminiscent of San Francisco—and stunning views from the craggy ridge that rises between St. George and Richmondtown characterize that portion of Staten Island nearest Manhattan. On leafy Todt, Emerson and Grymes hills, million-dollar homes look over the treetops to Brooklyn and Manhattan. Wood-frame Victorian houses, salted among the stucco mini-mansions and angular contemporary homes, are the darlings of homesteaders. You're more likely to find a rental apartment in a converted one-or two-family house than in an apartment building on Staten Island—although red brick apartment towers do exist.

The Staten Island Chamber of Commerce, 130 Bay Street, Staten Island, NY 10301, 718-727-1900, sells an excellent street map and the MTA's Staten Island Bus Map (free at the Chamber) is equally useful. Rental classifieds in the *Staten Island Advance*, 718-981-1234, www.statenislandadvance.com, are more numerous on Saturday and Sunday but this afternoon paper publishes real estate ads every day. In Manhattan, pick up a copy of the *Advance* at the newsstand located inside the ferry terminal. *The Village Voice* is also a good source for listings. Some Staten Island realtors are listed in the section on **Apartment Hunting**.

ST. GEORGE

Boundaries and Contiguous Areas: **North**: Richmond Terrace and the Kill Van Kull; **East**: Bay Street; **South**: Victory Boulevard and Stapleton; **West**: Jersey Street and The Narrows

Flags aflutter, the beguiling limestone and brick Borough Hall caps a rise to the right of St. George's ferry terminal. To the left as you exit the terminal, a stunning structure, at once public sculpture, bridge, and lighthouse-like tower, crowns a plaza, inviting visitors to climb to its glassy top for a smashing view of the harbor and lower Manhattan beyond. The two are symbolic of St. George's struggle against blight. The downtown sector, though quaint and historic, has defied gentrification, but uphill, within sight of the neo-Gothic spires of Curtis High School (between St. Mark's Place and Hamilton Avenue), you'll find restored Victorian, Tudor, and 1920s-stucco houses. Four formerly vacant apartment buildings there have been transformed into the Village on St. Marks with affordable rentals suitable for commuters to the Financial District. And the Saturday Greenmarket on St. Marks brings a village square feel to downtown St. George from May to December.

In contrast to the maple-shaded period homes, the three converted grain and coffee warehouses that comprise Bay Landing are certainly up-to-date. Arguably the borough's trendiest housing, these waterside condominiums located a five-minute walk east of the ferry terminal are the first stage in a projected harbor front revival. Here, black pines and juniper separate the public marina, esplanade, and the glass-enclosed Landing Cafe from the access road—shades of Sausalito. New rentals, rare in Staten Island, are to be found in moderately-priced waterfront mid-rises at Harbor View. Come spring, fishing enthusiasts flock to the charter boats tied up at the Landing's pristine docks. The Joseph L. Lyons Pool, one of Staten Island's four municipal swimming pools, and the George Cromwell Center, an indoor recreation center with tennis courts and a track situated on a pier, are both located near The Landing's complex. The new Richmond County Bank Ballpark is the home of exciting baseball action featuring the Staten Island Yankees, www.siyanks.com, a minor league affiliate of the Bronx Bombers. A lighthouse museum also remains in the planning stages for the warterfront area.

Check the classifieds and our list of Staten Island real estate brokers in the **Finding a Place to Live** chapter for rentals, and after filing off the ferry, walk through the gradually reviving community of St. George.

Web Sites: www.statenislandusa.com, www.statenislandadvance.com, www.si-web.com, http://community.silive.com, www.nyc.gov

Area Codes: 718, 347

Post Office: St. George Station, 45 Bay Street, Staten Island, NY 10301; Ferry Terminal Station, St. George Ferry, Staten Island, NY 10301, 800-275-8777

Zip Code: 10301

Police Precinct: One Hundred Twentieth, 78 Richmond Terrace, Staten Island, NY 10301, 718-876-8500

Emergency Hospitals (nearest): Bayley Seton Hospital, 75 Vanderbilt Avenue (at Bay Street), Staten Island, NY 10304, 718-818-6000; St. Vincent's Medical Center of Richmond, 355 Bard Avenue, Staten Island, NY 10301, 718-818-3186

Library: St. George Library Center of the New York Public Library, 5 Central Avenue, Staten Island, NY 10301, 718-442-8560, www.nypl.org

Public School Education: School District #31 in region 7, 715 Ocean Terrace, Staten Island, NY 10301, 718-556-8350, www.nycenet.edu

Adult Education: College of Staten Island, St. George campus (part of the City University of New York), 2800 Victory Blvd., Staten Island, NY 10301, 718-982-2000, www.csi.cuny.edu

Community Resources: Richmond County Bank Ballpark, 75 Richmond Terrace, Staten Island, NY 10301, 718-720-9265; Snug Harbor

Cultural Center, 1000 Richmond Terrace, Staten Island, NY 10301, 718-448-2500, www.snug-harbor.org, is located in a clutch of handsome Greek Revival buildings on 80 tree-filled acres. Once a haven for indigent sailors, the colonnaded buildings are now the locus of Staten Island's cultural rebirth; concerts, art exhibits, and plays fill the high-ceilinged halls. Also on the grounds you'll find the Staten Island Botanical Garden, 718-273-8200, and the Staten Island Children's Museum, 718-273-2060. The Staten Island Institute of Arts and Sciences, 75 Stuyvesant Place, Staten Island, NY, 718-727-1135, a museum offering tours and cultural events, and the Noble Maritime Collection, 718-447-6490.

Transportation—Train: the Staten Island Railway train costs $1.50 one way and provides service between the St. George Ferry Terminal and Tottenville at the southern tip of the 13.9-mile-long island. The second stop, Tompkinsville Station, is used for Bay Street Landing. Call 718-966-SIRT for information.

Transportation—Bus: local buses cost $2 one way. Express buses to Manhattan via the Verrazano Bridge and Brooklyn Battery Tunnel cost $4 one way. Call 718-330-1234 for bus information.

Transportation—Ferry: free passenger ferries run every 15 or 20 minutes during rush hours, every half hour at other times, every hour from 11 p.m. to 6 a.m. Service is less frequent on holidays and weekends. Car ferry service is available between 4:30 a.m. and 11 p.m. and costs $3 per car. Call 718-815-2628 for information.

STAPLETON

Boundaries and Contiguous Areas: **North**: Victory Boulevard and St. George; **East**: Bay Street and Upper New York Bay; **South**: Canal and Broad Streets; **West**: Louis Street, Van Duzer Street and Grymes Hill

Bordering Bay Street, Stapleton boasts a batch of more-collectibles-than-antiques stores and a few somewhat upscale watering holes. These cafes, tarted up with Tiffany style lamps, polished brass, and old-fashioned bottle vases, point to the presence of newcomers in Stapleton's craggy hills.

Located only two stops from the ferry terminal on the SIRT train, Stapleton for some time has attracted artists and young families looking for a third bedroom. Now, here come bankers and stockbrokers from Lower Manhattan. Sturdy 19th century homes characterize housing in **Stapleton Heights** and adjacent **Ward Hill**. Asphalt shingles sheath houses down on the flats near the gourmet takeout shops, the library, and handsome Tappan Park. The Mud Lane Society, a group of community boosters, promotes Stapleton with an annual house tour.

The area, still quaint and serene, has seen some modest growth on Beach and Van Duzer streets with the recent opening of new coffee shops, yoga schools, beauty salons, and Japanese restaurants. A new community center is in the works and a few townhouses have cropped up along Beach Street.

Web Sites: www.statenislandusa.com, www.si-web.com, http://community.silive.com, www.nyc.gov

Area Codes: 718, 347

Post Offices: Stapleton Station, 514 Bay Street, Staten Island, NY 10304; Rosebank Station, 567 Tompkins Avenue, Staten Island, NY 10305; 800-275-8777

Zip Code: 10304

Police Precinct: One Hundred Twentieth, 78 Richmond Terrace, Staten Island, NY 10301, 718-876-8500

Emergency Hospital (nearest): Bayley Seton Hospital, 75 Vanderbilt Avenue (at Bay Street), Staten Island, NY 10304, 718-818-6000

Library: New York Public Library, Stapleton Branch, 132 Canal Street, Staten Island, NY 10304, 718-727-0427, www.nypl.org

Public School Education: School District #31 in region 7 (see **St. George**).

Adult Education (nearby): St. John's University, 300 Howard Avenue, Staten Island, NY 10301, 718-390-4545, www.stjohns.edu

Community Resources (nearby): The Jacques Marchais Center of Tibetan Art houses Tibetan monastery artifacts at 338 Lighthouse Avenue in Richmondtown, call for an appointment, 718-987-3500, www.tibetanmuseum.com; the Richmondtown Restoration, a historic village comprised of 14 buildings operated by the Staten Island Historical Society at 441 Clarke Avenue, Staten Island 10306, 718-351-1611; The Conference House, a pre-Revolutionary manor house, at 7455 Hylan Boulevard, Staten Island 10307, 718-984-2086; Alice Austen House Museum and Garden, 2 Hylan Boulevard, Staten Island 10305, 718-816-4506.

Transportation—Train: the Stapleton Station is the third stop on the SIRT train (details under **St. George**).

Transportation—Bus: the #74, #76, and #51 travel Bay Street as far as Canal; the #78 runs along Van Duzer Street and St. Paul's Avenue in Stapleton Heights (details under **St. George**).

GRYMES HILL AND SILVER LAKE

Boundaries and Contiguous Areas: **North**: Louis Avenue; **East**: Stapleton, Van Duzer Street, and Vanderbilt Avenue; **South**: Clove Road and the Staten Island Expressway; **West**: Victory Boulevard

On blustery autumn days, salty sea breezes rattle maple and birch branches, garnishing **Grymes Hill** with russet leaves. Save for the outline of Wall Street's mist-shrouded skyline, the place feels a lot more like Westchester. Interspersed with narrow blacktop lanes and imposing houses, the hills of Staten Island radiate a rustic sub-urbanity.

The higher you climb any one of the island's myriad hills, the more imposing the homes become. Four-hundred-foot high **Todt Hill**, the tallest of Staten Island's peaks, is the toniest. Grymes Hill, nearer the ferry terminal, is the most intellectual: St. John's University and Wagner College cluster its slopes; the College of Staten Island lies in an adjacent valley. Though 12-story Sunrise Tower is co-op, there are 475 two- and three-bedroom rental apartments in the Grymes Hill Apartments Complex, built by Donald Trump's father in the 1940s. In addition, rental apartments can be found in remodeled one-family homes.

Silver Lake combines with Clove Lakes Park to form a sylvan greenbelt. There are tennis courts, bridle paths, an ice skating rink, and a municipal golf course laid out around the reservoir, and between Clove Road and Broadway a small, accessible zoo with a first-rate reptile collection.

Web Sites: www.statenislandusa.com, www.si-web.com, http://community.silive.com, www.nyc.gov

Area Codes: 718, 347

Post Offices: St. George Station, 45 Bay Street, Staten Island, NY 10301; Stapleton Station, 514 Bay Street, Staten Island, NY 10304; 800-275-8777

Zip Codes: 10301, 10304

Police Precinct: 120th, 78 Richmond Terrace, Staten Island, NY 10304, 718-876-8500

Emergency Hospitals (nearest): Bayley Seton Hospital, 75 Vanderbilt Avenue (at Bay Street), Staten Island, NY 10304, 718-818-6000; St. Vincent's Medical Center of Richmond, 355 Bard Avenue, Staten Island, NY 10310, 718-818-1234

Library (nearest): New York Public Library, Stapleton Branch, 132 Canal Street, Staten Island, NY 10304, 718-727-0427, www.nypl.org

Public School Education: School District #31 in region 7 (see **St. George**).

Adult Education: College of Staten Island, Sunnyside campus (nearby), 715 Ocean Terrace, Staten Island, NY 10301, 718-982-2000; St. John's University, 300 Howard Avenue, Staten Island, NY 10301, 718-390-4545, www.stjohns.edu; Wagner College (and Wagner College Planetarium), 631 Howard Avenue, Staten Island, NY 10301, 718-390-3100, www.wagner.edu

Community Resources: Staten Island Zoo, 614 Broadway, Staten Island, NY 10310, 718-4423100, www.statenislandzoo.org (see also **Stapleton**).

Transportation—Train: A steep climb is required to reach Grymes Hill from Stapleton, the nearest stop on the SIRT line (details under **St. George**).

Transportation—Bus: the #74 bus traverses Van Duzer Street along the base of Grymes Hill; the #61, #62, #66, and #67 traveling Victory Boulevard connect with the #60 shuttle bus at Clove Road. The shuttle follows Howard Avenue as far as the St. John campus (details under **St. George**).

You might also want to consider...

- **Port Richmond**, just south of West New Brighton on the Kill van Kull, offers reasonably priced housing, much of it pre-War, one- and two-family homes and a 50-minute commute by express bus or bus/ferry from Manhattan. Community Board 1, 718-981-6900, or Staten Island Chamber of Commerce, 718-727-1900, www.sichamber.com
- **West New Brighton** is a stable community across the Kill van Kull from New Jersey and southwest of the ferry. Here Victorian houses and apartments offer golf, tennis and extensive parkland in Silver Lake Park and Clove Lakes Park, which includes the Staten Island Zoo. The Snug Harbor Cultural Center is nearby. Bus to the ferry to the subway to work, about 50 minutes. Community Board 1, 718-981-6900, or Staten Island Chamber of Commerce, 718-727-1900, www.sichamber.com

NEW JERSEY

FORT LEE AND EDGEWATER

Boundaries and Contiguous Areas: North: Englewood and Englewood Cliffs; **East**: Hudson River; **South**: Cliffside Park and West New York; **West**: Leonia and Palisades Park

Apartment towers in **Fort Lee** ride the Palisades above the Hudson like so many schooner masts making their way up the river. Beneath the rocky cliffs sits the small community of Edgewater, where George Washington and his Continental Army landed in November of 1776, after the battle of Washington Heights. General Charles Lee had supervised the fortifications on the site that bears his name, and their remnants are still to be found there. Fort Lee remained a sleepy little town with a ferry landing throughout most of the 19th century. Civil War gunboats used the volcanically formed Palisades for target practice, and these same cliffs provided the Belgian paving stones for the streets of Manhattan. In the late 1800s an amusement center and resorts flourished on The Bluffs, as they were known, but as business waned and ferry service finally ceased, Fort Lee declined.

The location of a nascent movie industry here from about 1910 into the 1920s offered a reprieve, but Hollywood won the climate competition, and the village languished. Completion of the George Washington Bridge in 1931 gave Fort Lee a suburban future. The tallest high-rise in Bergen County rose in Fort Lee in 1972 and such buildings grew rapidly along Palisade Avenue. Fort Lee straddles the approach to the bridge, but the most sought-after housing lies south of the bridge. An estimated 80% of its approximately 35,000 inhabitants commute to jobs in the city, largely by Jersey Transit to the Port Authority Bus Terminal in Manhattan.

No longer sleepy, Fort Lee has maintained a small-town feel, despite its having grown faster—and taller—than it could plan for. Along the quiet streets off Palisade Avenue, tidy homes nearly fill their lovingly manicured postage-stamp lots (they're expensive, nonetheless). It's the view—Manhattan afloat on the Hudson—that determines the price of real estate and rentals. Apartments with a view fetch near-Manhattan prices, whether they are co-ops, condos, or rentals; but you use the same pool and health club at a lower rent without the view. Away from the edge, garden apartments and two-family houses are less expensive.

At the eastern, river end of Main Street in 33-acre Fort Lee Historic Park visitors trace the Revolutionary history of the area in the museum and discover the remnants of Continental Army dugouts. The park lies within the greater Palisades Interstate Park, a narrow strip of wooded land stretching for miles between the Hudson and the Palisades Parkway, with marinas, picnic areas, and a scenic drive. Known to few outside the immediate area, the park constitutes an extraordinary recreation asset for residents of Fort Lee and Edgewater.

Main Street winds down the steep hill into River Road in **Edgewater**, one of the more unusual small towns in New Jersey. A blue-collar pocket with an industrial history, Edgewater hunches under the Palisades along steep, narrow streets, some of whose modest houses have recently been replaced by clutches of tidy condos. There's a somewhat funky feel to the town.

Construction of upscale, high- and low-rise condo and rental developments along the river side of River Road has brought a wave of affluent young professionals, and change, to Edgewater and the adjoining riverside towns directly to the south, North Bergen, West New York, and Weehawken (see below). Sprawling handsomely at water's edge, or suspended over it on piles, housing complexes with aquatic names such as Admiral's Walk, Mariner's Cove, and Jacob's Ferry offer all the amenities—tennis, pool, health club—and the view, at a price. Clustered about are cinemas, a supermarket, restaurants, a restaurant/club in a restored old Hoboken Ferry boat, and hotels; and Yaohan, a Japanese mall complete with a Japanese supermarket, restaurant, and specialty shops, attracts shoppers from throughout the tri-state area. Interspersed helter-skelter between these waterside centers, are the occasional industrial site, a golf driving range, a tennis club, and marinas.

Edgewater is growing, with rental and condo projects proliferating, along with retail space and now a cineplex. Office complexes are being carved out of abandoned industrial sites. And with this critical mass, the megastores—Bed, Bath & Beyond, Barnes & Noble, Staples, etc.—have ventured in, Starbucks, too.

Although there is commuter bus service to the Imperial Ferry in Weehawken and to the Port Authority, a car is a necessity here in the relative isolation of Edgewater's narrow, winding River Road. Realtors handling Fort Lee and Edgewater properties are listed in the **Finding a Place to Live** chapter. It's advisable to drive around first to determine your proximity to the part of the city in which you work as the commute to lower Manhattan can be longer than the view might suggest.

Web Sites: www.newjersey.com, www.fortleenj.org, www.njtowns.com
Area Code: 201
Post Offices: Main Branch, 229 Main Street, Palisade Station, 1213 Anderson Avenue, Fort Lee, Edgewater Station, 33 Hilliard Avenue, Edgewater; 800-275-8777
Zip Codes: Fort Lee, 07024; Edgewater, 07020
Police Stations: Fort Lee Police Station, 1327 16th Street, Fort Lee, 201-

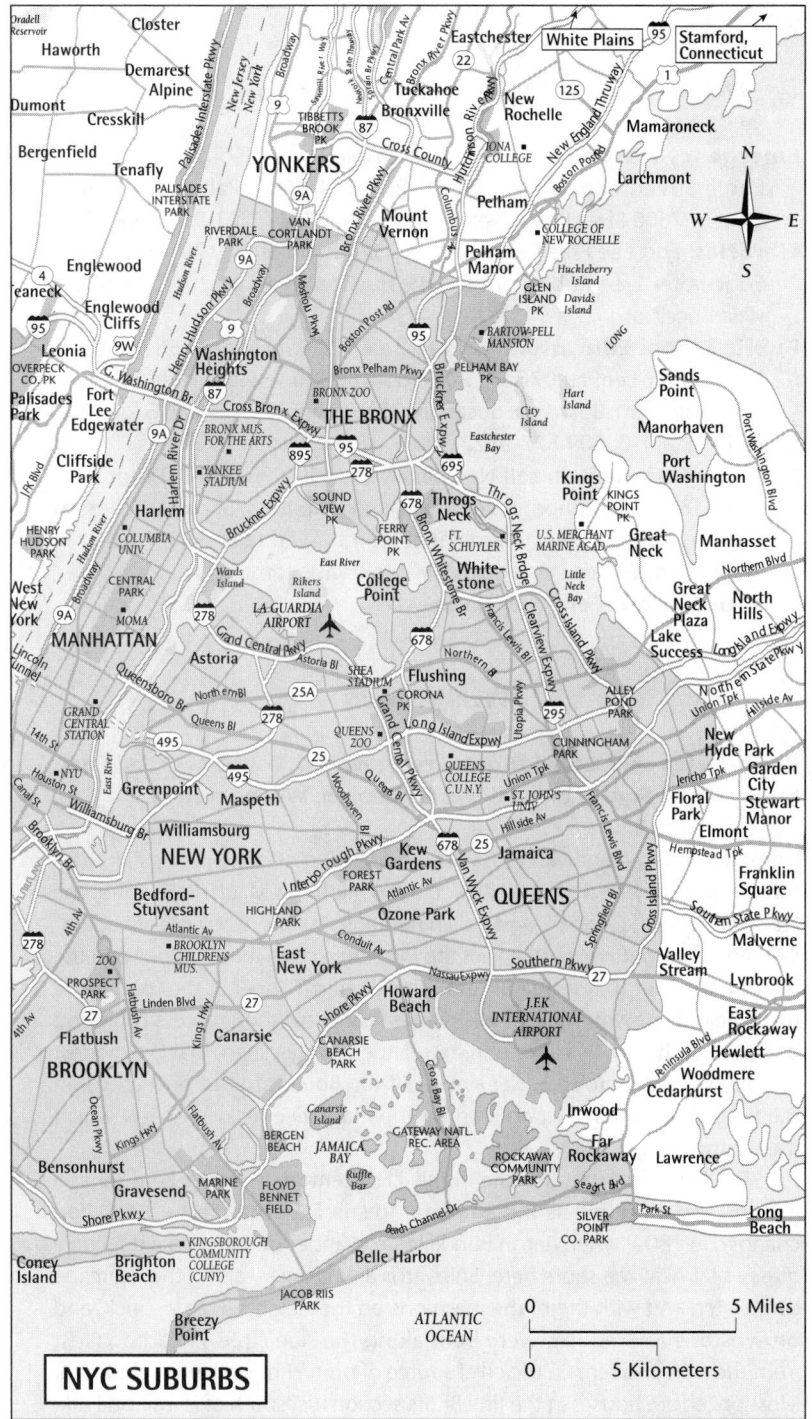

NYC SUBURBS

592-3500; Edgewater Police Station, 916 River Road, Edgewater, 201-943-2200

Emergency Hospitals: Englewood Hospital and Medical Center, 350 Engle Street, Englewood 07631, 201-894-3000; Palisades Medical Center, 7600 River Road, North Bergen, NJ 07047, 201-854-5000

Libraries: Fort Lee Free Public Library, 320 Main Street, 201-592-3614; Edgewater Free Public Library, 49 Hudson Avenue, 201-224-6144; www.bccls.org

Public School Education: Fort Lee Board of Education, 255 Whitman Street, Fort Lee, NJ 07024, 201-585-4600, www.atfortlee-boe.net; Edgewater Park Board of Education, 25 Washington Avenue, Edgewater Park, NJ 08010, 609-877-2122, www.edgewaterpark.k12.nj.us

Transportation—Bus: call New Jersey Transit, 973-762-5100 or 212-564-8484 (Port Authority), for routes and schedules, or pick up same at the Port Authority Bus Terminal at Eighth Avenue and 41st Street in Manhattan. You can also go to www.njtransit.com.

Transportation—Ferry: see Weehawken.

WEEHAWKEN

Boundaries and Contiguous Areas: **North**: West New York; **East**: Hudson River; **South**: Union City and Hoboken; **West**: Union City

Compact little Weehawken (.85 square miles) crests the Jersey Palisades three watery miles across the Hudson from midtown Manhattan. Longtime residents of Irish, German, and Italian heritage, the more recent Latino families, and commuter expatriates of the Big Apple prize that distance and the peace and quiet that it guarantees. The Lincoln Tunnel at the foot of the rocky heights provides Weehawken an enviable half-hour access (on good days) to Manhattan by car or mini-bus. Little wonder, then, that the modest mansions shoulder to shoulder along cliff-top Boulevard East fetch prices in the neighborhood of $1.5 million for the magnificent skyline view which they command.

The Dutch bought this site in the 17th century from the Leni Lenape Indians and modified its Indian name to suit Dutch tongues. Little had changed in 1804, when Aaron Burr killed Alexander Hamilton in a duel on a grassy plot near the shore here. Shipyards and industry along the shoreline came later, and with them, the mansions on the Heights. Frame, brick, and brownstone row houses were built along the side streets heading west from the cliffs and remain the chief source of prime housing in Weehawken. Most prized are houses in the tiny Bluffs section just south of Hamilton Park.

The housing stock in Weehawken was increased a few years ago by what's now called Gregory Commons, the conversion of a factory complex to 177 condos with Manhattan views. Hartz Mountain's 95-acre, mixed-use Lincoln Harbor development has transformed Weehawken's southern shore with two 10-story blue glass office buildings, restaurants, a hotel, and marina. The residential component, pricey beige-and-pastel Riva Pointe wrapped around a courtyard on a 1,000-foot pier, has attracted an affluent young clientele with its amenities and adjacent commuter ferry, not to mention the view. Just to the north at Port Imperial, developer Arthur Imperatore operates NY Waterway, continuous ferry service to Manhattan with connecting van service to midtown and the Wall Street area. (Two area ports also send ferries on 17-minute trips to destinations in lower and midtown Manhattan.) His grander plan for a "Venice-on-the-Hudson" comprised of a convention center, commercial and residential complex has been limited so far to a marina, golf driving range, and restaurant. Expect further expansion from this and other projects along the waterfront. Also planned is an 18.5-mile walkway along Weehawken's shore from the George Washington Bridge to Bayonne.

Many Weehawken properties are handled by Hoboken real estate brokers, or by their owners. Check the ads in the *Jersey Journal* (see **Jersey City**) and in the *Weehawken Reporter* (available locally in stores and apartment building lobbies), as well as the list of real estate brokers in the **Finding a Place to Live** chapter.

Web Sites: www.njtowns.com, www.newjersey.com
Area Codes: 201, 973
Post Offices: Weehawken Substation, 3504 Park Avenue; Park Avenue Branch, 4708 Park Avenue; 800-275-8777
Zip Code: 07087
Police Station: 400 Park Avenue, Weehawken 07087, 201-863-7800
Emergency Hospital (nearest): Palisades Medical Center, 7600 River Road, North Bergen 07047, 201-854-5000
Library: Weehawken Free Public Library, 49 Hauxhurst Avenue, Weehawken 07087, 201-863-7823, www.bccls.org
Public School Education: Weehawken Board of Education, 53 Liberty Place, Weehawken, NJ 07047, 201-867-2243
Transportation—Bus: mini-buses troll Boulevard East for passengers to the Port Authority Bus Terminal in Manhattan continuously weekdays, less frequently on weekends. New Jersey Transit service is also 10 minutes to the terminal; call 973-762-5100 or 212-564-8484 for routes and schedules, or pick up same at the Port Authority Bus Terminal, Eighth Avenue and 41st Street in Manhattan. You can also go to www.njtransit.com.

Transportation—Ferry: service by NY Waterway between Port Imperial and midtown Manhattan and Whitehall runs every 40 to 60 minutes on weekdays from 6 a.m. to 10 p.m. with a slightly different hourly schedule on weekends. Call 800-533-3779 for information or go to www.nywaterway.com.

HOBOKEN

Boundaries and Contiguous Areas: North: Weehawken; **East**: Hudson River; **South**: Jersey City; **West**: Jersey City and Union City

At the turn of the millennium, Hoboken was reinventing itself. Most of this tidy, small (population 33,000) "Mile Square City" sandwiched between the Hudson River and Jersey bluffs was built between 1860 and 1910. By 1900, Hoboken was famous as the first American port of call for tens of thousands of immigrants, many of whom stayed close by, finding jobs in the city's numerous light manufacturing plants. Industrious working- and middle-class citizens built the simple, unadorned brownstone and brick row houses that comprise most of Hoboken's real estate. These large families pushed Hoboken's population to 70,000 at its peak. The patrician Stevens family, who bought what was to become Hoboken soon after the Revolution, lived in relative isolation and splendor in the Castle Point section of town. This tract is now occupied by the Stevens Institute of Technology, the engineering school founded by the family.

Laid out in a grid that encompasses several pleasant, leafy squares, much of Hoboken retains a comfortable blue-collar feel. However, there is a solid presence of Manhattan refugees who are content to gaze back at a Manhattan skyline visually afloat on the river, gleaming in the afternoon sun and ablaze with lights at night. It began in the early 1970s when a tide of disaffected New Yorkers, many of them singles, were attracted to this community just ten minutes from Manhattan by subway (PATH). Artists and rock musicians as well as young professionals discovered Hoboken, and the row house renovations, the cafes, interesting shops, and galleries dotting the original downtown and Washington Street neighborhoods show it. Where homesteaders pioneer, serious developers almost always follow. Certainly, the conversion to condos of tenement blocks along Monroe, Adams, and the other "presidential" streets west of Washington, as well as the Curling Club, the Hudson Tea, and Hudson Park complexes, among other luxury rental developments on once-industrial land in the northwest quadrant, bear witness to that fact. To the south new brownstone lofts and luxury single-family brownstones stand occupied in formerly "undesirable" streets. Families are a strong presence in Hoboken, and private and charter schools, popular clothing and home furnishing shops, and health clubs proliferate.

Long awaited development of Hoboken's moribund mile-long riverfront began with the construction of the Shipyard, which now features 1,100 apartments in two towers, one for rentals and one for condos, along the southern waterfront. The Vanguard is one such state-of-the-art high-end rental residence, featuring indoor and outdoor children's play areas, a fitness center, easy access to the riverfront promenade, and a five-minute PATH train ride to Manhattan. Development of the 24-acre Maxwell House property as a mixed-use, housing/commercial complex on the waterfront will complete the process. Meeting the needs of area residents, the Hoboken Ferry plies the Hudson from two Hoboken piers to Battery Park. The main terminal, which it shares with PATH and Jersey Transit trains, is gloriously restored to its beaux-arts splendor, with Tiffany glass skylights, buff limestone, and ornamental plaster. Hoboken is now connected by electric trolleys along the 34-mile Hudson-Bergen Light Rail Transit System. The award winning system provides a clean and efficient way for passengers to commute locally or to make major connections.

The *Hoboken Reporter*, 201-798-7800, www.hobokenreporter.com, available in shops along Washington Street, is an excellent source of rentals, which tend to run 10% or more below comparable Manhattan dwellings. Condos are about one half the cost of comparable Manhattan apartments. For names of local brokers and a shares agency, refer to the **Finding a Place to Live** chapter.

Web Sites: www.newjersey.com, www.hobokenj.com, www.njtowns.com
Area Codes: 201, 973 (North and Central New Jersey)
Post Offices: Main Office, 89 River Street, Hoboken, 07030; Castle Point Station, Stevens Institute of Technology; Uptown Station, 57 West 14th Street; Washington Street Station, 734 Washington Street; West Side Station, 502 Grand Street; 800-275-8777
Zip Code: 07030
Police Station: #1 Police Plaza, 108 Newark Street, Hoboken 07030, 201-420-2100
Emergency Hospital: St. Mary's Hospital, 308 Willow Avenue Hoboken, 07030, 201-418-1000
Library: Hoboken Public Library, 500 Park Avenue, Hoboken 07030, 201-420-2346, www.bccls.org/hoboken
Public School Education: Hoboken Board of Education, 1115 Clinton Street, Hoboken, NJ 07030, 201-356-3610, www.hoboken.k12.nj.us
Community Resources: The Hoboken Chamber Orchestra gives concerts at the Demarest Grammar School. Membership in the Hoboken-North Hudson YMCA, with its tiled pool, workout rooms, and movement class-

es, is an inexpensive alternative to the health and fitness centers proliferating here: 1301 Washington Street, Hoboken 07030, 201-963-4100.

Transportation—PATH trains, 800-234-7284, shuttle between the Hoboken Station next to the Conrail (old Erie and Lackawanna Railroad) Terminal and Manhattan every 10 minutes from about 6:30 a.m. to 8:30 p.m., every 15 minutes between 8:30 p.m. and 11:45 p.m. and from then every 30 minutes until 6:30 a.m. Weekend times vary. A direct line runs between Hoboken and West 33rd Street in Manhattan, also makes stops at Christopher near Hudson Street, then at 9th, 14th, and 23rd streets, all on Sixth Avenue. The fare is $1.50 one way. For more details, go to www.pathrail.com.

Transportation—Bus: frequent commuter bus service on the #126 line operated by New Jersey Transit, call 212-564-8484 for schedules; also provides connections from the Hoboken Terminal to Manhattan's Port Authority Bus Terminal at Eighth Avenue and 42nd Street.

Transportation—Ferry: service between Hoboken Station at the 14th Street Pier to Pier 11 at Wall Street or the World Financial Center in Manhattan. Tickets are $3 each way, $28 for 10 trips, $92 for a monthly pass. Call 800-533-3779 for information or go to www.nywaterway.com.

JERSEY CITY

Boundaries and Contiguous Areas: North: Hoboken; **East**: Hudson River; **South**: Bayonne; **West**: Brunswick Street

Directly across the Hudson River from Lower Manhattan, New York's "sixth borough" is a small city with big-city amenities. And they're all new, from the glossy financial centers to the trim apartment towers rimming the Hudson, to the high-tech trolleys gliding between them. A resurgent economy in the late 1990s accelerated the expansion of relatively inexpensive commercial office space and rapidly proliferating housing to add to the city's stock of 19th century brick and brownstone townhouses. All this within five minutes of Manhattan. Following September 11th, 2001, nearly 20,000 displaced workers found themselves commuting to work at new locations here. Many of the relocated companies are now back in Lower Manhattan but others have remained in Jersey City, taking advantage of local tax breaks.

New Jersey's first city—"settled in 1630" says the historical marker erected in **Paulus Hook**, the oldest section of town—was for the better part of three and a half centuries largely a working-class community. Today it has a heterogeneous population of 250,000 and an enviable position five minutes by PATH train under the Hudson to and from Lower Manhattan, slightly longer by ferry.

The arrival of brownstoners presaged the current Jersey City revival. Thirty years ago expatriate New Yorkers began buying and reclaiming townhouses in the historic districts bordering **Hamilton** and **Van Vorst parks**. Co-ops and condominium conversions sprung up in these neighborhoods and in the adjoining Paulus Hook historic district. And once Banker's Trust leased space at the vast Harborside Financial Center, it became clear that back-office operations of large Manhattan corporations would prove a boon to the local economy.

Now, gleaming skyscrapers soar along wide boulevards that connect Harborside with **Newport**, the enormous, $10-billion apartment, mall, business center, and townhouse-marina complex across the Hudson River from Manhattan's Battery Park City. The most recent building phase at Newport has added a hotel and nearly 2,000 apartment units, mostly rentals, to the original 1,500 that opened in 1986. Sears, J.C. Penney, and Macy's anchor the suburban-style shopping mall there. When the Lefrak Organization completes the planned 600-acre development around 2010, they expect to have 9,000 apartments on site, truly a city within a city. The size and energy of this project has driven development elsewhere in Jersey City.

South of Newport, the expanding **Avalon Cove** development offers one- to four-bedroom rentals with tennis and racquetball courts, a swimming pool and a riverfront walkway. A sugar factory has been transformed into luxury condominiums. And Jersey City has acquired its own acronymic artists' enclave, the **WALDO (W**ork **A**nd **L**ive **D**istrict **O**verlay); this eight-block area with buildings certified to rent space only to artists (availability is limited) is composed of warehouse conversions and loft-studios. In the historic district at the foot of **Washington Street**, Portside's luxury rentals feature mostly balconied studios to three-bedroom spreads, many with panoramic views of lower Manhattan, the harbor, the Statue of Liberty, and Ellis Island. Additional luxury condos at Port Liberté to the south have increased the range of waterfront choices.

West of the harbor developments and 35 minutes from Manhattan by PATH, a 1,176-unit condominium community, **Society Hill**, offers mid-priced town houses and apartments with a marina, tennis courts, and two pools. Further revitalization in the downtown section of Jersey City on Grand Avenue includes new construction of two-family homes. Meanwhile, in Paulus Hook, nearly 1,000 rental or condominium units are either newly finished or are being completed along the Hudson River. Among the many developments are the 105-unit Pier House Condominiums and the small, 32-unit Liberty Point Condominiums.

Electric-powered trolleys connect these various communities with one another, with Bayonne to the south, and with links to the PATH tubes and ferry connections. The latest phase of the Hudson-Bergen Light Rail Transit

System extends north to Hoboken and ultimately will continue north into Bergen County. These 90-foot cars, winding among the city's mix of glass towers and historic brownstones, are expected to spur further growth in this rapidly changing city.

The Jersey Journal, www.thejerseyjournal.com, is the best source for Hoboken or Jersey City classified rental ads. In Manhattan, buy The Journal at newsstands at the 14th Street Downtown PATH station and outside the 33rd Street PATH station. See **Finding a Place to Live** for names of brokers.

Web Sites: www.newjersey.com, www.cityofjerseycity.com, www.njtowns.com

Area Codes: 201, 973

Post Office: The main Post Office, 69 Montgomery Street is located in downtown, 800-275-8777

Zip Codes: 07302 covers the downtown area; Port Liberté, 07305; Newport, 07310

Police Station: East District, 207 Seventh Street, 201-547-5408

Emergency Hospital: St. Francis Hospital, 25 McWilliams Place, Jersey City, 07302, 201-714-8900

Library: Jersey City Public Library (main branch), 472 Jersey Avenue, 07302, 201-547-4500

Public School Education: Jersey City Board of Education, 346 Claremont Avenue, Jersey City, 201-915-6000, www.jerseycityboe.org

Adult Education: St. Peter's College, 2641 Kennedy Boulevard, 201-915-9000, www.spc.edu; New Jersey City University, 2039 Kennedy Boulevard, 201-200-2000, www.njcu.edu; Jersey City branch of Hudson County Community College is headquartered at 168 Sip Avenue, 201-656-2020 or 201-714-2139 (registrar's office)

Community Resources: The Jersey City Museum, 350 Montgomery Street, Jersey City 07302, at the corner of Monmouth, 201-413-0303, www.jerseycitymuseum.org; Liberty Science Center, 25 Phillip Street, Liberty State Park Jersey City, 07305, 201-200-1000, www.lsc.org

Transportation—PATH trains, 800-234-7284; it takes 20 minutes at most from Journal Square or Grove Street to 33rd Street in Manhattan (with stops at Sixth Avenue and Christopher, 9th, 14th, and 23rd Streets in between). PATH trains also run to Hoboken and Newark from all four Jersey City stations. Go to www.pathrail.com for more information.

Transportation—Bus: the Red & Tan Bus Co., 201-876-9000 or 212-564-8484, operates frequent service between Jersey City and Wall Street or the Port Authority Bus Terminal in Manhattan.

Transportation—Ferry: New York Waterway, 800-533-3779, www.nywaterway.com, operates passenger ferries stopping at the Liberty Harbor Marina, Harborside and Colgate, and the World Financial

Center in Lower Manhattan, between Port Liberté and Wall Street and between Colgate and West 38th Street.

NEW JERSEY SUBURBS

Check www.njtowns.com or www.newjersey.com for more about New Jersey communities.

- **Bayonne**; a working class city of 62,000 south of Jersey City on Upper New York Bay, affordable and now just 20 minutes from Jersey City and the PATH tubes to Manhattan thanks to the Hudson-Bergen Light Rail system. www.bayonnenj.org
- **Cliffside Park**, on the Palisades just south of Fort Lee, is an affordable family neighborhood with an ethnically mixed population. www.cliffside parkchamberofcommerce.com
- **Englewood**, cosmopolitan with its ethnically diverse population and housing that ranges from low-income to redone turn-of-the-century estates. Traditionally home to affluent business executives, it boasts good shopping and restaurants and a 30-minute bus commute to Manhattan. Chamber of Commerce, 201-567-2381, www.englewoodchamber.com
- **Leonia**, west of Fort Lee but less glitzy and not as high rise; middle-class with a village-like feel. Proximity to the George Washington Bridge makes it a quick commute by bus to the city. Borough Clerk, 201-592-5752
- **Montclair**, cosmopolitan and affluent, enjoys a hilly perch from which Manhattan is visible at a distance to the east. Single-family housing is shaded by towering oaks. The bus commute takes about 30 minutes. Borough Clerk, 973-744-7660
- **Ridgewood**, a 60-minute commute northwest of the city, houses a homogeneous white-collar population of families along manicured, tree-shaded streets. Schools are excellent, taxes high, and the downtown shopping district seems not to have changed in 50 years. The Paramus malls nearby make up for that. Chamber of Commerce, 201-445-2600; also on the web at www.webridgewood.com.
- **Summit** is an affluent community of handsome homes along winding, hilly streets now just 50 minutes from Manhattan on the Midtown Direct train to Penn Station. On the web at www.cityofsummit.com
- **Teaneck**, just west of Englewood and without the estates, is similarly hilly and tree-shaded, more middle-class and proud of its ethnic diversity; a 30-40-minute commute. Chamber of Commerce, 201-801-0012; homepage, www.ziva.com/teaneck
- **Tenafly**, north of Englewood and a more homogeneous suburb, boasts a nice village center clustered around the railroad station and an excellent high school; also an easy commute. Borough Clerk, 201-568-6100

- **South Orange**, with its downtown railroad station, is convenient and quaint. Housing is varied, from modest to upscale up the hill, and 60 acres of parkland with three town pools add to the comfort level. Chamber of Commerce, 973-762-4333
- **Westfield** nestles among the rolling Watchung hills of Union County, about an hour by bus or 35 minutes by train and PATH tubes from midtown. A strong sense of community, excellent schools, extensive sports and recreation activities in three county-run parks make this culturally rich old town attractive to commuters. Chamber of Commerce, 908-233-3021; also on the web at www.westfieldnj.com/wacc.

LONG ISLAND SUBURBS

- **Garden City** was once a summer resort for the Morgans and Vanderbilts, and it's still expensive, tidy, and manicured. Squarely in the middle of the island, it's an easy 40 minutes to Penn Station. Chamber of Commerce, 516-746-7724
- **Great Neck**, just over the Queens border on the northern part of Long Island, is one of the jewels of the island. The quiet Village of Great Neck sports exclusive real estate and it's only a 40-minute commute to Manhattan. Chamber of Commerce, 516-487-2000, www.greatneck chamber.org
- **Manhasset** residents enjoy the option of choosing between single-family homes and condos. The former are most attractively and expensively set around Manhasset Bay in Plandome to the north. Because of the department stores along Miracle Mile, real estate taxes are low here. About 35 minutes from Manhattan on the LIRR. Call North Hempstead Town Hall, public affairs office, at 516-627-0590 for more details about the area. www.manhasset.org
- **Old Westbury** once housed the North Shore estates of high society and still has 25 miles of horse trails and a polo club. Besides its rolling hills, the high cost of living here gets you good schools, three colleges, and Old Westbury Gardens. Village clerk, 516-626-0800
- **Port Washington**, formerly a glamorous summer resort on a peninsula in the Long Island Sound, is still attractive to boaters and boasts harbor events like the annual Harborfest. The 40-minute train commute is a relatively easy one. Chamber of Commerce, 516-883-6566; web site, www.portwashington.org
- **Rockville Centre**, 30 minutes from Manhattan by the Long Island Railroad, provides easy access to Long Island beaches, an arts guild, eight parks, a thriving shopping center, and a variety of housing. But it is best known for its municipal power plant, which gives its residents the

cheapest electricity on the island. Village administrator's office, 516-678-9212; Rockville Centre web site, www.ci.rockville-centre.ny.us

WESTCHESTER COUNTY (NY) SUBURBS

- **Bronxville**, on the city's northern border and hilly, feels rather English and looks rather Tudor. There are also co-ops and condos, quite elegant ones near the railroad station. Known for its good schools. Chamber of Commerce, 914-337-6040
- **Dobbs Ferry** on the Hudson just to the north, and about 40 minutes by Metro North's Hudson line from the city, also offers a variety of housing possibilities and a heterogeneous population. Appealing to academics and people in the arts. Town Clerk, 914-693-6161
- **Edgemont**, a hamlet within the town of **Greenburg**, is adjacent to Scarsdale but less known and more affordable. Its good schools have attracted a growing foreign-born population, especially Japanese. Houses are traditional in style; co-ops and condos are relatively plentiful and reasonable. Greenburg town clerk, 914-993-1500
- **Mamaroneck**, which includes **Larchmont**, houses a heterogeneous population just west of tony Rye on a neck of land in Long Island Sound. You'll find co-ops, condos, and single-family homes, with few rentals. Waterfront is what it's about, with good recreational facilities including boating and beaches on Harbor Island Park; a 35-minute commute. Town administrative offices, 914-381-7810
- **Mt. Kisco** sports hilly terrain, good schools, a variety of restaurants, a town park, and a shopping area featuring The Gap, Starbucks, and other chain favorites. Single-family homes, several condo developments, and apartment rentals can all be found in this northern Westchester hub. Chamber of Commerce, 914-666-7525, www.mtkisco.com
- **New Rochelle**, just 32 minutes from midtown on Metro North, is a suburban city of 67,000, with an exceptional variety of housing choices, nine miles of shoreline and 35 parks. www.newrochelleny.com
- **Pelham**, just over the Bronx County line and a 20-minute train ride north from the city, is cosmopolitan and relatively unknown. Fine old trees line its winding roads, and you can walk to everything, which includes beaches, a golf course, woodland hiking, and fishing. Taxes are high. Town Clerk, 914-738-0777
- **Scarsdale**, rocky, wooded, and upscale, has few rentals or co-ops, but it does have beautiful homes along winding, wooded roads and lots of open land. Its highly competitive public schools attract a diverse population into this family-friendly neighborhood. The commute to Manhattan is about 45 minutes. Chamber of Commerce, 914-722-1110, and on the web at www.village.scarsdale.ny.us

- **Tarrytown** sits at the gateway to the Tappan Zee Bridge (which leads to Rockland County) and meanders above the Hudson River. This diverse white- and blue-collar town is rich with history from the Revolutionary War, where a number of battles were fought, to which a Historical Society Museum, among other landmarks, now pays tribute. The commute is 30 minutes and housing runs the gamut from single-family homes to large condominium developments. The Sleepy Hollow Chamber of Commerce includes Tarrytown information at 914-631-7105 or www.sleepyhollowchamber.com.
- **White Plains**, 35 minutes from the city, offers a quick commute by train or express bus, good shopping, ethnic restaurants, a variety of housing choices, and relatively low taxes. Recreational facilities include a golf course, outdoor pools, tennis, and an ice skating rink. Chamber of Commerce, 914-948-2110; and on the web at www.city ofwhiteplains.com

CONNECTICUT SUBURBS

- **Greenwich** (pronounced Gren-itch) is a 45-minute train commute from the city and offers genteel seclusion for the very wealthy, the bustle of corporate headquarters, as well as upscale shopping and eateries, excellent schools, beaches, and recreational facilities. Less expensive than the Greenwich "backcountry" is the downtown area with some more moderate rentals. Nearby **Cos Cob**, **Byram** and **Old Greenwich** are also somewhat more affordable. www.greenwichct.org
- **Norwalk** is a diverse community and generally less expensive than surrounding towns. Partially rehabilitated, south Norwalk, with its condos, galleries, and restaurants, appeals to a young crowd, many of whom work in nearby corporate offices. Boating, fishing, beaches, tennis, and paddle tennis are also a draw. **Silvermine** to the west and **Rowaton** on the southwestern tip are more upscale. www.norwalkct.org
- **Stamford**, 40 minutes from Grand Central on Metro North, is a city of 111,000 with a bustling downtown on the banks of the Mill River and the Long Island Sound, and there is lots of upscale housing here, including sprawling estates to the north. Housing styles are varied, parks and beaches plentiful. www.ci.stamford.ct.us
- **Westport** on Long Island Sound became a colony of artists and writers in the 1930s and 1940s, and it is still popular with the sophisticated set, more like New York City than the rest of Connecticut. There is a summer theater, and the arts are still a presence, as are pricey boutiques and good shopping in nearby Stamford. Water and woods, a variety of single-family homes, a few rentals and condos characterize the town. The train to New York takes about an hour. www.ci.westport.ct.us

Newcomers' shock at housing prices is nearly universal; living in New York City *is* expensive. And renting an apartment in New York City can be a daunting task. But you're not alone: according to the latest US Census, 70% of New York City residents rent rather than own.

Over the last year, the rental market has tightened considerably, even at the high end, and rents are rising. According to a recent *New York Times* article, one-bedroom apartments below 100th Street in Manhattan averaged nearly $2,500, up three percent from the previous year. In that same time period, vacancy rates slipped to below two percent. Less expensive apartments (affordable one- or two-bedrooms) are increasingly hard to find, even outside Manhattan. And recently, the New York Rent Guidelines Board approved a 7.5% rent increase for two-year leases (to learn more go to www.housingnyc.com). Making matters worse for would-be renters is, in the face of dramatically rising housing prices, many would-be-homeowners are opting to rent rather than buy, shrinking an already small market.

In Manhattan's established neighborhoods, location doesn't influence price much. One rental expert estimates that in Greenwich Village and the neighborhoods between 15th Street and 96th Street (Chelsea, the Upper East and West sides, Murray Hill, Gramercy Park), the price difference between comparable apartments is negligible. If cost is a serious concern, it is best to search in the developing Manhattan neighborhoods, over the bridges in Brooklyn, Queens, The Bronx, or Staten Island, or in the suburbs. Another option, especially attractive at the studio and one-bedroom level, is to purchase a condo or a co-op. At this writing, mortgage rates remain low, and with the income tax deduction for mortgage interest factored in, these apartments may be less expensive than renting an equivalent space, plus you build equity. To see what's involved in buying an apartment or a house, turn to **Buying** at the end of this chapter.

All that said, however, in return are all the riches the Big Apple has to offer, both tangible and intangible, including higher earnings, incomparable cultural resources, dynamic street life, incredible social diversity, and unparalleled personal opportunity.

To compare cost of living analysis of US cities, visit www.bestplaces.net. Data covers quality of life, cost of living, and comparative salary information for 3,000 US cities.

APARTMENT HUNTING

First, renting—with fortitude and imagination, you can find an acceptable place to live in an appropriate neighborhood. Various strategies for doing so are listed below in order of conventionality and practicality. But to start, some golden generalities:

- **Don't panic**. Don't be immobilized by what you may have heard. Negativism will get you nowhere. If possible, start your search a couple of months before you expect to move. Through newspapers, rental agents, word of mouth, and posted "apartments for rent" signs, get an idea of which areas have the greatest turnover in rental apartments.

- **Be prepared for high rents**. In the long run, it may indeed be possible to find that charming, sun-drenched apartment in the neighborhood of your dreams for a reasonable sum, but such gems take time, contacts, more contacts, and a little luck, so brace yourself.

- **Be adventuresome but prudent**. The housing squeeze has intensified gentrification of neighborhoods throughout the city. Yesterday's marginal areas are meccas for today's trendsetters. One realtor notes that the hardest apartments to find are now the ones south of 14th street, which was certainly not the case just a decade ago. Behind dusty facades from the Bowery to upper Broadway lurk attractive apartments, but before getting too carried away, realize that not all areas are suitable, especially not for single women. If you are looking around Midtown or Wall Street, be sure to visit at night to see if these areas become too desolate after offices close.

- **Inquire about a neighborhood**. Local police precincts (see listings under **Neighborhoods**) can supply valuable safety information about a particular neighborhood, street, or block within their boundaries. Stop by the precinct for candid and well-founded opinions about the characteristics and police problems of a particular area. Also, talk to store owners and doormen.

- **Consider subletting or sharing to start**. If you are in desperate need of a roof and have not discovered a feasible rental, seriously consider these alternatives. Subletting is a great way to get comfortable in the city while buying yourself time to find the optimum situation in the most suitable neighborhood. And, should you find a good roommate, sharing affords companionship and a more affordable start to life in the Big Apple.

Generalities out of the way, on to ways of finding your space.

NEWSPAPER CLASSIFIED ADVERTISEMENTS

Start here, on paper or online, to get a sense of what's available, where, and at what price. In fact, it's a good idea to begin in advance of your move by scanning the online classifieds to get some idea of neighborhoods and prices. Because individual landlords, as well as brokers, place ads, classifieds sometimes are a way to avoid brokerage commissions. Chances are, however, you will end up using a broker. The classifieds provide a good way of finding one and of discovering which brokers are active in a particular neighborhood.

- The **Sunday *New York Times'* Real Estate section,** printed Friday night and delivered to dealers sometime on Saturday, contains the best rental listings in the city. The *Times* actively discourages sale of the Sunday edition before the multi-sectioned paper is completed Saturday evening. However, many outlets sell the sections they have on hand (often for full newspaper price) Saturday morning. While far fewer in number, daily ads in the *Times* are also worth checking. Since the race is to the swift, the cyber-connected will do well to check the *Times'* web site, www.nytimes.com, where the Sunday ads appear before 5 a.m. Saturday morning, with daily updates.
- The ***Village Voice*** is a good source of rental listings for Manhattan as well as other boroughs. Newsstand deliveries are made around 5 a.m. Wednesdays; the newsstand on the island beside the Seventh Avenue IRT Uptown Christopher Street subway entrance at Sheridan Square is one of the first places to receive delivery. Also, you can get early copies Tuesday night at the Village newsstand on Astor/Lafayette. Easier yet, the *Voice* listings are online, www.villagevoice.com; updated at 1 p.m. Tuesday, and 12:01 a.m. Wednesday-Saturday.
- The ***Wall Street Journal's*** Friday edition lists apartments for rent in "The Mart" classified section.
- The ***New York Post's*** rental classifieds are best consulted on Friday. The Friday edition is printed Thursday night and delivered to all-night newsstands in the mid-Manhattan area (try stands at Grand Central or Pennsylvania stations Thursday night around midnight). The *Post* is a particularly good source for apartments in Queens, Brooklyn, and The Bronx. The *Post's* web site, www.nypost.com, is updated daily.

- The **Daily News'** Brooklyn and Queens editions carry numerous rental classifieds for those boroughs. Listings in the Manhattan edition are negligible. On the web at www.nydailynews.com.
- **Newsday**, published daily in Garden City, Long Island, and available in Manhattan, is the best source of listings in Queens and Long Island. On the web at www.newsday.com.
- **New York Press**, a somewhat offbeat free weekly, is distributed each Wednesday, and is a good source for sublets and shares. Look for it in restaurants, stores, and street boxes all over town. Press listings are online, www.newyorkpress.com at 10 a.m. Tuesday.
- **Jersey Journal**, published in Jersey City Monday-Saturday, is the paper to consult for rentals in Hoboken and Jersey City. The _Journal_ can be purchased at newsstands adjoining the 14th Street and 33rd Street PATH stations in Manhattan.
- New York City neighborhood newspapers—**The Villager**, **Chelsea Clinton News**, **The Spirit** (West Side), **Our Town** (East Side), **The Flatiron News**, **Tribeca Trib**, and others—occasionally carry a rental ad or two but are not prime sources. In Brooklyn, however, two weeklies, the **Brooklyn Heights Press**, 129 Montague Street, second floor, and **The Phoenix**, 33 Flatbush Avenue, carry sublet and rental advertisements. First copies of the _Press_ are delivered to the office around 2 p.m. Thursday afternoon, and _The Phoenix_ reaches Brooklyn newsstands early Friday morning.

ONLINE LISTINGS—APARTMENT HUNTING

Increasingly, renters and buyers are going online to find an apartment, house, or broker to suit their needs before venturing forth streetward. We've mentioned newspaper classifieds above. Oddly, unlike other major US cities, New York City has no multiple-listing service giving buyers and renters access to available properties citywide in one composite listing. Nonetheless, there are several web sites that specialize in New York real estate. Also, you can have success just using a major search engine to find listings for a particular city neighborhood.

New York City Realty, www.cityrealty.com, for example, offers detailed listings, photos, and floor plans of houses, co-ops, condos, and apartments for rent or sale in the city. They're updated hourly. You can search by location, price-range, and size, with e-mail notification as properties in your categories come online. The site includes excellent, detailed neighborhood descriptions, and application forms. The computer-challenged can call 212-755-5544 for this site's information. It may also be worth your while to visit the web sites of some of the major rental agencies, such as **Citi Habitats**, www.citi-habitats.com, and **Halstead/Feathered Nest Realty**, www.halstead.com, and large owner/management firms such as **Rockrose**, www.rockrosenyc.com, all to be found in the *Times* real estate ads. These sites are virtual data banks of each firm's entire listings. For apartment listings you might go to www.nyc-apartments.net. See also **No Fee Apartments Online**, below.

REAL ESTATE BROKERS

Generally, New York City's real estate brokers focus on sales rather than rentals. However, some agencies specialize in rentals, and many have brokers who handle nothing else. Below, we've listed the names of real estate brokers as a service. Their presence in this book does not indicate an endorsement. Rather, firms and the neighborhoods they cover are given as possible starting points for your search.

Real estate agencies tend to concentrate their efforts on one or a series of contiguous neighborhoods, for example: the Upper East Side and Yorkville; Chelsea, the Village, and SoHo; Gramercy Park and Murray Hill. If your heart is set on one location, it is important to discover the savviest brokers in that area. If any neighborhood will do, make sure you list with several knowledgeable firms to get the coverage you need.

Count on spending some time and effort discovering a broker sympathetic to your needs and capable of showing you suitable places. In the long run, a broker may well be the best route to a decent apartment, and she (the majority seem to be women) can save you hours of calling and traipsing on your own. Broker commissions for unfurnished apartments currently run 15% of one year's rent, which you pay up front, but this may vary depending on the broker, landlord, neighborhood, availability, etc. Get some ground rules and ask how the commissions work before agreeing to work with someone. In New Jersey, where rentals are more generally available, the broker commission usually equals one month's rent; sometimes there is no commission at all.

Recommendations for finding a real estate broker:
- Ask friends, colleagues, your firm, and family for recommendations of brokers who are particularly helpful. As previously mentioned, not all capable agents with good lists advertise widely.
- Gather names from appealing classified listings.
- Do a web search for real estate brokers in your neighborhood or neighborhoods of choice.
- If your heart is set on one locale, try some of the smaller firms whose storefronts you'll notice while pounding the pavement. These firms seldom advertise but are often good sources for listings in the immediate vicinity.

As a start, we've compiled a list of brokers who handle rentals in Manhattan, parts of The Bronx, Brooklyn, Queens, Staten Island, and New Jersey:

MANHATTAN REAL ESTATE BROKERS

- **Citi Habitats**, 30 East 33rd Street, NYC 10016, 212-685-7777, and on the web at www.citi-habitats.com: all Manhattan
- **Coldwell Banker Hunt Kennedy**, 1200 Lexington Avenue, NYC 10028, 212-327-1200, www.cbhk.com: all Manhattan
- **Coldwell Banker Hunt Kennedy**, 401 Avenue of the Americas, NYC 10014, 718-624-7000, www.cbhk.com; all of Manhattan
- **Corcoran Group**, 2112 Broadway, NYC 10023, 212-877-2711, www.corcoran.com: primarily Upper West Side
- **Dwelling Quest Corp.**, 360 Lexington Avenue, Suite 1601, NYC 10022, 212-681-9200: Upper East and West sides
- **Eychner Associates Inc.**, 44 Greenwich Avenue, NYC 10012, 212-807-0700, www.eychner.com: Greenwich Village and downtown
- **Halstead/Feathered Nest**, 770 Lexington Avenue (HQ), 212-253-9300, four Manhattan locations, www.halstead.com: handles all Manhattan
- **Green Real Estate**, 4310 Broadway, NYC 10033, 212-795-0144: Washington Heights, Inwood, and North Harlem
- **Gumley-Haft-Klier, Inc.**, 415 Madison, NYC 10022, 212-371-2525, www.ghkrealty.com: luxury rentals, Upper East Side
- **Home Realty**, 206 West 99th Street, NYC 10025, 212-864-0016, ask for Yolanda Chang, specializes in Harlem and Uptown Manhattan
- **Hudson View Associates, Inc.**, 159-00 Riverside Drive West, NYC 10032, 212-928-0508, www.hudsonview.com: Washington Heights
- **Insignia Douglas Elliman, Rental and Relocation Division**, 3 East 54th Street, NYC 10021, 212-350-8500, www.elliman.com: all of Manhattan
- **Kain Realty**, 37 West 84th Street, NYC 10024, 212-877-5100: Upper East and West Side and Midtown
- **Macklowe**, 515 East 72nd Street, NYC 10019, 212-988-5551, www.macklowe.com: all Manhattan
- **M. Woods and Associates**, 212-645-7158, by appointment only: brownstones primarily, Chelsea, Greenwich Village, and downtown.
- **Alice F. Mason, Ltd.**, 635 Madison Avenue, NYC 10022, 212-832-8870, www.alicefmasonltd.com: luxury rentals, primarily on the Upper East Side
- **Manhattan Apartments, Inc.**, rental office at 225 West 57th Street, NYC 10019, 212-378-2680; you can also contact Chris Hornsby at 347-

423-7339. Sales office at 1780 Broadway, NYC 10019, 212-378-2360, www.manhattanapts.com. Will provide corporate relocation services.
- **New Heights Realty**, 632 West 207th Street, NYC 10034, 212-567-7200: primarily Inwood, some Washington Heights
- **Salon Realty Co.**, 338 East 92nd Street, NYC 10128, 212-534-3131, www.salonrealty.com: Upper East Side
- **Sandra Greer Real Estate**, 201 East 77th Street, NYC 10021, 212-472-1878: mostly Upper East Side
- **Simone Song Properties**, 241 Cabrini Boulevard, NYC 10033, 212-928-5100, www.simonesong.com: Washington Heights, especially Hudson Heights, Inwood, Northern Manhattan
- **Spencer Realty**, 353 Lexington Avenue, NYC 10016, 212-661-9440, www.spencerny.com: all Manhattan
- **Stein-Perry Real Estate**, 740 West 181st Street, NYC 10033, 212-928-3805, www.steinperry.com: Washington Heights
- **Stribling & Associates**, www.striblingny.com, 924 Madison Avenue, NYC 10021, 212-570-2440: Uptown, Tribeca, and Chelsea; 340 West 23rd Street, NYC 10011, 212-243-4000: all of Manhattan
- **Webb & Brooker Realty Inc.**, 2534 Seventh Avenue, NYC 10039, 212-926-7100: Harlem

BRONX REAL ESTATE BROKERS

- **Aztec Realty**, 2006 Williamsbridge Road, Bronx 10461, 718-822-9100, www.aztecrealty.com: The Bronx
- **Re/Max Deal-Finders**, 2366 Westchester Avenue, Bronx 10462, 718-829-3325: The Bronx
- **Robert E. Hill, Inc.**, 279 West 231st Street, Bronx, 10463, 718-884-2200, www.robertehill.com: Riverdale and Kingsbridge
- **Spero Real Estate**, 33 South Broadway, Yonkers, 10701, 914-968-7862: Riverdale, Westchester County, and Putnam County
- **Susan Goldy Real Estate**, 6114 Riverdale Avenue, Bronx 10471, 718-549-4116: Riverdale, Spuyten Duyvil
- **Trebach Realty Inc.**, 3801 Greystone Avenue, Riverdale 10463, 718-543-7174, www.TrebachRealty.com: Riverdale, Spuyten Duyvil, Fieldston, Kingsbridge, Van Cortlandt Village

BROOKLYN REAL ESTATE BROKERS

- **Coldwell Banker Hunt Kennedy**, 155 Seventh Avenue, Brooklyn 11215, 718-622-7600
- **David Perlman**, 16 Court Street, Brooklyn 11241, 718-855-8708: Brooklyn Heights, Park Slope, Cobble Hill, Boerum Hill, Carroll Gardens

- **Flood Company**, 464 Bay Ridge Avenue, Brooklyn 11220, 718-238-9800, www.floodcompany.com: Bay Ridge, Fort Hamilton, Benson Hurst, Sunset Park
- **Frank Manzione Real Estate**, 223 Columbia Street, Brooklyn 11231, 718-834-1440, www.fpmre.com: South Brooklyn
- **Kenn Firpo Realty Corp.**, 158 Bedford Avenue, Brooklyn 11211, 718-384-4949, www.kennfirpo.com: Greenpoint and Williamsburg
- **Kline Realty**, 599 Lorimer Street, Brooklyn 11211, 718-361-1776: Greenpoint and Williamsburg
- **Park Slope Office of the Corcoran Group**, 125 7th Avenue, Brooklyn 11201, 718-935-9800, www.corcoran.com: Brooklyn Heights, Cobble Hill, and vicinity
- **Renaissance Properties**, 71 Hoyt Street, Brooklyn 11201, 718-875-5650, www.renaissanceproperty.com: primarily Boerum Hill
- **William B. May Co.**, www.williambmay.com, 150 Montague Street, Brooklyn 11201, 718-875-1289: Brooklyn Heights, Cobble Hill, Carroll Gardens; 100 7th Avenue Brooklyn 11215, 718-230-5500: Park Slope, Prospect Park

QUEENS REAL ESTATE BROKERS

- **Bay Benjamin**, 212-89 26th Avenue, Bay Terrace Shopping Center, Bayside 11360, 718-225-0800, www.baybenjamin.com: Bayside
- **Castle Realty, Inc.**, 21-77 31st Street, Astoria Boulevard, Astoria 11105, 718-545-7669: Astoria
- **Century 21 Tri-Boro Realty**, 31-08 Astoria Boulevard South, Astoria 11102, 718-721-2700, www.c21triboro.com: Astoria
- **Coldwell Banker/Owner's Club Realty**, 33-06 Ditmars Boulevard, Astoria 11105, 718-956-5757: Astoria, Long Island City, Sunnyside
- **Dynasty Realty**, 34-16 30th Avenue, Queens 11103, 718-204-4800: Astoria, Woodside, Long Island City
- **First Choice Real Estate**, 61-43 186th Street, Fresh Meadows 11365, 800-875-4111, www.firstchoicerealty.com: Flushing, Forest Hills, Kew Gardens, Rego Park, Bayside.
- **Golden Choice Realty**, 37-11A Prince Street, Flushing 11354, 718-359-1700: Queens, especially Flushing
- **Nu Place Realty**, 120-10 Queens Boulevard, Kew Gardens 11415, 718-793-9500: Forest Hills, Kew Gardens, Rego Park, Briarwood
- **Re/Max Today**, 32-75 Steinway Street, LIC 11103, 718-274-2400, www.seenyhomes.com: Astoria, Long Island City, Sunnyside
- **Terrace Realty**, 16 Station Square, Forest Hills 11375, 718-268-1045, www.foresthillsrealestate.com: Greater Forest Hills, Rego Park, Kew Gardens

- **Welcome Home Real Estate**, 46-15 Skillman Avenue, Sunnyside 11104, 718-706-0957, www.welcomehomerealestate.biz: Sunnyside, Woodside, Astoria

STATEN ISLAND REAL ESTATE BROKERS

- **Gateway Arms Realty**, 285 St. Marks Place, St. George 10301, 718-273-3800, www.gatewayarmsrealty.com: St. George, Snug Harbor
- **Prudential Appleseed Realty**, 2043 Richmond Avenue, New Springville 10314, 718-698-9797, www.pruappleseedrealty.com: North Shore
- **Rachel Gannon Realty, Inc.**, 963 Post Avenue, SI 10302, 718-273-9200: all Staten Island
- **Rainbow Agency**, 364 Decker Avenue, Port Richmond 10302, 718-720-2002: Victorian properties in St. George, Stapleton, Snug Harbor, and Port Richmond
- **Vitale-Sunshine Realty**, 1671 Highland Blvd., SI 10305, 718-979-3333, www.vitalesunshine.com: all Staten Island

NEW JERSEY REAL ESTATE BROKERS

- **Action Agency**, 4301 Bergenline Avenue, Union City 07087, 201-348-8741: Fort Lee, Edgewater, Weehawken
- **Apartments & Homes of NJ, Fort Lee Inc.**, 214 Main Street, Fort Lee 07024, 201-947-6464: Fort Lee, Edgewater, Weehawken
- **Boyne Real Estate**, 303 Grove Street, Jersey City 07302, 201-451-0950: Jersey City
- **Hoboken Brownstone Co.**, 1125 Hudson Street, Hoboken 07030, 201-792-0100, www.hbrownstone.com: Hoboken, Weehawken, Jersey City
- **McAlear Cavalier Realtors, GMAC**, 327 Broad Avenue, Leonia 07105, 201-944-4660, www.mcrealtors.com: Leonia
- **Oppler-Ketive Realtors**, 2050 Center Avenue, Fort Lee 07024, 201-585-8080, www.classic-realty-group.com: all Bergen County
- **Severino Realty**, 830 Washington Street, Hoboken 07030, 201-653-1800: Hoboken
- **Singleton and Galmann**, 1106 Washington Street, Hoboken 07030, 201-656-5400, wwww.singletongalmannrealestate.com: Hoboken
- **Sky-Line Realty, Inc.**, 3506 Park Avenue, Weehawken 07087, 201-863-6090, www.sky-linerealty.com: Weehawken

NO-FEE APARTMENTS ONLINE

You may have noticed among the newspaper listings ads for no-fee services, and if you're determined to avoid a broker's fee one of these may help. Here's how they work: pay a flat fee, detail your specifications online, and receive a list of no-fee apartments being offered by management companies and private owners. Updates are daily or weekly, and you do the rest of the work. However, listings can be wrong or out-of-date. We mention six services that may be useful:

- **Apartment Source**, apartmentsource.com, online only, lets you search their database for apartments according to price, size, location, and amenities, in addition to which you receive daily e-mail updates with new vacancies to meet your specifications. You may also occasionally find sublets and short-term rentals, and there is access to roommateclick.com, a roommate matching service. The site also offers a credit check.
- **Apartment Store**, www.nyaptstore.com, lets you search thousands of apartments. You can specify number of rooms, neighborhoods, etc. Moving services, insurance, and other services are also available. Membership is $49.99 and listings are updated frequently. You can elect to receive daily updates via fax or e-mail.
- **Citi Rent**, 36 West 20th Street, 6th floor, NYC 10011, 212-691-8300, www.citirent.com; a clearinghouse of listings from management companies. Subscribers ($49.95 for six months) can search apartments by price and neighborhood.
- **Craig's List**, www.craigslist.org, is a national site with NYC listings; you can search vacancies provided by area landlords, or sublets, shared housing, or temporary accommodations as posted by individuals. No fee.
- **Metro List Xpress**, 212-220-4663, extension 224, www.mlx.com, is a Manhattan-wide database with no-fee and fee listings. For $169, the subscriber receives an account number and a personal identification number. Search specifications include desired location, apartment size, whether pets are allowed, maximum rent, etc. Members receive a list, by fax or e-mail, of all the apartments in the database fitting the requested specs, with updates on request for as long as necessary. You can change specifications to receive listings in other categories: different neighborhoods or rent limits, for example. A free membership gives access to more limited services. Included among the listings, which are updated daily, are properties handled by some 200 brokerage companies—these would involve fees. Also included: co-ops, condos, and houses for sale by owners as well as brokers, photos.
- **Rent-Direct**, 166 Fifth Avenue, 4th floor, NYC 10010, 212-645-9797, www.rent-direct.com, has perhaps the deepest list of apartments in the

city and New Jersey, as well as seven-day customer support and a walk-in office with computers for customer use. You pay $195 to access the service for three months. Service includes access to their database of some 5,000 buildings, with photos of street panoramas and interior views. New apartment listings are provided via e-mail or, once you are an established user, you can go online to check out all listings.

A word about no-fee apartment guides sold in book form at bookstores and some newsstands. They tend to be unreliable and out-of-date.

NEW BUILDINGS

Renovated factories, warehouses, and other commercial buildings occasionally add new rental units to the city's supply. Apartments in reconstructed or totally new buildings command top dollar. However, it is often possible to avoid brokers' commissions in these buildings when landlords and managers pay on-site rental agents to fill the buildings as quickly as possible. You'll need to have the inside track to get on these buildings' short lists. Be sure to check that the unit is zoned for residential space as you may be denied renter's insurance if you live in a non-residentially zoned building.

DIRECT ACTION

In a town where single-minded apartment hunters have been known to read the obituary columns with as much intensity as the real estate classifieds, no one need feel self-conscious about approaching landlords, managing agents, superintendents, or local merchants in order to locate a place in a particular neighborhood or building.

Additional strategies include:

- **Call the managing agent of a likely building**. The firm's or agent's name is usually posted near a building's entrance. If no telephone number is given, check the phone book.
- **Speak with the superintendent directly**. To find him, check the building directory, buzzer listings or, in the case of the smaller brownstones with shared part-time supers, your man could be the person sweeping the steps or putting garbage cans out on the sidewalk. If an apartment is available, the super or manager will sometimes send you to a broker to gain access. If a vacant apartment is found through independent efforts, you are not liable for the broker's fee. However, since reasonable apartments are in short supply, need usually overrides the fine points of the legal situation; most people prefer to pay the commission rather than go without the apartment. Once secure in your nest, if you want redress, you can file a complaint with the Division of Licenses,

New York Department of State, 123 Williams Street, 19th floor, NYC 10007, 212-417-5747. This might eventually result in a settlement.

- **Pavement pounding** accompanied by incessant querying of merchants, stoop sitters, dog walkers, postmen—indeed anyone who looks like a resident of the neighborhood—can also yield results. Some hunters go building to building and strike up conversations with doormen.
- **Driving around** in the boroughs can give you the feel of a neighborhood (in Manhattan, walking is easier). You will likely see some rental signs on buildings. Take down phone numbers even if it is not a building or an area you are interested in. You never know what other buildings that rental agent or landlord can recommend.

WORD OF MOUTH

The grapevine approach—broadcasting your need through a network of local friends—is often an effective means to a desired apartment and certainly to a sublet or share that may get you into town and buy you several more months of happy hunting. However, when you're new to town the chances of having such a network are usually slim. Nonetheless, use any contacts available. Parents can call old college chums; who knows, their son or daughter may be leaving a desirable place. In any case, personal contacts are often a shot at the type of high-demand place that never makes it as far as the *Times* or a broker's office. In sublet situations, check to make sure the lease allows the tenant to sublet.

BULLETIN BOARDS

Certain neighborhoods, particularly the more homogeneous communities such as SoHo and Tribeca, some of the larger buildings, as well as in the more "old-world neighborhoods" of Brooklyn and Queens, have bulletin boards where an occasional apartment turns up among the sheets offering tutoring, a ride to California, or opportunities for self-improvement. Inquire locally to find out which cafe, supermarket, or grocery store serves this neighborhood function. Bulletin boards in university areas also include valuable information, notably New York University, Columbia, Cooper Union, and Hunter College. If you know someone in NYC in an apartment building, call ahead and ask him/her to check the building bulletin board for vacant apartments, sublets, or sharing options.

HOUSE ORGANS

Many corporations and organizations publish newsletters or magazines for their personnel that print employee advertisements. Sublets and the occasional rental turn up in these columns, and it is worth asking friends working for likely concerns to check their in-house publication for leads.

COLLEGE RELATED ASSOCIATIONS

Some New York alumni associations try to address the difficulty graduates have settling or relocating in the city. Contact your alumni office or local group to see if they can help. Some university clubs also offer advice and an occasional lead. Alumni magazines and newsletters may also offer sublet opportunities.

EMPLOYERS AND RELOCATION FIRMS

Frequently, large companies pay for the services of relocation firms to find suitable long- and short-term apartment rentals for their mid- and upper-level hires and to help solve the various problems associated with moving and settling in. The fortunate employee is saved money and headaches in the bargain. Presumably the company you are working for will inform you if it is prepared to offer help with your search for living quarters.

A variety of relocation services are also available to individuals through real estate firms, which are part of nationwide franchise networks such as Re/Max, Century 21, Prudential, and Coldwell Banker or networks of independent brokers such as Genesis, First Choice Real Estate, and Relo. Also, there are independent services such as Relocation Consulting Services, located in Bedford, NY. While they exist primarily to service relocating homeowners or potential homeowners, these services are sometimes available to renters. Contact a broker near you affiliated with one of these networks before you move; they can help you sell your home and put you in touch with a realtor here. Particularly if you are new to NYC, having a relocation advisor is a good idea. He/she will take you in hand, provide you with local real estate information and show you communities which interest you, find you a place, get you pre-qualified for a mortgage, help you with insurance, get you a mover at a discount, help your spouse find a job, find a veterinarian for your cat, a painter for your bathroom, and a school for your children.

SUBLETS AND SHORT-TERM FURNISHED RENTALS

Even without the services of a relocation firm, you still have access to the same resources, but you're on your own. Most brokers offer long-term sublets, furnished and unfurnished, and advertise them, together with regular rentals, in local newspapers and online; expect to pay a broker's fee. You may also find an un-brokered sublet offered among the classifieds by the owner or lessee. In recent years, ads have proliferated for short-term furnished rentals without broker's fees but at higher rental rates; these are not sublets, but are specifically marketed as short-term furnished rentals. Consider either of these useful interim measures, providing the time needed to discover the optimum rental apartment. Note: leaseholders of rent stabilized or exceptionally reasonable apartments have been known to ask for fixture fees or key money in a sublet situation. While some people do pour money and energy into rehabilitating an inexpensive rental apartment and may deserve compensation for their efforts when they move, fixture fees that reflect no real value are tantamount to key money, which is illegal.

Prime **sources for sublets and short-term furnished rentals** include:

- The **Village Voice** with its special "Sublets" classified section, www.villagevoice.com; available at newsstands throughout the city.
- The **New York Times**, which lists sublets under "Apartments—Furnished" and "Apartments—Unfurnished," www.nytimes.com.
- **New York Press** is a free weekly distributed each Wednesday. Look for it in restaurants, stores, and street boxes all over town. Good source for sublets.
- **Brokers**: a number of sublet specialists advertise in the *Voice* and *New York Times*. Typically, commissions on furnished rentals run between one-half and one whole month's rent for periods of less than nine months. Most agencies charge 15% for longer sublets. Four brokers and one service currently specializing in sublets:
  - **Apartment Placement Services**, 575 Lexington Avenue, 4th floor, NYC 10022, 212-572-9609, specializes in short-term furnished sublets and unfurnished prime lease rentals for a fee; also places young professionals in shared apartments throughout the city. Call for an appointment.
  - **Gamut Realty Group**, Inc., 301 East 78th Street, NYC 10021, 800-437-8353 or 212-879-4229, on the web at www.gamutnyc.com.
  - **Insignia Douglas Elliman** Rental and Relocation Division, 3 East 54th Street, NYC 10021, 212-645-4040, www.elliman.com
  - **New York Habitat**, 307 Seventh Avenue, Suite 306, New York 10001, 212-255-8018, on the web at www.nyhabitat.com; specializes in sublets, short-term and long-term rentals, a no fee service.
  - **Senter Sublet**, 510 Madison Avenue, NYC 10022, 212-935-8730, www.sentersublets.com, call for appointment.
- **Bulletin boards** in large buildings, bars or other neighborhood locations. Large apartment complexes have waiting lists for rental apartments the proverbial block long. However, leaseholders arrange sublets directly and occasionally post notices on community bulletin boards. Check with the management of these big units to see if they have a central sublet source.

- **In-house publications** tend to be a better source of sublets than of rentals.

SHARING

One of the best solutions to high housing costs, particularly for young, single people, is an apartment-share. But if you are just arriving in the city and don't know anyone, you may not have anyone to share with. If networking with old college buddies fails to turn up anything, your best bet is probably the newspapers or a roommate-finding service.

To find a room in someone else's apartment check the *Times* ads under "Apartments to Share," #1696, and the *Voice's* "Shares." Some leaseholders prefer to have roommates pre-screened and list with agencies that arrange apartment shares for a flat fee up front. Reputations ebb and flow; we can't guarantee satisfaction. But if you want to investigate this option, two of the firms in Manhattan are:

- **Roommate Finders**, 253 West 72nd Street, Suite 1711, NYC 10023, 212-489-6862, www.roommatefinders.com; open Monday-Friday noon to 7:30 p.m., Saturday and Sunday noon to 6 p.m. For the $300 fee, the client, after filling out a registration sheet covering personal habits and preferences and discussing specifications in a half-hour interview, is given information sheets on prospective apartments and/or roommates. You can call daily for new listings for up to one year, and if you find your own roommate or apartment, you are entitled to a 50% refund. Listing is free.
- **New York Habitat**, 307 Seventh Avenue, Suite 306, NYC 10001, 212-255-8018, www.nyhabitat.com; open 9 a.m. to 6 p.m. This firm, which also handles sublets and rentals, charges the renter only when he/she agrees to rent an apartment share. The fee, a minimum of 30% of one month's rent, maximum of 15% of one year's rent, is based on length of stay.

Also popular is the national service, **Craig's List**, which features a wide range of roommate listings for numerous cities. The New York section includes a wealth of room shares with price and location. Click on the individual listing for more details. Then, through e-mail or in some cases by phone, you'll contact the individual. Craig's List also has extensive listings of apartments for rent. Keep in mind that anyone can post on Craig's List (meaning ads are not screened carefully, only categorized), so use some caution when following up leads. It's always a good idea to first meet with a prospective roommate or the person you will be subletting from in a public space, and bring along a friend to view the apartment.

CHECKING IT OUT

You've found what appears to be the perfect, sunny apartment in a pleasant neighborhood and, best of all, you're the first person to see it! You want to shout, "I'll take it," but you should restrain yourself and spend a few minutes looking it over first. We suggest you bring a checklist of your musts and must-nots. In addition, you should make a quick inspection to make sure the apartment's beauty is not just skin deep. A little time and a few questions asked now can save you a lot of time, money, and headache later. Specifically, you may want to look for the following:

• Are the kitchen appliances clean and in working order? Do the stove's burners work? What about the oven? Is there enough counter and shelf space? Does it smell funny in the kitchen space—or anywhere else? Does the refrigerator work?
• Do the windows open, close, and lock? Do they open onto a noisy or potentially dangerous area?
• Are there enough closets and is there enough storage space?
• Are there enough electrical outlets for all your needs? Do the outlets work?
• What about laundry facilities, are they in the building or nearby?
• When was the apartment last painted? Is it lead free paint? In the event you will stay longer than a year, who is responsible for painting the apartment?
• Do the bathroom fixtures work? Look for leaks under pipes.
• Is there a bug problem in the building? Look in the kitchen cabinets.
• Is the building wired for cable TV service? If not, what, if any, reception is there without cable, and can you have direct or satellite television installed?
• Is the superintendent easily accessible? Ask neighbors about the building staff. Are they helpful, trustworthy, competent, available?
• What about building security and cleanliness: check the building entry, lobby, and public areas.
• If you own a car, what is the parking situation like? Is there a long waiting list for garage space?
• Do you feel comfortable in the area? Will you feel safe here at night?
• What about public transportation and shopping? Is it nearby?
• How close is the nearest emergency hospital and police precinct?

Also, try to visit apartments during non-business hours when more people are home to get a feel for how noisy a unit will be. This will also give you a feel for the comings and goings of the building, specifically: is the front entrance locked, and is there a 24-hour doorman?

Ed Sacks' *Savvy Renter's Kit* contains a thorough renter's checklist for those interested in augmenting theirs.

If it all passes muster, be prepared to stake your claim without delay.

STAKING A CLAIM

It may seem to newcomers that securing an apartment, after having found one suitable, can be as difficult as gaining membership in an exclusive club. In a tight market, that's not far off the mark. You have to be found acceptable. For starters, arrive on time and be presentably dressed for appointments. Even in this city of "attitude," a little politeness goes a long way. Also, be sure to come armed with as many of the following as possible:

- A certified check, bank check, or money order to cover a deposit equivalent to one to two months' rent. Without this, none of the rest will matter.
- Most recent W-2 form.
- Letter from current employer verifying that you are employed and, if possible, will continue to be; lacking that, your employer's business telephone number.
- Pay stubs showing a yearly income(s) equivalent to 40 to 50 times the monthly rent.
- A credit report or money to cover the fee for having a credit-check done.
- Reference letters (sometimes necessary), business and personal, and one from your current landlord stating you are prompt with rent payments.
- Recent statements from checking, savings, and investment accounts.
- A guarantor, parents for example in the case of youthful renters, with documents showing an income 80 to 100 times the monthly rent, if you do not have an income adequate to satisfy the landlord.

Having successfully navigated these shoals and been accepted, you are ready to sign a lease. First, a word of caution: there are fraudulent real estate and rental agents who take advantage of eager and unwary apartment seekers. To avoid them, meet real estate and rental agents only in an office, not on the street. Ask for a Department of State identification card and a photo ID. Give a deposit only to the landlord, and be wary of agents who can be reached only by cell phones.

TENANT/LANDLORD RELATIONSHIP, LEASES, SECURITY DEPOSITS

TENANT/LANDLORD OBLIGATIONS

Whether you are renting or subletting, before you sign a lease it's a good idea to investigate tenant/landlord obligations and rental restrictions. Specifics can be found at the **NYC Rent Guidelines Board** web site, www.housingnyc.com. The **New York Attorney General's** Office, 120 Broadway, NYC 10271, 212-416-8000, has a comprehensive web site that addresses tenant rights, ordinances, and lease information: www.oag.state.ny.us/realestate/tenants_rights_guide.html. The state **Division of Housing and Community Renewal's** rent information line, 718-739-6400, can also provide information. A membership group called the **New Jersey Tenants Organization (NJTO)** provides tenant-related information in that state. It assists with organizing local tenant associations in New Jersey, offers legal guidance to its members, and works for pro-tenant legislation. Individual membership is $22 a year. Ask about their publication, available for $21. The NJTO is located at 389 Main Street, Hackensack, NJ 07601, 201-342-3775. Also in New Jersey, the **New Jersey Department of Community Affairs, Office of Landlord Tenant Information**, 101 South Broad Street, Trenton, NJ 08625, 609-292-4174, www.state.nj.us/dca, sets regulations for renters and landlords. Their "Truth in Renting" booklet ($1.50) is available at their office or send a check or money order to Treasurer, State of NJ, Office of Landlord Tenant Information, Truth in Renting, P.O. Box 805, Trenton, NJ 08625-0805. Finally, online you can go to the national site, www.rent law.com, which provides renters with information regarding landlord/ tenant law by state.

Additional resources include:

- **Metropolitan Council on Housing**, 212-979-0611, tenants union
- **New York City Rent Guidelines Board**, 212-385-2934, www.housing nyc.com
- **Rent Stabilization Association**, 212-214-9200, www.rsanyc.org
- **TenantNet**, www.tenant.net

DEPOSITS

The first written check undoubtedly will be a deposit held by the broker or landlord while credit references are being researched. Some landlords require certified check or bank check rather than personal check, so inquire in advance. The first person to put down a deposit (customarily one month's rent) stands the best chance of signing the lease. The credit investigation should take no more than a couple of days if you have supplied the documentation outlined above. Once you are pronounced credit-worthy, the deposit check should be accepted as your first month's rent (some landlords require two months' rent in advance). The interest-earning security deposit, also generally one month's rent, will be refunded at the end of your lease, providing the apartment is left in the same condition in which it was found. (Now is the time to walk through with the landlord to record any existing damage.) If a real estate broker is involved, your third payment will be the broker's fee, which currently averages about 15% of the first year's rent. In some cases, the owner will pay all or part of the fee.

LEASES

Read the lease carefully *before* signing it or giving a security deposit. Married couples should have both names on the lease, especially if they go by different last names; unmarried couples should try to get both names on the lease, though the landlord is not legally obliged to do so. A standard form is customary. Be familiar with the content of the entire lease, but pay special attention to the end of the form where the qualifying clauses are printed. The document should specify any special arrangements made with the landlord about alterations, repairs, painting, and new appliances. Before signing is the time to ask questions or have uncertain terms clarified. Terms in leases can sometimes be negotiated, but be sure to get any such alterations in writing and initialed by the landlord. Ask about making alterations within the apartment, notification of moving, if pets are allowed, responsibility for repairs, and what, if any, responsibilities you have for public areas. Also, make sure to inquire about any extra fees, such as application fees for condo or co-op sub-leases or move-in/move-out deposits. Determine how the building is heated and who pays the bills. If the landlord is responsible, there must be a clause in the lease to this effect. Traditionally, especially in the pre-war buildings, landlords pay for steam heat and hot water so you only pay for gas (for cooking) and electricity. In newer buildings without boilers, tenants customarily pay for the more costly electrical heat.

Since 1982, smoke detectors, essentially one per sleeping area, have been mandatory in New York apartments. Tenants are responsible for the repair and maintenance of these alarms. Apartments with children are required by law to have window guards.

Your landlord is legally responsible for ridding your apartment of cockroaches. Some provide routine exterminator services; others simply take care of the matter as it crops up. Obviously, the ounce of prevention method is preferable and you should know in advance if regular service is included in your lease.

Check for a sublet clause. Subletting is allowed "with the landlord's permission." This means he or she can say no. To avoid permission being withheld capriciously, the clause should mention that the apartment can be sublet with written permission from the landlord and that "permission shall not be unreasonably withheld."

Conversely, if you are subletting an apartment from the original lessee, determine whether or not you have a legal right to be there. To address this and other questions, **Tenants & Neighbors** offers a useful 22-page booklet, *A Tenant's Guide to Subletting and Apartment Sharing*, available for $12. Write to Tenants & Neighbors, 105 Washington Street, 2nd Floor, NYC 10006; or save $2 by picking it up at the office. Call 212-608-4320 for information about membership ($20 per year). The guide details the practical and legal ramifications of apartment sharing, and the ins and outs of subletting to, as well as from, another individual. The **New York State Rent Guidelines** web site, www.housingnyc.com, is useful, and includes an online guide to renting. If you have questions about the propriety of a subtenancy and the apartment falls under city or state-enforced guidelines, try calling one of the organizations listed below under **Additional Resources** (Rent Guidelines Board, the New York Loft Board, or the Office of the DHCR) with your concerns.

Subletting a cooperative apartment can be daunting. Not only is it necessary to prove yourself to the landlord but you must also pass the scrutiny of the building's board of directors. Unfortunately, the traditionally restrictive subletting practices of many cooperative buildings are still in effect. If you are very fortunate, you will meet with a rare co-op board that focuses on realistic concerns for their building and will consider a sublet situation. Keep in mind that if you sublet a co-op without the board's approval you could be evicted. Individually-owned condominium apartments can typically be sublet at the owner's discretion.

Finally, for a comprehensive guide to the ins and outs of renting in the city, including housing laws, a list of agencies and resources for tenants, recent articles, and links to related sites, go to TenantNet, www.tenant.net.

RENT STABILIZATION AND RENT CONTROL

While municipal rent controls have been eliminated in most of the country, they have survived in New York City. Few if any of the **rent controlled** apartments ever reach the market; they are either passed among qualifying members of one family like heirlooms or, once vacant, automatically become **rent stabilized** (apartments in large buildings) or decontrolled (apartments in buildings with five units or less). The Office of Rent Administration's web site states: "In New York City, rent control tenants are generally in buildings built before February 1, 1947, where the tenant is in continuous occupancy prior to July 1, 1971. Tenants who took occupancy after June 30, 1971, in buildings of six or more units built before January 1, 1974, are generally rent stabilized." Rents in condominiums and cooperative apartments are left to market forces. Under rent control guidelines, apartments in buildings with six or more units could only see limited increases (in 2004, rents increased 4.5% for one-year leases and 7.5% for two-year leases). After the $2,000 mark, apartments no longer qualify as rent controlled units, and can be rented by the landlord at the market rate. To speed up this process, landlords are renovating many of the remaining low-rent apartments to push their value above $2,000, which allows these units to be taken off the rent control market. In short, rent control is becoming a thing of the past in New York City. The **Rent Stabilization Association** (the landlord group), 1500 Broadway, NYC 10036, will answer questions about tenants' rights under rent stabilization. Call 212-214-9200 or go to www.rsanyc.org. If your apartment is rent controlled or rent stabilized, call the **Office of Rent Administration, State Division of Housing and Community Renewal (DHCR)** in your borough with any questions or problems: Upper Manhattan, above 110th Street, 163 West 125th Street, 212-961-8930; Lower Manhattan, below 110th Street, 25 Beaver Street, Fifth Floor, 212-480-6238; The Bronx, 1 Fordham Plaza, 718-563-5678; Brooklyn, 55 Hanson Place, Room 702, Brooklyn 11217, 718-722-4778; Queens, 92-31 Union Hall Street, Jamaica 11433, 718-739-6400; Staten Island, 60 Bay Street, Seventh Floor, Staten Island 10301, 718-816-0278; web site, www.dhcr.state.ny.us.

LOFTS

During the 1960s, the trickle of hardy artists working and living illegally in industrial lofts located in manufacturing districts became a stream. Living in a vast, often high-ceilinged space à la bohème became a desirable alternative life style. Add a few partitions, a restaurant gas stove, some antiques—instant chic.

Illegal loft tenancies proliferated throughout the 1970s, but an amendment to the state's Multiple Dwelling Law legalized loft living in manufacturing buildings (buildings with no residential Certificates of Occupancy) containing three or more rental units. Some areas of the city were exempted, but in Chelsea and lower Manhattan, in the Fulton Ferry area of Brooklyn, and Long Island City in Queens, loft dwellers breathed a legal sigh of relief.

The loft law did not, however, create complete order out of chaos, and the legality of some loft-living situations is still in doubt. Anyone considering renting or subletting a loft is well advised to check with the **New York City Loft Board**, 49-51 Chambers Street, Room 1006, NYC 10007, 212-788-7610, before signing the lease. This is the city agency charged with overseeing the legalization of residential lofts.

Look for a Certificate of Occupancy for the building and check to see if you're signing a commercial or residential lease.

ADDITIONAL RESOURCES—RENTERS

- **Gas** or **Electric service shutoff hotline**, 800-342-3355
- **Housing Authority**, 250 Broadway, NYC 10007 212-306-3000, www.nyc.com
- **Housing Discrimination** for New York (and New Jersey): Fair Housing Hub, US Department of Housing and Urban Development, 26

Federal Plaza, Room 3532, NYC 10278-0068, 212-264-9610 or 800-496-4294; housing discrimination hotline, 800-669-9777, www.hud.gov/complaints/housediscrim.cfm
- **Landlord/Tenant Fact sheet** (NY State Attorney General) 120 Broadway, NYC 10271, 212-416-2000, www.oag.state.ny.us
- **Loft Board**, 49-51 Chambers Street, Room 1006, NYC 10007, 212-788-7610, www.nyc.gov/html/loft/
- **New York City Rent Guidelines Board**, 51 Chambers Street, NYC, 10007, 212-385-2934, www.housingnyc.com
- **NYC Heat Hotline**, 311
- **NYC Urban League**, 204 West 136th Street, 212-926-8000, www.nyul.org
- **Office of Rent Administration, State Division of Housing and Community Renewal** (**DHCR**): Upper Manhattan, above 110th Street, 163 West 125th Street, 212-961-8930; Lower Manhattan, below 110th Street, 25 Beaver Street, Fifth Floor, 212-480-6238 (see above under **Rent Stabilization** for additional borough listings), www.dhcr.state.ny.us.
- **Rent Stabilization Association** (the landlord group), 212-214-9200 or go to www.rsanyc.org.

If you're settling in the Lower East Side of Manhattan or the East Village, **GOLES** (stands for **Good Old Lower East Side**), is the tenant association, and is one of the best run tenants groups in the city: 525 East 6th Street, NYC 10009, 212-533-2541.

RENTER'S/HOMEOWNER'S INSURANCE

Your neighbor upstairs has a grease fire in his kitchen, which gets out of hand. There is no fire damage to your apartment, but smoke and water damage from extinguishing the fire have rendered your furniture unusable, your walls in need of new paint, and your television and computer are out of commission. The cost of replacing all this stuff is covered by the owner's building insurance, right? Wrong. You're out of pocket, unless you have renter's insurance.

While events such as this are relatively rare, when they occur they can be financially devastating. If your possessions are few, it may be worth the gamble to skip the insurance. However, your possessions can be insured against fire, water damage, and theft. Rates vary from company to company; be sure to shop around. It's a good idea to pay the additional cost for replacement coverage, and be sure your premiums provide personal liability coverage, protecting you and your family against lawsuits resulting from injuries to others, on or off the premises. If you own a dog, be sure the personal liability covers dog bites as well. Insurance is even more important for apartment owners, who will also need to be covered for structural improvements or alterations as well as loss of personal possessions in the event of a disaster. Some co-ops and condo buildings require such coverage. When seeking insurance from an insurance agent (Yellow Pages under "Insurance" or online under keywords "Renters Insurance" or at www.insure.com), it's a good idea to get quotes from at least three providers. One company will be more competitive than another in a specific neighborhood, or in rentals, say, than in condos. If you want to check your insurance record, contact **ChoicePoint Asset**, P.O. Box 105108, Atlanta, GA 30348-5108, www.choicetrust.com, to order your CLUE (Comprehensive Loss Underwriting Exchange) report. This national database of consumers' automobile and homeowner's insurance claims is used by insurers when determining rates or denying coverage. Contact ChoicePoint if you find any errors.

Some companies which sell renter's/homeowner's insurance in the metropolitan area:

- **Aetna Inc.**, 800-273-0123, www.aetna.com
- **Allstate**, 877-634-5317, www.allstate.com
- **Chubb**, 908-903-2000, www.chubb.com
- **CAN**, 800-CAN-HELP, www.can.com
- **Fireman's Fund**, 800-227-1700, www.firemansfund.com
- **The Hartford**, 860-547-5000, www.thehartford.com
- **Liberty Mutual Group**, 617-357-9500, www.libertymutual.com
- **Prudential** (homeowners insurance), www.prudential.com
- **Travelers**, 800-252-4633, www.travelers.com

For more information or if you have a problem with your insurer, contact the **New York State Department of Insurance**, 212-480-6400, www.ins.state.ny.us; in New Jersey go to www.state.nj.us/dobi/homepage.

BUYING

In a city of renters, why buy? Real estate values have risen sharply since the late 1990s, but so have rents. Factoring in the income tax exemption for mortgage interest, which is highest in the early years of the mortgage, the cost of renting now can approach, or even exceed the cost of buying, especially in the studio and one-bedroom apartment category. For many, the idea of having home equity, as opposed to paying rent to someone else, has a strong appeal. For others, it's the satisfaction and security of home ownership. Keep in mind, however, home ownership in New York City is quite different compared to much of the US. The $400,000 that might buy a four-bedroom, three-bathroom house with plenty of greenery in parts of the US, in NYC may buy you a studio apartment with an alcove—if you're lucky.

That said, the newcomer to New York City would be well advised to rent or sublet for a year at least before buying: become comfortable in the city, familiar with some of its neighborhoods, and develop a sense of how you use the city. Furthermore, the case can be made that, given the expenses incidental to buying (described below) and the fact that real estate values tend to rise and fall in roughly ten-year cycles, it makes sense to buy only if you expect to spend at least ten years in the city. Even if the market goes soft for a while, New York real estate values will eventually rise again. New Yorkers whose parents bought brownstones in the 1940s or '50s for several thousand dollars can attest to that from their now inherited multi-million dollar homes.

As with renting, the search for a condo, a co-op, or a house generally begins online or in the classified ads in the *New York Times*, the *Wall Street Journal*, or the *New York Observer*, a weekly newspaper distinctively pink in color and available at most newsstands. The ads lead the seeker to realtor web sites where one can browse through the images and specs. Web sites on the internet offering national real estate listings proliferate, many with virtual tours. Below, a few that may be useful:

- **Homes & Land Magazine**, www.homes.com
- **Netprop**, www.netprop.com, especially strong in the New York/New Jersey area.
- **Owners.com**, www.owners.com, a "For Sale by Owners" site, excluding brokers, with area listings in New Jersey and Connecticut
- **Realtor.com** and **Homestore.com** are affiliated sites controlled by the National Association of Realtors, a huge listing nationwide.
- **RealtyGuide**, www.xmission.com/~realtor1, with links to broker web sites, lenders, for-sale-by-owner directories, and home-for-sale magazines.
- **YahooRealestate**, http://realestate.yahoo.com/realestate, national real estate and rentals listings; relocation advice
- **ZipRealty**, www.ziprealty.com is a national site that combines internet service with the personal attention of an agent. No cost to register to view listings.

Those looking online to buy a co-op, condo, or house in the city may probably be more successful at city-specific sites, most of which provide neighborhood profiles, comparative prices and mortgage information:

- **MLX**, www.mlx.com, co-ops and condos, as well as rentals, by neighborhood in Manhattan only
- **New York City Real Estate Exchange**, www.cityrealty.com, with condos, co-ops, and houses in all boroughs

- **New York Today**, www.nytimes.com or www.nytoday.com; the *New York Times'* site with extensive real estate listings, which automatically searches the databases of the city's major brokers

For those who are contemplating buying, a few considerations now, which apply whether you are looking for a house, a co-op, or a condo. First, what can you afford to pay? The rule of thumb, and one which lenders use: it is safe to pay three or four times the buyer's yearly income, depending on a variety of factors. The required down payment will generally be 20% of the purchase price; it may go as low as 10%, in which case origination fees (points) to the bank will probably be higher. Be prepared for a thorough examination of your finances, your credit record, and your employment status. This, of course, assumes the buyer is not paying cash but will be obtaining a mortgage from a bank.

Know that the transaction you are about to make is going to cost more than the agreed upon price. How much more? Generally, in New York, closing costs run five- to eight-percent of the purchase price. This includes points, attorney's fees, title insurance, a title search, inspection and survey, recording tax, various fees, and the deposit of some real estate tax payments and homeowner's insurance premiums in escrow. The lender (bank or mortgage company) is required to give a good-faith estimate of closing costs. In New York, the seller pays the broker's fee.

Whatever and wherever you are looking to buy, you'll need a good broker who listens to you, knows the neighborhoods, and can put you in touch with potential lenders and mortgage brokers. (See **Recommendations for finding a real estate broker**, above.) A buyer's broker, who represents only the buyer, is becoming common, particularly in the suburbs. It's a good idea to get pre-approved for a mortgage before looking; in today's market it can make the difference in your bid winning out against competing bids for a property. And in popular neighborhoods, you may need to act fast. Without being pre-approved, you can lose out on the apartment you want. You must also have a good real estate lawyer, whom you can find through the recommendations of friends, your own lawyer, or your broker. If you have no idea where to find an attorney who handles real estate transactions, call legal referral, 212-382-6600, at the **Association of the Bar of the City of New York**, 42 West 44th Street.

If you are buying a **house**, you will do well to hire a building engineer to check the structure of the house, the heating and plumbing systems, fireplaces, etc.; a thorough inspection may save you thousands of dollars or prevent you from making a disastrous purchase. In New York City, there are lead paint disclosure forms that are to be filled out by the seller. In the case of a co-op, or condominium, it is important to check out the financial stability of the board of directors. In all buying scenarios, it is in the best interest of the buyer to have everything reviewed by a competent real estate attorney.

When you buy a **co-op** (cooperative apartment) you are buying shares in the ownership of a building, the other shareholders of which must approve your purchase through their board. And, should you choose to sell or rent your apartment later, the same approval process must be repeated, which can be a problem. In the most desirable buildings, approval may be more difficult than getting a mortgage, as shareholders attempt to guarantee the financial reliability and the "social acceptability" of their new partner. Your finances will be scrutinized, and your life-style may be considered. Try to get an idea about governing attitudes of the co-op board and check recent board decisions regarding upkeep and repair of the co-op before committing to an apartment. The wrong co-op board, with a list of onerous rules and regulations, can make life less than pleasant. Also, get a prospectus, minutes of the last meeting of the board, board/building rules, and a financial statement from the cooperative, and go over them with your broker and your lawyer. If your purchase is rejected, expect no explanation. Be aware that co-op size may affect your ability to get a mortgage; in co-ops with fewer than 12 units, lenders may be more likely to reject a mortgage application because the relatively small number of shareholders in such buildings raises the collective risk of default. Also, keep in mind that co-op maintenance fees (the cost of upkeep for everything outside the walls of your apartment) can be more than your mortgage, depending on the building, and only some of the maintenance fee (the portion of the fee that is allocated for property tax payments) is tax deductible. Forty to fifty percent is a ballpark figure.

The purchase of a **condo** involves fewer hurdles, though some condo management organizations request letters of recommendation from prospective buyers. Here you are buying an apartment outright, with the right to rent or re-sell when and as you choose. Of course, this means neither you nor the other residents have any control over who your neighbors are. In making this purchase you will also want your lawyer to examine a prospectus and financial statement on the building to avoid buying into a financially unstable property.

In either situation, condo or co-op, if you're the kind of person who likes to be left alone or has trouble getting along in a group with strict rules, purchasing a condominium or co-op could be a mistake. If such possible limitations are not an issue, then take the plunge.

Questions to ask about a co-op or condo:

- What percentage of the units are owner-occupied?
- How much are the association dues and projected assessments?

- What are the rules and regulations?
- Who manages the property?
- Have there been any lawsuits involving the association in the past five years?

These and many other issues are covered in the "Condominium/ Townhome Guide," published by Re/Max Real Estate, 800-878-8404. The guide provides information about different styles of housing, associations, and comprehensive checklists to use to evaluate developments.

Finally, a word about **mortgage brokers**. In the competition to win new mortgage clients, banks offer a confusing array of loans. Mortgage broker to the rescue! Think of a mortgage broker as a financial advisor who helps his/her client get a suitable mortgage. At no charge to you, he/she will examine your financial situation (age, income, assets, debt load, etc.) and the type of property you want to buy, and then recommend the most likely lender and the best type of mortgage for your needs. Given the mortgage broker's relationship with various banks, he/she can ease your way through the process, especially on co-op loans. If you're the ruggedly independent sort, keep in mind that in New York City your chances of getting a good mortgage are much higher with a qualified mortgage broker than without.

ADDITIONAL RESOURCES—HOMEBUYERS

You might check out the quasi-governmental agency **Fannie Mae**, 800-834-3377, www.fanniemae.com or www.homepath.com, for credit counseling, assistance with finding low-cost mortgages, and advice for low-income and first-time buyers.

Once a New York City tenant, if necessary, you can contact the **Central Complaint Bureau** of the **New York City Department of Housing and Preservation**, 100 Gold Street, NYC 10038, by dialing 311.

Five books that we found useful:

- *100 Questions Every First Time Homebuyer Should Ask: With Answers from Top Brokers From Around the Country*, 2nd edition (Times Books) by Ilyce R.Glink
- *The 106 Common Mistakes Homebuyers Make (And How to Avoid Them)*, 3rd edition (Wiley) by Gary W. Eldred
- *The Co-Op Bible: Everything You Need to Know About Co-Ops and Condos: Getting In, Staying In, Surviving, Thriving* (Griffin) by Sylvia Shapiro
- *Opening the Door to a Home of Your Own*, a free pamphlet by the Fannie Mae Foundation, 800-834-3377
- *Your New House: the Alert Consumer's Guide to Buying and Building a Quality New Home*; (Windsor Peak) by Alan and Denise Fields

HAVING FOUND AND SECURED A PLACE TO LIVE, YOU NOW HAVE the task of getting your stuff there and perhaps storing some of it because a New York apartment is smaller than you had expected.

TRUCK RENTALS

The first question you need to answer: am I going to move myself or will I have someone else do it for me? If you're used to doing everything yourself, you can rent a vehicle, load it up, and hit the road. Look in the Yellow Pages under "Truck Rental" and call around and compare; also ask about any specials. Below we list four national truck rental companies and their toll-free numbers and web sites. For the best information, you should call a local office. Note: most truck rental companies now offer one-way rentals as well as packing accessories and storage facilities. Of course, these extras are not free and if you're cost conscious you may want to scavenge boxes in advance of your move and make sure you have a place to store your belongings upon arrival (see **Storage** below). Also, if you're planning to move during the peak moving months (May through September) call well in advance, at least a month ahead, of when you think you'll need the vehicle.

Once you're on the road, keep in mind that your rental truck may be a tempting target for thieves. If you must park it overnight or for an extended period (more than a couple of hours), try to find a safe place, preferably somewhere well-lit and easily observable by you, and do your best not to leave anything of particular value in the cab. Make sure you lock up and if possible use a steering wheel lock or other easy-to-purchase safety device.

Four national self-moving companies to consider:

• **Budget**, 800-428-7825, www.budget.com

- **Penske**, 800-222-0277, www.penske.com
- **Ryder**, 800-297-9337, www.ryder.com (now a Budget company, still operating under the Ryder name)
- **U-haul**, 800-468-4285, www.uhaul.com

Not sure if you want to drive the truck yourself? Commercial freight carriers, such as **ABF**, 800-355-1696, www.upack.com, offer an in-between service; they deliver a 28-foot trailer to your home, you pack and load as much of it as you need, and they drive the vehicle to your destination (often with some other freight filling the remaining space). Keep in mind though, if you have to share truck space with another customer you may arrive far ahead of your boxes—and bed. Try to estimate your needs beforehand and ask for your load's expected arrival date. You can get an online estimate from some shippers, so you can compare rates. If you aren't moving an entire house and can't estimate how much truck space you will need, keep in mind this general guideline: two to three furnished rooms equal a 15-foot truck; four to five rooms, a 20-foot truck. Due to New York's narrow streets and overnight parking restrictions, self-moves may be best suited to those moving outside Manhattan.

MOVERS

INTERSTATE

First, the good news: moving can be affordable and problem-free. The bad news: if you're hiring a mover, the chances of it being so are much less. Probably the best way to find a mover is by personal recommendation. Absent a friend or relative who can recommend a trusted moving company, you can turn to what surveys show is the most popular method of finding a mover: the **Yellow Pages**. Then there's the internet: just type in "movers" on a search engine and you'll be directed to hundreds of more or less helpful moving-related sites.

In the past, ***Consumer Reports***, www.consumerreports.org, has published useful information on moving. You might ask a local realtor, who may be able to steer you towards a good mover, or at least tell you which ones to avoid. Members of the American Automobile Association have a valuable resource at hand in **AAA's Consumer Relocation Services**, which will assign the member a personal consultant to handle every detail of the move free of charge and which offers discounts with premier moving companies. Call 800-839-MOVE, www.aaa.com.

But beware! Since 1995, when the federal government eliminated the Interstate Commerce Commission, the interstate moving business has degenerated into a wild and mostly unregulated industry with thousands of unhappy, ripped-off customers annually. (There are so many reports of unscrupulous carriers that we no longer list movers in this book.) Since states do not have the authority to regulate interstate movers and the federal government has been slow to respond, you are pretty much on your own when it comes to finding an honest, hassle-free mover. That's why we can't emphasize enough the importance of carefully researching and choosing who will move you.

To aid your search for an honest and hassle-free **interstate mover**, we offer a few general recommendations. First get the names of a half-dozen movers and check to make sure they are licensed by the US Department of Transportation's **Federal Motor Carrier Safety Administration (FMCSA)**. With the mover's Motor Carrier (MC) numbers in hand, call 888-368-7238 or 202-358-7000 (offers the option of speaking to an agent) or go online to http://fhwa-li.volpe.dot.gov, to see if the carrier is licensed and insured. If the company you're considering is federally licensed, your next step should be to check with the Better Business Bureau, www.bbb.org, in the state where the moving company is licensed as well as with that state's consumer protection board (in New York call 800-697-1220 or go to www.consumer.state.ny.us), or attorney general. Assuming there is no negative information, you can move on to the next step: asking for references. Particularly important are references from customers who did moves similar to yours. If a moving company is unable or unwilling to provide references or tells you they can't because their customers are all in the Federal Witness Protection Program, eliminate them from your list. Unscrupulous movers have even been known to give phony references who will falsely sing the mover's praises—so talk to more than one reference and ask questions. If something feels fishy, it probably is. One way to learn more about a prospective mover: ask them if they have a local office (they should) and then walk in and check it out.

Once you have at least three movers you feel reasonably comfortable with, it's time to ask for price quotes (always free). Best is a binding "not-to-exceed" quote, of course in writing. This will require an on-site visual inspection of what you are shipping. If you have *any* doubts about a prospective mover, drop them from your list before you invite a stranger into your home to catalog your belongings.

Recent regulations by FMCSA require movers to supply five documents to consumers before executing a contract. These include a brochure called *Your Rights and Responsibilities When You Move*; a concise and accurate written estimate of charges; a summary of the mover's arbitration program; the mover's customer complaint and inquiry handling procedure; and the mover's tariff containing rates, rules, regulations, classifications, etc. For more about FMCSA's role in the handling of household goods, you can go to their consumer page at www.fmcsa.dot.gov/factsfigs/moving.htm.

Additional moving recommendations:

- If someone recommends a mover to you, get names (the salesperson or estimator, the drivers, the loaders). To paraphrase the NRA, moving companies don't move people, people do. Likewise, if someone tells you he/she had a bad moving experience, note the name of the company and try to avoid it.
- Remember that price, while important, isn't everything, especially when you're entrusting all of your worldly possessions to strangers.
- Ask about the other end—subcontracting increases the chances that something could go wrong.
- In general, ask questions, and if you're concerned about something, ask for an explanation in writing. If you change your mind about a mover after you've signed on the dotted line, write them a letter explaining that you've changed your mind and that you won't be using their services. Better safe than sorry.
- Ask about insurance; the "basic" 60 cents per pound industry standard coverage is not enough. If you have homeowner's or renter's insurance, check to see if it will cover your belongings during transit. If not, ask your insurer if you can add that coverage for your move. Otherwise, consider purchasing "full replacement" or "full value" coverage from the carrier for the estimated value of your shipment. Though it's the most expensive type of coverage offered, it's probably worth it. Trucks get into accidents, they catch fire, they get stolen—if such insurance seems pricey to you, ask about a $250 or $500 deductible. This can reduce your cost substantially while still giving you much better protection in case of a catastrophic loss.
- Whatever you do, do not mislead a salesperson/estimator about how much and what you are moving. And make sure you tell a prospective mover about how far they'll have to transport your stuff to and from the truck as well as any stairs, driveways, obstacles or difficult vegetation, long paths or sidewalks, etc. The clearer you are with your mover, the better he or she will be able to serve you.
- Think about packing. If you plan to pack yourself, you can save some money, but if something is damaged because of your packing, you may not be able to file a claim for it. On the other hand, if you hire the mover to do the packing, they may not treat your belongings as well as you will. They will certainly do it faster, that's for sure. Depending on the size of your move and whether or not you are packing yourself, you may need a lot of boxes, tape, and packing material. Mover boxes, while not cheap, are usually sturdy and the right size. Sometimes a mover will give a customer used boxes free of charge. It doesn't hurt to ask. Also, *don't* wait to pack until the last minute. If you're doing the packing, give yourself at least a week to do the job;

two or more is better. Be sure to ask the mover about any weight or size restrictions on boxes.

- You should transport all irreplaceable items such as jewelry, photographs, or key work documents. Do not put them in the moving van! For less precious items that you do not want to put in the moving truck, consider sending them via the US Postal Service or by UPS.
- Ask your mover what is not permitted in the truck: usually anything flammable or combustible, as well as certain types of valuables.
- Although movers will put numbered labels on your possessions, you should make a numbered list of every box and item that is going in the truck. Detail box contents and photograph anything of particular value. Once the truck arrives on the other end, you can check off every piece and know for sure what did (or did not) make it. In case of claims, this list can be invaluable. Even after the move, keep the list; it can be surprisingly useful.
- Movers are required to issue you a "bill of lading"; do not hire a mover who does not use them.
- Consider keeping a log of every expense you incur for your move, i.e., phone calls, trips to New York, etc. In some instances, the IRS allows you to claim these types of expenses on your income taxes. (See **Taxes** below.)
- Be aware that during the busy season (May through September), demand can exceed supply and moving may be more difficult and more expensive than during the rest of the year. If you must relocate during the peak moving months, call and book service well in advance (a month at least) of when you plan on moving. If you can reserve service way in advance, say four to six months early, you may be able to lock in a lower winter rate for your summer move.
- Listen to what the movers say; they are professionals and can give you expert advice about packing and preparing. Also, be ready for the truck on both ends—don't make them wait. Not only will it irritate your movers, but it may cost you. Understand, too, that things can happen on the road that are beyond a carrier's control (weather, accidents, etc.) and your belongings may not get to you at the time or on the day promised.
- Treat your movers well, especially the ones loading your stuff on and off the truck. Offer to buy them lunch, and tip them if they do a good job.
- Before moving pets, attach a tag to your pet's collar with your new address and phone number in case your furry friend accidentally wanders off in the confusion of moving. Your pet should travel with you and you should never plan on moving a pet inside a moving van.
- Be prepared to pay the full moving bill upon delivery. Cash or bank/cashier's check may be required. Some carriers will take VISA and

MasterCard but it is a good idea to get it in writing that you will be permitted to pay with a credit card since the delivering driver may not be aware of this and may demand cash. Unless you routinely keep thousands in greenbacks on you, you could have a problem getting your stuff off the truck.

INTRASTATE AND LOCAL MOVERS

According to Section 191 of the New York State Transportation Law, all companies involved in the moving business must be insured and hold a license that permits them to provide intrastate moving services within New York State. Licenses are issued by the **New York State Department of Transportation (DOT)**, www.dot.state.ny.us. To verify certification of your chosen mover, call 800-786-5368 and punch in the state license number listed on the mover's literature. Consumers can also call this number if they wish to file a complaint. According to the DOT, nearly 12,000 consumers use the service every year. New York's Better Business Bureau also estimates that three out of every ten moves into New York City each year result in the filing of a complaint; all the more reason to be careful about the company you hire.

CONSUMER COMPLAINTS—MOVERS

If a **move goes badly** and you blame the moving company, you should first file a written claim with the mover for loss or damage. If this doesn't work and it's an intrastate move, contact the **New York State DOT Carrier Certification Unit**, 47-40 21st Street, Long Island City, 11101, 718-482-4810, 800-786-5368 (complaints); also, New York State's **Motor Carrier Compliance Bureau**, 518-457-4600, can inform you of a mover's certification and can field complaints. Still not satisfied? Contact the **New York State Attorney General's Office**, locally at 55 Hansen Place, Brooklyn, NY 11217-1523, 718-722-3949, or the **New York State Consumer Protection Board**, 5 Empire State Plaza #2101, Albany, NY 12223-1556, 518-474-3514, www.consumer.state.ny.us, and you can call the Governor's **consumer hotline**, 800-697-1220. For consumer-related questions within New York City, dial 311 to be directed to the appropriate office. Remember, for moves within the state of New York, the DOT can provide assistance only when you have used a licensed mover. Hire an unlicensed firm and you're on your own in case of damage or loss.

If your grievance is with an **interstate carrier**, your choices are limited. Interstate moves are regulated by the Federal Motor Carriers Safety Administration (FMCSA), www.dot.fmcsa.gov, an agency under the Department of Transportation, with whom you can file a complaint against a carrier. While their role in the regulation of interstate carriers historically has been concerned with safety issues rather than consumer issues, in response to the upsurge in unscrupulous movers and unhappy consumers, they have issued a recent set of rules "specifying how interstate household goods (HHG) carriers (movers) and brokers must assist their individual customers shipping household goods." According to their consumer page, carriers in violation of said rules can be fined, and repeat offenders may be barred from doing business. In terms of loss however, "FMCSA does not have statutory authority to resolve loss and damage of consumer complaints, settle disputes against a mover, or obtain reimbursement for consumers seeking payment for specific charges. Consumers are responsible for resolving disputes involving these household goods matters." They are not able to represent you in an arbitration dispute to recover damages for lost or destroyed property, nor enforce a court judgment. If you have a grievance, your best bet is to file a complaint against a mover with FMCSA (call 888-DOT-SAFT or go online to www.1-888-dot-saft.com) and with the Better Business Bureau, www.bbb.org, in the state where the moving company is licensed, as well as with that state's attorney general or consumer protection office. To seek redress, hire an attorney.

STORAGE WAREHOUSES

Storage facilities may be required when you have to ship your furniture without an apartment to receive it or if your apartment is too small for all your belongings. If your mover maintains storage warehouse facilities in the city, as many do, you may want to store with them. Some even offer one month's free storage. Most warehouses are in Queens, Brooklyn, or New Jersey. Look in the Yellow Pages under "Storage Warehouses" and shop around for the best and most convenient deal. Below we list two major moving/storage companies. Listing here does *not* imply endorsement by First Books.

- **Approved Moving and Storage**, 718-622-2660, www.approved movers.com; has a fireproof warehouse in Brooklyn. Estimates are based on the number of rooms of furniture and household goods to be stored.
- **Moishe's**, 800-536-6564, www.moishes.com, has warehousing in Brooklyn and in Long Island City, for goods hauled by their trucks and those of others. They also own self-storage facilities in Manhattan and Queens.

The **New York City Department of Consumer Affairs** licenses storage—but not self-storage—warehouses. Dissatisfied? Call the city's all-purpose complaint number, 311.

SELF-STORAGE

The ability to rent anything from 3' x 3' lockers to small storage rooms is a great boon to urban dwellers. Collectors, people with old clothes they can't bear to give away, and those with possessions that won't fit in a sublet or shared apartment all find mini-warehouses a solution to too-small living spaces.

Rates for space in Manhattan self-storage facilities are competitive: expect to pay at least $70 a month for a locker 4' x 4' x 7', $175 a month for an 8' x 8' x 8' space, and so on. Some offer free pick-up, otherwise you or your mover delivers the goods. If you're looking for lower rates, check the prices for storage units located in the suburbs and boroughs other than Manhattan.

As you shop around, you may want to check the facility for cleanliness and security. Does the building have sprinklers in case of fire? Do they have carts and hand trucks for moving in and out? Do they bill monthly, or will they automatically charge the bill to your credit card? Access should be 24-hour or nearly so, and some are air conditioned, an asset if you plan to visit your locker in the summer.

Finally, a word of warning: unless you no longer want your stored belongings, pay your storage bill and pay it on time. Storage companies may auction the contents of delinquent customers' lockers.

Here are a few area self-storage companies. For more options, check the Yellow Pages under "Self-Storage."

- **Chelsea Mini Storage**, 626 West 28th Street, Manhattan 10001, 877-902-9751, www.chelsea-mini-storage.com; also offers moving services.
- **Manhattan Mini Storage**, 212-786-7243 and 212-255-0482, www.manhattanministorage.com; with 13 locations including: 520 West 17th Street corner of Tenth Avenue, 524 West 23rd Street, 600 West 58th Street corner of Eleventh Avenue, and 570 Riverside Drive, corner of 134th Street, among others. Offers private storage rooms from 5' x 5' to 10' x 25' (the size of some NYC studio apartments).
- **Public Storage**, 800-447-8673, www.publicstorage.com; facilities in Brooklyn and New Jersey
- **Storage Deluxe**, 800-869-7605, www.storagedeluxe.com; three Bronx storage locations, plus one on Long Island and one in Connecticut.
- **Storage USA**, www.sus.com; facilities in Manhattan, Brooklyn, and Queens
- **U-haul Moving and Storage** has a mini-warehouse located at 562 West 23rd Street, 212-620-4177, www.uhaul.com, with rooms 4' x 8'

for $65 and 8' x 12' for $175, as well as facilities in Brooklyn, The Bronx and Queens, among others.

CHILDREN

Studies show that moving, especially frequent moving, can be hard on children. According to an American Medical Association study, children who move often are more likely to suffer from such problems as depression, low self-esteem and aggression. Often their academic performance suffers as well. Aside from not moving more than is necessary, there are a few things you can do to help your children through this stressful time:

- Talk about the move with your kids. Be honest but positive. Listen to their concerns. To the extent possible, involve them in the process.
- Make sure children have their favorite possessions with them on the trip; don't pack "blankey" in the moving van.
- Make sure you have some social life planned on the other end. Your children may feel lonely in your new home and such activities can ease the transition. If you move during the summer you might find a local camp (check with the YMHA or YMCA) in which they can sign up for a couple of weeks in August to make some new friends.
- Keep in touch with family and loved ones as much as possible. Photos and phone calls are important ways of maintaining links to the important people you have left behind.
- If your children are school age, take the time to involve yourself in their new school and in their academic life. Don't let them fall through the cracks.
- Try to schedule a move during the summer so they can start the new school year at the beginning of the term.
- If possible, spend some time in the area prior to the move doing fun things, such visiting a local playground or playing ball in a local park or checking out the neighborhood stores with teenagers. With any luck they will meet some other kids their own age.

For children ages 6-11, ***The Moving Book: A Kids' Survival Guide*** by Gabriel Davis is a wonderful gift. For general guidance, read ***Smart Moves: Your Guide Through the Emotional Maze of Relocation*** by Nadia Jensen, Audrey McCollum, and Stuart Copans.

TAXES

If your move is work-related, some or all of your moving expenses may be tax-deductible—so you may want to keep those receipts. Though eligibility varies, depending, for example, on whether you have a job or are self-employed, generally, the cost of moving yourself, your family, and your belongings is tax deductible, even if you don't itemize. The criteria: in order to take the deduction your move must be employment-related, your new job must be more than 50 miles away from your current residence, and you must be at your new home for at least 39 weeks during the first 12 months after your arrival. If you take the deduction and then fail to meet the requirements, you will have to pay the IRS back, unless you were laid off through no fault of your own or transferred again by your employer. It's probably a good idea to consult a tax expert regarding IRS rules related to moving. However, if you're a confident soul, get a copy of IRS Form 3903 (www.irs.gov) and do it yourself!

ADDITIONAL RELOCATION AND MOVING INFORMATION

- **www.firstbooks.com**; relocation resources and information on moving to Atlanta, Boston, Chicago, Los Angeles, Minneapolis-St. Paul, San Francisco, Seattle, Washington, D.C., as well as London, England.
- *How to Move Handbook* by Clyde and Shari Steiner; an excellent general guidebook
- **http://houseandhome.msn.com**; online quotes
- **www.allamericanmovers.com**, 800-989-6683; online quotes
- **www.american-car-transport.com**; if you need help moving your car
- **www.erc.org**, the Employee Relocation Council, a professional organization, offers members specialized reports on the relocation and moving industries.
- **www.homestore.com**
- **www.usps.com**, relocation information from the United States Postal Service.

AFTER FINDING YOUR NEW PLACE OF RESIDENCE, YOUR FIRST ORDER of business probably will be opening a bank account. The following information about personal savings and checking accounts, credit unions, and credit cards and credit resources should make the task less daunting. And, for your edification come April 15, we've included information about federal, state, and city income tax procedures, as well as details for those wanting to start or move a business.

BANK ACCOUNTS AND SERVICES

While most people tend to choose their bank for its location, services, interest rates, and minimum balance requirements can be important determinants as well. If the services a bank offers are more important to you than location, particularly now that ATMs provide easy access to cash and account information outside the branch, be sure to shop around for the best deals for your banking needs. The city's two largest retail banks, Citibank and JP Morgan Chase & Co., operate more than 100 branches in Manhattan alone, plus more in the outer boroughs. However, fees at large interstate banks can be significantly higher than smaller banks. The Yellow Pages contain some five pages of financial institutions. Below, we list eight banks with multiple branches. When deciding which one to choose, consider branch locations and hours of operation. Some banks are now open seven days a week:

- **Citibank**, 212-627-3999, www.citibank.com
- **Commerce Bank**, 888-751-9000
- **JP Morgan Chase & Co.**, 800-CHASE-24, www.chase.com
- **Merchants Bank of New York**, 212-973-6600
- **Apple Bank**, 800-722-6888, www.theapplebank.com
- **Fleet**, 800-841-4000, www.fleet.com

- **HSBC**, formerly Marine Midland, 800-975-4722, www.hsbc.com
- **Republic National**, 718-488-4050, www.republicbank.com

Technology has transformed banking and continues to do so daily. Most banks offer the option of banking via your home computer, although the majority of customers still feel more comfortable banking the old fashioned way. What's more, traditional distinctions between commercial banks, savings banks, and brokerage houses have become blurred. And financial software has crossed all these lines. In this fluid situation, "It's a consumer's market," says one bank officer.

Services offered by financial institutions include, but are not limited to, the following:

- **Checking**; take a completed application—two references are required, usually the name of your current bank and that of your employer—to the branch where you intend to bank, together with two signed pieces of identification: driver's license, credit card, student ID with photo. Some banks require a minimum start-up deposit. Your account can be opened immediately, but checks and deposit slips won't be issued until your signature is verified. "Regular" non-interest-bearing personal checking accounts typically carry no charges as long as a minimum daily balance is maintained. A certificate of deposit, money market or savings account linked to your regular checking account may also get you free checking. Institutions offering interest-earning NOW checking accounts charge a fee if the accounts fall below required minimum balances. Generally, **debit cards** are issued automatically to new customers. Most can be used to make withdrawals through the nationwide network of CIRRUS and NYCE ATMs and can be used at retail outlets to pay for goods and services, debiting your checking account directly. You can arrange to have your paycheck go straight to your checking account via direct deposit. Be sure to inquire about fees and shop around before opening a checking account.
- **Savings**; follow the procedures detailed above for checking accounts to apply for a "statement" savings account, which provides monthly statements of all transactions and can be linked to your checking account. Most banks require an average minimum balance of at least $1,500 to avoid maintenance charges. Again, inquire about fees.
- Today, it is rare when a bank does not offer **online banking**. Generally, this includes simple balance and other account information, making transfers, paying bills, and even applying for loans from the comfort of your own home. Security should be a chief concern when accessing your private financial information over the internet. While banks should encrypt your personal information and password, the user should also take standard precautions as well. Don't share your

password with anyone, and change it often; don't send confidential information through e-mail or over unsecured web space; and restrict your banking interactions to private computers—not a work computer with a shared network or at an internet café. Online access services and fees may vary from bank to bank, so check with individual institutions for information. Sometimes access is directly through the bank's web site; sometimes you'll first need to download a program or use specialized banking software.

- **Banking by phone**; a touch-tone telephone gives access to all the banking services performed by an ATM, except deposits and cash withdrawals: you can check account balances and make transfers between accounts. For a small monthly charge (or free with a minimum combined balance of, say, $10,000) the bank will make scheduled bill payments such as rent, mortgage or car payments, as well as payments on request to designated payees such as stores, credit card companies, and utilities. A year-end annual statement may be provided on request. Again, inquire about the latest refinements and fees, if any.

CREDIT UNIONS

According to the **National Credit Union Administration (NCUA)**, "A federal credit union is a nonprofit, cooperative financial institution owned and run by its members." Organized to serve, democratically controlled credit unions provide their members with a safe place to save and borrow at reasonable rates. Members pool their funds to make loans to one-another. The volunteer board that runs each credit union is elected by the members. According to *American Banker*'s annual survey, credit unions continually rank high in customer satisfaction. Because credit unions limit membership based on set criteria, you'll need to investigate a few for a match. Organizations such as employers, unions, professional associations, churches, and schools (alumni associations) typically provide membership. A few, such as the **Lower East Side Peoples' Federal Credit Union**, 37 Avenue B, NYC 10009, 212-529-8197, www.lespfcu.com, have community charters enabling them to serve anyone who works or lives in that community. And some, such as the **Progressive Credit Union** at 370 Seventh Avenue, NYC 10021, 212-695-8900, www.progressivecu.org, might contact your employer with an offer of free credit union services for company employees, which would qualify you. Credit unions lack the convenience of multiple branches but offer considerable financial benefit in exchange. For a complete list of local credit unions or information about them, you can visit the **National Association of Credit Union Service Organizations**, www.nacuso.org, or the **NCUA**, http://ncua.gov.

CONSUMER COMPLAINTS—BANKING

Federal and state governments regulate bank policies on discrimination, credit, anti-redlining, truth-in-lending, etc. If you have a problem, you should first attempt to resolve the issue directly with the bank. Should you need to **file a formal complaint** against your financial institution, you can do so through the Board of Governors of the **Federal Reserve System, Division of Consumer and Community Affairs**. For specifics, call 202-452-3693 or go to www.federalreserve.gov/pubs/complaints/. You can also pursue the issue with the following agencies:

- Nationally chartered commercial banks go through the **US Comptroller of the Currency**, Customer Assistance Group, 1301 McKinney Street, Suite 3710, Houston, TX 77010, 800-613-6743, www.occ.treas.gov.
- **US Office of Thrift Supervision**, 1700 G Street NW, Washington, D.C. 20552, 202-906-6000, www.ots.treas.gov; for thrift institutions insured by the Savings Association Insurance Fund and/or federally chartered (i.e., members of the Federal Home Loan Bank System).
- For federally chartered credit unions or state chartered credit unions with federal insurance, contact the **National Credit Union Administration**, 9 Washington Square, Washington Avenue Extension, Albany, NY 12205, 518-862-7400, www.ncua.gov.

CREDIT CARDS

On the off chance that your mailbox hasn't been filled with credit card applications, you can call to request one. Many cards now offer various "rewards" as incentives to use them, the most common being frequent flyer miles. Shop around for the one that best suits your needs.

- **American Express**, 800-528-4800, www.amex.com; once famous for issuing charge cards that must be paid off every month, American Express now offers nearly two dozen different cards, including credit cards and airline affinity cards that accumulate frequent-flyer miles. With the exception of a student card, all Amex cards have minimum income requirements, and all but the Optima True Grace Card charge annual fees.
- **Diner's Club**, 800-234-6377, www.dinersclub.com; with annual fees and income requirements, the Diner's Club card is accepted mainly in travel and hospitality circles; cardholders have access to special amenities at most major airports.
- **Discover/Novus**, 800-347-2683, www.discovercard.com; Discover cards and affiliated Novus/Private Issue cards offer an annual rebate based on the amount you charge, and some plans let you accumulate credit at various hotels or retail chains.

- **VISA** and **MasterCard** can be obtained from a variety of financial service organizations, usually banks. Interest rates vary, annual fees may even be waived, and many cards offer frequent flyer miles. It pays to shop around, especially if you don't pay off your balance every month.
- **Department store credit cards** can offer advantages over other forms of payment: advance notice of sales, mail or phone orders, no annual fee. Accounts may be approved instantly upon application. Macy's and Bloomingdales cards are popular among New York shoppers.

For a handy way to compare rates and to learn more about credit cards, visit **bankrate.com**. **Cardweb.com** is an online directory of credit cards; search or browse by interest rates, fees, special offers, or affinity features such as frequent-flyer miles or charity donations based on the amount you charge. The same information can be retrieved by phone at 800-344-7714. And finally, you can visit the personal finance section of **epinions.com** for customer reviews of specific institutions' credit cards.

BANKING & CREDIT RESOURCES

For a list of articles about trends in banking and links to the Federal Trade Commission and other consumer protection agencies, visit the **National Institute for Consumer Education** web site at www.nice.emich.edu. To look up current interest rates on deposits, go to www.rate.net or www.bankrate.com.

If you're buying a car or boat, renovating your new fixer-upper, or sending the kids to college, you can still shop for loans the old-fashioned way, using the Yellow Pages and the financial section of the newspaper, but the internet can make the job a lot easier. Online loan calculators let you experiment with different payment plans. There are several loan calculators on bankrate.com but you can look at other sites as well:

- **www.myfico.com**
- **www.411-loans.com**
- **Eloan**, www.eloan.com
- **Financial Power Tools**, http://financialpowertools.com
- **Women's Financial Network**, www.wfn.com
- **The Motley Fool**, www.fool.com (an excellent place to learn about money, investing and banking. They offer online seminars, well-written articles, and an active discussion board.)

Obtain copies of your **credit report** from the three major credit bureaus at **www.icreditreport.com**. Avoid ordering your credit report more than once a year, as frequent requests could adversely affect your credit rating.

INCOME TAXES

Heralded by freshly painted H&R Block signs and black-bordered boxes in the newspapers warning "Only 10 more days to file your income tax returns," April 15 arrives promptly every 365 days. In New York City, the Internal Revenue Service and New York Department of Taxation and Finance provide literature and taxpayer information services via telephone. In case you did not know it before moving here, the bad news is that New York City takes a yearly income tax bite out of your earnings, along with the state and federal government. The good news is that it is not the highest taxed state in the country.

- **Federal income tax** forms can be obtained by calling 800-829-3676; they are also available in most Post Offices and libraries at tax time. Call 800-829-1040 to obtain explanatory literature as well as answers to specific questions, such as which of the three tax forms—1040EZ, 1040A or 1040—you should use. Many opt to visit the IRS's helpful web site www.irs.gov, where you can find answers to tax questions as well as downloadable tax forms and information on filing electronically. The staff at the Internal Revenue Service office (hours are weekdays 7:30 a.m. to 4:30 p.m.) downtown at 120 Church Street provides instruction in the fine art of calculating your federal income tax but won't do it for you.
- **New York State and New York City** use a combined income tax form. If you have not received forms by mail, call 800-462-8100 to order. If you use either IRS 1040EZ or 1040A, choose the IT 100, which you fill in and let the state tax people calculate for you, or the IT 200, which you calculate yourself. For those filing the Federal 1040 long form, you'll need the IT 201. The number for taxpayer assistance in New York State is 800-CALL-TAX. A number of federal forms are available at the IRS web site, www.irs.gov, and New York State tax forms can be downloaded from www.tax.state.ny.us/forms/. Your federal adjusted gross income is the tax base for state and city taxes. New York State taxable income is calculated by adding and subtracting various New York State "modifications" and then the New York City Resident's income tax is based on your state taxable income. New Jersey residents can get tax information and download state tax forms from www.state.nj.us/treasury/taxation/.

ONLINE FILING AND ASSISTANCE

Filing your taxes online can save you time, especially if you already keep your personal financial records using compatible software such as Turbot, Quicken or Quickbooks. Visit www.irs.gov/elec_svs for details, including a list of companies that make tax software. For some, it may be advisable to get assistance in calculating and preparing your tax return. See the Yellow Pages under "Tax Returns" if you do not have a tax preparation firm recommendation from an acquaintance, or look up the nearest H & R Block location. Remember to keep all receipts, be prepared to spend some time, and don't show up on April 14th. Questions? Call the IRS helpline, 800-829-1040, to speak to an IRS representative. Automated information is available 24/7 at 800-829-4477; this is also the number to call to find out the status of your return if you have filed and have been waiting more than four weeks, or you can visit the IRS web site: www.irs.gov.

If you need help with a tax problem or are suffering some hardship due to the tax law, you can contact the **Taxpayer Advocate Service**, an independent agency within the IRS designed to help taxpayers resolve tax problems; contact them at www.irs.gov/advocate.

Taxpayer assistance in filing on paper or electronically is available for simple returns at no cost at Manhattan IRS offices: 290 Broadway, 110 West 44th Street and 55 West 125th Street; Bronx IRS: 3000 White Plains Boulevard; Brooklyn IRS: 625 Fulton Street; Queens office: 1 Lefrak City at 59-17 Junction Boulevard in Rego Park, Queens. No appointment is necessary at these sites, which are open Monday-Friday, 8 a.m. to 4:30 p.m., but don't wait until April, unless you like standing in long lines. Assistance in preparing and filing returns, electronically at some sites, is provided by volunteers under the **VITA (Volunteer Income Tax Assistance)** program throughout the city and in New Jersey. To find the site nearest you call 800-829-1040 (customer assistance hotline).

For questions concerning New York State income tax call the **New York State Department of Taxation and Finance**, 800-225-5829.

STARTING OR MOVING A BUSINESS

A Deloitte and Touche survey found that, in terms of taxes, New York City ranked as the second most expensive city in the country in which to operate a small business. But if proximity to power, money, and a diverse and deep talent pool is important to you, then New York City can't be beat as a place to locate a business. You need to do a great deal of research before setting up shop in New York City. Competition is fierce and customer expectations are high. Things like "family friendly," "good customer service" and "flexibility" are among the ingredients necessary to be a successful business owner in New York City.

If you are looking to set up a business that does not need to be based in Manhattan (such as phone sales, mail order or manufacturing) you will find more space for your money by heading into Brooklyn, Queens, or neighboring New Jersey. Unless a Manhattan presence will help your business, you might want to avoid high office rents.

If you are setting up shop, you may choose to hire an attorney who is familiar with the process, but if you want to begin your research on your own, the following resources should help you get the ball rolling:

- **Association of the Bar of the City of New York**, Legal Referral Service, 212-382-6600, www.abcny.org
- **Better Business Bureau**, www.newyork.bbb.org
- **Business to Business Yellow Pages**, which lists all wholesalers and manufacturers, is free of charge and can be obtained by calling your local telephone office. Call 800-426-8686 to order.
- **Internal Revenue Service**, 800-829-1040, with whom you will need to talk to get an employer tax ID number.
- **New York City Department of Finance Home Page**, www.ci. nyc.ny.us/finance
- **New York Department of State, Division of Corporations**, 41 State Street, Albany, NY 12231, 518-473-2492, www.dos.state.ny.us; in order to incorporate in New York, you must first reserve a name here (do an advance name search). You can obtain information and fee schedules regarding filing for C Corporation, S Corporation, Limited Liability Company, or Limited Partnership status. Discuss your options first with your attorney and/or accountant.
- **US Small Business Administration home page**, www sba.gov; from counseling and training to start up guidelines to SBA loans, the SBA is ideal for finding small business information.

ET'S SEE. YOU'VE SIGNED A LEASE OR MORTGAGE PAPERS AND opened a bank account. So now, keys in hand, it's time to have utilities connected, telephone installed, and to choose your cable and internet service providers. You can make yourself at home once you can cook and call, and really feel like a local once you possess a library card, are registered to vote, and have found a doctor. Here are some of the important how-to's.

UTILITIES

CONSOLIDATED EDISON

Call **Consolidated Edison's** customer service to have gas and electricity turned on: 800-75-CON-ED. In New Jersey, call **PSE&G (Public Service Electric and Gas**), 800-436-7734, for service. A personal visit from either is not necessary unless the prior tenant's service was cut off for non-payment. Expect to wait at least one business day before service commences; note that PSE&G is open for new accounts Monday-Friday only. Deposits are no longer required for residential accounts unless a credit check indicates the need.

TELEPHONE

You have several choices for local and long distance phone service in New York City, and many of the companies that offer local service also offer long distance. Verizon (the largest local carrier), AT&T, MCI, Sprint, and RCN Communications (in Manhattan and Queens on a building by building basis) all offer local and long distance service and are among the many companies offering internet, cellular, and digital service. Cable television giants are also now offering telephone and internet service in the form of bundled telecommunications over their fiber optic cables. When calling to inquire about service, ask about weekday, evening, and weekend rates, specials, and the costs of installation. Whichever local phone service you choose, you will be offered a bouquet of extra features, each carrying an extra monthly fee, among them: Call Waiting (the most popular), Call Forwarding, Call Answering, Voice Dialing, Call Return, 3-Way Calling, and Caller ID. If you are looking to set up DSL service for your computer, inquire about the additional cost and ask about special deals.

In New York, widely used **long distance service providers** also provide local service. To institute new **local service** contact: **Verizon**, 212-890-2550, www.verizon.com; **AT&T**, 800-222-0300, www.att.com; **Sprint**, 800-877-7746, www.sprint.com; **MCI**, 800-444-3333, www.mci. com; or **RCN**, 800-891-7770, www.rcn.com.

Verizon no longer requires a deposit from most customers; when required, the deposit accumulates interest and is refunded after a year. MCI and RCN typically require a credit check but no deposit. The set-up charges for all phone companies will vary depending on your needs. For example, if you need additional jacks you will pay more. It is advantageous to ask the superintendent or someone who works in the building where the phone lines come into the building. This will expedite the process of getting phone service.

For help comparing long distance calling plans see below. **Bundling** is the current buzzword in communications: i.e., charging one rate on one bill for two or more services, for example for long distance calls made from home phones and internet or cable television service. Other service plan variables include volume discounts, monthly minimums, and overseas service. Check around.

A word about **slamming**, being switched to a different long distance carrier without your knowledge or consent, or **cramming**, charges billed to you for calls you did not make: while these practices have been largely eliminated in recent years, should you notice such discrepancies on your bill you should contact your local service provider and report the problem. The next step is to report the offense to the FCC, should you wish to do so, 888-225-5322 or their consumer assistance number at 202-418-0200. To inform the New York Public Service Commission, call 800-342-3377 or contact the New York State Consumer Protection Board at 800-NYS-1220, or better yet, consult their extensive web site, www.consumer.state.ny.us, an encyclopedically useful resource covering every conceivable consumer problem, including slamming and cramming. Web sites for the Federal Trade Commission, www.ftc.gov, and for the Federal Communications Commission, www.fcc.gov, have tips on combating cramming. (See **Rip-off Recourse** in **Helpful Services** for more on consumer protection.)

TELEPHONE DIRECTORIES

Most New Yorkers aren't aware of how much good information can be found in the city's telephone books. The **White Pages** includes extensive listings of community service numbers as well as government listings and an emergency care guide. The **Yellow Pages** is almost in itself a guide to doing business or getting whatever you need in New York City. Seek it as a reference for historical sites and landmarks, public transportation maps, a yearly calendar of events, and even sports stadiums and concert hall seating charts! The **Business to Business Yellow Pages**, which lists all wholesalers and manufacturers, is free of charge and can be obtained by calling your local telephone office.

In today's web-oriented world, **directory assistance** does not have to cost a lot of money. Numerous sites are dedicated to providing telephone listings and web sites, including:

- **Verizon's Super Pages** at www.bigbook.com
- **www.anywho.com** (AT&T's site, includes searches for toll-free numbers)
- **www.infospace.com**
- **www.optonline.net** (from Cablevision has a link to their own yellow pages)
- **www.people.yahoo.com**
- **www.smartpages.com** (from Sprint)
- **www.switchboard.com**
- **www.whowhere.lycos.com**
- **www.worldpages.com**

Dialing 411 for directory assistance is available, for $1.25 plus tax (more for out of state directory assistance). You can also call either 212-555-1212 or 718-555-1212; each call costs 80 cents. Information about city related services is available by dialing 311 (outside New York City, 212-639-9675). Operators are ready to assist 24/7.

AREA CODES

Until recently, all Manhattan was in area code 212, while the other boroughs were in area code 718. Now, new landline phones in Manhattan are given area code 646, and in Manhattan and the boroughs, area code 917 generally serves wireless phones and beepers. Boroughs previously reached at 718 have been extended code 347; and 631 has been added to 516 on Long Island; in New Jersey, part of the 201 area, South Orange for example, has become 973; Westchester remains primarily 914. Until recently, you only needed to dial area codes when dialing between boroughs. Now, all calls within New York City require 11-digit dialing: "one," plus the area code, plus the seven-digit number.

CELL PHONES

Cell phone technology continues to change rapidly, and costs are falling, so much in fact, that some users have dispensed with landlines altogether. If you are considering a cell phone purchase, find out as much as possible before signing a contract. Better yet, try to find a service that does not require a long-term contract. And be sure to determine whether the cell phone you want to purchase is only operable if you subscribe to a particular service plan. The Better Business Bureau, www.bbb.org, has a page on their web site dedicated to complaints against cell phone service providers.

Currently, six major companies provide cellular service in the metropolitan area:

- **AT&T Wireless**, 800-IMAGINE, www.attws.com
- **MCI**, 800-444-2222, www.mci.com
- **Nextel**, 800-639-8359, www.nextel.com
- **Sprint PCS**, 800-480-4PCS, www.sprintpcs.com
- **Verizon**, 800-256-4646, www.verizonwireless.com
- **T-Mobile**, 800-937-8997, www.t-mobile.com

If you want to compare long distance pricing, go to **SmartPrice** at www.smartprice.com or call 877-550-5317, Monday-Friday 7 a.m. to 7 p.m. CST. You will be asked questions regarding your phone usage, your area code, and the first 3 digits of your phone number, and then be provided with a free analysis of the carriers available in your area. Or contact **Telecommunications Research and Action Center** (**TRAC**); unaffiliated with the communications industry, TRAC is a consumer organization that compares long distance and wireless calling plans and prices: www.trac.org, 202-263-2950.

INTERNET SERVICE PROVIDERS

Choices in internet service providers (ISPs) in the metro area are numerous, varied, and changing rapidly as technology advances. Newspaper ads occasionally offer deals.

When picking your provider, be sure to call around, as plans and pricing vary. Some ISPs currently available in the metropolitan area are:

- **America Online**, 800-827-6364, www.aol.com
- **AT&T WorldNet**, 800-967-5363, www.att.com/net
- **Compuserve**, 800-848-8199, www.compuserve.com
- **Earthlink**, 800-719-4332, www.earthlink.net
- **Juno**, 877-665-9995, www.juno.com
- **MSN**, 800-386-5550, www.msn.com
- **NetZero**, 877-665-9995, www.netzero.com

- **SBC Internet Services**, 800-776-3449
- **RCN**, 800-RING-RCN, www.rcn.com
- **Verizon**, 888-638-6100, www.verizon.com; offers wireless internet coverage

And now, **broadband**, high-speed (almost) always-on internet connection via cable, telephone, or satellite. Cable TV subscribers can access this speedy connection for about $40 monthly, plus the cost of installing the cable modem; non-TV subscribers will pay more. Call **TimeWarner Cable**, 212-674-9100, or go to www.twcnyc.com; in Brooklyn and The Bronx call **Cablevision**, 718-252-3700; Jersey City, 201-217-0800, www.optimumonline; or **RCN**, 800-891-7770, www.rcn.com. **DSL** delivers high-speed internet connection over regular phone lines without disrupting simultaneous phone service. Where available, it costs $40-$50 per month usually with a one-time installation charge, but there may be a bundling advantage if you buy the service from your phone service provider. Go to www.dslreports.com to evaluate local plans. If this service is important to you, when looking for a place to live, be sure to inquire about which service is available in prospective apartments you are viewing. Where neither is available, satellite service may be the answer; for which, you will need to pay for the installation of a special dish antenna and receiver. Two-way satellite service is available through StarBand ("if you can see the southern sky, you can get StarBand"), 800-4Starband, www.starband.com. The other metropolitan area provider is Direcway at 800-347-3272, www.direcway.com.

CITY WATER

Considering the quantity of commercially bottled water consumed by its residents, you might think that New York City water is either unpalatable or unsafe. In fact, city water, which flows from vast supply systems north of the city in Westchester, the Catskills, and the Delaware River watershed, is both safe and exceptionally tasty when compared to water in other cities. Except in the infrequent years of extreme drought, the supply is ample and unrationed. Tenants are not charged for water but are encouraged to avoid water waste, especially in the summer months.

A slight rust-colored tint appears occasionally in water drawn from the Croton system (10% of the total water supply), caused by a bloom of microorganisms, which are tasteless and harmless, if unappealing. If the pipes have not been used for a while when you first move into your new apartment, let the water run for about ten minutes to clear out rust and the water will then be fine. Filtration of this water system, soon to be completed, should prevent discoloration. Questions about water quality or about the water system should be addressed to the **NYC Department of Environmental Protection**, Bureau of Public and Intergovernmental Affairs, 59-17 Junction Boulevard, Corona, NY 11368. Or contact the department's 24-hour Communications Center through the city's new 311 information line, where you can also address concerns about air quality, noise, hazardous materials, sewers or any number of city related problems. Visit the Department of Environmental Protection at www.nyc. gov/dep or contact them through the city's 311 call center.

Most of the eastern and northern parts of New Jersey, closest to New York City, are served by **United Water New Jersey**, www.unitedwater.com/uwnj. Problems/concerns are handled by their customer service center, 190 Moore Street, Hackensack, NJ 07601, 800-422-5987; emergencies: 800-422-5987.

For more on area water quality, go to the EPA's site, www.epa.gov, and read their guidelines on microbiological contaminants. Or call the **Safe Drinking Water Hotline**, 800-426-4791.

GARBAGE AND RECYCLING

Garbage service is provided by the city and is collected curbside in covered garbage cans or secured black plastic bags two to three times a week, depending on your location. Bulk trash, such as furniture and appliances, is picked up on the last day of regular garbage collection weekly. Garbage disposal for those living in large apartment buildings will most likely entail locating the trash chute in your hall. Check with your building super with any questions. To find out the pick-up days for your neighborhood call 311. (People in private homes in the boroughs, Westchester, and Long Island will need to supply their own trashcans and move them to the curb on specific pick-up days.)

Recycling is a part of life in New York City and, as with garbage collection, the service is provided by the city. Pick up is weekly and is scheduled on one of your garbage collection days. Items to be recycled include paper: writing, copier, construction paper, glossy paper, envelopes, junk mail, postcards, smooth cardboard, wrapping paper, paperback books, and flattened boxes (no carbon paper, candy wrappers, take-out containers, napkins, paper towels, or hardcover books); glass; metal, including empty metal cans, aluminum foil trays, and general household items and appliances that are at least 50% metal; and number one and number two plastics. FYI: returnable bottles and cans should be redeemed; in many neighborhoods they can be left neatly outside for the homeless to collect: often, it's their living. Or contact We Can, a non-profit group that collects redeemable bottles and cans from businesses and apartment buildings, donating all proceeds to the homeless. For more information, call 212-262-2222.

For drivers with a New York driver's license and registration, the sanitation department operates self-help bulk sites (for large items) in four boroughs; call 311 for locations and hours. The Sanitation Department's "Digest of Codes," outlines regulations, penalties, and procedures for trash deposal. For more specifics, visit the department's web site, www.nyc.gov/sanitation. Fines for improper trash disposal range from $25 to over $250.

In New Jersey, garbage collection and recycling is provided municipally. The department to call for these services and the telephone number are listed here:

- **Edgewater**: Department of Public Works/Recycling, 201-943-2626
- **Fort Lee**: Department of Public Works, 201-592-3634
- **Hoboken**: Hoboken Environmental Services, 201-420-2385
- **Jersey City**: Waste Management, 201-435-1345
- **Weehawken**: Department of Recycling, 201-319-6070

CONSUMER COMPLAINTS—UTILITIES

If you have problems with a utility company (gas, electric, phones, water, steam, cable TV) you can contact the New York State Public Service Commission. By law, the commission is responsible for setting rates and ensuring that the public receives adequate service. You can file a complaint on the internet at www.dps.state.ny.us/complaintdept.html or by calling one of several hotlines including (contact New York Relay Service at 800-662-1220 for TDD assistance with these hotlines):

- **New York Public Service Commission's** helpline: 888-697-7728; regulates telephone, cable TV, and energy utilities
- **Gas** or **Electric service shutoff hotline**: 800-342-3355

In New Jersey, contact **PSE&G** at 800-436-7734. If you have any questions about your rights as a consumer, you can also call the **New Jersey Board of Public Utilities** (**BPU**), which is responsible for regulating natural gas, water, telecommunications, and cable television, and for handling customer complaints: 800-221-0051 or 800-624-0241.

PRINT AND BROADCAST MEDIA

TELEVISION

LOCAL NETWORK CHANNELS

In Manhattan, you'll need cable to get any reception. In the boroughs, you can get away without cable, but reception will not be great. The major networks in New York City are: Channel 2—WCBS; Channel 4—WNBC; Channel 5—WNYW (Fox); Channel 7—WABC; Channel 9—WOR, the UPN Network during prime time hours (otherwise local programming); Channel 11—WPIX, offers the WB Network during prime time evening hours (otherwise local programming). Two PBS channels are available: Channel 13—WNET (Public Broadcasting System) and Channel 21—WLIW (Long Island's public network channel). They broadcast similar PBS programming but at different times.

You'll find weekly programs for the broadcast channels as well as cable channels (including HBO, Showtime and the like) printed in *TV Guide* and the Sunday *New York Times'* "Television" section. This supplement also carries a complete "Station Guide" detailing the ownership and/or focus of broadcast and cable stations.

CABLE TELEVISION AND THE DISH

Expanded programming and famous skyscrapers make cable an attractive and often necessary option in New York City. Like the telecommunications industry, the cable industry is in the throes of change. Currently, service in Manhattan is provided by Time Warner and RCN. The boroughs are covered by Time Warner and Cablevision, which also serves Queens, Long Island, and Westchester; Staten Island Cable is the sole server on Staten Island. The eastern and northern portions of New Jersey, closest to New York, are handled primarily by Cablevision New Jersey and Comcast.

If your building isn't already wired, the owner or manager must request hookup, which has been known to take anywhere from several months to a year. In Manhattan, call **Time Warner Cable**, 212-674-9100 or go to www.twcnyc.com; for **RCN** service, dial 800-RING-RCN, or go to www.rcn.com. Queens and Brooklyn call **Time Warner Cable** at 718-358-0900; The Bronx and Brooklyn call **Cablevision** at 718-617-3500, www.cablevision.com; **Staten Island Cable** is at 718-816-8686, www.statenislandcable.com.

The latest alternative to lousy reception via the rabbit ears and the tyranny of the cable companies is **direct broadcast satellite (DBS)**, more commonly known as "the dish." DBS provides the clearest reception available and hundreds of channels, now including the local channels, though only if you are in a position suitable for mounting an 18- to 36-inch dish outside your home, a difficult proposition for most Manhattanites. Basically, you'll need to own your building so you can use the roof—or have a southwest-facing balcony on which to mount the thing, and there can be no taller building to block the signal from the southwest. Clearly, TV junkies in the outer boroughs and the suburbs, where buildings are lower and spread out, have the advantage here. Currently two DBS signal providers compete in the metropolitan area: **DirecTV**, 800-347-3288, www.directv.com, and **Dish Network**, 800-333-3474, www.dishnetwork.com. You buy the receiver and dish, pay a one-time installation fee, and a monthly programming fee. Watch for occasional ads in the *Times* offering free installation with a one-year programming contract.

Along with pay cable networks such as HBO, Showtime, and Cinemax, plus numerous basic cable offerings, New York City has several of its own channels including New York One, which provides round the clock New York news, weather, and information for Time Warner customers, and The YES Network, owned and operated by the New York Yankees, among others. Public access also allows for several channels to be set aside for pay-as-you-go programming, most of which is less than mediocre and some of which is more than a bit risqué.

RADIO

RADIO STATIONS

Music lovers are best served by their FM dials; news and talk shows dominate the AM band. However, on either broadcast frequency most stations specialize further still, emphasizing one specific format. Check below to find your station. For program details, consult *Time Out New York's* "Radio" page, which is particularly good; The *New York Times'* daily "Radio Highlights;" and "Radio Highlights" in *New York* magazine's "Cue" entertainment guide.

AM STATIONS

- **AM news, sports, talk**: WCBS 880—"News Radio" and WINS 1010— two round-the-clock news stations plus sports, weather, traffic reports, etc. WCBS also carries the Yankees. WFAN: sports; WABC 770 and WOR 710 are talk radio stations with popular talk radio personalities; WLIB 1190 provides Air America—progressive talk radio; WNYC 820 features cultural and consumer-oriented broadcasts, as well as National Public Radio's "All Things Considered;" WWRC 1660 provides Spanish talk radio; WABC and WOR also carry Jets football.
- **AM Spanish news, talk, sports**: WALDO 1280

- **AM Christian radio**: WMCA 570; WTHE 1520 for gospel
- **AM easy listening music**: WHLI 1100
- **AM sports**: WFAN 660 and ESPN sports radio 1050: both offer sports talk, WFAN is also home to the Mets, Knicks, Giants, and Rangers, while ESPN has Islanders hockey.
- **AM children**: WQED "Radio Disney" 1560, pop favorites for children

FM STATIONS
- **FM big band** and **standards**: WRTN 93.5
- **FM news/talk public affairs and NPR**: WNYC 93.9
- **FM urban**: WQHT "Hot 97" 97.1; WRKS "KISS-FM" 98.7; WWPR "Power 105.1" 105.1; WBLS 107.5; contemporary stations featuring hip-hop and R&B.
- **FM adult contemporary**: WLTW "Lite FM" 106.7; WFAS 103.9; WALK 97.5
- **FM classical**: WQXR 96.3, the *New York Times'* mostly-classical music.
- **FM current hits**: WPLJ (Power 95) 95.5; WQHT 97.1; WHTZ "Z-100" 100.3; WKTU 103.5
- **FM jazz**: WBGO, "Jazz 88" 88.3 and WQCD 101.9
- **FM listener sponsored radio**: WBAI 99.5; WNYC 820
- **FM oldies**: WCBS 101.1; hits from the 1960s and '70s; WKHL "Kool" 96.7
- **FM rock**: WXRK 92.3 "K-Rock," plus the always controversial Howard Stern Show; WAXQ 104.3
- **FM Spanish**: WPAT 93.1 and WCAA, 105.9 for Spanish contemporary hits; Salsa and Merengue: WSKQ "Mega" 97.9

In addition, nearly a dozen New York college radio stations between 88.1 and 90.9 on the FM dial offer a wide variety of musical styles and occasionally some interesting talk.

OWNING A CAR IN NEW YORK

DRIVER'S LICENSES, AUTOMOBILE REGISTRATION (AND STATE IDS)

New residents with valid foreign or out-of-state licenses have 30 days to apply for a New York State driver's license and to register their cars and/or motorcycles. Licenses and vehicle registrations are issued by the District Office of the New York State Department of Motor Vehicles, 141-155 Worth Street, corner Centre Street, NYC 10013, open Monday-Friday 8:30 a.m. to 4 p.m. Pick up a license application (which will have a convenient voter registration form attached), driver's manual and, if necessary, an automobile registration form at the District Office or have them sent by calling 212-645-5550 (if you can get through), or simply download the form from the DMV web site (see below). A valid out-of-state license exempts you from the road test, but you must pass the vision, road sign, and written tests, which means waiting on line at the DMV. You cannot drive in NYC with an out-of-town learners permit.

Unless you get lucky and the examiner has a time slot open, you must make an appointment in advance to take the written test. You can stop by your borough's Preliminary Test Office of the Department of Motor Vehicles to schedule your test appointment or call the New York State Road Test Scheduling System at 518-486-6639, or go to www.nysdmv.com/roadtest. The written tests, based on the driver's manual, are given between 9 a.m. and 3 p.m. The best place for information on rules and regulations for obtaining a driver's license, plus motorcycle licenses, address changes, and more is at the **DMV web site**, www.nysdmv.com.

Tests are scored upon completion of your exam and, if you pass, you are issued a temporary license allowing you to drive immediately. Your official license, the one with the photograph, is mailed to you. On testing day, you must have the completed application form and your current license, and pay a fee of $40, which includes the written test fee, license validation fee, and picture (taken at the time your license is issued). New York State licenses are valid for four years.

If your license has lapsed or this is your first, you'll need to pick up the materials and take the vision, road sign, and written tests noted above at the DMV, which also means waiting on line. You'll then be eligible for a learner's permit. With this in hand, after a three-hour course at a licensed driving school, it is possible to take the road test, the ultimate qualification for the New York Driver's License. Examiners can be finicky, but the most frustrating aspect of the road test is getting an appointment to take it. If you can arrange to take the test out of Manhattan, do so. If you make road test arrangements, pay $40, and then have to cancel, make sure you provide them with 72-hours notice or they will charge you another $40.

If you do not drive but wish to have a **state identification card**, visit any DMV office with at least two original identification documents, a combination of passport and Social Security card, for example, at least one of which must show date of birth and one with your signature. You can have your picture taken on site and receive a temporary ID. Yes, you'll wait on line. The permanent ID will arrive by mail in four to six weeks. For more details go to www.nysdmv.com.

To register your car or motorcycle you will need: a registration application or title (completely filled out), proof of ownership, proof of insurance, proof of vehicle inspection, sales tax clearance, and proof of your identity and birth. Read the back of the registration application to determine what "proofs" are acceptable. The registration fee depends on vehicle weight. New York State requires **liability insurance** on all automobiles, upon the purchase of which, from a licensed insurance company, you will be provided with an FS-20 card, which is your proof of insurance. New York is a no-fault insurance state. Auto emission tests are part of the annual inspection procedure necessary for operating a registered vehicle.

You may find it easier to do your DMV business at one of these offices (all can be reached at 212-645-5550 or 718-966-6155):

- 2110 Adam Clayton Powell Boulevard, at 126th Street, NYC 10027, 212-645-5550, Monday-Friday, 8:30 a.m. to 4:40 p.m., Thursday, 10 a.m. to 6 p.m.
- 625 Atlantic Avenue, Brooklyn 11217, Monday-Friday, 8:30 a.m. to 4 p.m., Thursday, 10 a.m. to 6 p.m.
- 2875 West 8th Street, Brooklyn 11224, Monday-Friday, 8:30 a.m. to 4 p.m., Thursday, 10 a.m. to 6 p.m.
- 696 East Fordham Road, Bronx 10458, Monday-Friday, 8:30 a.m. to 4 p.m., Thursday 8:30 a.m. to 6 p.m. No original license, permit or non-driver ID transactions
- 1350 Commerce Avenue, Bronx 10461, Monday-Friday 8:30 a.m. to 3:30 p.m. License or non-driver IDs only.
- 168-46 91st Avenue, Jamaica, Queens, 11432, Monday-Friday, 8:30 a.m. to 4 p.m.
- 168-35 Rockaway Boulevard, Jamaica, Queens, 11434, Monday-Friday, 8:30 a.m. to 4 p.m., Thursday, 10 a.m. to 6 p.m.
- 30-56 Whitestone Expressway, Flushing 11354, Monday-Friday, 8:30 a.m. to 4:15 p.m., Thursday, 10 a.m. to 6 p.m.
- Showplace Bowling Center, 141 East Service Road, Staten Island 10314, Monday-Friday, 8:30 a.m. to 4 p.m., Thursday, 10 a.m. to 6 p.m.

Long lines are a Department of Motor Vehicles tradition. Best time to go is early in the week, but bring reading material along, *War & Peace* perhaps. Fridays are particularly busy. The last workday of any month can find the line spilling out onto the sidewalk and is to be avoided. Note: for a quickie (10-minute) renewal of your New York State driver's license or car registration, go to the DMV office at 300 West 34th Street between Eighth and Ninth avenues, Monday-Wednesday, 8 a.m. to 5:30 p.m., Thursday to 7 p.m. The fee for a renewal is $28 and is good for five years.

For information about the **New Jersey DMV**, go to www.state. nj.us/mvs.

PARKING

Signs such as "Don't even think of parking here" give you an idea of how difficult it is to park in parts of New York City—particularly Manhattan. You can park legally on city streets if you are prepared to spend several hours a week switching parking spots to conform to the city's alternate side of the street parking laws. In addition, you will need a crash course in reading the complex street signs that regulate parking on every block—often you'll find several signs regulating various sections of the same block. Call 311 to find out what regulations are in effect on any given day or, better yet, get a free copy of the Department of Transportation's calendar showing the days your car doesn't have to be moved. Send a stamped, self-addressed envelope to Calendar, NYC Department of Transportation, 40 Worth Street, NYC 10013.

In the boroughs, you'll find street parking in residential areas much easier and private homes generally have driveways and garages. Along main thoroughfares and in commercial shopping areas, such as Forest Hills in Queens, you may have to find garage space if you own a car. While many apartment buildings have garages, some have very long waiting lists. In Manhattan, monthly garage rates rival the price of monthly rent in other cities. There are alternatives, however, to be found in garages around the fringe of town, on the Lower East Side, south of Greenwich Village along, and to the west of the West Side Highway, and north of Morningside Heights. A favorite for the budget-conscious below 14th Street is Standard Parking, Pier 40, West and Houston streets, 800-494-7007. More Than Parking has relatively inexpensive indoor parking at 540 West 59th Street, 212-307-7886, and at 627 West 125th Street, 212-280-7487. Open lots are cheaper although some are better guarded than others.

Note: city residents are exempt from 8% of the 18.25% parking tax. To apply for the exemption call or write the **NYC Department of Finance**, 25 Elm Place, 3rd Floor, Brooklyn 11201, 718-935-6000. You must send the name and license number of the lot or garage you use and proof of residence, which can be a copy of your car registration and driver's license. The process must be repeated yearly, but the savings make it worth the trouble.

If you use a car only occasionally, consider a private garage in a nearby community that is easily accessible by public transportation.

If you are frequenting Manhattan—other than midtown—for shopping or other purposes for a day or evening visit, you can usually find meters (outside of rush hours: 7 a.m. to 10 a.m. and 4 p.m. to 7 p.m.). Have plenty of quarters ready. Nighttime parking gets easier in many parts of the city where parking limits are not in effect between 7 p.m. and 7 a.m.

Many Manhattanites don't bother owning a car since lack of parking coupled with heavy traffic throughout Manhattan makes driving to and from the office stressful and inefficient. The cost of renting a car for the few times you really need one—such as taking a trip out of town—is cheaper than paying for parking, car insurance, taxes and fees, and maintenance. Using mass transit or taxis is the preferred method of getting around the city—especially on weekdays. See the **Transportation** chapter for information about car rentals, including ZipCar, an hourly car rental subscription service. For tips on auto services and repair, go to **Helpful Services**.

PARKING TICKETS AND TOWING

What's the price if you get caught? To help you decide whether to take that parking chance or not, keep in mind that parking tickets issued below 96th Street in Manhattan range from $65 to $180, depending on the violation. (Note: the web site for the New York City Department of Finance Parking Violations Operations, www.ci.nyc.ny.us/html/dof/, includes a wealth of parking information, including specifics about how to pay your ticket online, requesting a hearing, and information about towed vehicles.) Should you decide to take a chance and let your meter run over or block a crosswalk for a quick errand, you can be sure that a ticket will be waiting on your windshield. A recent article in the *Times* reported that, in an effort to raise $69 million dollars for the city, an additional 300 traffic agents are now out cruising the streets. If you do get a ticket, you may pay by mail for the cost of a postage stamp; pay online at www.nyc.gov for $1.50 service charge; or pay by phone for $3 at 718-422-7800, using VISA, MasterCard, Discover, or American Express.

But tickets are only a part of the penalty. The real deterrent to joining the ranks of New York's parking scofflaws is the threat of having your automobile towed. It costs $185 to retrieve your car from the pound on Pier 76 (Twelfth Avenue and 38th Street) in Manhattan, plus $20 a day (not including the day your car was towed) for storage. To retrieve your auto, you must produce the car's registration and your driver's license. If your name is on the registration papers, you can pay by check. Otherwise, or if you have accumulated traffic tickets, you must produce cash, certified check, or traveler's check for payment. The pound is open 7 a.m. to 6 p.m., seven days a week. Call 212-971-0773 to determine if your car has been towed. If it isn't in the pound (and you haven't misplaced it), your car has been stolen, and you should report it to the police. To find out if you have an accumulation of tickets (they sometimes blow off the windshield or are taken by other drivers who put them under their windshield wipers in order to fool the cops), all five boroughs have Help/Redemption Centers where you can get a free computer printout of your tickets or where you can pay to redeem a towed car: 150 Nassau Street, Manhattan; 1400 Williamsbridge Road, 1st floor, and 1932 Arthur Avenue, The Bronx; 144-06 94th Avenue, Jamaica, Queens; 210 Joralemon Street, 9th floor Brooklyn; 350 St. Mark's Place, 3rd floor, Staten Island. Residents outside of New York City should check with their municipality for information regarding traffic/parking citations. In New Jersey, you can pay parking citations online by going to www.judiciary.state.nj.us/atswep/njmc/directmain. To contact the New Jersey Motor Vehicle Commission, call 609-292-6500. For car safety, it is best not to leave any valuables in the car or any items in plain sight. A Chapman lock or the popular "Club" (a steering wheel lock) are also suggested. On quiet side streets, you are better off parking as close to a doorman building as possible, although such parking is generally limited.

KEEPING PETS

Can you bring your Portuguese water dog and your Burmese cat to New York? Will that pose a problem? Yes and maybe. The biggest hurdle to clear will be the first: finding an apartment that will accept pets (fish don't count). As a general rule, landlords and co-ops prohibit pets in their buildings, which means you may have to choose between the perfect apartment and the perfect pet. Be sure to inquire as you search for a pet-friendly home, and don't plan to sneak one in where they are prohibited. One web site, www.nycdoglife.com, is worth checking for its listing of pet-friendly rentals, condos, and co-ops, as well as other pet-related information. Dogs and cats being the most common city pets, we'll address their needs here. If yours is an exotic pet, say a miniature pig, you're on your own.

You will want to have a vet lined up before you need one. Start by calling the **Veterinary Medical Association of New York City**, 212-246-0057, for a list of accredited vets in your neighborhood. Visit the dog run, park, or vacant lot in your neighborhood where dogs and their owners frequent to glean information on local vets and the whole range of dog-owner concerns. Choosing a vet, like choosing a physician, is largely a subjective thing. Beyond the cleanliness and friendliness of the establishment, you and your pet will want to be comfortable with this vet. You may want to inquire to be sure your vet is available or covered after hours by an answering service. In case of a serious emergency after hours, the **Manhattan Veterinary Group**, a private animal hospital at 240 East 80th Street between Second and Third avenues, 212-988-1000, is open until 1 a.m. daily; the **Animal Medical Center** at 510 East 62nd Street at York Avenue, 212-838-8100, is open 24-hours and is one of the premier pet facilities in the city.

Dogs must be licensed by the city's Department of Health, 212-676-2120, for which you will need proof of rabies vaccination. Dogs must be leashed, except inside fenced dog runs; they may not enter playgrounds. Note: besides keeping your dog leashed, you must clean up after your dog.

Dogs typically need to be walked at least three times a day, not a problem if you work at home or someone is at home during the day. Being social animals they suffer more than cats from being left alone for long periods. Consider the proposition that two dogs are not much more bother than one, and both are happier together than one alone. In any case, if you are away for more than eight hours a day, you will probably need a **dog walker**, a person who has your keys and who will come in and take your dog out for 15 to 60 minutes. Expensive? Yes. To find a reliable walker check with other dog owners and your vet for recommendations. Some of the better pet-care establishments keep a list of walkers whose credentials they can vouch for. Some dog walkers will also pet-sit when you are away, either staying in your home to care for your pets and plants or visiting three times a day to feed, water, play with, and walk your pet. The price? Currently a minimum of $22 a day for cats, $25-$35 a day for dogs, more in some neighborhoods. There are kennels in the city, at least one without pens; those out of town, most of which will pick up and deliver your dog, tend to be roomier and less expensive.

Dog runs, fenced-in enclosures in which dogs can play off-leash, have proliferated in the city in recent years. At this writing there are 33 in the five boroughs, with more planned. Most, such as those in Riverside Park, are open to all non-aggressive dogs that are not in heat. Others, such as the run at West Houston and Mercer Streets in the Village, are by membership only and often have a waiting list to get in. Carl Shurz Park on the Upper East Side has the city's only small-dog enclosure, in addition to space for large dogs. To find a dog run in your neighborhood go to www.urban hound.com/houndplay, which also has useful information on dog-friendly getaways, transportation with dogs, and links to other canine sites.

If you're looking to **acquire a dog or cat** you might consult the classified ads in the Sunday "Sports" section of the *New York Times*. There are purebred rescue groups in the city for most breeds; they find homes for animals of a particular breed that need to be placed, usually at less cost than from a breeder. Of course, if you adopt a pet from the **Center for Animal Care and Control** (**CACC**), the largest animal adoption organization in the city, you are saving it from almost certain euthanasia. For about $75 to $100 you can adopt a mixed breed dog ($150 for purebreds) or a cat, complete with vaccinations and spaying/neutering, at any of the CAC adoption centers in the five boroughs. In Manhattan the shelter is at 326 East 110th Street, 212-722-3620, open for adoptions daily, 11 a.m. to 6 p.m. Call 212-442-2076 for the location and hours of the other four shelters or visit their web site at www.nycacc.org; with links to petfinder.org it allows you to search other shelters in the metropolitan area. The **ASPCA Shelter and Adoption Center**, 424 East 92nd Street at First Avenue, 212-876-7700, www.aspca.org, also offers animals for adoption. The **Bide-A-Wee Manhattan Shelter** at 410 East 38th Street east of First Avenue, 212-532-4455, www.bide-a-wee.org, does not destroy animals and offers dogs and cats for adoption at minimal cost.

Now available is the pet HMO, Pet Assure, which offers members 25% off all medical care and supplies for pets using participating veterinarians and 10% to 50% off the cost of pet foods, supplies, training, grooming, and boarding at participating establishments in the five boroughs, Manhattan especially. Call 888-789-PETS, www.petassure.com. Or, for straight medical coverage try Veterinary Pet Insurance, 800-872-7387, www.petinsurance.com.

Dog owners may find useful information, training advice, and links to other dog-related web sites at www.canine.org and www.urbanhound.com.

Two books that offer useful information for New York City dog owners:
* **The Great New York Dog Book** by Deborah Loven (HarperCollins)
* **The Dog's Guide to New York City, With Jack, the City Dog** by Jan Rohman (Richmond Press)

FINDING A PHYSICIAN

"What about how to find a doctor?" a plaintive reader inquires, adding, "It's been tough." Indeed. They're out there, more than 13,000 of them in Manhattan alone, but choosing a personal physician is more like choosing a mate than buying a car. You're looking for a doctor who has graduated from an excellent medical school, done residency in a good teaching hospital, is board-certified, has practiced long enough to know what he/she is doing but not so long as to be out of touch with the latest research and technology, and has just the right professional manner—concerned, straightforward, a listener with, perhaps, a good sense of humor. In short, you want a doctor you can rely on. If you put it off until you need one, you're apt to wind up sitting miserably in the nearest emergency room, followed by a big bill.

If you are enrolled in an HMO through your employer or independently, you are probably limited in your choice of physicians to those listed by that HMO. This makes choosing somewhat easier, but the criteria for choosing remain the same. More about HMOs below.

You may choose a physician as many do, on the basis of the recommendation of friends, which can be a good start. Question your friend closely on what exactly he/she does and does not like about a doctor. Or, if you had a physician you liked before moving here, he may be able to recommend a colleague here who will suit you.

Conventional wisdom says that one should have a doctor who is on staff or is an attending physician at one of the **teaching hospitals**. These physicians have been carefully screened and their credentials certified, the reasoning goes, and the teaching hospitals tend to offer a wider range of services and sophisticated procedures than do the smaller community hospitals. Bear in mind also, that as a patient in a teaching hospital, you may be poked and probed by students and residents, and some care may be provided by residents without additional supervision. In any case, these hospitals have referral services, which is one place to start your search. Referrals are based on medical specialty and location. The major academic hospitals in Manhattan, with their physician referral lines, are:

- **Beth Israel-St. Luke's-Roosevelt**, First Avenue at 16th Street, NYC 10003, 888-445-0338
- **Columbia-Presbyterian Medical Center**, 622 West 168th Street, NYC 10032, 800-227-CPMC
- **Mount Sinai Medical Center**, Fifth Avenue at 100th Street, NYC 10029, 800-MD-SINAI
- **NY Presbyterian Hospital-Cornell Medical Center**, 525 East 68th Street, NYC 10021, 800-822-2NYH
- **NYU Medical Center**, 550 First Avenue, NYC 10016, 888-7-NYU-MED
- **St. Luke's-Roosevelt Hospital Center**, 1000 Tenth Avenue, NYC 10019, 888-445-0338
- **St. Vincent's Hospital and Medical Center**, 153 West 11th Street, NYC 10011, 888-478-4362

Some of these hospitals also have treatment centers elsewhere, and their doctors practice throughout the metropolitan area. See the Yellow Pages for more hospitals in Manhattan and in the other boroughs.

Another source of referrals is the county medical society, which in Manhattan (NY County Medical Society, 12 East 41st Street, NYC 10016, 212-684-4670, www.nycms.org) has some 6,000 members. The caller can specify the area of choice, hospital of choice, specialty, sex, and be given three names. Note: you can also check on the credentials, training, and board specialties of a physician.

Referral(s) in hand, call the specific doctor's office to ask about an introductory visit. Inquire about office hours and their procedure for an introductory interview, which may be by phone or in person, and what the charge will be. Is the office staff helpful? Before talking with the physician have your questions written down: in which hospital does he/she practice, who covers for him/her when he/she is unavailable, can he/she be reached by phone after hours if need be, what are his/her billing procedures, etc. You may also want to discuss such sensitive issues as his/her views on abortion and life support. If you are satisfied so far, you'll probably make an appointment for a physical exam and some tests to establish a baseline profile. Ask about that and what it will cost. If you are not satisfied, go elsewhere.

A word about **HMOs**; if you are not covered by some form of health insurance and are not in an HMO connected with your place of employment, you can join one directly yourself on a "direct pay" basis. That means you pay, and it isn't cheap, at least until you consider the alternative, should you or a family member become ill or injured. Competition between HMOs is intense, and the field is rapidly changing. It's a good idea to request information from a number of organizations in order to determine what is available and what best suits your situation and your pocketbook. Some unions and associations that you may belong to also have HMO plans, which will be less costly for members than if you joined one as an individual.

To assist in this and/or in the choice of a physician or hospital, one book, known as "Best Doctors," is especially useful. Based on extensive surveys of health care professionals, statistics and other data, *How to Find the Best Doctors, New York Metropolitan Area* by John Castle and John Connolly is available in bookstores and in area library reference rooms. *New York* magazine also runs an annual "Best Doctors in the City" issue, in which you can gather names of physicians in various fields of medicine.

Should you have a **serious complaint**, which you cannot resolve with your physician, contact the **NY State Board for Professional Medical Conduct**, NY State Department of Health, Office of Professional Medical Conduct, 433 River Street, Suite 303, Troy, NY 12180, 518-402-0855, www.health.state.ny.us. In New Jersey, contact the **NJ State Board of Medical Examiners**, 140 East Front Street, Second Floor, Trenton, NJ 08608, 609-826-7100, www.state.nj.us/lps/ca/medical.htm.

VOTER REGISTRATION

Registering to vote is as simple as calling the New York State Board of Elections voter registration hotline, 800-FOR-VOTE, to request a voter application. You can also call the **Manhattan Board of Elections** at 212-868-3692, www.vote.nyc.ny.us, for an Application for Registration and Enrollment by mail. Complete this form and return it to the board. If you live in another borough, the Manhattan Board will pass the completed application along to the appropriate borough board: Bronx, 718-299-9017; Brooklyn, 718-797-8800; Manhattan, 212-886-3800; Queens, 718-392-8989; and Staten Island, 718-876-0079. Under the 1995 "Motor Voter" law, the pre-stamped applications are also available now in post offices, libraries, and some public agencies. If you enroll in a political party, the form must be received by the Board of Elections 25 days before the primary or general election. You can also register in person during specific central registration periods at Election Board headquarters, 32 Broadway, NYC 10013.

For information on voter registration in New Jersey, start with the League of Women Voters of New Jersey, 204 West State Street, Trenton, NJ 08608, 609-394-3303, http://www.lwvnj.org.

LIBRARY CARDS

The New York Public Library, www.nypl.org, with four research libraries, numerous special divisions for various disciplines, famous reference collections, and over 80 branches in Manhattan, The Bronx, and Staten Island, is one of the city's great treasures. Residents of Brooklyn and Queens, however, aren't bookless: the Brooklyn Public Library has 59 branches, the Queens Borough Public Library, 60. Neighborhood branch libraries are listed at the end of each neighborhood profile in the **Neighborhoods** section.

Library cards are free and entitle you to borrow or request circulating books from any branch in the system. To obtain a card, give your name, address and proof of residence to the librarian at the return desk of the nearest branch library. In New York City, call 212-661-7220 for library hours—which vary widely from branch to branch.

A wonderful resource is New York Public's **Telephone Reference Service**, 212-340-0849. Library researchers try to answer all possible questions and, if they cannot, will refer you to the department most likely to have the required data. If the Manhattan number is busy, try the Brooklyn number, 718-230-2100, or Queens, 718-990-0714.

In New Jersey, library information is available at the New Jersey Library Association's web site: www.njla.org/resources, or try one of the following contacts:

- **Edgewater Public Library**, 49 Hudson Avenue, Edgewater, NJ 07020, 201-224-6144, www.bccls.org/edgewater
- **Fort Lee Public Library**, 320 Main Street, Fort Lee, NJ 07703, 201-592-3614, www.bccls.org/fortlee
- **Hoboken Public Library**, 500 Park Avenue, Hoboken, NJ 07030, 201-420-2280, www.bccls.org/hoboken
- **Jersey City Public Library**, 472 Jersey Ave, Jersey City, NJ 07302, 201-547-4500, www.jclibrary.org
- **Weehawken Public Library**, 49 Hauxhurst Avenue, Weehawken, NJ 07087, 201-863-7823, www.bccls.org/weehawken

For more on New York's fabulous literary traditions and opportunities, see **Literary Life** in the **Cultural Life** chapter.

PASSPORTS

Whether you are applying for a passport for the first time or renewing, do not wait until just before your summer or Christmas vacation to do so. Apply early and relax. First, call New York City **Passport Agency** at 212-206-3500 for recorded passport application information and to schedule an appointment. For detailed information and to download the proper mail-in forms, you can visit the **US Department of State Bureau of Consular Affairs**' link: http://travel.state.gov/get_forms.html, or call them at 877-487-2778, TDD 888-874-7793, Monday-Friday 8 a.m. to 8 p.m. EST. General travel information and advisories are available at the bureau's home page, www.travel.state.gov.

If you are applying for a passport for the first time, you must have (1) proof of citizenship: an original or copy of your birth certificate with a raised seal, or naturalization papers, and (2) proof of your identity: a driver's license or other ID with a photograph and signature. (If you don't have these papers, call the number above for alternatives.) You will need two passport photos (which can be made while you wait in most neighborhood photo shops) and $85 if you are age 16 or older, $70 for those under age 16; renewals are $55. For expedited service, add $60. New applications for passports use form DS-11, and for minors under age 14 an additional consent form, DS-3053. You will find the necessary forms at many post offices and libraries, at the county court offices (listed below) or online at the State Bureau of Consular Affairs. You must appear in person to get your first passport; this includes minors. To **renew a passport**, pick up form **DS-82** at the address listed above and mail it as directed with two passport pictures, and your expired passport. Allow four to six weeks, more if you're applying in high summer season, or mention the date of your departure on the form; passports are processed on the basis of departure date. A passport is good for ten years and can be renewed within two years after expiration.

Visit the New York City Passport Agency for passport processing only if you have an appointment for a priority passport (see below). These government centers can process your application:

- **New York State Supreme Court County Offices**: (Manhattan) New York County Clerk, Supreme Courthouse, 60 Centre Street, 10007; (Brooklyn) Kings County Clerk, Supreme Court Building, 360 Adams Street, 11201; (Bronx) Bronx County Clerk, Supreme Courthouse, 851 Grand Concourse, Bronx 10451; (Queens) Queens County Clerk, Supreme Courthouse, 88-11 Sutphin Boulevard, Jamaica, 11435; (Staten Island) Richmond County Clerk, 130 Stuyvesant Place, SI 10301.

Many **Post Offices** have passport acceptance services; call the USPS, 877-275-8777, or go to www.passportinfo.com/Local/NY.htm (New York) and www.passportinfo.com/Local/NJ.htm (New Jersey) to locate a passport acceptance facility.

If you must leave the country in a hurry, it is possible to obtain or renew a passport in three days by calling 212-206-3500 from a touch-tone phone to make an appointment at the **New York City Passport Agency**, 376 Hudson Street, 10th floor at West Houston Street, open 7:30 a.m. to 3:30 p.m. You will punch in your Social Security number, the date of your travel ticket, and other information and be given a choice of three appointments. To your appointment, bring your ticket and other necessary papers and cash or check for the full fee, plus extra cash for priority handling fees, and be prepared to return for your passport. In high season (April through June, just before Christmas, Easter and other school holidays) an applicant with an appointment made by phone is likely to need two hours to get to the head of the line.

Suppose you've got to go to Botswana on short notice, you don't even know what documents and shots you need, and you're too busy to get it together. What to do? For a fee (up to $150 for a same-day passport renewal) a knowledgeable staff at Passport Plus, 20 East 49th Street, 212-759-5540, www.passportplus.net, will handle it for you, as will Red Tape Cutters, 1 Beekman Street, Suite 401, 212-406-9898.

BUILDING STAFF

New Yorkers rely on the staff of their buildings in ways that are unique to the city—and they reward their staff in an equally unique manner.

Most multi-unit residences have a superintendent (the "super") who is responsible for the maintenance and day-to-day operation of the building. Many superintendents may be assisted by porters and hallmen. There are also doormen (and today, the occasional doorwoman) in many buildings, and in luxury buildings, perhaps a concierge.

Because many New Yorkers do not rely on their cars to accomplish their daily tasks, goods and services are delivered by businesses to the consumer's home even when they are not there, hence the importance of the building staff. Other staff duties may include hailing cabs, supplying important building information, directing repair people, door holding and—in some buildings—even mail delivery. Most of all, your staff, particularly the doorman, is the first line of security in your building, making certain that anyone who desires entrance truly belongs there.

In addition to the generally higher rents found in staffed buildings, there is an unspoken cost associated with the extra service. It is widely expected that a building's residents tip the staff at Christmas-time for general services rendered throughout the year. (Anything beyond a general service, such as pet-walking or heavy lifting, is best attended to at the time the service is performed.) The tip is by no means mandatory but individual service has been known to decline precipitously for those tight-fisted residents. The custom varies widely from building to building both in terms of cost and how the money is dispersed. It is a good idea to find out what is customary in your building and budget for the holiday season accordingly.

CITY SAFETY

The incidence of violent crime in New York City has declined significantly in the last decade. In fact, according to a recent FBI Uniform Crime Report, New York City had the lowest overall crime rate of large cities in the US (cities with more than one million people). Despite this good news, it is still prudent to pay attention to your surroundings and be cautious, particularly for those new to an urban environment. Consider the following:

- Always remain alert to what is around you (in front and in back); if you don't pay attention to your surroundings, you make yourself a target for crime.
- Trust your instincts; they are usually right.
- Stay clear of deserted areas such as empty streets, uninhabited subway cars or platforms and lonely automatic teller machines.
- If you must take the subway late at night, always get in the car that houses the brakeman (generally one of the middle cars). Typically, there is a black and white "zebra" sign marking the spot where the brakeman's car stops.
- Look for children playing outside or women walking on their own as signs that an area is safe.
- If you do find yourself on an ominous-looking block, avoid the sidewalk and walk directly in the street to be in view of traffic.
- If you feel you are being followed, walk into the nearest restaurant or store, or flag a cab.
- Conceal your valuables, and if you wear a diamond ring turn it around so only the band is showing. Cover watches and necklaces or put jewelry away when riding the subway.
- Hold your handbag close to you, wearing the strap across your chest, keeping the bag in front of you. Don't hang a purse on a restaurant chair or restroom hook. Men, don't put your wallet in your back pocket.
- Do not count your money in public or use big bills. Tuck your money in a safe place before leaving an ATM vestibule.
- If you're walking alone, or even as a pair, avoid crowds of teens (or any groups) congregated or hanging out on street corners. Cross the street and walk on the other side.

- Beware of operators working as a team: someone who tells you she just dropped her contact lens might well have a friend who is reaching in your handbag.
- Do not hold or open doors that are supposed to be locked in your apartment building for anyone you do not know.
- Remember: you do not owe a response to anyone who asks for one. This may seem callous but it is better to err on the side of bad manners rather than bad judgment. Go with your instincts.

The New York City Police Department publishes free brochures on safety. These booklets include safety precautions addressed to men, women, children, and the elderly—even to runners. Brochure topics also include how to safeguard your apartment, car, and small business. See the final section of this book for emergency phone numbers. Residents outside of New York City should contact their local police station for similar pamphlets and safety initiatives.

If your security desires can only be satisfied by hi-tech gadgetry, you may want to pay a visit to the Counter Spy Shop at 444 Madison Avenue or in the lobby of the Waldorf-Astoria.

Finally, become involved in your neighborhood. All over town, people organize block associations to monitor crime and make stronger communities by helping out and working together. To find out if a block association exists in your neighborhood, or to set one up, call **Citizen's Committee for NYC** at 212-989-0909, www.citizensnyc.org.

Contrary to popular belief, when it comes to the good of the common cause, New Yorkers have shown a remarkable ability to go above and beyond. In numerous instances, including the citywide power outage in 2003, during transit strikes, paralyzing snow storms, and of course the tragedy of September 11th, 2001, New Yorkers pull together and help each other.

I T SHOULD COME AS NO SURPRISE THAT THE INTERNATIONAL SERVICE capital is as energetic in supplying the needs of New Yorkers as it is of those the world over. Multitudinous talents and supremely innovative minds combine to provide a mind-boggling array of services, for individuals as well as for industry. Local magazines and newspapers seldom let an issue go by without feature articles about umbrella repair specialists, third-generation tapestry re-weavers, or the pair of clever Upper East Side women available to organize your closets and your life. We'll leave these summaries of the city's more *recherché* services to the press and provide instead the names of a few representative firms and organizations which supply basics such as house cleaning, mail and shipping services, auto or computer repair, as well as organizations to contact for consumer protection, or which address the concerns of the lesbian and gay communities, the needs of senior citizens, people with disabilities, and immigrant newcomers.

Note: listing in this book is merely informational and is *not* an endorsement or recommendation by First Books.

HOUSE CLEANING

Word of mouth is your best bet for finding a cleaning person (women have no monopoly on the profession here). Ask friends and neighbors if they know of someone with a few hours available. If this doesn't work, you might try one of the services listed below. The hourly rates typically include dusting, changing linens, mopping, vacuuming, laundry, cleaning bathrooms, and washing dishes. The same firms provide specialists to handle floor waxing, washing walls, and other heavy-duty jobs at higher fees. For more help with domestic concerns refer to the listings under **Au Pairs and Nannies** and **Baysitters** in **Childcare and Education**. The *Irish Echo's* classifieds, published in the city and available at newsstands throughout the city, are a good place to look for house-cleaning personnel.

- **Lend-A-Hand, Inc.**, 627 East 11th Street, 212-614-9118, www.lahny. com; housecleaning is one of the many services provided by this agency's actors, musicians, and dancers. They also offer party services, clerical services, and childcare.
- **Maid in NY**, 200 Park Avenue South, 212-777-6000, www.maidin newyork.com; homes as well as industrial sites and business offices are serviced by some 100 employees. Times and schedules are arranged to suit the client: weekly, bi-weekly, or just once for a thorough spring cleaning. Provides online estimates.
- **Maids Unlimited**, Flatiron Services, 230 East 93rd Street, 212-369-9100, www.flatironcleaning.com; for regular service, the same person will be sent when possible. One or two days' notice required. Help is bonded. Maids use your supplies. Provides online estimates.

MAIL AND SHIPPING SERVICES

The General Post Office has sat prominently at 421 Eighth Avenue between 31st and 33rd streets since 1913. It is open 24-hours, seven-days a week. Post boxes rent from about $82 (including tax and $10 key deposit) for a standard size box for four months. To snag a box at a high-occupancy station line up early on the 15th of the month, when leases expire. If you need more than just a box, a mail service center, which will also forward mail and typically offer fax and copy service, may be your best bet. Such services have even been known to accept dry cleaning and flowers for their customers. The UPS Store (formerly Mail Boxes Etc.) is the most prolific chain in the city. Check the Yellow Pages under "Mail Receiving Services" for a comprehensive list. Less expensive are the neighborhood businesses that take in mail and offer no services beyond renting boxes and notifying their occupants of package arrival.

Need to send a set of golf clubs to your brother in Kansas? Then you need a shipping service. The Yellow Pages under "Delivery Service" lists a host of them, from local to national and overseas shipping services. National package delivery services include:

- **Airborne Express**, 800-247-2676, www.airborne.com
- **DHL Worldwide Express**, 800-225-5345, www.dhl.co.id
- **Craters & Freighters**, 800-736-3335, www.cratersandfreighters.com; for especially heavy or bulky items they claim they're the best. Locations in New York City and New Jersey.
- **FedEx, and FedEx Ground**, 800-238-5355, www.fedex.com
- **United Parcel Service (UPS)**, 800-742-5877, www.ups.com
- **US Postal Service Express Mail**, 800-222-1811, www.usps.com

JUNK MAIL

Junk mail will surely follow you to your new locale. In order to curtail this kind of unwanted mail we suggest you send a written note, including name and address, asking to be removed from the **Direct Marketing Association's** list (Direct Marketing Association's Mail Preference Service, Box 643, Carmel, NY 10512). Some catalogue companies will need to be contacted directly with a purge request. For **junk e-mail**, you may also go to their web site, www.dmaconsumers.org, and request an opt-out service for your e-mail address. The service will accept three non-business e-mail addresses at a time. This should reduce the amount of e-mail you receive from national e-mail lists. Another option is to call the "opt-out" line at 888-567-8688, and request that the main credit bureaus not release your name and address to interested marketing companies. (**Curb phone solicitations** by going to the government's do not call registry, www.donotcall.gov, and registering your phone number—or call 800-382-1222, TTY 866-290-4236.)

AUTOMOBILES

AUTO SERVICES AND REPAIR

There are hundreds of auto repair shops throughout the city, and many of them are competent and honest. Which ones? Alas, there is no consumer rating system for auto repair shops. Talk to friends and colleagues for their recommendations before you have a problem; you may find a gem of a repairman. If so, try to establish a good rapport—they're often just as valuable as a good doctor. Recommendation in hand, before taking your car in, it's still a good idea to check with the Better Business Bureau to see if any complaints have been filed against a repair shop. Membership in AAA (American Automobile Association), $55 for the first year, $45 thereafter, is probably the best investment you can make in your car in the city. The emergency road service alone, with free battery charge and free towing within a three-mile radius to an AAA-affiliated service station, is worth the price of admission. Their list of affiliated stations is a valuable starting point. Members also receive free maps, trip-planning services, trip interruption insurance, the service of AAA travel agents, travel discounts, and a host of products and services highlighted in their monthly magazine, *Car and Travel*. Drop in to their Manhattan branch at 1881 Broadway at 62nd Street or call 212-586-1166 or 718-224-2222. In Brooklyn, AAA has an office at 2334 Ralph Avenue between avenues M and N, 718-279-7272; in Queens, 186-06 Hillside Avenue, Jamaica, 718-279-7272. They are open from

Monday–Friday 8:45 a.m. to 5:30 p.m., Saturday from 9 a.m. to 5 p.m. They're also on the web at www.aaany.com. When all else fails, try calling "Car Talk" 888-CAR-TALK, NPR's popular radio show where the entertaining Click and Clack brothers (Tom and Ray) try to diagnose your car's problems and then offer advice. On their web site, http://cartalk.cars.com, they have a useful "find a mechanic" section.

COMPUTER REPAIRS

Of course, you should always back up your files. So when the crash comes ... well, you know. But that won't save you from unscrupulous computer repair shops. Stories abound, but in fact there are reliable repair shops out there—usually found by word of mouth. We list a few that *New York* magazine rated highly. First, a few guidelines: if you have a problem with your computer and you are still under your manufacturer's warranty, call the company directly to see if they can help. If that doesn't work, call a repair shop and describe the problem; a good shop may be able to talk you through a diagnosis and self-repair. Before taking the computer in, ask if the shop stocks spare parts for your system, how long repairs typically take, if there is a diagnostic fee and if that fee will be applied toward any work they do to fix the computer. Be sure to get an estimate and make them understand that they are not to do any work until it has been authorized by you. If the technician seems vague or intimidating, call someone else. As with auto repair shops, be sure to check with the Better Business Bureau to see if any complaints have been filed against a particular shop before you take your computer in for repairs.

- **CompUSA**, 420 Fifth Avenue, 212-764-6224, www.compusa.com
- **Machattan**, 381 Park Avenue South, 212-242-9393, Macintosh only
- **Tekserve**, 155 West 23rd Street, 212-929-3645, fourth floor, www.tekserve.com, Macintosh only

CONSUMER PROTECTION—RIP-OFF RECOURSE

It goes without saying that the best defense against fraud and consumer victimization is to avoid it. You read all contracts down to the smallest print, save your receipts and canceled checks, get the name of telephone sales and service people with whom you deal, check a contractor's license number with the Department of Consumer Affairs for complaints. But you've been stung. A dry cleaner returns your blue suit, but now it's purple and he shrugs. A shop refuses to refund as promised on the expensive gift that didn't suit your mother. Your landlord fails to return your security deposit when you move. After $733 in repairs to your automobile's engine, the car now vibrates wildly, and the mechanic claims innocence.

Negotiations, documents in hand, fail. You're angry, and embarrassed because you've been had. *There is something you can do*:

- File a complaint with the **New York State Consumer Protection Board**, 800-NYS-1220, www.oag.state.ny.us or the NY State Consumer Frauds and Protection Bureau, Office of the Attorney General, 120 Broadway, NYC 10271. You may want to call the bureau's complaint line, 212-416-8000, first for advice or a complaint form. Or go in to the office in person, third floor, open Monday-Friday 9:30 to 4:30. Again, have all your documentation organized and in hand.
- Call the **NYC Department of Consumer Affairs**, Complaints Department, 212-487-4444, for information on filing a complaint; have all your information organized before calling, and be prepared to spend some time on the phone. Better yet, file a complaint online at www.nyc.gov.
- File suit for relief, up to $3,000, in **small claims court**. You do not need a lawyer, and some 60,000 New Yorkers use this resource annually. There are six small claims locations in the city, two of them in Manhattan, all open one evening until 10 p.m. For details, call New York City's civil information line, 212-791-6000; ask for two excellent booklets, *A Guide to Small Claims Court* and *Preparing for the Collection of a Small Claims Judgment*. Be advised that winning in small claims court is much easier than ever collecting on a judgment.
- In New Jersey, file a complaint with the **New Jersey State Office of Consumer Protection**, 124 Halsey Street, Newark, NJ 07102, 973-504-6200, www.state.nj.us/lps/ca/.

Before doing any of the above, inform your adversary of your intentions, politely but firmly. You may force a settlement, thereby saving yourself the trouble of following through.

IMMIGRANT NEWCOMERS

Those new to the US may find the following information useful.

CONSULATES

There are over 20 consulates in New York City. Here are a few:
- **Consulate General of Australia**, 150 East 42nd Street, 34th floor, NYC 10017, 212-351-6501, www.australianyc.org
- **Consulate General of Brazil**, 1185 Avenue of the Americas, 21st floor, NYC 10036, 917-777-7777, www.brasilny.org
- **Consulate General of Canada**, 1251 Avenue of the Americas, NYC 10020, 212-596-1628, http://canada-ny.org

- **Consulate General of China**, 520 12th Avenue, NYC 10036, www.nyconsulate.prchina.org
- **Consulate General of the Federal Republic of Germany**, 871 United Nations Plaza, NYC 10017, 212-610-9700, www.germany-info.org
- **Consulate General of France**, 934 Fifth Avenue, NYC 10021, 212-606-3680, www.consulfrance-newyork.org
- **Consulate General of Great Britain**, 845 Third Avenue, NYC 10022, 212-745-0200, www.britainusa.com/ny
- **Consulate General of Italy**, 690 Park Avenue, NYC 10021, 212-439-8600, www.italconsulny.org
- **Consulate General of Japan**, 299 Park Avenue, NYC 10171, 212-888-0889, www.ny.us.emb-japan.go.jp/
- **Consulate General of Mexico**, 27 East 39th Street, NYC 10016, 212-217-6400, www.consulmexny.org
- **Consulate General of New Zealand**, 222 East 41st Street, Suite 2510, NYC 10017, 212-832-4038, www.un.int/newzealand
- **Consulate General of Poland**, 233 Madison Avenue, NYC 10016, 212-686-1541, www.polandconsulateny.com
- **Consulate General of Russia**, 9 East 91st Street, NYC 10128, 212-348-0926, www.ruscon.com
- **Consulate General of Spain**, 150 East 58th Street, NYC 10155, 212-355-4080, www.spainconsul-ny.org
- **Consulate General of Taiwan**, 90 Park Avenue, NYC 10016, 212-557-5122, www.taipei.org

IMMIGRATION & NATURALIZATION SERVICE

US Citizenship and Immigration Services (CIS) for New York City is in lower Manhattan: BCIS New York City District Office, Jacob Javits Federal Building, 26 Federal Plaza 3rd floor, NYC 10278, 800-375-5283, www.uscis.gov.

IMMIGRATION RESOURCES

- **Bureau of Immigration and Customs Enforcement**, www.bice.immigration.gov
- **Customs & Border Protection**, www.cbp.gov
- **Department of Homeland Security**, www.dhs.gov; www.whitehouse.gov/deptofhomeland
- **General Government Questions**, 800-688-9889, www.firstgov.gov

- **International Center in New York**, 50 West 23rd Street, 7th floor, NYC 10010, 212-255-9555, www.intlcenter.org; English conversation and American culture for immigrant newcomers.
- **Social Security Administration**, 800-772-1213, www.ssa.gov
- **US Bureau of Consular Affairs**, www.travel.state.gov
- **US Department of State, Visa Services**, http://travel.state.gov/ visa_services
- **US Immigration Online: Green Cards, Visas, Government Forms**, www.usaimmigrationservice.org

PUBLICATIONS

- ***The Immigration Handbook***, 3rd edition, by Henry Liebman (First Books)
- ***Newcomer's Handbook for Moving to and Living in the USA*** by Mike Livingston (First Books)

MOVING PETS TO THE US

Cosmopolitan Canine Carriers out of Connecticut, 800-243-9105, has been shipping dogs and cats all over the world for over 25 years. Contact them with questions or concerns regarding air transportation arrangements, vaccinations, and quarantine times.

LESBIAN AND GAY CONCERNS

In a city with large and established lesbian and gay communities, there are many organizations, businesses, and publications which address their various needs and interests—too many to detail here. We mention one important umbrella organization and six other resources as starting points.

- **The Lesbian & Gay Community Services Center**, 208 West 13th Street, NYC 10011, 212-620-7310, www.gaycenter.org; is just that, and it offers numerous services seven days a week in a newly-renovated, 150-year-old former schoolhouse in Greenwich Village. Besides social, cultural, and recreational offerings and events galore there are alcohol and substance abuse counseling; adoption and parenting support; a gender identity project; a variety of HIV/AIDS-related services, counseling and bereavement support; couples mediation; and public policy programs, among others. Center orientation provides newcomers to the city with "a map of New York's organized lesbian and gay community"; it offers a monthly open house known as the "Orientation Welcome Wagon" and a "Welcome Packet" for gay, lesbian, bisexual, and transgender tourists, which includes entertainment guides listing gay bars, clubs, and restaurants, fliers on cultural programs, and a monthly calendar of events. The center's web site is updated daily and hyper-linked with most New York City and national gay organizations, and contains a daily calendar of events and a bimonthly newsletter.

- **Callen-Lorde Community Health Center**, 356 West 18th Street, NYC 10011, 212-271-7200, www.callen-lorde.org, is the largest primary health care center in the country devoted to lesbians, bisexuals, gay men, and transgenders. Patients pay on a sliding scale, according to their income.
- **Creative Visions**, 548 Hudson Street, NYC 10014, 212-645-7573, the city's largest locally owned Gay, Lesbian, Bi, and Trans book and video store.
- **Gay Women's Focus** at Beth Israel Medical Center, 10 Union Square East, Suite 2B, NYC 10003, 212-844-8500, is a full service internal medical practice with links to OB-GYN, psychiatric, and social work specialists.
- **Oscar Wilde Bookshop**, 15 Christopher Street, 212-255-8097, www.oscarwildebooks.com; said to be the world's first gay and lesbian bookshop.
- **Rainbow Roommates**, 268 West 22nd Street, NYC 10011, 212-627-8612, www.rainbowroommates.com, is an apartment share referral service for the gay and lesbian community throughout the city and in New Jersey.
- **Senior Action in a Gay Environment (SAGE)**, 212-741-2247, www.sageusa.org, is a non-profit community support agency, which offers workshops, discussion groups, and day trips for gay seniors, many of them for free. With an annual membership one receives a monthly newsletter, information on lectures, day trips and excursions, plus extensive social services for GLBT seniors.

RESOURCES AND SERVICES
FOR PEOPLE WITH DISABILITIES

Living in New York City with a disability has never been easy, but after passage of the federal Americans with Disabilities Act (ADA) in 1990 it became easier as the city began to address the needs of the disabled more seriously. Increasingly, street curbs and public buildings were modified to become wheelchair accessible. Following are some New York services, organizations, and resources that make life safer, easier, and more pleasant for people with disabilities. (In New Jersey, call 888-285-3036 or go to the **New Jersey Department of Human Services**, Disabilities services section: www.state.nj.us/humanservices/disable/index.html)

GETTING AROUND

- **Buses**: all buses operated by the Metropolitan Transit Authority (MTA) are wheelchair-accessible, with lifts at the rear door. If you have a qualifying disability or are 65 years of age or older you are eligible for reduced fare travel on MTA buses and subways. To get the reduced fare card and for more information, call 718-243-4999, TTY 718-596-8273, or go to www.mta.info.

- **Subway**: there are *Accessible Transfer Points* within the New York City subway; a pamphlet of the MTA lists all the subway stations and transfer points in the system which are wheelchair-accessible by elevator, with a map of the system. Reduced fare by token or MetroCard as described above also applies to the city's subway system and to the Long Island and Metro-North Railroads, except at peak morning hours. The pamphlet, also in large type and on audiotape, is available from customer assistance, MTA NYC Transit, 370 Jay Street, 8th Floor, Brooklyn 11201, or by calling the MTA customer service line, 718-330-3322.

- **CITY ACCESS** is a city program that contracts with private carriers to provide rides for customers who are unable to use city bus or subway service for some or all of their trips. For more information, go to www.nyc.gov.

- **Parking Permits for People with Disabilities** (**PPPD**): the city Department of Transportation issues two types of permits for citizens with disabilities: the New York State permit, which allows the driver to park in spaces marked by the International Symbol of Access, which in the city are all off-street in parking lots; and the NYC permit, which allows the driver to park on city streets in all "no parking" and "restricted parking" zones. For more information and to request an application for either or both permits write: Parking Permits for People with Disabilities (PPPD), NYC Department of Transportation, 28-11 Queens Plaza North, 8th Floor, Long Island City, NY 11101-4008, or call 718-433-3100; TTY 718-433-3111.

COMMUNICATION

The Verizon Communications Center for People with Disabilities, 204 Second Avenue at 13th Street, NYC 10009, offers information, services, and a variety of adaptive communications equipment necessary or useful to people with various disabilities. Some of these devices, such as enlarged number rings, are free; others, such as Weak Speech Handsets, may be rented, leased, or purchased. The Teletypewriter Device for the Deaf, alternately referred to as TTY or TDD and available at cost through Verizon, sends typed words over the phone lines to the New York Relay

Center, from which special operators relay conversations verbally 24-hours a day. The service is confidential and free of charge, except for the cost of the call. Hearing callers to TTY users reverse the process, calling a number (below) from which a special relay operator types the message to the TTY recipient, etc. To qualify for this and other services you must be certified at the center after providing an approved application and a letter from a doctor or an authorized social service agency.

- **Verizon Communication Center for People with Disabilities**, 800-974-6006; TTY users call 888-663-0363
- **New York Relay Center**, TTY 800-835-5515; others 800-421-1220

OTHER RESOURCES

- **Andrew Heiskell Library for the Blind and Physically Handicapped**, 40 West 20th Street, 212-206-5400, TTY 212-206-5458, www.nypl.org/branch/lb; wheelchair accessible, offers books in Braille and recorded books, an extensive collection of large-print books, print and non-print materials on disabilities. Also here, a collection of community information services on resources for people with disabilities, as well as recreational, cultural, and service-oriented programming for and about people with disabilities. Materials are for use on site or by postage-free mail to those who are homebound, 212-621-0564, TTY 212-621-0553.
- **Associated Blind**, 135 West 23rd Street, NYC 10011, 212-766-6800, operates 205 apartments for the blind and wheelchair bound at this address, but there is a long waiting list. Non-resident blind also have access to social workers, recreation, and the fitness center here.
- **Con Edison Concern Program** for the hearing-impaired and sight-impaired, 800-872-8846, TTY 800-642-2308, www.conedison.com.
- *Exceptional Parent Magazine*, 800-372-7368, www.eparent.com, is a guide for parents of children and young adults with disabilities or health problems. Also publishes an annual resource guide available in bookstores or through the magazine.
- **Goodwill Industries International**, 4-21 27th Avenue, Astoria, Queens 11102, 718-728-5400, www.goodwill.org, offers a host of job training and computer classes for people with physical and mental disabilities.
- **Hospital Audiences Inc. (HAI)**, 548 Broadway, 3rd floor, NYC 10012, 212-575-7660, www.hospaud.org, provides access to the arts for New Yorkers with disabilities. They also provide the indispensable *Access for All: A Guide to New York City Cultural Institutions for People with Disabilities*, which lists 300 cultural venues accessible to the handicapped, including major galleries and historical monuments; available online at no charge.

- **International Center for the Disabled** (**ICD**), 340 East 24th Street, NYC 10010, 212-585-6250, TTY 212-585-6060, provides primary medical care, vocational evaluation, job training and placement for learning and physically disabled.
- **League for the Hard of Hearing**, 71 West 23rd Street, NYC 10010, 917-305-7700, www.lhh.com, provides a range of services including hearing rehabilitation. Call for their resource manual ($5) or get information on their programs and services from their web site.
- **Learning Disabilities Helpline**, 212-645-6730, operated by the Learning Disabilities Association of New York, 27 West 20th Street, Suite 303, NYC 10011, provides information and referrals in English and Spanish from their database of resources for the learning disabled.
- **The Lighthouse, Inc.**, 111 East 59th Street, NYC 10022, 212-821-9200 or 800-829-0500, www.lighthouse.org, provides vision rehabilitation and other services to the visually impaired. Services include readers, mobility training, computer training, career services, a child development center, and adaptive skills classes.
- **Mayor's Office for People with Disabilities**, 52 Chambers Street, Room 206, NYC 10007, 212-788-2830, TTY 212-788-2838; for information and referrals.
- **Metropolitan Museum of Art**, 1000 Fifth Avenue at 81st Street, NYC 10028-0198, 212-535-7710, TTY 212-570-3828, www.metmuseum.org, is wheelchair accessible and has programs with sign language interpretation for the hearing impaired; guides by appointment only for the visually impaired; tours and programs for the developmentally disabled.
- **National Center For Learning Disabilities**, 381 Park Avenue South, Suite 1401, NYC 10016, 212-545-7510, www.ncld.org; provides information and referrals concerning learning disabilities in children and adults at 888-575-7373, and on their web site, which has links to related organizations and resources, publications, and recent events. Their concerns include dyslexia and adult literacy.
- *New York Able*, a monthly newspaper "Positively For, By and About the Disabled," with news, commentary, a calendar of events, and ads of interest to people with disabilities. Write P.O. Box 395, Old Bethpage, NY 11804, or call 516-939-2253 or 718-792-3533.
- **New York Public Library Branches** (see also Andrew Heiskell Library above). Most Manhattan, Bronx, Queens, and Staten Island libraries are wheelchair accessible as are more than a dozen Brooklyn libraries with more upgrading underway. Call the local branch first and ask, or go to www.nypl.org. Included on the list are: The Donnell Library Center, 20 West 53rd Street, 212-621-0618; the Library for the Performing Arts, 40 Lincoln Center Plaza at 65th Street, 212-870-1630;

Mid-Manhattan Library, 455 Fifth Avenue at 40th Street, 212-340-0833; Science, Industry, and Business Library, 188 Madison Avenue at 34th Street, 212-592-7000; the Fordham Library Center, 2556 Bainbridge Avenue, The Bronx, 718-579-4244; and St. George Library Center, 5 Central Avenue, St. George, SI, 718-442-8560, among others. Project ACCESS, by appointment at the Mid-Manhattan, St. George, and Fordham branches, uses Kurzweil Personal Readers to give sight-impaired readers access to the full range of the library services and materials. Other helpful technology, such as Braille writers, is available here and at some other branches. For information about these and other services call 212-340-0843, TTY 212-340-0931.

- **New York Society for the Deaf**, 817 Broadway at 11th Street, 7th Floor, NYC 10003, 212-777-3900, www.nysd.org, provides multiple services for the deaf.
- **Resources for Children With Special Needs**, 116 East 16th Street, NYC 10003, 212-677-4650, www.resourcesnyc.org
- **Rusk Institute of Rehabilitation Medicine's** driver training program, 400 East 34th Street, Room RR312, 212-263-6028; offers technicians to evaluate the particular needs of prospective drivers with physical handicaps, adapting each car with special devices, and train the driver to operate the adapted car.
- **Technology Resource Center**, operated by United Cerebral Palsy of New York City, 120 East 23rd Street, NYC 10010, 212-979-9700. Come here to the demonstration center to view, learn about, and try a range of adaptive products and get information about others through a resource specialist and catalogues. Products range from adapted toys to augmentative communication devices, computers, home products, and accessibility modifications.
- **TAP, Theater Access Project of the Theatre Development Fund**, 1501 Broadway, 21st floor, NYC 10036, 212-221-1103, TTY 212-719-4537, www.tdf.org, offers signed performances of selected shows and discounted tickets for people with physical disabilities.
- **Visions Services for the Blind and Visually Impaired**, 500 Greenwich Street, 16th Floor, NYC 10005, 212-625-1616, www.visionsvcb.org; offers free and low-cost rehabilitation and social services to the blind and multi-handicapped, including those who are non-English speaking. Self-help audio guides at cost teach life skills, and there are peer support groups and recreation year-round at Vacation Camp for the Blind in Rockland County, transportation provided.
- **Walter Reade Theater**, 70 Lincoln Center Plaza at 67th Street, 212-875-5600, www.filmlinc.com, shows first-run features with open captions for the deaf once a month. Call after 3 p.m. for details.

RESOURCES AND SERVICES FOR SENIORS

If you are or are soon to be a senior and living in New York City get yourself a copy of *Take Charge! A Complete Guide to Senior Living in New York City* by John Vinton (New York University Press), a comprehensive reference to services, resources, and some practical advice you didn't know you'd need. It includes guidance on avoiding rip-offs in home repair and other areas in which seniors are targeted, where to get help with financial/estate planning, resources for long-term care, end-of-life concerns such as hospice, assisted death and burial. Another good resource for young seniors is *Retire in New York City—Even If You're Not Rich* by Janet Hays (Bonus Books).

The prime source of services and assistance for seniors here is the city's **Department for the Aging (DFTA)**, whose web site, www.ci.nyc.ny.us/aging, is useful in discovering and accessing these services. Write or call the department at 2 Lafayette Street, NYC 10007, 212-442-1000.

The Department for the Aging also operates 335 senior centers throughout the boroughs, where meals are served, cultural trips originate, and outreach gives access to other services. The department offers guidance on government benefits and referral to community services; provides transportation for health care, social services and necessities; arranges home care for the qualified; helps victims of elder abuse; offers job training for the employable unemployed; subsidizes part-time employment; offers computer training and customer service skills and placement in jobs in private industry; arranges legal assistance to those in need; and more.

Some useful numbers:

- **Alzheimer's and Long Term Care Services**, 212-442-3086, offers counseling and referrals for families of seniors with Alzheimer's disease.
- **Elder Pharmaceutical Insurance Coverage (EPIC)**, 800-332-3742, www.health.state.ny.us/nysdoh/epic/, offers savings on the cost of drugs for qualified individuals.
- **Health insurance information and counseling**, 212-333-5511
- **Housing,** for the department's *Alternatives in Senior Housing: A Comprehensive Guide for New York City*, call 212-442-1384. In recent years complexes for senior "assisted living" at market prices have sprung up throughout the city and in the greater metropolitan area; see ads in the *New York Times*.
- **Legal assistance**: Call the Manhattan office at, 212-426-3000 and ask for information regarding Queens and The Bronx; in Brooklyn, call 718-645-3111; Staten Island, 718-273-6677.
- **Reduced fare** for seniors: people with disabilities and those 65 and older can purchase a MetroCard at half-price. Write MTA, Reduced Fare, P.O. Box 023158, Brooklyn 11202-0064, or call the reduced fare line at 718-243-4999, TTY 718-596-8273.

- **Senior Citizen Rent Increase Exemption (SCRIE)** is for those over 62 whose income falls below $20,000; this is a city subsidy. Call 212-442-1000 for more information.
- **State School Tax Relief (STAR)** offers reduced school property taxes for homeowners (condos and co-ops included) on limited incomes. Write STAR Program, Office of Real Property Services, 16 Sheridan Avenue, Albany, NY 12210, or call 518-474-9276 (www.orps.state.ny.us/star)

Under state law **new rental housing** in the city is frequently classified **80/20**, which means that 20% of the apartments are reserved for seniors at below-market rents. Applicants are chosen by lottery, and the waiting list is long. Get on the list before you need the apartment. To find out if you are eligible and to get on line, call the **New York State Housing Finance Agency (HFA)**, 212-688-4000.

The city abounds in culture at a discount for seniors. Most notably, the **Senior Cultural Discount Program**, administered by Hospital Audiences, Inc. (HAI) provides $10 tickets to events on Broadway, at Lincoln Center, BAM, and elsewhere. Call HAI to register for this benefit on their "tickets to go line" at 212-284-4100 or HAI at 212-575-7676 or visit www.hospaud.org. Museums, movie theaters, and some theaters discount admission for seniors as well. State parks and historic sites are free to seniors who present a photo ID that includes date of birth.

Exercise programs for seniors, free or at low cost, are widely available. Exercise classes, stress management, and walking clubs are located in many of the senior centers. Call **Health Promotion Services (HPS)**, 212-442-0954, to find out more. The Parks and Recreation Department operates 25 recreation centers in the city (membership, $25 annually), some of which offer senior aerobics and other classes. The Parks Department also sponsors concerts in the parks and other activities. For all parks information call the citywide information line 311 or visit www.nyc parks.org. And, finally, there are exercise programs for seniors at many YMCAs and YMHAs (see **Health Clubs, YMCAs, YWCAs, and YMHAs** in the **Sports and Recreation** chapter).

Access to college courses on a "space available" basis is offered to seniors at a discount by most of the major universities and colleges in the city. To name some:

- **Brooklyn College**, "Institute for Retired Professionals and Executives," 718-951-5647
- **City University of New York**, "Quest" Program, 212-925-6625, www.cuny.edu, offering free course auditing to those 60 and older in the four-year colleges, enrollment courses (for credit) in the community colleges.

- **College of Staten Island**, "Options for Older Adults," 718-982-3772, www.csi.cuny.edu
- **Columbia University**, "Life Long Learners," 212-854-2820, www.columbia.edu
- **Fordham University**, "College at 60," 212-636-6740, www. fordham.edu
- **New School**, "Institute for Retired Professionals," 212-229-5682, www.newschool.edu
- **NYU School of Continuing Education**, 212-998-7080, www.nyu.edu
- **Pace University**, "Adult Resource Center," 212-346-1288, www.pace.edu
- **Queens College**, "Center for Unlimited Enrichment," 718-997-3635, www.qc.edu
- **St. John's University**, Queens, 718-990-6161, www.stjohns.edu

A host of volunteer opportunities are available to seniors (see **Volunteering** chapter) and some of the resources detailed above (**Resources and Services for People with Disabilities**) are valuable for seniors as well. A few other resources are worth noting:

- **Alzheimer's Association**, 212-983-0700, www.alz.org; useful for those who are diagnosed with the disease and for their families.
- **Con Edison**, 800-872-8846, in their "Concern" program for seniors age 62 and older provides a newsletter and advice on bill payments, financial assistance, a Home Energy Assistance Program (HEAP), and turn-off protection for seniors who are blind or disabled.
- **New York Foundation for Senior Citizens**, 212-962-7559, offers a free home safety audit to homeowners (condos and co-ops included) 60 and older. They also have a home repair program, providing minor electrical, plumbing, masonry, and carpentry repairs.
- **SAGE, Senior Action in a Gay Environment**, is a non-profit community support agency described above under **Lesbian and Gay Concerns**, 212-741-2247, www.sageusa.org.

IF YOU'RE PLANNING TO RAISE CHILDREN IN NEW YORK CITY, FRIENDS and relatives (from out of town) may look at you with concern. And it is a challenge to raise children here. But it is also richly rewarding, for child and parent alike. In fact, it isn't so much difficult as it is just different here in the Big Apple. This chapter attempts to make it a little easier by describing the available options in childcare, nursery schools, primary and high schools—public, private, and parochial—with information to help parents choose between them. We begin with baby sitters and infant care and wind up with high schools. For a more in-depth look at raising kids in the city, you may want to read *Living with Kids in Manhattan* (Grownup's Guide Publishing) by Diane Chernoff-Rosen.

Please note: listing in this book is merely informational and is *not* an endorsement or a recommendation. Always be careful when entrusting your child with strangers.

CHILDCARE

Quality day care, now typically called childcare, can be hard to find and is usually more expensive in New York than anywhere else in the country, thanks to the tremendous cost of real estate and the need for stringent standards governing the operation of day care centers. Asked what is required to open a day care center here, Frances Alston, former program director of the not-for-profit Day Care Council, says, "First thing is, rob a bank. You can't start a day care center in New York for less than a quarter million dollars." According to Runzheimer International (www.runzheimer.com) in 2004, daycare costs in New York City averaged over $900 a month; only Boston ranked higher.

High prices aside, there are many options, and not all are with such high price tags; some take into consideration your financial situation and childcare needs. Non-profit agencies, which act as go-betweens for parents and day care providers, are proliferating. We list some below under **Information Sources**. Your employer may have day care information and some even offer on premises facilities.

Also below, you'll find thumbnail descriptions of the kinds of pre-school care (and education) available in New York City. Arranged chronologically by ages covered—from birth through six years—these categories are followed by the names of organizations that provide specific day care recommendations.

New York State establishes the eligibility requirements for publicly funded day care, be it family day care in a private home or group care at a center. To be eligible, a family must meet established maximum income requirements. Almost all those entitled to assistance still pay something; currently fees range from a low of $1 per week, per child, up to $99 per week.

The US Department of Education provides a useful source of parenting information covering such topics as children's television viewing habits, sleep problems, childcare, and behavioral issues, with a library of articles and book abstracts and links to special interest organizations; visit www.ed.gov, or call 800-USA-LEARN. KinderStart's web site at www.kinderstart.com has a handy "childcare locator," which can help you find childcare in your neighborhood. For a daycare safety-hazard checklist and safety recalls, you can call the Consumer Product Safety Commission, 800-638-2772 or go to www.cpsc.gov. Available free in school lobbies, pediatricians' offices and laundromats, a variety of monthly parent magazines, the most ubiquitous of which is *BigAppleParent* (as well as *QueensParent* and *WestchesterParent*), offer useful advice and information on everything from nutrition to single parenting, day care, schools, and child health and recreation. *BigApple's* web site, www.parentsknow.com, has links to current and past articles, an extensive monthly calendar of events for parents and children, and a bulletin board worth checking for baby sitters, nannies, playgroups, Spanish classes for children ... the list goes on.

AU PAIRS AND NANNIES

When it comes to sitters, New York's no different than the suburbs. Neighborhoods are filled with reliable teenagers looking for jobs. But it takes time to meet them. As with many personal services, the best sources for good baby sitters or nannies are recommendations from friends, relatives, or colleagues. You can also stop by a crowded playground and talk to the many nannies that you'll find watching the neighborhood children. Naturally, before hiring anyone to watch your children, you should carefully screen applicants and check all references. In case networking fails, we've listed a number of alternatives. Some of the agencies also provide full-time, sleep-in or day only help.

Au pairs are young women (between 18 and 25), usually European, who provide a year of in-home childcare and light housekeeping in exchange for airfare, room and board, and a small stipend ($110 to $150 per week). Less expensive than nannies, they are also less experienced, may be less mature, and are gone in a year. The program is certainly valuable for the cultural exchange it offers the host family and the au pair. The US Information Agency oversees and approves the organizations that place au pairs. Either of the national agencies listed below will connect you with a local coordinator who will match up your family with a suitable au pair:

- **Au Pair in America**, 800-928-7247, www.aupairinamerica.com
- **Interexchange**, 800-479-0907, www.interexchange.org

Good fortune is having a friend who passes on to you her excellent **nanny**, her children having outgrown the need, just when you need one. Failing that, there are want ads, the internet, and nanny agencies to fall back on. An invaluable source of full- and part-time nannies, both live-in and out, as well as house-cleaning personnel is the classified ad section in the *Irish Echo*, published in the city and available at newsstands throughout the city. Those seeking positions are not necessarily Irish, and some of the ads under "situations wanted" are placed by the satisfied employers of nannies whose services they no longer need. On the internet, www.4nannies.com carries classified nanny listings allowing you to avoid agency fees, which can run $800 to $3,000. You simply pay the application fee. The site has links to firms that do background checks and some that provide nanny tax advice and/or service.

An agency, on the other hand, will have checked the nanny's background, perhaps by detective, her Social Security record, driving record, credit record and so far as possible, any chance of criminal record. Note that there are no national criminal records available to investigators. But the agency will also have interviewed the nanny, in person or by phone, and will have checked her references. The agency can inform you about necessary nanny tax procedures and insurance and should provide a detailed contract. The **International Nanny Association** maintains a useful web site, www.nanny.org, which provides information about nanny agencies and the nanny selection process. Another site, which is advertiser supported, www.nannynetwork.com, contains a database of nanny placement agencies and referral services, nanny insurance services, and background verification services as well as a library of articles.

However you find your nanny, be sure to check at least two of the prospective nanny's references, questioning them carefully, and repeatedly, if necessary. You will also want to interview the nanny in your home if possible in order to insure a good fit.

NANNY AGENCIES

- **Best Domestic**, a national agency at 10 East 39th Street, #1005, 212-683-3070, www.bestdomestic.com, handles nannies, live-in or out, as well as housekeepers and other domestic help. Weekly wage for a nanny runs $450 to $600, with a two-month guarantee, and an agency fee of 12% of one year's salary, paid one week after the nanny starts work.
- **Fox Agency**, 30 East 60th Street, NYC 10022, 212-753-2686, providing baby nurses and nannies since 1936. Rates are hourly, daily, or weekly. Nannies, screened by the agency, run $400 and up weekly, higher for living in (the rate may or may not include the legally mandated Social Security taxes and unemployment insurance).
- **Irish Agency**, 10 East 39th Street, 212-473-5263 (IRE-LAND), and 43 Center Drive, Old Greenwich, CT, 800-462-6697, provides full-time nannies throughout the metropolitan area, living in or out, starting at $550 per week, with an agency fee of four weeks' salary, a minimum of $2,200 up front. As their nannies, not necessarily Irish, have been with them for some time, they do not do a background check unless it is requested, however they do check references.
- **NY Nanny Center, Inc.**, 31 South Bayles Avenue, Port Washington, NY 11058, 516-767-5136, www.nynanny.com, has both live-in and out nannies in the tri-state area. The nannies are evaluated by the director, a former social worker. Nannies in this program attend a monthly support meeting. Weekly wages start at $500, with an agency fee of four weeks' salary starting at $2,000 and a 60-day guarantee.
- **Pavillion Agency, Inc.**, 15 East 40th Street, NYC 10016, 212-889-6609, www.pavillionagency.com, specializes in nannies (as well as butlers, domestics and chauffeurs) who negotiate their rates depending on the needs of their clients. Currently nannies, living in or out, cost $500 and up weekly, plus Social Security taxes and unemployment insurance. The agency fee is 15% of the annual salary.

BABYSITTERS

AGENCIES

Most babysitting is via word of mouth, short of that, try:
- **Avalon Nurses Registry**, 162 West 56th Street, 212-245-0250, www.avalonhealthcare.com; rates start at $15 per hour and there is a four-hour minimum plus travel pay, which increases after 8 p.m. and then after midnight. You can call them 24/7. Fees include the agency commission.

- **Baby Sitters' Guild**, 60 East 42nd Street, 212-682-0227, www.baby sittersguild.com, hourly fee for one or two children starts at $20, higher for more children. With enough advance notice, a sitter with a nursing background is provided for children under one year. There is a four-hour minimum plus travel pay, which varies depending on time of day. The guild can provide a babysitter fluent in one of 16 languages for an additional fee. All fees include the agency's commission. Call between 9 a.m. and 9 p.m. seven-days a week. While requests made the day of can usually be filled, it is better to call a day prior. The guild was established in 1940.
- **Pinch Sitters**, 799 Broadway, NYC 10003, 212-260-6005; babysitters, on short notice if necessary, starting at $14 per hour, plus transportation at night, four-hour minimum. Call Monday-Friday, 7 a.m. to 5 p.m.

NON-PROFIT

- **Parents League**, 115 East 82nd Street, 212-737-7385, www.parents league.org; the league's babysitting service is just one of several benefits included in the $90 annual membership fee. Sitters are students, ages 13 to 18, who attend league member schools or who are the children of members. Riffle through the sitter files, arranged by neighborhood, in the league's office between 9 a.m. and 4 p.m., Monday-Wednesday, 9 a.m. to 7 p.m. on Thursday, until noon on Friday. The league also provides plenty of information on city schools: see **Nursery Schools** below.

SCHOOLS

- **Barnard College Babysitting Service**, 117th and Broadway, 212-854-2035, www.barnard.edu; to pre-register, call in your name, address, phone number and name of your pediatrician. Once you are in their file, call Monday, Thursday, Friday between 10 a.m. and 4 p.m., and between 10 a.m. and 7 p.m. Tuesday and Wednesday, two days in advance of your needs. A student will call you back. Rates start at around $8 per hour but most parents pay more in this competitive market. There is also a $20 annual fee.
- **St. Vincent's Hospital School of Nursing**, 27 Christopher Street: mail or bring a notice to be posted on the school's bulletin board. Negotiate a rate with the student who calls you.

FAMILY DAY CARE

More and more middle-class parents are electing family care for their toddlers. Here in New York City the Health Department and/or other agencies involved in the field certify and supervise individuals caring for infants and toddlers in their apartments. These "providers," often mothers of young children drawn to childcare as a means of remaining at home with their own youngsters, are allowed to oversee up to six children—no more than two of whom can be infants—in their dwelling at one time. Typically, parents who do not qualify for assistance pay between $40 and $50 per child for a six- to eight-hour day. To obtain a list of licensed day care facilities in New York City, write to NYC Department of Health, Bureau of Daycare, 2 Lafayette Street, 22nd floor, New York, NY 10048 or call 212-676-2444. The city site, www.nyc.gov, has a link to the bureau if you type in day care. The bureau also has a complaint hotline at 800-732-5207.

GROUP DAY CARE CENTERS

These city-licensed facilities, be they in the private or public sector, offer educational as well as care-taking programs for groups of children primarily, but not exclusively, between the ages of two and six years for an extended (beyond normal nursery school hours) or a full eight-hour day.

- **Publicly funded day care centers** are usually found in, or contiguous to, neighborhoods with the greatest economic need. Even with an income above the maximum allowed by the state, parents proving "social" need—those working full-time qualify—can apply to publicly funded daycare centers, if they are prepared to pay the full cost for their child's care. Depending on the facility, this now runs about $600 a month.
- **Private centers** tend to be either nursery schools, which have added full-day care to the regular school curriculum, or centers established to supply childcare, which also offer education. Private daycare centers in New York City can easily run $800 a month.

Contact the city's **Agency for Child Development** through the city information line, 311, during business hours or the **Department of Health, Bureau of Day Care**, 212-676-2444, for a list of publicly funded daycare centers. Ads for private centers and for the occasional playgroup will be found in parent magazines such as *Big Apple Parent*, which are distributed free in school lobbies.

INFANT CARE

Formal programs for the two-month-old to two-year-old set are almost all publicly funded and appended to day care centers. Call the New York City Health Department's Bureau of Day Care, 212-676-2444, for the names of city-licensed facilities. Infants can also be placed in family day care homes.

PLAY GROUPS

Neighborhood parents often band together informally, usually in cooperative fashion, to care for a small group of pre-schoolers for a half-day or so, one, two or three times a week. Do some networking, a little research and use your best judgment about such existing groups, or start your own.

INFORMATION SOURCES

New York Parents' Book by Lois Gilman (Penguin) covers everything from having the baby to care and entertainment. Several non-profit organizations as well as the Agency for Child Development, jointly sponsored by the city, state and federal governments, provide information about local facilities. To determine the most suitable day care solution for your family's needs, consult these sources while pursuing the other leads suggested below.

- **Agency for Child Development**, 30 Main Street, Brooklyn 11201, dial 311 for pre-school information and referrals from the ACD's Vacancy Information Service. Their staff provides names and addresses of private as well as publicly funded and Head Start childcare facilities located in the five boroughs. This information is supplied to ACD by the Department of Health's Bureau of Day Care, 212-676-2444, the group charged with licensing pre-school facilities. Their "Directory of Day Care Services in New York City" is available by mail free of charge.
- **Day Care Council of New York, Inc.**, 12 West 21st Street, NYC 10010, 212-206-7818, www.dccnyinc.org, has 50 years' experience as a non-profit providing free information, counseling and referrals on all types of childcare, including baby sitters, nannies and day care throughout the five boroughs.
- The **New York Public Library's Early Childhood Resource Center** at the Hudson Park Branch on Leroy Street off Seventh Avenue in Greenwich Village, 212-929-0815, devotes one whole floor to resource materials for parents and a playroom for kids, open Tuesday-Saturday afternoons.
- **The Parents League of New York**, 115 East 82nd Street, NYC 10028, 212-737-7385, www.parentsleague.org, provides parenting help, support, babysitting, after school activities, tutors and special workshops and programs for a $90 annual membership fee.

OTHER LEADS

Check out some of the following resources for referrals in your particular neighborhood: **churches** and **temples**, large and small; old-fashioned, wall-mounted **bulletin boards**, most often found in the larger supermarkets; **private schools**, ask the admissions director for the names of feeder schools, day care centers or playgroups; **pediatricians**; **hospitals**, talk with the administrative officer in charge of residents and interns; and, last but perhaps most accessible and knowledgeable of all, **playgrounds** and **neighborhood parents**.

SCHOOLS

NURSERY SCHOOLS

It is at this point, typically, that parental anxiety sets in. And it needn't. In Manhattan alone there are more than 175 privately run pre-school programs, generally geared to three-, four-, and five-year-olds, often including toddlers' groups and sometimes all-day care as well. They vary widely in educational philosophy and style, and admission to none of them is essential to a child's later success at Harvard. *The Manhattan Directory of Private Nursery Schools* by Linda Faulhaber (SoHo Press) is a detailed listing of more than 150 nursery and all-day programs plus other useful information. It's a good place to start. Meanwhile, talk with mothers in the parks you frequent and with parents of children in neighborhood nursery schools. The search process typically begins just after Labor Day preceding application, and many schools will have open houses; this is also the time to request information from the schools you might wish to consider. And finally, in helping you decide what might be the best school for your child (and for you), the two sources below should be helpful:

• **The Independent Schools Admissions Association of Greater New York (ISAAGNY)** publishes the "New York Independent Schools Directory" containing page-long descriptions of more than 120 private member schools, from pre-school through high school. Nursery schools and toddler groups, as well as numerous elementary and secondary schools, along with pre-school groups, are listed, and a useful geographical index is included in the appendix. This directory provides an excellent overview of New York's varied private schools. Copies cost $20 and can be picked up at the office of the Parents League of New York, 212-737-7385, or ordered from them by mail ($23)

• **Parents League of New York, Inc.**, 115 East 82nd Street, NYC 10028, 212-737-7385; with 106 member schools, mainly in Manhattan, the Parents League is an excellent source of private school information. One counseling session with a specialist from their School Advisory Service—for example, their expert on toddlers' groups and nursery schools—is well worth the league's annual $90 membership fee. A panoply of other child-related services, not the least of which is their reliable Baby Sitter-Young Helper listing, a great boon to any newcomer with kids, also comes with league membership, as does their "Toddler Activities Directory."

GRADE SCHOOLS

Here, decision-making can become more difficult because there are so many options. To begin with, there is the choice between public, private, and parochial school. For some it is a choice easily made; they know they want one or the other, or they can't afford private school. A word to the undecided: know that there are some excellent public schools in the city, just as there are some dreadful ones.

Those opting for a **private school** will find the resources above under **Nursery Schools** helpful. *The Manhattan Family Guide to Private Schools* by Victoria Goldman and Catherine Hausman (SoHo Press) offers an independent evaluation of the specific schools; however the focus is distinctly uptown, giving scant attention to some excellent downtown schools. They do provide useful information and advice on navigating the admissions process. When trying to determine which school is right for your child—public or private—it is possible to do a lot of research on your own. For starters, you can go to the each school's web site, which will offer a lot of preliminary information. Ask parents whose children attend area schools. Contact schools directly and arrange a time to visit, and be sure to ask the administrators and staff about school philosophy, structure, and performance indicators. Read the school literature carefully. Examine the physical facility. Observe the relationships between children, staff, and administration. Consider the program, in theory and in practice. Finally, what is your gut reaction? Remember, you and your child may spend the next eight to twelve years here, and no decision is irrevocable. Just hard. In the case of private schools, school advisors are available, for a fee.

Catholic **parochial schools**, which cost considerably less than many of the city's private schools, have found favor in recent years with non-Catholics as well as Catholics as an attractive alternative to public schools. The Archdiocese of New York operates 144 elementary and 39 high schools in Manhattan, The Bronx, and Staten Island. For information about Catholic schools in your neighborhood or beyond, call 800-SCHOOL4 or 212-371-1000. The Roman Catholic Diocese of Brooklyn and Queens operates 156 elementary schools and 22 high schools. Contact the Superintendent's office, 718-965-7300, www.archdioceseofbrooklyn.org, for more information. There is no source of comparative evaluation of the parochial schools, which are independently run, so interested parents are left to make their own evaluation on a school by school basis.

Parents considering **public school** should begin by contacting the community school board in their district (see **Neighborhoods**) for a list of schools and to find out in which school zone they reside. Many school boards have brochures from which it is possible to get a sense both of the character of the district and its schools. When visiting schools, try to get a grasp of teacher-student interaction, school safety, PTA involvement, class size, and the overall feel of the school. Ask questions.

It is often possible to send a child to a school outside of his/her zone, space permitting, and if the process is begun early enough. One reason to do this is if your workplace is in a different district; inquire with that district about the required variance procedure.

In recent years several grade groupings have evolved among the city's schools, making choice more complicated. And within these groupings are schools with varying focus. The most common configurations below the high school level are:

- **Early childhood schools**, pre-kindergarten to second or third grade, popular for their focus on the needs of young children.
- **Elementary schools**, K-fifth or -sixth grade, are the most common configuration. Many districts are now shifting sixth grade to middle schools to avoid crowding.
- **Grammar schools**, K-8, are very rare but can serve as an alternative to middle school.
- **Middle schools** or **intermediate schools**, containing sixth through eighth grades or, sometimes, seventh and eighth. Some of these are theme schools, focusing on a particular subject area, such as the performing arts or technology; some require entry exams. These are the most common schools following K-5 and have essentially replaced the junior high school. Middle school is often where crowding, social issues, and transportation issues (children taking buses and even subways to get to school) begin. It is, therefore, a time when some families head for the boroughs or the suburbs, or opt for private schooling for their kids. This is not to say there aren't good public middle schools. It just takes perseverance to find the right one.

For further guidance and encouragement in choosing public schools for your child, you can turn to three books from SoHo Press written by Clara Hemphill, a researcher at the Public Education Association. In *New York City's Best Public Elementary Schools: A Parents' Guide* (updated in 2002), she profiles the top 100 elementary schools in the city. In *Public Middle Schools: New York City's Best*, and *New York City's Best Public High Schools*, she takes a similar look at middle and high schools, providing excellent descriptions and ratings of schools in each district of the city. You can also find much of this information on the web site of Advocates for Children at www.advocatesforchildren.org, which includes digests on more than 50 schools and a complete list of programs for gifted children and their admissions criteria.

HIGH SCHOOLS

Decisions at this level, however fraught with anxiety, are made somewhat easier by the guidance procedures at your child's current school, as well as by the fact that your about-to-be-a-high-schooler will participate in the decision. Again, public or private? Information sources for the private schools are as noted above.

Admission to many of the public high schools is citywide, a trend which is increasing as theme schools proliferate at this level. Parents and students often find themselves in a mad scramble for entry into the "best school." Competition can be fierce, as the number of good high schools—particularly in Manhattan—is limited. Depending on the high school and the specific program, students may be selected by audition (for performing arts programs), by test scores, middle school grade averages, or a combination thereof. If not applying to a specific school, students are selected by lottery or in some cases (typically in the boroughs outside of Manhattan) they attend the school nearest them. Typically, parents of Manhattan middle school students start scouting high schools much in the manner of college selections. Key concerns are safe transportation to and from the school, special programs, and how the school rates both academically and in terms of student safety. According to the *Times*, in 2004 about 34% of students were assigned to their first school choice.

The various categories of high school include the following major groupings:

- **Audition schools**, such as Fiorello LaGuardia High School of Music and Art and the Performing Arts, and High School of Art and Design, to which the student must be recommended and must audition or present a portfolio for admission.
- **Competitive schools** to which admission is by competitive exam; Bronx High School of Science, Brooklyn Tech, Hunter High School, and Stuyvesant are the most well known and desirable schools in this group.
- **District schools**, which range from abysmal to excellent.
- **Special interest schools** include the School of Fashion Industries and the New York School of Printing, among others.

INFORMATION SOURCES

The annual public school options fair, with workshops and guides to schools in several Manhattan districts, at the 92nd Street YMHA, 212-996-1100, is worth a visit. The Parenting Center there has a variety of seminars on public and private schools, and one need not be a member to attend. Call the center for particulars.

- **New York City Department of Education**, 52 Chambers Street, New York, NY 10007, 718-935-2000, www.nycenet.edu; contact them for a free "Public High School Directory."
- **The Division of Assessment and Accountability of the Board of Education**, 52 Chambers Street, Rooms 309 & 310, NYC 10007, 212-374-3990, www.nycenet.edu/daa, publishes an annual report, commonly known as the "Report Card," which describes each of the public schools statistically for the previous year. It's a source of information on enrollment, ethnic composition, reading scores, etc.
- **The Manhattan Borough President's Office**, 1 Centre Street, 19th Floor South, NYC 10007, 212-669-8300, www.cvfieldsmbp.org, will send a *Parent's Guide to Choosing a Public Elementary School in New York City*, on request, free.
- **The Toussaint Institute**, 212-422-5338, offers an annual spring seminar on New York City public schools for African-American and Hispanic parents. Call for details.
- **School Match**, 5027 Pine Creek Drive, Westerville, OH 43081, 800-992-5323, www.schoolmatch.com, is a private organization which, for $97.50, will send a ranked list with descriptions of 15 schools, public or private (or both for $87.50 each), in a specific area, which best suit your requirements as determined by a questionnaire.

BIG CITY LIVING ENCOURAGES IDIOSYNCRATIC LIFE STYLES. AND New Yorkers pursue their interests and goals singularly unencumbered by considerations as to "what the neighbors might think." Home decoration is a striking case in point. Anything (within the terms of the lease) goes, and when it comes to providing all the goods and services necessary for us to feather our wildly divergent, albeit mainly minuscule, nests, the city really comes through for its residents. Generally speaking, there are at least three approaches to shopping in Manhattan: (1) largish, fairly priced, standard sources; (2) famous signature shops and upscale boutiques; and (3) discounters, warehouse-style superstores, and/or alternative resources such as wholesale districts and sample sales.

Note from the shopping strategies department: unless you are literally sitting and sleeping on the floor of your new apartment, it pays to wait until winter for the annual, city-wide furniture and housewares sales to make those major purchases. In both department stores and specialty shops, the savings in January and February are considerable, 20% to 50% off. Watch for the ads in the *Times*. And it's worth noting, especially if you anticipate making a major purchase, the **sales tax** in New York City is 8.625%, but the tax bite in New Jersey is six percent and most clothing items are exempt. Depending on the "spree," the savings in New Jersey may more than pay the toll to cross the Hudson.

While most stores are open on Sundays, except in Paramus, New Jersey, where blue laws are still in effect, store hours will vary, with many stores cutting hours during the summer and staying open late as the end of year holiday season approaches. Many run specials during Memorial Day, President's Day, Independence Day, etc.—check ads and call stores for hours and sales. In some cases you can get on their e-mail or mailing lists to find out about sales and other happenings.

FULL SERVICE DEPARTMENT STORES

As designer sections fragment the more traditional uniform displays of merchandise, one-stop shopping at full-service department stores has lost some of its cohesiveness. Still, it beats 15 stops in a 20-block neighborhood. Although more difficult than it once was, it's comforting to take a 15-item list—electronic organizer through silk sheets—and pass the afternoon under one roof. So, we lead off with the royalty of New York's department store scene:

- **Bloomingdale's**, between Third Avenue at 59th Street, 212-705-2000, www.bloomingdales.com (coming soon to SoHo on Broadway); for all the zap and glitter, Bloomie's has a sturdy core: you can leave your watch for repair, order Christmas cards, shop the best white sales in town—January and August—buy a TV, a mattress, and sweat socks, as well as try out glittery shoes to a funky beat, or nosh the food of the moment at one of several chic cafés. The main floor offers a full array of make-up and makeovers, plus exquisite jewelry and other top-of-the line items. Once above the initial frenzy of the main floor, you'll find designer clothing and much more in calmer environs. Services include Beatrice Dale personal shoppers, 212-705-2380, translators, a bridal registry, decorators, dining, and 24-hour telephone order service.
- **Century 21**, 22 Cortlandt Street, 212-227-9092; 472 86th Street, Bay Ridge, Brooklyn, 718-748-3266, www.c21stores.com; not the nationwide real estate broker but something that is unique to New York City—a full service department store where nearly everything is discounted. There are many bargains here and the service is pleasant and no-nonsense. Beware: the Manhattan store can be a zoo around Christmas-time.
- **Filene's Basement**, 620 Avenue of the Americas (Sixth Avenue) between West 18th and 19th Street, 212-620-3100; other locations at 2222 Broadway at 79th Street, 212-873-8000, and 187-04 Horace Harding Expressway in Fresh Meadows, 718-479-7711, www.filenes basement.com. Some good bargains at busy locations. Don't expect a lot, or any, personal attention.
- **Kmart**, 770 Broadway at 8th Street, 212-673-1540, www.kmart.com; essentially the antithesis of Bloomingdale's, the big "K" offers practical goods at reasonable prices. Fairly comprehensive, including even a houseplants department as well as clothing, furniture, housewares, and appliances, not to mention Martha Stewart linens, paints and furniture. Another Kmart at 1 Penn Plaza, 34th Street between 7th and 8th avenues, 212-760-1188, is much smaller, not really a department store in the true sense.

- **Lord and Taylor**, 424 Fifth Avenue, 212-391-3344, www.lordand taylor.com; wide selection and helpful sales staff. Lots of women's clothing including formal wear and smart business suits.
- **Macy's**, Broadway at 34th Street, 212-695-4400, www.macys.com; enormous! Complete! The crown jewel of New York City department stores. And, yes, it can be overwhelming! First-timers take advantage of the multilingual assistance and location maps at the first floor information booths. Others might opt for Macy's By Appointment, the personal shopping service, and the 24-hour telephone ordering service, 212-494-4181. Included are special events and a bridal registry. A total revamp of the beloved behemoth began at the basement level with the creation of the superb Cellar, a bazaar-like warren of individual food and housewares shops, and moved skyward as each floor was completely redone with pizzazz and flair: a merchandising *tour de force*. Even if you're not setting out with a specific shopping goal, Macy's is a great place to browse and browse and browse ...
- **Macy's** at 420 Fulton Street, Brooklyn, 718-875-7200, www.macys. com; talk about full service! Lucky Brooklyn residents need travel no further than the Hoyt Street stop on the #2 or #3 train for practically any nicety or necessity. Macy's has both an optometrist and a podiatrist on duty and a fur storage and restyling service. From TVs, furniture and electronics on the lower level to fabric on six, this rather reserved, nononsense institution also heeds the latest fashions with up-to-the-minute styles from leading designers on three.
- **Macy's**, 90-01 Queens Boulevard, Elmhurst, 718-271-7200, www.macys.com; not as vast as Herald Square, but it provides full service and is convenient to the entire borough from a Queens Boulevard location.
- **Saks Fifth Avenue**, 611 Fifth Avenue at Rockefeller Center, 212-753-4000, www.saksfifthavenue.com; carefully coifed customers, calm and self-assured, and elaborate bouquets that cascade nonchalantly into the glowing, wood-paneled aisles characterize Saks Fifth Avenue. So do the most refined escalators in New York. They float you silently past eight well-lit shopping floors against a backdrop of perfectly placed plants, mirrors and pinky-beige marble. Luxurious Saks exudes well-being from every tasteful counter. Departments are stylish and help is generally available. Saks also harbors a useful set of shops along 49th and 50th streets. Housewares, luggage, bathing suits, and sportswear, the bath and linen shop, and the art gallery all have private entrances. Recently, the store has made a fetish of personalized service. The Fifth Avenue Club, on the third floor, shelters five personal shopping services, among them the Executive Service for women executives.

- **Sears**, Cross County Parkway and Route 87, Yonkers 10704, 914-377-2100, www.sears.com; other Sears stores at 50 Mall Drive West in the Newport Mall, Jersey City, NJ, 201-420-5300; 2307 Beverly Road, Brooklyn, 718-826-5800; 96-05 Queens Boulevard, Rego Park, Queens, 718-830-5900; 137-61 Northern Boulevard, Flushing, 718-460-7000; 5200 Kings Plaza, Brooklyn, 718-677-2100, call for hours. For those with wheels this reliable old standby represents convenience and good value with plenty of selection. Parking is free, and in the New Jersey store just outside the Holland Tunnel the sales tax bite is less painful.
- **T.J. Maxx**, 620 Avenue of the Americas (Sixth Avenue) between West 18th and 19th streets, 212-229-0875, www.tjmaxx.com; again, not one of the grand old department store dames, but it's more than just off-price clothing. You'll find housewares and some small furniture items. The location upstairs over Filene's Basement (clothing only) doesn't hurt.
- **Target**, 135-05 20th Avenue, College Point, Queens, 718-661-4346, and 543 River Road, Edgewater, NJ, 201-402-0253, www.target.com; new to the metropolitan area in 1998, this popular department store, nestled in a shopping center among other national chain giants, lacks only a full furniture department. Everything else, from clothes to appliances and their exclusive line of household products for the garden, kitchen, and living room, designed by architect Michael Graves is here; check their cryptic newspaper ads.

The city is full of stores that specialize in any and every type of product you might want. Some of these stores provide savings and offer minimal customer service while others will practically hold your hand through the purchase—of course you'll spend a little more. Either way, you can find a vast selection of goods throughout the city, so don't settle—shop around and get what you want. Most stores also have web sites so you can go online to view and even make purchases.

APPLIANCES, ELECTRONICS, CAMERAS

These three categories have been lumped together because many of the stores listed below cross merchandise lines.
- **Macy's**, see **Full Service Department Stores**, above.
- **Sears**, see **Full Service Department Stores**, above.
- **Olden Camera**, 1265 Broadway, at 32nd Street, 2nd Floor, 212-226-3727, lots of camera and even computer equipment.
- **Sharper Image**, 900 Madison Avenue, 212-794-4974; 89 South Street Seaport @ Pier 17, 212-693-0477; 4 West 57th Street, 212-265-2550, www.sharperimage.com; okay, so they are more in line with

electronic toys and James Bond paraphernalia, but they're still great stores for browsing and finding electronic gadget gifts ... and some practical stuff, too.

- **Willoughby's Konica Imaging**, 136 West 32nd Street, 800-378-1898 or 212-564-1600, www.willoughbys.com; offers phone quotes. Complete rental and service departments complement the most extensive new and used photographic stock in the city. Willoughby's also has a computer department.

SPECIALTY SHOPS

- **Alkit Image Express**, 820 Third Avenue at 50th Street, 212-832-2101; 222 Park Avenue South at 18th Street, 212-674-1515; 830 Seventh Avenue near 53rd Street, 212-262-2424, www.alkit.com; full video and stereo line but fame rests on the quality and quantity of the professional and amateur cameras and other photographic equipment offered, along with Alkit's custom order department, rental, and repair services.
- **Harvey Electronic**, 2 West 45th Street, 212-575-5000, and Broadway at East 19th Street inside ABC Carpet & Home, 212-228-5354, www.harveyonline.com; "the best of the best for everybody," they say. High-end audio equipment, including free at-home consultation.
- **Innovative Audio**, 150 East 58th Street between Lexington and Third avenues, 212-634-4444, www.innovativeaudiovideo.com; perhaps a bit higher-end, but they offer a full range of quality equipment. They are noted for their helpful sales staff.
- **Lyric High Fidelity**, 1221 Lexington Avenue at 83rd Street, 212-439-1900, www.lyricusa.com; "Only the finest stereo components." A good selection of speakers.
- **Sound by Singer**, 18 East 16th Street, 212-924-8600, www.soundbysinger.com; full range of audio equipment, quiet listening rooms and an extremely knowledgeable sales staff. Specializes in American brands.
- **Stereo Exchange**, 627 Broadway at Houston Street, 212-505-1111; this established sound emporium specializes in home theater, audiophile stereo and new components. Used high-end components, expertly repaired in-house and sold at 60% to 70% off what they might cost new, are a real draw.

DISCOUNT STORES

The Lower East Side doesn't have a monopoly on good buys any longer. Appliances and electronics are sold all over the city at less than retail. A few of the many discounters in Manhattan:

- **ABC Trading Co.**, 31 Canal Street near Essex, 212-228-5080; call for hours. Offers photographic equipment, small as well as major appliances, audio equipment and supplies, TVs and DVD players.
- **Adorama**, 42 West 18th Street near Sixth Avenue, 800-223-2500; mail order: 212-741-0052, www.adoramacamera.com, is a favorite of professional photographers and filmmakers. Carries a staggering array of cameras, accessories, video equipment, lighting, lenses, VCRs, and more. Call for their specialty catalog or drop by for one.
- **B&H Photo-Video-Pro Audio**, 420 Ninth Avenue at 34th Street, 800-606-6969, 212-444-6670, www.bhphotovideo.com; whether you need an English-made Billingham photographer's vest, a point-and-shoot, or a Hasselblad, professional lighting and movie equipment, or camcorder, you'll find it in this sprawling audio-video bazaar with knowledgeable sales staff, a large professional clientele, and an encyclopedic catalog. Biggest price breaks are on professional equipment.
- **Circuit City**, 2232 Broadway, NYC, 212-362-9850; 232 East 86th Street #240, NYC, 212-734-1694; 52 East 14th Street at Union Square, 212-387-0730; 625 Atlantic Avenue, Brooklyn, 718-399-2990, 369 Gateway Drive, Brooklyn, 718-277-1611; 9605 Queens Boulevard, Rego Park, 718-275-2077; 13603 20th Avenue, College Point, Queens, 718-961-2090; and 2505 Richmond Avenue #2535, Staten Island 718-982-1182, www.circuitcity.com; one-stop shopping for computers, telephones, appliances, CD players, televisions, VCRs, car stereos, and video games.
- **J&R Music World**, 31 Park Row across from City Hall for audio-video hardware, and 27 Park Row for kitchen and small personal appliances and fitness equipment, 212-238-9000, www.jandr.com. It's definitely not all music, though their stereo selection is perhaps the best among the discounters. This string of outlets along Park Row also draws shoppers from all over for CDs, cameras, camcorders, cellular phones, television and video equipment, home office equipment, computer hardware and software (see **Computers** below).
- **P.C. Richard & Son**, 120 East 14th Street between Third and Fourth avenues, 212-979-2600; 205 East 86th Street between Second and Third avenues, 212-348-1287, www.pcrichard.com; also at more than 40 other locations in Brooklyn, Queens, Westchester, Long Island, and New Jersey. Home appliances, digital cameras, DVDs, and video games.
- **Vendome Trading Corp.**, 345 Seventh Avenue at 29th Street, 212-279-3333; offers phone quotes. A member of a cooperative buying group that has its own warehouse, Vendome sells air conditioners, washing machines and other major, as well as small, appliances, computers, TVs, and stereos.

BEDS, BEDDING, AND BATH

Department stores can take care of all your bedding needs under one roof. Lay in supplies during January and August, traditional white sale months. Bloomingdale's becomes particularly generous at these times, stocking irregular Martex towels and name brand sheets at great savings.

SPECIALTY SHOPS

- **Bed, Bath & Beyond**, 620 Sixth Avenue at 18th Street, 212-255-3550; 410 East 61st Street at First Avenue, 646-215-4702; 96-05 Queens Boulevard, Rego Park, Queens, 718-459-0868; 459 Gateway Drive, Brooklyn, 718-235-2049; Edgewater Commons Mall at 489 River Road, Edgewater, NJ, 201-840-8808, www.bedbathand beyond.com; this popular and affordable chain store has almost everything for your household needs. Helpful service too. The Manhattan store boasts wide aisles, plenty of departments, easy checkout and a special escalator for your shopping cart.
- **Dixie Foam**, 104 West 17th Street, 212-645-8999, www.dixiefoam. com; in this factory/showroom, 4" and 5 1/2" thick foam mattresses are the forte. Choose standard sizes or have irregular sizes cut and covered to order. Closed Sundays.
- **Futon Warehouse**, 113 University Place at 13th Street, 212-473-4400; mecca for students and first apartment furnishers and conveniently located near NYU, this is probably the largest futon merchant among many. The cotton and foam futons come in all sizes, in stock and custom-covered, with a selection of frames as well as shelving, loft beds and occasional tables.
- **Gracious Home**, 1220 Third Avenue between 70th and 71st streets, 212-517-6300; imported linens for the Upper East Side, bathware, fabrics, stationery, and giftware. Free gift-wrapping and delivery in Manhattan, not to mention phone orders.
- **Sleepy's**, 962 Third Avenue at 58th Street, 212-755-8210; huge chain offering beds, beds, beds of all kinds, frames and headboards, mattresses as well. Call 800-SLEEPYS or go to www.sleepys.com for a location near you.
- **Laytner's Linen & Home**, 2270 Broadway at 81st Street, 212-724-0180, www.laytners.com; outfit your bedroom and bath here, and then some. Besides a limited selection of handsome cotton drapes, you'll find bedding, feather beds, duvets, spreads, towels and bathroom and closet supplies, tablecloths, chenille throws and scatter pillows, but none of it in overwhelming quantities. Scattered among these soft goods, are items of Mission-style furniture, also for sale.

ALTERNATIVE SOURCES

Household linens on the **Lower East Side** are squashed into two blocks on Grand Street between Allen and Forsyth. An uptown look has intruded on the cram-jammed bargain basement fustiness always considered *de rigeur* in the city's most raffish bazaar area. The uninitiated will find comparatively sleek **Harris Levy**, 278 Grand Street, 212-226-3102, a satisfying shopping opportunity with goods from Laura Ashley, Marimekko, Martex, Wamsutta, Cannon, and Stevens, in addition to the scores of other stores along Grand. All closed Saturday, open Sunday. Department store white sale prices match those you're likely to find on the Lower East Side but, if you avoid the Sunday crush, you'll discover sales personnel often more knowledgeable and helpful than their uptown counterparts.

- **ABC Carpet & Home**, 888 Broadway at East 19th Street, 212-473-3000; 1055 Bronx River Parkway, Bronx (warehouse outlet), 718-842-8770; 20 Jay Street, Brooklyn, 718-643-7400; www.abccarpet.com; it's certainly not just carpets anymore. Imported and domestic designer lines, spreads and towels, along with a fetching array of country furniture, folk art objects, decorative pieces, and scatter pillows. Now there's crystal, earthenware, Limoges, bone china, and flatware as well. Sink into the Pipa Restaurant and refuel when energy flags, or book a reservation at Lucy, their Mexican-themed café, also on the main floor.
- **Dial-A-Mattress**, showroom at 31-10 48th Avenue, Long Island City, 11101, 718-628-8737, www.dialamattress.com; but you don't go there, unless you want to personally try out a mattress or look at their bedding, sofa beds, frames or accessories. Simply dial, 24-hours a day, and a bedding consultant will help you choose among discounted Sealy, Simmons, Serta, or Spring Air mattresses according to size, firmness, and price range. Delivery is within 24 hours, on approval, with a 36-day comfort exchange (softer or firmer). It's hard to beat if you're busy and want a mattress for that aching back in a hurry.
- **J. Schacter Corp.**, 5 Cook Street, Williamsburg, Brooklyn, 718-384-2732, Sunday by appointment only, closed Saturday. New York's leading feather merchants, famous for standard and custom-made pillows and comforters in various mixes of feathers and down and for reprocessing and cleaning already fabricated down bedding and garments.

CARPETS AND RUGS

For an overview, check the department stores, in particular Macy's for broadlooms, and Bloomingdale's for imports.

- **Einstein Moomjy Inc.**, 141 East 56th Street between Third and Lexington avenues, 212-758-0900; also New Jersey locations. At this self-described "Rug Department Store" located in the Architects and Designers Building, the very best broadlooms share floor space with luminous Orientals as well as domestic and imported carpets of all kinds. Don't worry about missing an Einstein Moomjy sale: newspapers and the television are flooded with ads.
- **Safavieh**, 238 East 59th Street, 212-888-0626; 902 Broadway at 20th Street, 212-477-1234; 153 Madison Avenue, 212-683-8399, and other city locations, www.safavieh.com. They sell a variety of handmade Oriental rugs new and antique, silk and wool, and an assortment of Aubusson weaves. Watch for their sales. See their web site for stores in Connecticut, Long Island, and New Jersey, some of which also sell antique reproduction furniture.

DISCOUNT STORES

- **Central Carpet**, 81 Eighth Avenue at 14th Street, 888-731-6100, 212-741-3700, www.centralcarpet.com; the self-proclaimed "Grand Palais of Rugs," they have been in business for over 50 years, supplying New Yorkers with antique and semi-antique Oriental rugs—from earthy Kilims to elegant Kashans. Go upstairs for more mundane mill ends and discounted broadlooms. The downtown store, resplendent in a landmarked former bank building, has a larger selection of machine-made rugs and wall-to wall carpeting, and all but the smallest rugs are hanging, not stacked.

ALTERNATIVE SOURCES

Carpets and rugs also turn up at thrift shops, auctions, and flea markets. See **Furniture** for details.

COMPUTERS AND SOFTWARE

Personal computers can be bought in a variety of places, from comparatively cozy neighborhood centers to barn-like discount warehouses. Many outlets offer courses as well as literature on the subject. For an overview of current prices and trends, check the "Circuits" section of the Thursday *New*

York Times, where the weekly computer columns are flanked by ads for hardware, software, and allied services.

- **The Apple Store**, 103 Prince Street, SoHo, 212-226-3126; lovely store in which to browse the newest and coolest Macs. Classes available.
- **Circuit City**: see **Appliances, Electronics, Cameras** above.
- **CompUSA**, 420 Fifth Avenue at 37th Street, 212-764-6224; 1775 Broadway at 57th Street, 212-262-9711, www.compusa.com; in addition to a vast selection of PCs and computer peripheries, offers many courses, from PC fundamentals to advanced graphics.
- **J&R Computer World**, 15 Park Row across from City Hall, 212-238-9100, www.jandr.com; a knowledgeable sales staff and a showroom with all the major computer hardware lines available to try out, in stock and discounted, have made this the largest single (non-chain, that is) computer store in the country. They'll install your upgrades for you or repair your old PC. Call for a catalogue, and if you know what you want, phone order, 800-221-8180.
- **RCS Computer Experience**, 575 Madison Avenue at 56th Street, 212-949-6935, www.rcseshop.com; an experienced sales staff at these service-oriented stores handle the major computer lines, Apple included, desktop and notebook, as well as accessories, peripherals, software and digital cameras at competitive prices. The bonus is a service staff prepared to make home and office calls and telephone help technicians to talk you out of digital blind alleys.
- **Staples**, 488-92 Broadway at Broome, 212-219-1299; 5-9 Union Square at 14th Street, 212-929-6323; 425 Park Avenue at 56th Street, 212-753-9640; 1280 Lexington Avenue at 86th Street, 212-426-6190; 2248 Broadway at 81st Street, 212-712-9617, www.staples.com; and at many other locations. Everything for the (home) office, including computers, peripherals, and software.

FABRIC–DECORATING

Ringed around the **Decoration & Design Building**, 979 Third Avenue between 59th and 60th streets, wholesale fabric showrooms marked "To The Trade Only" usually require shoppers to be accompanied by a decorator or to possess a decorator's card. No entrée? Try the department stores or the retail fabric importers or discount merchants listed below, all of whom stock dress goods as well as slipcover, curtain and upholstery fabrics. For more information, call 212-759-5408 or go to www.ddbuilding.com. You can buy yardage as well as decorative accents, clothes, and accessories from **April Cornell**, 487 Columbus Avenue between 83rd and 84th streets, 212-799-4342, which specializes in hand-stamped and hand-woven Indian cottons and an outstanding Dhurrie rug selection.

DISCOUNT STORES

- **Martin Albert Interiors**, 9 East 19th Street, 212-673-8000; formerly located on Grand Street, this discounter still sells uptown fabric at downtown prices.
- **K Trimming & Zippers**, 519 Broadway at Spring, 212-431-8929; dig through boxes stuffed with grommets, braids, and hundreds of buttons for low, low prices on all the trimmings.
- **Beckenstein Home Fabrics**, 150 Fifth Avenue, entrance at 4 West 20th Street, 212-366-5142; for over 80 years the place to go on Orchard Street, now this Lower East Side bastion of discount fabric has moved uptown and is somewhat upscale. With fabric on racks now and some furniture as well, the selection in decorating fabric remains broad and the prices still represent a saving over the uptown boutiques.
- **Long Island Fabric**, 406 Broadway at Canal Street, 212-925-4488; right in the heart of the fabric wholesale district between SoHo and City Hall, this ramshackle three-story outlet houses notable bargains.
- **Paterson Silks**, 151 West 72nd Street, 212-874-9510; 300 East 90th Street at Second Avenue, 212-722-4098; besides a wide selection of fabrics, this old standby specializes in custom draperies, slipcovers and re-upholstery. Call 800-522-5671 for shop-at-home decorating.
- **Baranzelli/Silk Surplus**, 1127 Second Avenue between 59th and 60th streets, 212-753-6511; while noted for Scalamandre seconds, heavy embroideries and other elegant coverings, including silks, are stocked here, along with some traditional furniture. Closed Sundays.

ALTERNATIVE SOURCES

Long a mecca to home decorators and seamstresses, the Lower East Side fabric shops clustered on **Grand Street** at the Eldridge Street intersection (between Forsyth and Allen), like the household linen outlets adjacent, are open Sunday-Friday, closed on Saturday. But just as uptown shops are moving downtown, so Lower East Side is moving uptown. Three of the major fabric discounters have decamped for uptown locations. The remaining grand old man, **Harry Zarin Company**, 318 Grand Street, 212-925-6112, holds the fabric fort. Prices for the curtain, upholstery and slipcover fabrics in stock are almost always a better bargain than materials you select from the sample books. But these too are discounted. You'll find stellar names printed on the selvages of velvets, embroideries, cottons, and tapestries: Brunschwig & Fils, Givenchy, Schumacher, and Stroheim & Roman among them.

FURNITURE

Antique furniture dealerships tend to cluster. Rare pieces from the 17th, 18th, and 19th centuries, the quality found at the Winter Antiques Show held late each January at the Seventh Regiment Armory, are most likely to be found in elegant shops along Madison Avenue north of 67th Street. Increasingly, retail outlets for less prestigious pieces are infiltrating the wholesale "to the trade only" antique district located in the quadrant formed by University Place, Broadway, East 9th and East 11th streets in the Village. Art deco dealers and those specializing in the Depression era, in retro furniture, and the now-fashionable Fifties clump together in SoHo and NoHo. A handful of good sources can also be found in Greenwich Village. The more upscale antique stores, dealing mostly in Early American and French country furniture, line Bleecker west of Seventh Avenue.

Look for furniture sales post-Christmas. Those held by New York department stores at their warehouses in the boroughs and suburbs offer especially large savings for anyone with a car and enough stamina to brave the stampede.

- **Carlyle Custom Convertibles**, main store 1056 Third Avenue near 62nd Street, 212-838-1525; clearance at 122 West 18th Street between Sixth and Seventh avenues, 212-675-3212, www.carlylesofa.com; offers quality custom-made sofas in a variety of fairly conservative styles and fabrics. Allow four to six weeks for delivery.
- **Crate & Barrel**, 650 Madison Avenue, 212-308-0011 and 611 Broadway, 212-780-0004, www.crateandbarrel.com; somewhat incongruously located at the base of a sleek office tower, this emporium of handsome, countryish furniture, dish and cookware, decorative items, and linens is theme-decorated in natural pine. The earth tones are muted, and the selection of reasonably priced glassware is extensive. It's affordable and stylish one-stop home furnishing.
- **The Door Store**, 1 Park Avenue at 33rd Street, 212-679-9700; 1201 Third Avenue at 58 Street, 212-421-5273; 123 West 17th Street west of Sixth Avenue, 212-627-1515; www.doorstorefurniture.com; an excellent source of reasonably priced contemporary furniture, especially desks, computer tables, wall units, chairs and tables in oak, teak and pine—but no doors. Their sales are well worth the wait.
- **Ethan Allen**, 192 Lexington Avenue at 32nd Street, 212-213-0600; 103 West End Avenue, 212-201-9860; 1107 Third Avenue at 65th Street, 212-308-7703; 2275 Richmond Avenue, Staten Island, 718-983-0100, among other locations, www.ethanallen.com. Handsome, well-made traditional furniture for the whole house. Watch the *Times* for their sales.
- **Ikea**, 1000 Ikea Drive, Elizabeth, NJ, 908-289-4488; Broadway Mall, Hicksville, Long Island, 516-681-4532, www.ikea.com; worth the trip

from the city for excellent deals. Take the LIRR from Penn Station to the Hicksville station, or better, bring a car to stock up. Selections range from inexpensive pine dressers, kitchen tables, beds, and living room furniture, all designed Swedish-style with clean lines and natural materials. Pick up sheets, glasses, wallpaper, lamps and more—for less. At the Jersey store have a Swedish meatball lunch for less than $5 in the spacious, clean (if slightly antiseptic) cafeteria, also open for breakfast and dinner. Delivery is available.

- **Jennifer Convertibles**, 1430 Third Avenue at 79th Street, 212-535-1242; 1014 Second Avenue at 54th Street, 212-751-1720; 153 East 57th Street, 212-752-2078; 750 Broadway, 212-677-1539; 902 Broadway, 212-677-6862; 2424 Broadway, 212-787-8507; 181 Eighth Avenue at 20th Street, 212-924-8828, 893 Broadway, 212-674-1338, leather only; plus stores in Brooklyn, the Bronx, Queens, Staten Island and Long Island: www.jenniferfurniture.com. No question, stores in this chain, which bills itself "America's largest sofa bed specialist," have the city's widest selection of relatively inexpensive convertible sofas, including Sealy and Simmons models.
- **Jensen-Lewis**, 89 Seventh Avenue at 15th Street, 212-929-4880, www.jensen-lewis.com; famous for deck chairs, satchels, backpacks, and other canvas products in lots of zippy colors. In big, bright quarters puffy sofas and easy chairs, beds, and an expanding housewares department fill the showroom.
- **Maurice Villency**, 949 Third Avenue, corner of 57th Street, 212-725-4840, www.mauricevillency.com; if sleek and modern, embellished with glass and brass, is the look you favor, then head for this sparkling showroom, where furniture lines exclusive to Maurice Villency are displayed.
- **Pottery Barn**, 600 Broadway at West Houston Street, 212-219-2420, 1965 Broadway at 67th Street, 212-579-8477, 127 East 59th Street, 917-369-0050, www.potterybarn.com; where's the pottery? Mostly gone now. This former emporium of tableware has evolved into a design studio and catalogue operation focusing on home furnishings in a fairly country mode. Reasonably priced sofas and chairs often covered in tough cotton, rugs, dining and occasional furniture, drapes, and decorative items fill their catalogs and the stores. There's also a selection of inexpensive to moderately priced imported glassware, china, and table settings, augmented by quality cookware, sometimes below list price, and occasional gourmet items. Their periodic sales of specific merchandise are worth catching.
- **Restoration Hardware**, 935 Broadway at 22nd Street, 212-260-9479, plus stores in New Jersey and Long Island, www.restoration hardware.com. Hardware? In fact, there are some drawer pulls, some bathroom hardware, fireplace and cleaning supplies, but these spa-

cious showrooms, part of a nationwide chain, are furniture and house-wares emporiums. You can buy sturdy garden furniture and the garden clogs and tin floral buckets to go with it, rugs, picture frames and the like, but the draw here is the mission-style furniture with its clean lines and sturdy oak construction.

- **Seaman's Furniture**, 133 East 14th Street, 212-473-8157, www.furniture.com; also stores in the outer boroughs, Long Island, and Westchester. For over 70 years they've been selling furniture. Prices are generally good, particularly during their many holiday sales. Wide selection of styles including kids' furniture. Sales help is hit or miss.
- **George Smith**, 75 Spring Street in SoHo, 212-226-4747, www.georgesmith.com; it's quiet here in two vast rooms just steps from the bustle of lower Broadway, perhaps because all the large sofas, chairs and stools are down/feather filled, muffling sound. This is high-end, meticulously English-made furniture in the classic style and requiring space most city apartments haven't got. Upholstered to order in your fabric or theirs, in cotton brocades, florals, checks, antique kilim or leather, they'd all look splendid in a paneled home library. Custom orders take 10 to 12 weeks, or you can buy off the floor.

ALTERNATIVE SOURCES

- **Salvation Army**, main store: 536 West 46th Street between Tenth and Eleventh avenues, 212-757-2311, www.thesalvationarmy.org, and seven other outlets. Credit cards accepted for purchases over $50. For those of humbler means, the two huge warehouse floors on 46th Street contain everything a homemaker needs to set up housekeeping. Some fine bargains and clothes, too. Closed Sunday.
- **Thrift shops**: charities and hospital research programs benefit from the proceeds of these stores, just as donors benefit from the tax deductions and buyers benefit from the bargains on everything from designer clothes to silver pitchers and down sofas. Head to Third Avenue between 80th and 86th streets and east to Second Avenue for new and gently used goods. **Spence-Chapin Corner Shop**, 1850 Second Avenue between 95th and 96th streets, 212-426-7643; and **Memorial Sloan-Kettering Cancer Center Thrift Shop**, 1440 Third Avenue at 82nd Street, 212-535-1250, are just a couple of the many thrift stores concentrated in this neighborhood.
- **Housing Works Thrift Shops**: 143 West 17th Street at 7th Avenue, 212-366-0820; 202 East 77th Street between Second and Third avenues, 212-772-8461; 306 Columbus Avenue between 74th and 75th streets, 212-579-7566, and 157 East 23rd Street, 212-529-5955, www.housing works.org; sell clothes, books, records, bicycles and whatever, but furni-

ture is the best buy here, where proceeds go to house and service home-less people with AIDS/HIV. Come at 10 a.m. for the best buys.

- **Atlantic Avenue**, Brooklyn: the *Village Voice* describes this as the best strip in the five boroughs for vintage furniture above the junk category. Beware of pricey delivery costs, the *Voice* warns, and think about rent-ing a van. Atlantic Avenue between Nevins and Bond streets.

- **Auction houses**: diverting, and occasionally rewarding, auctions are another way of obtaining basic necessities such as mattresses, as well as moth-eaten moose heads, which, in fact, make poor hat-racks. Check the auction pages at the back of the "Arts and Leisure" section of the Sunday *Times* for sale descriptions and viewing hours. The big three: **Christie's**, 20 Rockefeller Plaza, 212-636-2000, www.christies.com; **Phillips, de Pury & Luxembourg**, 415 West 15th Street, 212-940-1200; and **Sotheby's**, 1334 York Avenue, 212-606-7000, www.sothebys.com, hold specialty auctions of interest to collectors and connoisseurs (and voyeurs) once or twice a week in season. The second tier, including **Christie's East**, 219 East 67th Street, 212-606-0400 (weekly); **William Doyle Galleries**, 175 East 87th Street, 212-427-2730, www.doylenewyork.com (every other Wednesday); and **Sotheby's Arcade Auctions**, 1334 York Avenue, 212-606-7000, usu-ally auction off a varied selection of household goods in a single session. These are typically not places for the price conscious consumer. Designers prowl the tag sale operation where Doyle's disposes of high-class flotsam from the adjacent gallery, 8:30 a.m. to 4:30 p.m., Monday-Friday, 10 a.m. to 5 p.m., Saturday; you can too. For erratic quality, more fun and lower prices try **Swann Galleries**, 104 East 25th Street, 212-254-4710, www.swanngalleries.com, and **Tepper Galleries**, 110 East 25th Street, 212-677-5300, www.teppergalleries.com.

- **Flea markets**—this raffish country custom adapts well to New York's jostling sidewalks. Check the "Art & Antiques" classified column near the back of the "Weekend Fine Arts and Leisure" section in the Friday *Times* for flea market listings. All but the hardiest markets (and those held indoors) shut down from late fall until spring. The **Annex Antiques Fair**, Avenue of the Americas at 26th Street, 212-243-5343, 9 a.m. to 5 p.m. Saturday and Sunday, levies a small admission charge, but 80 to 100 dealers make it the largest and best of the lot. The same management runs the **Annex Flea Market** two blocks south at 24th Street, where new and used clothing and housewares are sold. The west twenties on a Saturday afternoon are chock full of flea markets in every outdoor parking lot and available space. Arrive early and don't even think about parking in the immediate vicinity.

- **Public school PTAs** sometimes sponsor flea markets on school grounds in order to raise funds. These are rain-or-shine affairs; sometimes they take place on Saturdays and Sundays and sometimes they don't. The most consistent markets include the one in the Greenwich Avenue school yard of P.S. 41 between Seventh Avenue and 10th Street, in the P.S. 183 yard on East 67th Street between York and First avenues—also indoor in the cafeteria where jewelry dealers abound with good prices, and in the Columbus Avenue yard of Intermediate School 44, between 76th and 77th streets.

- **The street**: a *New York Times* "Home" section featured the apartment of a dedicated young middle-class scrounger who furnished his two rooms with street finds. The comfortable living room looked just like home in the heartlands, traditional with overstuffed chairs, a coffee table, and standing lamp. Resourcefulness, a strong back, and willing cabbies are all that's required for street shopping—well, that and a knowledge of the Sanitation Department's collection days for whatever area you're combing. It's legal to put large items on the sidewalk after dark the evening before any regular collection day. The Upper East Side tends to be fertile territory for found furniture, so if that's your game, Sunday, Tuesday, and Thursday evenings after 8 p.m. are the time to canvas. For other neighborhood collection days, call the 24-hour Sanitation Department line, 212-219-8090, and navigate the menus. Be careful. If an item has been sitting outside on the street for more than a few hours it may not be something you want to bring into your home ... or touch for that matter.
- *Art & Antiques Magazine* can also be helpful. Pick up their magazine at newsstands or check out their web site, www.artandantiques.net, for a list of New York City antique dealers.

HARDWARE, PAINTS AND WALLPAPER

On Saturdays, slow-moving lines make local hardware stores as good a way of meeting people as local bars later that night. But once you've made new friends along with those seemingly endless purchases, you may require more than the good old, all-purpose neighborhood reliable to fill decorating needs. Some specialty resources, then (the behemoth **Home Depot** is listed below under **Superstores**):

- **Gracious Home**, 1217 & 1220 Third Avenue at 70th Street, 212-517-6300, and 1992 Broadway at 67th Street, 212-231-7800; www.gracioushome.com; the sprawling hardware/houseware/home-furnishings center for the Upper East Side, and slightly smaller Upper West Side version, are both well organized and staffed. From screws to decorative bathroom fixtures, paints, electrical fixtures, and power tools, to glassware and hard-to find-vacuum cleaners.

- **Kraft Hardware**, 316 East 62nd Street between First and Second avenues, 212-838-2214, www.kraft-hardware.com; just the place to find those special pewter or bronze drawer pulls, mahogany switch plates, elegant hinges and door knobs, fluted porcelain sinks, and the like.
- **Janovic Plaza**, 1150 Third Avenue at 67th Street, 212-772-1400; 2680 Broadway at 102nd Street, 212-769-1440; 159 West 72nd Street between Broadway and Columbus Avenue, 212-595-2500; 771 Ninth Avenue at 52nd Street, 212-245-3241; 215 Seventh Avenue between 22nd and 23rd streets, 212-645-5454; 161 Avenue of the Americas at Spring Street, 212-627-1100; 80 Fourth Avenue at 13th Street, 212-477-6930; 292 Third Avenue at 22nd Street, 212-777-3030; and 136 Church Street in Tribecca, 212-349-0001, www.janovicplaza.net; the Bloomingdale's of the paint-and-wallpaper scene, Janovic's image is as glossy as its enamels and printed foil papers. For the latest colors and trends, as well as an overall view of what's available, Janovic can't be beat.
- **Simon's Hardware and Bath**, 421 Third Avenue near 30th Street, 212-532-9220; join the inevitable throng of contractors and decorators shopping Simon's first-rate stock of brass, bronze, pewter, plastic, wood, steel—whatever!—decorative hardware. They've recently expanded to include tile, bath fixtures and lighting as well.

ALTERNATIVE SOURCES

Hardware and plastics—nuts and bolts made dingy by neighboring bright, bouncing baubles—overflow rows of cut down cardboard boxes that alternate with the racks of surplus and flea market clothing lining Canal Street between West Broadway and Broadway. Most of this sidewalk hardware and pretty plastic bric-a-brac is useful only to the professional handyman or collage artist, but inside, generalists revel in complete selections of quality merchandise at exceptionally fair prices. Try any of the stores sitting side by gray dilapidated side on Canal, west of Broadway.

- **Pearl Paint Co.**, 308 Canal Street, 212-431-7932, www.pearl paint.com; listed here because of the discounted house paints, including Benjamin Moore. Pearl Paint is in fact renowned for art-related materials and accessories, and its four upper floors are usually swamped with an international array of fine artists.

HOUSEWARES

Of course, any department store or furniture store will offer scads of traditional and funky housewares, particularly Crate & Barrel, the Pottery Barn, Ikea, as well as Target, Kmart, the list goes on (see above). Those specializing in housewares include:

- **Design Within Reach**, 142 Wooster Street, NYC, 212-475-0001; 408 West 14th Street, NYC, 212-242-9449; 76 Montague Street, Brooklyn, 718-643-1015; www.dwr.com
- **Jonathan Adler New York**, 47 Greene Street and 465 Broome Street, 212-941-8950; contemporary home furnishings.
- **Moss**, 146 Greene Street, NYC, 212-204-7100, www.mossonline.com; cool, sleek designs for every room of the house.
- **Pier One Imports** 1550 Third Avenue, NYC, 212-987-1746; 461 Fifth Avenue, NYC, 212-447-1610; and other locations, www.pier1.com; glassware, crystal, housewares, plenty of gift items and even some furniture at reasonable prices.
- **Third Avenue Bazaar**, 125 West Third off Sixth Avenue, 212-673-4138; an all-purpose emporium with adequately tasteful, moderately priced rattan chairs, painted glasses, curly plastic cords, greeting cards, black pressboard stacking tables, aluminum and enamel pots, etc., etc., etc.
- **Zabar's**, 2245 Broadway at 80th Street, 212-787-2000, www.zabars.com; housewares department on the mezzanine. Expansive Zabar's, mecca to millions for unequaled edibles, houses an equally esteemed and often bargain-priced selection of supplies for the home and kitchen in four rooms on the mezzanine. Try to avoid weekend forays there.

SPECIALTY SHOPS

- **Bridge Kitchenware**, 214 East 52nd Street off Third Avenue, 212-688-4220; purveyors of durable, professional-quality kitchen equipment—for example, chrome-topped glass shakers found on every luncheonette counter worth its salt, an enviable selection of French tinlined copper pots, huge Hobart dough mixers—to the city's food establishment and serious cooks the world over.
- **Broadway Panhandler**, 477 Broome at Wooster Street, 212-966-3434; discounted cookware (Calphalon, All Clad, Le Creuset) and quality kitchen tools for the serious cook. Hit the **Gourmet Garage** at 453 Broome for your ingredients.
- **Fishs Eddy**, 889 Broadway at 19th Street, 212-420-9020, and 2176 Broadway at 77th Street, 212-873-8819, www.fishseddy.com; offers surplus restaurant china where you can buy just one piece. Everything guaranteed chip and crack-free.

- **Hammacher Schlemmer**, 147 East 57th Street, 212-421-9000, www.hammacher.com; a department store of sorts for the eclectic, has plenty of off-beat luxury item, gadgets, electronic toys, and a premier collection of quality kitchen and bar ware.
- **Hold Everything**, 2109 Broadway at 73rd Street, 212-595-5639; 1309 Second Avenue at 69th Street, 212-535-9446; 104 Seventh Avenue at 15th Street, 212-633-1674, www.holdeverything.com; organize your closets, your kitchen, your drawers, your desk, your life! This Williams-Sonoma subsidiary is the last word in containers: garment bags, shelving, shoe holders, drawer dividers, wicker boxes, closet accessories.
- **S. Feldman Housewares, Inc.**, 1304 Madison Avenue near 93rd Street, 212-289-7367, www.wares2u.com; upscale cookware, including Calphalon, LeCreuset, and All-Clad, as well as the popular Miele vacuum cleaners. Watch for their sales.
- **Tiffany and Co.**, 727 Fifth Avenue at 57th Street, 212-755-8000, www.tiffanys.com; stand up straight, speak softly and be on your best behavior when entering the hallowed halls of the famous high end department store. The main floor jewelry draws oohs and ahs from a multitude of tourists, but if you ask the elevator operator for "three please," you'll find shimmering ivory walls and plates by Picasso nudging Royal Crown Derby place settings. The selection of fine china and glassware is exquisite. Tired of jelly glasses? Crystal's to your right. And if you're getting married, for many this is *the* place to register.
- **Williams-Sonoma**, 110 Seventh Avenue, 212-633-2203; 121 East 59th Street, 917-369-1131; 1175 Madison Avenue, 212-289-6832, www.williams-sonoma.com; known through their appealing catalogue to serious cooks nationwide, this California-based firm specializes in quality cookware, handsome glassware, and mostly imported country-style tableware. The familiar pieces, and then some, are available here, along with gourmet food items and cookbooks. For lovers of blue and color-coordinated kitchens, it's a treasure trove.

ALTERNATIVE SOURCES

- **The Restaurant Supply District**: as the use of professional kitchenware in the home increases, the wholesale restaurant strip along the section of Bowery between West Houston and Broome streets has become an accepted destination for retail shoppers. Pots, pans, butcher block, Robot Coupes, Garland ranges, bar ware and thick, nigh on to unbreakable dishes are available from most stores at less than uptown retail. Outlets include **Bari Restaurant Equipment Corp.**, 240 Bowery, 212-925-3786, for a grand assortment of pots, pans, strainers, stirrers and such must-haves as pizza ovens and gigantic wooden pizza spatulas; and **Chef Restaurant Supply**, 294 Bowery, 212-254-6644, "unbelievably cheap" and favored by uptown chefs.

- **Secaucus Outlet Center**, Secaucus, NJ and Flemington, NJ; don't visit during the Christmas rush without armor plate. At other times, values obtained in these two discount giants may well be worth the schlep. To get to Secaucus, located about 15 minutes from the Lincoln Tunnel, follow signs to Route 3 West continuing about six miles to the "Meadowlands Parking" exit, take the down ramp to the light, then a left and continue past two more sets of lights to American Way, take another left and you will be confronted by a number of warehouses. Bring boxes for your gleanings and a companion to watch them as you gather. Get a booklet containing a map and brand names by merchandise category from the first warehouse. Mikasa and Copco both have large outlets here. While you're at it, if you've the stamina, load up on discount Gucci shoes, Liz Claiborne goodies, Oleg Cassini, and the like.

LAMPS AND LIGHT FIXTURES

You can't beat the department stores for variety and choice; wait for the winter sales if you can. But if you want better prices or the newest imports, shop some of the sources below.

SPECIALTY SHOPS

- **Gracious Home** (see above listing under **Beds, Bedding, and Bath**)
- **Just Bulbs Ltd.**, 5 East 16th Street, 212-228-7820; an eclectic and funky mix of bulbs (and more bulbs!). Can make you a little "light" headed.
- **The Lighting Center**, 240 East 59th Street at Second Avenue, 212-888-8383; although a large selection of mainly American contemporary lighting fixtures crams the center's small, gray-walled retail shop, the specialty is track lighting. Have a system custom designed or choose from the Halo, Lightolier, Lighting Services, or Altalite lines already on hand. Not for the bargain conscious. Closed Sundays.
- **Lightforms**, 168 Eighth Avenue, 212-255-4664; 509 Amsterdam Avenue, 212-875-0407; interesting, moderate to expensive contemporary light fixtures.
- **Oriental Lampshade Company**, 816 Lexington Avenue near 62nd Street, 212-832-8190, www.orientallampshade.com; hand-made shades to order and less expensive ready-mades in a great variety of colors, shapes and styles. Lamp repair too.
- **Rosetta Lighting & Supply Co.**, 49 West 45th Street, 212-719-4381; a wide variety of lighting fixtures along traditional lines, at reasonable prices makes this a source worth investigating.

ALTERNATIVE SOURCES

The **Lamp and Light Fixture District** concentrated on The Bowery between Broome and Canal streets abuts wholesale restaurant supply stores that begin at Broome and end a few blocks north at Houston. If you know what you want, don't be daunted by lurid window displays of fantasy fixtures. Push on past high kitsch, find a salesman and describe your product. Chances are the fixture can be ordered or will be in stock at less than retail. But don't count on tender loving care. That's reserved for large wholesale buyers. Try **Bowery Lighting Corp.**, 132 Bowery, 212-941-8244, one of the largest stores in the district, or **Just Shades**, 21 Spring Street, 212-966-2757, covers the gamut from burlaps to fine pleated ivory silks in all sizes.

SUPERSTORES

Well established in the suburbs and rural areas across the country, big box stores such as Home Depot arrived in the outer boroughs in the late 1990s, and now with one location in Long Island City. The cost of space and community resistance to their establishment poses the ultimate challenge to these warehouse-style behemoths. For those who have the stamina to roam their vast aisles and the storage space at home for, say, 32 rolls of toilet paper, they represent real savings, though some require yearly membership fees. Note: a car is a definite asset, if not a necessity, when shopping these outlets.

- **BJ's Wholesale Club**, 137-05 20th Avenue, College Point, Queens, 718-359-9703, 396-420 Marin Boulevard, Jersey City, 201-798-0500, www.bjs.com; sells everything from tires to oven mitts to peanut butter—in the gigantic family size. Bring some muscle to carry everything to and from the car—or van or rental truck. Members pay $40 annually for access.
- **Costco**, 32-50 Vernon Boulevard, Long Island City, Queens, 718-267-5500; 2975 Richmond Avenue, Staten Island, 718-982-9000; 976 Third Avenue, Brooklyn, 718-965-7600; also at four New Jersey locations: www.costco.com. Vast stores housing books, jewelry, computers, cameras, hardware, the list goes on. Membership is $45 per year.
- **Home Depot**, 50-10 Northern Boulevard, Long Island City, 718-278-9031, 550 Hamilton Avenue, Brooklyn, 718-832-8553; 131-35 Avery Avenue, Flushing, Queens, 718-358-9600; 112-20 Rockaway Boulevard, Jamaica, Queens, 718-641-5500; 124-04 31st Avenue, Flushing, 718-661-4608; 1806 East Gunhill Road, Bronx, 718-862-9800; 635 Zerega Avenue, Bronx, 718-518-8811; 2501 Forest Avenue, Staten Island, 718-273-5069; 75-09 Woodhaven Boulevard, Glendale,

718-830-3323; 1055 Peterson Plank Road, Secaucus, 201-271-1200; 440 Route 440, Jersey City, 201-521-9437, www.homedepot.com. This mecca for do-it-yourselfers offers clinics on how to build it, paper it, paint it, wire or plumb it, and plant it; and they stock everything you'll need to do it from nuts and bolts to toilets and hot tubs. Make a list before you go.

SAMPLE SALES

These are special sales of a designer's leftover inventory (from jewelry to furniture to upscale bathroom fixtures), and they offer considerable savings for the determined shopper. Typically, designers do not advertise their sample sales, but predominant sale months are November, December, April, and May. Scan *New York* magazine's "Sales & Bargains" section for some sale times and locations. Better yet, subscribe to the **S&B Report**, 877-579-0222, a monthly publication stating every major designer showroom sale in the city. A one-year subscription is $124 ($75 for the online subscription): www.lazarmedia.com.

FOOD

New York eats, but in ways that take some getting used to. The city is host to some of the finest and some of the most expensive restaurants in the world, as well as hundreds of excellent eateries of every ethnic and national persuasion, large and small. For this you're on your own to explore the city's restaurant riches as far as your pocketbook permits, and with perhaps a *Zagat's Restaurant Guide* or the "Food" section of the *New York Times* in hand. You're also on your own to explore the possibilities of take-out, which has become a ubiquitous part of the city's food-life. It seems you're never more than a block away from a source of take-out; many New Yorkers depend on it. And the host of corner delis throughout the city providing late night sandwiches, coffee, milk, beer, and snack food, needs no chronicling. You have one in your immediate neighborhood. Chances are, you also have an open-air fruit and vegetable stand operated nearly round-the-clock and stocked with beautifully displayed, fresh but somewhat pricey produce. These islands of color, almost invariably operated by Korean-Americans, brighten the city streets while they offer convenience and a sense of neighborhood. New York is sometimes referred to "the city that never sleeps," perhaps that's because New Yorkers have too much fine food available 24-hours a day.

Sooner or later, though, you'll need that jar of spaghetti sauce, a steak, a box of rice, salt, not to mention some toilet paper. Thanks to the high cost of space here, the city is not supermarket proud. They're scarce in some neighborhoods, lackluster in others. The best of them are clean but crowded, with narrow aisles and often selections that run dry much faster than their sprawling suburban counterparts. Depending on where you live, specialty shops may provide the best selection for fresh meats and produce, and summer finds many New Yorkers shopping for the freshest fruits and vegetables at sidewalk carts. If stocking up suits you, but you don't have access to a car, consider signing up with the online grocery delivery service **Fresh Direct** at www.freshdirect.com. More reasonably priced than you might imagine, this company delivers to much of Manhattan and has plans to begin service to Queens and Brooklyn.

As far as **local grocery chains**, we begin with **D'Agostino's**, www.dagnyc.com, which is perhaps the best in terms of cleanliness, quality of selection, and consumer friendliness. Additionally, we list the main chains that operate multiple supermarkets in the city. Within chains, some outlets are better than others:

- **Associated Food Stores and Supermarkets**, www.afstores.com
- **Food Emporium**, www.thefoodemporium.com
- **Gristede's**, www.gristedes.com
- **Met Food**, www.metfoods.com
- **Pioneer**, www.pioneerspmkt.com

You want some good French or Italian bread, a decent paté, fresh smoked salmon, and some frisee for Sunday brunch? Manhattan especially is well served by excellent bread bakers in just about every neighborhood, and by gourmet shops, which carry good breads and every other imaginable edible, at a price. Listed in the Yellow Pages under "Gourmet Shops," you'll find some of the finest shops in the world offering any tasty delicacy you have in mind. Here are just a few:

- **Agata & Valentina**, 1505 First Avenue at 79th Street, 212-452-0690
- **Balducci's**, 155 West 66th Street, 212-653-8320
- **Citarella**, 2135 Broadway at 75th Street and 1313 Third Avenue at 75th Street, 212-874-0383
- **Dean & Deluca**, 560 Broadway at Prince Street, 212-226-6800; 1150 Madison Avenue, 212-717-0800; 235 West 46th Street, 212-869-6890; 75 University Place, 212-473-1908; www.deandeluca.com
- **E A T Gourmet Foods**, 1064 Madison Avenue between 80th and 81st streets, 212-772-0022
- **Fairway**, 2127 Broadway at 74th Street, 212-595-1888; and 2328 12th Avenue at 132nd Street, 212-234-3883
- **Garden of Eden Farmers Market**, 162 West 23rd Street, 212-675-6300, and 314 Third Avenue at 23rd Street, 212-228-4681
- **Gourmet Garage**, 117 Seventh Avenue South at Christopher, 212-414-5910; 453 Broome Street at Mercer, 212-941-5850; 301 East 64th Street between First and Second avenues, 212-535-6271; and 2567

Broadway between 96th and 97th streets, 212-663-0656, www. gourmetgarage.com
- **Grace's Marketplace**, 1237 Third Avenue at 71st Street, 212-737-0600
- **Jefferson Market**, 450 Sixth Avenue between 10th and 11th streets, 212-533-3377
- **The Vinegar Factory**, 431 East 91st Street, 212-987-0885
- **Todaro Brothers**, 555 Second Avenue at 30th Street, 212-532-0633
- **Whole Foods Market**, 250 Seventh Avenue at 24th Street, 212-924-5969; new location at 59th Street and Columbus Avenue, www.wholefoods.com.
- **Zabar's**, 2245 Broadway at 80th Street, 212-787-2000, www. zabars.com

Vegetarians and those in search of organic foods find the farmers' markets a good source, and the better gourmet stores have organic sections as well as good selections of soy and grain products. But there are also stores catering to this market. They can be found in the Yellow Pages under "Health and Diet Food Products—Retail." Some of the better-known **health food stores** are listed here:
- **Commodities Natural Market**, 165 First Avenue between 10th and 11th streets, 212-260-2600
- **Gary Nulls Whole Foods**, 2421 Broadway at 89th Street, 212-874-4000
- **Healthy Pleasures**, 93 University Place between 11th & 12th streets, 212-353-3663
- **Integral Yoga**, 229 West 13th Street between 8th and 9th avenues, 212-243-2642
- **LifeThyme**, 410 Sixth Avenue at 8th Street, 212-420-9099
- **Park Slope Food Co-op**, 782 Union Street, Brooklyn, NY 11215, 718-622-0560, www.foodcoop.com; provides fresh organic foods and household supplies to community members, who now number over 6,000. Each member pays a one-time $25 joining fee and then contributes a $100 investment to the co-op (returnable when the member leaves the co-op) and each member must do a minimal work share. The co-op buys food and sells it to members for much less than competing grocery stores.
- **Westerly Natural Market**, 911 Eighth Avenue at 54th Street, 212-586-5262

ETHNIC FOODS

The ongoing immigration history of New York is displayed in the sidewalk stalls and food markets of its ethnic neighborhoods. For every conceivable item of **Chinese** vegetable, ingredient, and condiment, not to mention fish, and **Korean, Japanese, Thai,** and **Malaysian** food items, all very reasonably priced, New Yorkers go to Chinatown, on either side of Canal Street downtown, or to Flushing on either side of Main Street, or to Sunset Park in Brooklyn. For the ultimate in Japanese food shopping, Yaohan on River Road in Edgewater, NJ, is the place to go. Little **Italy**, just north of Chinatown, isn't the only place to buy Italian food items, it just feels more authentic. In fact there are pockets of Italian specialty stores in the Village, on Ninth Avenue in the Thirties, and along legendary Arthur Avenue in The Bronx. Pungent **Indian** spices scent the air along Lexington Avenue between 23rd and 28th streets. **Polish** and **Ukrainian** foods hold their ground among other ethnic outlets along First and Second avenues between 14th and Houston streets, but Greenpoint, Brooklyn, is the Polish food capital of the city. **Latino** food specialties are to be found throughout the city, especially in East Harlem along 116th Street, along Broadway in Washington Heights, and in Jackson Heights, Queens. No city outside Israel has more to offer in the way of **Jewish** foods than New York, in parts of The Bronx, Brooklyn, and Queens. In Manhattan, aficionados go to Broadway on the Upper West Side, East Houston Street near Orchard, and elsewhere in the Lower East Side especially for "the best" bagels, lox, pastrami, smoked whitefish, stuffed derma, etc. It's Brighton Beach, Brooklyn, no question about it, for **Russian** food (and some more Jewish, as well).

GREENMARKETS/FARMERS' MARKETS

One of the surprises and joys of New York shopping has been the great success of the many greenmarkets that now take place throughout the city. The **Council of the Environment of New York City**, 212-477-3220, www.cenyc.org, sponsors these affairs by arranging for farmers and bakers from the tri-state area to sell their produce and goods at various outdoor locations within the five boroughs. In addition to fruit and vegetable growers, the council invites suppliers of beef, pork, lamb, poultry, eggs, honey, dairy, breads, wine, flowers, maple syrup, and other delectable items. Prices are competitive and the offerings are fresher than anything else except homegrown. All this and a general air of festivity is the reason why so many urbane New Yorkers—as well as some of the city's top chefs—have made greenmarkets a regular part of their shopping routine, especially at Union Square, the mother of all greenmarkets. (Personal tours may be arranged of the Union Square greenmarket on Wednesdays, Fridays, and Saturdays; a tour takes about 90 minutes. Call the council for more information.) Because the produce does come from the tri-state area, the warmer months are the most bountiful time to shop the markets. Market hours typically start at 8 a.m. and end anywhere from 2 p.m. to 6 p.m. Check the council's web site for a comprehensive list of greenmarket locations and accompanying map.

THE INCREDIBLE DIVERSITY AND DEPTH OF THE CITY'S CULTURAL, intellectual, and artistic life is a magnet for many. Nowhere else can such an enormous range of interests and avocations be accommodated on so many levels. While it is impossible to cover all the opportunities New York offers, we can help the newcomer, young and old alike, access this cultural smorgasbord by providing a compilation of ticket, subscription, and membership information for leading opera companies, symphony orchestras, dance companies, theatrical repertory groups, and museums. And we've added cultural opportunities for children, a section called **Literary Life**, and at the end, listings of major colleges and universities in the city, with the emphasis on Manhattan. In addition to graduate degrees and an inviting array of evening courses, these schools also offer lectures and workshops of interest, not to mention musical and theatrical performances. For more cultural life and opportunities see the community resources that are listed at the end of each neighborhood profile at the beginning of the book.

First, what is showing, where, and when? Two particularly useful sites for tracking down event details are the *New York Times'* www.nytoday.com or www.nytimes.com, and the extensive web site of the Alliance for the Arts, **NYC Arts On Line** at www.allianceforarts.org. The latter comprehensive compendium lists concert halls, galleries, museums, theaters, historical structures, monuments, and parks throughout the five boroughs, with links to web sites, information about hours and admissions, timely articles, performance calendars, and a culture guide for children. Area publications offering **event information** include:

- **"Weekend,"** *New York Times'* Friday edition, in two sections, features reviews, articles, and tips on the endless arts and entertainment possibilities for Friday, Saturday, and Sunday. The "Performing Arts" section also contains an up-to-the-minute "movie clock," useful in a town where movie schedules are notoriously unreliable.

- **"Arts and Leisure,"** *New York Times'* Sunday edition, besides reviews and critical articles on current trends and upcoming events in the arts, includes listings for the arts with thumbnail reviews.
- **The *New Yorker*,** on the stands Wednesday, includes not just plays, opera, and museums in its comprehensive "Goings on About Town," but also poetry readings, sporting events, and nightlife. Most listings include abbreviated reviews. www.newyorker.com
- ***New York* magazine,** on the stands Monday, incorporates Cue, "A Complete Guide to Entertainment, the Arts, and Dining for the Week." Included are brief movie and theater reviews. Comprehensive. www.newyorkmag.com
- ***Time Out New York*,** on the stands Wednesday, offers comprehensive listings and reviews in all aspects of entertainment and the arts, as well as gay and lesbian features, and listings of events for children. www.timeoutny.com
- The ***Village Voice*,** free on the street Wednesday, is filled with entertainment ads and carries a "Listings" column of weekly free events. Particularly good for alternative events. www.villagevoice.com
- ***New York Press*** is distributed free in restaurants, stores, and in street boxes below 28th Street; sparsely uptown. A favorite with downtowners as a reference for what's going on in the arts and music, the weekly also includes restaurant reviews and feature stories. Attitude at no extra cost. www.nypress.com
- ***Club freetime*,** a monthly sold at a dozen Manhattan newsstands and by subscription, is indispensable for the culturally active but financially challenged New Yorker, listing as it does a host of free and cut-rate lectures, dance, and theater performances, concerts, walking tours, film screenings, poetry readings, street festivals, and the like, mostly in Manhattan. Just goes to prove you can pig out culturally in the city for free. You can join Club freetime on their web site at www.clubfreetime.com or subscribe by calling 212-545-8900.

For performance information by telephone try **New York City/On Stage** a service of the Theatre Development Fund. Dial 212-768-1818 for up-to-the-minute information and ticket availability. Once connected with this 24-hour recorded service, you are asked to choose a category: press "1" for theater and performance, "2" for dance and music, "4" for family entertainment, "5" for events accepting TDF vouchers, "8" for information on TKTS booths, and so on. Recorded information is also available in Spanish.

If you don't know which show you want to see or you want to buy a block of seats to a musical, call the **Broadway Show Line**, operated by the League of American Theatres and Producers, 888-292-9669, for descriptions of Broadway and off-Broadway shows, performance schedules, seat locations, and group sales information. You can also order tickets here, with service charges the same as from Telecharge. For New York Theater listings you can also check out Theatermania at www.theatermania.com.

TICKETS

How can you buy tickets to New York's plays, concerts, ballets, operas, and special mega-events? Let us describe the ways.

BOX OFFICE

To get the best seats for the day you want, go to the appropriate box office in person well in advance of the performance desired, cash or charge card in hand. Not only can you check the theater's seating diagram (usually posted near the ticket window), you won't pay a handling fee. When ordering by telephone or mail, you have no control over the exact row or seat issued because orders are filled automatically on a "best available" basis. Box offices are usually open from 10 or 11 a.m. until the evening performance. Note: sometimes producers, directors, or actors release their personal tickets and these go back to the box office for sale at the last minute, making it possible for the persistent to see a hot show which has officially sold out.

TELEPHONE ORDERS

Most theaters list a special number to call for reservations. Billed to credit cards, tickets are mailed if time allows; otherwise pick them up at the theater the day of the performance. **Telecharge.com**, 212-239-6200, represents some 20 Schubert Theaters in New York City and adds $5.50 per off-Broadway ticket and $6.50 per Broadway ticket to your bill plus a $2.50 handling charge for the entire order. **Ticketmaster**, 212-307-7171, www.ticketmaster.com, now handles theater productions as well, collecting $4 to $6 per ticket plus a handling fee of $2.50. It all adds up. While usually not at all convenient, the theater box office is much cheaper if you're buying more than one ticket to an event.

ONLINE ORDERS

Individual tickets and subscriptions to most major concert series, operas, dance programs, and the like can be ordered online from their web sites using a major credit card. Likewise, tickets to plays, sporting events, and popular entertainment generally can be ordered through www.tele charge.com or www.ticketmaster.com.

TICKETMASTER

Promoters determine how tickets to their events will be sold: at Ticketmaster outlets, by calling Ticketmaster, or both. First call 212-307-7171 or go to www.ticketmaster.com to find out what performances they are offering and whether tickets can be ordered by phone and charged to a credit card (fees range, depending on the venue and type of ticket) or whether they must be picked up in person and paid for in cash at one of Ticketmaster's 2,200 outlets in the US and Canada. There are 160 outlets in the tri-state area.

BROKERS

Unless you have a friend with a personal broker or an "in" with a hotel concierge, don't expect to walk into a ticket agency and get front row center for the town's hottest musical the day of the performance. These seats are held for valued clients. However, for most people, events brokers who usually handle only orchestra, mezzanine, and box seats, are still probably the easiest way to get into a show or sporting event in a hurry. Expect to pay 20% to 50% over the total price for their service. Note: deal only with licensed brokers in the city; out-of-town brokers operating with 800 numbers are not regulated, and you can get burned. See "Ticket Sales—Entertainment and Sports" in the Yellow Pages for names, among whom American Tickets and Continental Guests Services, operating out of major hotels, are large and well established. Scalping is illegal, so think twice before buying from the guy hawking tickets in the street. For seating charts of several major New York City venues check the Yellow Pages.

ALTERNATIVE SOURCES

At the **Times Square Visitor's Center**, 1560 Broadway between 46th and 47th streets, 212-869-1890, www.timessquarebid.org, open daily 8 a.m. to 8 p.m., you can buy same-day and advance sale tickets to Broadway and off-Broadway shows at box office prices (subject to availability) plus a per ticket service charge of up to $5. The center, in a renovated old movie theater, also sells MetroCards and tickets to sightseeing tours, and airport shuttles, and provides free internet access, multilingual tourist counselors, theater seats in which to rest, as well as clean, handicap-accessible public restrooms.

Tickets to sports events, tours, and other entertainment, as well as theater tickets, can be bought at a kiosk at the city's official **Visitor Information Center**, 810 Seventh Avenue at 53rd Street, 212-397-8200, www.nycvisit.com, Monday-Friday, 8:30 a.m. to 6 p.m., and Saturday and Sunday, 9 a.m. to 5 p.m. There is a service charge for these tickets. Also available here is the CityPass, a steeply discounted ticket to six major tourist attractions good for nine days, plus maps, brochures, and multilingual tourist counselors.

Suppose you've just got to have tickets to that hot show now, and cost is no object. Call the **Actors' Fund of America**, 212-221-7301, or **Broadway Cares/Equity Fights AIDS**, 212-840-0770, www.broadway cares.org, for the best seats at hard-to-get shows. The tariff? You'll pay twice the box office price, but half of that is tax-deductible.

DISCOUNTS

TKTS is one of the city's great bargains. The Theatre Development Fund operates two outlets for half-price and 25%-off day-of-performance tickets to Broadway and off-Broadway shows. Availability information is posted on large boards near ticket sales booths, and a small fee—currently $3—is charged for each ticket; cash or traveler's check only. Note: ticket selection is better and lines shorter early in the week. For a list of discounted tickets available that night go to www.newyork.citysearch.com or www.nyto-day.com after 4 p.m.

- **TKTS Times Square**, West 47th Street and Broadway, sells Broadway, off-Broadway, dance, and music event tickets for evening performances from 3 p.m. to 8 p.m., Monday-Saturday, and 11 a.m. to 7:30 p.m. on Sundays. Matinee tickets are on sale on Wednesdays and Saturdays only from 9 a.m. to 2 p.m. For more information go to the Theatre Development Fund web site at www.tdf.org or call or write: 212-768-1818, Theater Development Fund, 1501 Broadway, 21st floor, New York, NY 10036-5652.
- **Twofers** resemble theater tickets but are, in fact, passes. When exchanged at Broadway (and some off-Broadway) box offices, twofers entitle the bearer to two tickets for little more than the price of one. A convenient way to keep a show open after bad reviews or at the end of a long run, twofers can be found all over town. Try: restaurant cash registers, the city's official Visitor Information Center at 810 Seventh Avenue at 53rd Street, in college dorms, or hotels.
- The **Theatre Development Fund**, 1501 Broadway, 21st floor, Attention: TDF Membership, NYC 10036, 212-221-0013, www.tdf.org; offers tickets to a variety of plays, musicals, dance, and jazz performances at reduced prices, typically less than $30 for a Broadway play or musical

and under $25 for off-Broadway productions. Memberships are available to seniors (62 or older), students, teachers, performing arts professionals, union members, staff member of a non-profit organization, or members of the clergy or armed forces. Download the application from the TDF web site and mail it in. The annual membership fee is $22.50.

- **Audience Extras**, 61 Lexington Avenue, Ste. 1A, NYC 10010, 212-686-1966, www.audienceextras.com, provides free tickets to plays in preview and post opening (whose producers wish to "paper" the house, i.e., fill it with freebies to stimulate word-of-mouth) to its members in the theater industry. For $115 you get a one-year membership card, renewable for $85, with a reserve fund against which a $3 service charge per ticket is charged as well as access to their 24-hour hotline, which lists available shows. There is no limit on free shows.
- **Quicktix**; a small allotment of seats for each of the various performances at the New York Shakespeare Festival's Public Theatre on Lafayette Street (see **Theater** section) go on sale at 5:30 p.m. the day of performance for about half the price of regular tickets. You need to be a **Public Theatre** member. Call 212-260-2400 after 1 p.m. for information. The Public Theatre is online at www.publictheater.org.

 Student tickets at half price or less are often available to those holding bona fide student IDs as follows:
- **New York Philharmonic** at Avery Fisher Hall, Lincoln Center, has two arrangements. They sell $14 tickets for rehearsals about a month before the actual date. In the Student/Senior Rush Program, tickets are available two for $10 ($10 each for non-students) for shows that have high availability (call 212-875-5656 on Monday of the week of the performance in which you are interested). For more information go to www.newyorkphilharmonic.org.
- **New York City Opera**, also at Lincoln Center, sometimes has student tickets for those who line up at the theater by 10 a.m. on the morning of a performance, 11:30 a.m. on Sunday. Tickets, if available, are $10. Call the box office, 212-870-5570, for more information.
- **Carnegie Hall** sells $10 tickets, when available, on a first-come, first-served basis. You can call 212-247-7800 on the day of the concert starting at noon to see if tickets will be available. Day-of tickets are available at the box office from noon until one hour before the performance.
- **Grace Rainey Rogers Auditorium** at the Metropolitan Museum of Art sells standing room tickets for half price on the day of a concert. Call the box office at 212-570-3949 to check on availability.

High school students have access to the best deal of all on tickets to music, theater, museums, dance, and more through **High 5 Tickets to the Arts**. Students 13 to 18 years old can get $5 tickets to weekend (Friday-Sunday) performances, two for $5 for weekday performances by presenting school ID at any Ticketmaster outlet, including HMV, Tower Records, and other stores in the city and in much of New Jersey, at least a day before the performance. Museum admission is two for $5 any day, with ID, at the museum. Free catalogs of High 5 events are available at participating Ticketmaster outlets, public libraries, and at High 5's office, 1 East 53rd Street. Call 212-445-8587 for information or visit www.high5tix.org.

A few of the smaller to mid-size Manhattan theaters (generally off-Broadway and off-off Broadway) will exchange admission for volunteer ushering, a boon to the theater devotee who is light of wallet. Call around for participating theaters.

If you are a frequent theater-goer, sports fan, or classical music enthusiast, you might want to pick up **STUBS**, a paperback which publishes the seating plan of every concert hall, opera house, stadium, arena, and theater in town. STUBS in hand, you can immediately locate the seats being offered by TKTS booths, brokers, Ticketmaster outlets and others who have no seating diagrams available for ticket purchasers. The book sells for $12.95 and can be ordered on www.amazon.com or found in New York bookstores.

SUBSCRIPTIONS

Common practice dictates that new subscriptions to any series—symphonic, operatic, dance, theatrical—must wait to be filled until the previous season's subscribers are given an opportunity to renew. Once the renewal deadline is past, new subscriptions are processed on a first-come, first-served basis. The initial announcement of each new season's schedule is sent to everyone on the mailing list anywhere from six weeks to six months before performances are scheduled to begin. To assure a position near the beginning of the line, call whatever institution interests you well in advance of its season and ask to be put on the mailing list. Upon receipt of the announcement schedule, choose your series and return the coupon and a check quickly. Often this can be done online at the appropriate web site. Full-page ads in the New York Times Sunday "Arts and Leisure" section herald symphonic, operatic, and dance seasons five to six months before performances begin, but usually a week or two after the first public subscription mailers have been sent out.

Incidentally, certain nights are traditionally more popular than others. If good seats are more important than sitting next to the right people, find out which night or series has the best tickets available.

GRAND OPERA

- **Metropolitan Opera**, Metropolitan Opera House, Lincoln Center, NYC 10023, 212-362-6000, www.metopera.org; subscriptions range from $160 for an eight-opera series high up in the Family Circle to $2,300 for an eight-opera series in the Center Orchestra. The Met charges $35 per subscription for handling. Renewal notices are mailed to current subscribers, and once these orders are processed in the spring, new subscriptions are filled. The Met's season is broken into three periods for the sale of individual seats: fall, winter, and spring. Subscribers are given first crack, then seats for single performances are offered to the public, first through a mailing, then via newspaper ads about a month and a half before each of the three seasons begins. Standing room goes on sale the Sunday before performance. You might also catch the Met during their free concert series in the parks during the summer. They visit each of the five boroughs. Check their web site for a schedule as the summer approaches.
- **New York City Opera**, New York State Theater, Lincoln Center, NYC 10023, subscriptions, 212-496-0600 or 212-870-5580; box office, 212-870-5570; www.nycopera.com. The New York City Opera offers numerous two- to four-opera series for performances September-April. There are several different plans; ticket prices vary.
- **Opera Orchestra of New York**, 239 West 72nd Street, NYC 10025, 212-799-1982, www.oony.org; under the musical direction of Eve Queler, performs three non-staged (that is, concert style) operas per season at Carnegie Hall. Performed by singers of the first rank but not super-stars, these are usually operas by major composers, which are rarely staged. Subscriptions to the 2003-2004 season ranged from $75 for a seat in the rear balcony to $375 for parquet center and first tier, plus a suggested donation ranging from $18 to $80.

CLASSICAL MUSIC

- **New York Philharmonic**, Avery Fisher Hall, Lincoln Center, NYC 10023, 212-875-5656, www.nyphilharmonic.org; numerous series are available for a September-June season. Easiest to obtain are subscriptions to the three-concert mini-series. Fall schedules are announced in late February/early March.
- **Carnegie Hall**, 57th Street and Seventh Avenue, NYC 10019, 212-247-7800, www.carnegiehall.org; one hundred years old and still counting, Carnegie, featuring splendid acoustics, is still the concert hall preferred by many performers, and it continues to host programs by a

variety of virtuosos and orchestras, plus popular superstars and even chamber music, with age-given grace. Call Carnegie Hall for subscriber information.

CHAMBER MUSIC

Several halls traditionally host the extraordinarily popular chamber music groups that perform here regularly. The Guarneri Quartet, the Juilliard Quartet, and the Beaux Arts Trio might give three or more New York concerts during any given year, each at a different location. Only the Lincoln Center Chamber Music Society has a hall—Alice Tully Hall in Lincoln Center—that it can call home. Good seats go fast once the *Times* advertisements appear, so it's important to get on each group's mailing list. The following spaces are most likely to host chamber music performances. Call them or keep your eyes on the "Arts and Leisure" section of the Sunday *New York Times* in late spring and summer.

- **Abraham Goodman House**, Merkin Concert Hall, 129 West 67th Street between Broadway and Amsterdam Avenue, NYC 10023, box office, 212-501-3330, www.kaufman-center.org
- **Alice Tully Hall**, Lincoln Center, NYC 10023, 212-721-6500, www.lincolncenter.org; concerts by the Lincoln Center Chamber Music Society as well as other groups.
- **Brooklyn Academy of Music (BAM)**, 30 Lafayette Avenue, Brooklyn 11217, 718-636-4100, www.bam.org
- **Metropolitan Museum of Art**, Grace Rainey Rogers Auditorium, 83rd Street and Fifth Avenue, NYC 10028, 212-570-3949, www.metmuseum.org
- **92nd Street Y (YM-YWHA)**, Kaufmann Concert Hall, 1395 Lexington Avenue, NYC 10028, 212-427-6000

DANCE

It could be argued that New York is the dance capital of the world. Certainly it is possible to see a performance of some form of dance—ballet, modern, jazz, ethnic, avant-garde—just about any night of the week somewhere in the city. Dance enthusiasts watch the publications above to catch visiting troupes and local groups at alternative sites. Among the latter, for example, are **Dance Theatre Workshop** at 219 West 19th Street, 212-924-0077, www.dtw.org; **Danspace Project** at St. Mark's Church, 131 East 10th Street, 212-674-8112, www.danspace.org; **Performance Space 122**, 150 First Avenue at Ninth Street, 212-477-5288, www.ps122.org; **Joyce SoHo**, 155 Mercer Street, south of Houston Street, 212-431-9233; **Context Theater**, 28 Avenue A at East Third

Street, 212-613-8456; and **Theater of the Riverside Church**, 91 Claremont Avenue at 120th Street, 212-496-5497. Below we've listed the established troupes and theaters to which one can subscribe. Get yourself on one mailing list and others are likely to find you.

- **American Ballet Theater**, 890 Broadway, Third Floor, NYC 10003, 212-477-3030, www.abt.org; subscription series are offered for the ABT's spring season at the Metropolitan Opera House, April-June. The first announcement, mailed to friends in late December, is followed shortly by a new subscriber mailing, then a week or so later by the traditional January *New York Times* ad. Subscriptions for seats vary. Individual tickets at the box office and by phone from the Met Ticket Service go on sale in March.

- **New York City Ballet**, New York State Theater, Lincoln Center, NYC 10023, 212-499-0600 for subscriptions or 212-870-5570 for performance information; www.nycballet.com. Two seasons provide balletomanes the opportunity of feasting on dancing by Balanchine's company. Both the winter season, November-February, and the spring season, April-June, have sixteen four-performance series, and good seats are easiest to come by for weekend matinees. First announcements go out nine weeks before the season begins. A tip for Nutcracker ballet fanciers: first orders for single, non-subscription performances of the Nutcracker are accepted in late October and tickets go fast for this seasonal family favorite. Call 212-870-5500 for prices and dates, and if certain seats for special performances are important, make your order several weeks before that time.

- **The Joyce Theater**, 175 Eighth Avenue at 19th Street, NYC 10011, 212-242-0800, www.joyce.org; celebrating dance of all kinds—ballet, modern, flamenco—the Joyce is an elegantly revamped former Art Deco movie house in Chelsea. Your reward for buying tickets to performances by four different dance groups during the fall or spring season is a membership that entitles you to 40% off on all tickets purchased subsequently. Your membership card also entitles you to priority seating and various discounts at fifteen Chelsea restaurants located between 14th and 23rd streets and Sixth and Tenth avenues.

- **The City Center Theater**, 131 West 55th Street, NYC 10019, 212-581-1212, www.citycenter.org; dance companies once dominated the City Center's performance schedule; today they vie with a variety of musical comedy performances. The following **dance troupes** are among the major groups performing here regularly:
  - **Martha Graham**, 316 East 63rd Street, 212-838-5886, www.marthagrahamdance.org
  - **Alvin Ailey American Dance Theater**, 211 West 61st Street, 212-767-0590, www.alvinailey.org

- **Paul Taylor Dance Company**, 552 Broadway, 212-431-5562, www.paultaylor.org
- **Dance Theatre of Harlem**, 466 West 152nd Street, 212-690-2800, www.dancetheatreofharlem.com
- **American Ballet Theater**, 890 Broadway, Third Floor, NYC 10003, 212-477-3030, www.abt.org

As with the chamber music ensembles, it is best to get on each company's mailing list. Call the company direct or City Center's Subscription Department. Prices vary for each series.

THEATER

Broadway, besides designating Manhattan's longest avenue, refers to the midtown theater district on and around "the Great White Way," home to the greatest theatrical productions in the nation, ranging from grand musicals and comedies to classic dramas. It's the big time and a magnet for theater-lovers everywhere. But a high percentage of the most critically acclaimed plays and musicals produced in any given year originate off-Broadway, more often than not in theaters that offer subscriptions as a means of financing productions. Season tickets not only ensure exposure to new artists, playwrights and directors, but in most cases save money as well. A few of the most established groups are mentioned here, but please don't be limited by this list. Many more experimental but no less rewarding companies exist and should be explored.

- **Circle in the Square Theatre School**, 1633 Broadway at 50th Street, NYC 10019-6795, 212-307-0388, www.circlesquare.org; professional conservatory and acting and musical theater. Beginning in the 1950s in the Village, plays by Tennessee Williams and Eugene O'Neill premiered at Circle in the Square with such young actors as Jason Robards and George C. Scott. Uptown now, the theater continues to stage some of the best contemporary drama and comedy with first-rate actors and directors.
- **CSC Repertory Theater**, 136 East 13th Street, NYC 10003, 212-677-4210, www.classicstage.org; founded in 1967, CSC has been performing Ibsen, Strindberg, Brecht and other mostly-contemporary classics in this comfortably intimate theater since then. It's not a resident company, but three or four plays are performed in repertory throughout the season, with an occasional lecture bonus.
- **Joseph Papp Public Theater**, 425 Lafayette Street south of East 8th Street, NYC 10003, www.publictheater.org; members call 212-260-2400 for tickets; non-members call Telecharge at 212-239-6200. Joseph Papp, who died in 1992, was perhaps the single most impor-

tant figure in the post-WWII American theater. This venue, complete with the New York Shakespeare Festival's Public Theater and the cabaret, Joe's Pub, offers events that are hailed for their diversity as well as their excellence. A membership package plan allows the public inexpensive access to productions and flexibility in choosing which of the season's productions one wishes to see. A small allotment of the seats for any performance at The Public are held for same-day sale at a discount. The tickets, called Quicktix (see **Discounts** section), go on sale at 6 p.m. for about half the price of regular tickets.

- **Lincoln Center Theater**, 150 West 65th Street, Attention: Members Department, NYC 10023, 212-239-6277, www.lct.org; members in this innovative theater program have access to a potpourri of presentations from Shakespeare to Mamet, with an occasional first-rate musical thrown in, be it at Lincoln Center on Broadway or off-off-Broadway at the experimental LaMama. The $40 membership fee buys one year's access to Lincoln Center Theater plays already in progress around town and first crack at six new productions a year as they come up. Popular productions with outstanding casts have included *Our Town*, *Waiting for Godot*, and *Anything Goes*.

- **Manhattan Theatre Club**, 311 West 43rd Street, NYC 10036, 212-399-3030, www.mtc-nyc.org; has been producing critically acclaimed plays since its founding on the Upper East Side in 1972. After some years with one foot at City Center on West 55th Street, MTC has settled in there, at 299-seat Stage I and at 150-seat Stage II. Productions that prove to be especially successful typically move to larger Broadway or off-Broadway venues. Single tickets can also be purchased through City Tix: 212-581-1212.

- **Pearl Theatre Co.**, 80 St. Marks Place, NYC 10003, 212-598-9802, www.pearltheatre.org; a repertory theater company, it mounts regular productions of theater classics such as Ibsen, Chekhov, and Shakespeare for a loyal audience in an intimate East Village theater. Various subscription plans for three to five performances range from $102 to $145.

- **Roundabout Theatre Company**, 231 West 39th Street, Suite 1200, NYC 10018, 212-719-1300, www.roundabouttheatre.org; with a subscription base of some 20,000, this not-for-profit theater company is obviously doing something right. What that involves is presenting revivals such as Pinter's *Betrayal* and O'Neill's *Anna Christie* and musicals such as *Cabaret* with such stars as Natasha Richardson, Nathan Lane, Laura Linney, and Alan Cumming in their handsome new home, The American Airlines Theater, 227 West 42nd Street, as well as new plays by established writers off-Broadway.

ALL OF THE ABOVE

- **Brooklyn Academy of Music**, 30 Lafayette Avenue, Brooklyn 11217, 718-636-4100, www.bam.org; is a center for all the performing arts. Best known for its Next Wave Festival, which takes place September to December, BAM (as it is popularly known) is a prime showcase for cutting-edge dance, theater, music, and opera. From the intimate LeClerq Space to the magnificent Opera House and the rejuvenated Majestic Theater, BAM presents everything from small chamber performances to alternative new age music. With several series taking place year-round, it is best to call and get on the mailing list in order to have a shot at getting tickets. Subscriptions represent a real value here, and if you become a Friend of BAM you'll get priority seating.
- **Queens Theatre in the Park**, Flushing Meadow Corona Park, Flushing 11368, 718-760-0064, www.queenstheater.org; brings major dance companies, off-Broadway plays, and children's theater to its two theaters located in the Philip Johnson-designed New York Pavilion of the 1964-65 World's Fair. From *Charlie and the Chocolate Factory* to *Dames At Sea* to laser vaudeville to the Latino Culture Festival, Queens Theatre offers a variety of performances for a wide range of tastes.

FILM

New York is a movie buff's paradise. Screening of new filmmakers' works is a constant at the **Whitney Museum of American Art**, 945 Madison Avenue, 212-570-3676, www.whitney.org, and at the **Guggenheim Museum**, 1071 Fifth Avenue 212-423-3500, www.guggenheim.org, as well as at most of those all-encompassing, art-encouraging alternative spaces sprinkled throughout New York. **New School University**, 66 West 12th Street, 212-229-5600, www.newschool.edu, and the **Cinema Department of New York University**, 721 Broadway, 6th floor, 212-998-1600, www.nyu.edu/tisch/cinema, explore movies in depth through numerous seminars and courses and, almost every semester, sponsor a film series or two as well.

Some of Manhattan's remaining revival and art film showcases include: **Angelika Film Center and Cafe**, 18 West Houston Street, NYC 10003, 212-995-2000, www.angelikafilmcenter.com; **Anthology Film Archives**, 32 Second Avenue at Second Street, NYC 10003, 212-505-5181; **Cinema Village**, 12th Street east of Fifth Avenue, NYC 10003, 212-924-3363; **Film Forum**, 209 West Houston, NYC, 212-727-8110; **The**

Screening Room, 54 Varick Street, NYC 10013, 212-334-2100; and the **Walter Reade Theater**, 165 West 65th Street at Broadway, NYC 10023, 212-875-5600. Weekly schedules for these theaters are found in the "Arts and Leisure" section of the Sunday *Times* and *The New Yorker*. More comprehensive yet and including films shown in truly alternative venues is *Time Out New York's* "Film, Alternatives and Revivals" section.

Additional film societies and museums include:

- **The American Museum of the Moving Image**, 36-01 35th Avenue at 36th Street, Astoria 11106, 718-784-0077, www.movingimage.us, is a continuous movie, animation, and video art retrospective with exhibits, speaker series, symposia, celebrity appearances, and film series throughout the year to quicken the pulse of the true movie maven. Membership, $50 for individual, $75 for family, gives you admission, reservation privileges for screenings, a subscription to the Quarterly Guide, a 15% discount at the museum shop, and reduced admission to special programs and celebrity appearances. You need not be a member to visit; day rates available.
- **The Film Society of Lincoln Center**, 140 West 65th Street, NYC 10023, 212-875-5600, presents the New York Film Festival each fall (late September through October) at the Walter Reade Theater (see above) as well as the New Directors/New Films series in conjunction with the Museum of Modern Art each spring. Established in 1963, the Film Festival presents some 20 films during its annual run. A $50 membership in the Film Society ($35 for students) provides the following perks: right to buy two twelve-film subscriptions to the New York Film Festival and first crack at certain other festival tickets, discounts on tickets for New Directors/New Films at the Museum of Modern Art, and a free subscription to the society's bi-monthly magazine, *Film Comment*. If you're not interested in membership, it's a good idea to get on the society's mailing list before the Film Festival's program is announced the last week in August, in order to obtain the schedule before it appears in the papers. The box office for performances at **Alice Tully Hall** is at 1941 Broadway at 65th Street, NYC 10023, 212-875-5050. It opens the Sunday after Labor Day for single ticket sales to the public.
- **Tribeca Film Institute**, 375 Greenwich Street, NYC 10013, 212-941-2400, box office 212-941-1515, www.tribecafilminstitute.org; offers year-round cultural events, including comedy, film, music, and theater, as well as the annual Tribeca Film Festival held each spring. Established by Robert De Niro and Jane Rosenthal in an effort to make Lower Manhattan a "centerpiece for culture and the arts."

Of course, there are plenty of movie theaters around the city showing the latest in Hollywood's big screen hits. Theaters range from the small screens and tight seating in the multiplex theaters to the more spacious and comfortable Beekman on 66th and Second Avenue in Manhattan, where you might just catch a star studded opening night. The IMAX Theater on Broadway and 68th Street with a four-story screen is worth checking out, especially with children. New Yorkers love to get out to the movies so expect to find lines for the hottest new flicks. Call the **movie phone**, 777-FILM, or go to www.moviephone.com to find out what is playing in your neighborhood and when.

BROADCASTING

The Museum of Television and Radio, 25 West 52nd Street, 212-621-6800, www.mtr.org, shouldn't be missed as a chance to revisit your childhood and to experience American culture in video and audiotape form. "...The Shadow knows," Fred Allen on radio, "All in the Family," "I Love Lucy"—it's all there. The museum offers 96 video monitors for individual viewing of any television program in their collection. Call for schedule listings of special screening events. Annual memberships vary with special prices for students, which allow admission to the museum's theaters and screening and listening rooms. Membership also gives you a discount on museum seminars and magazines as well as all gift shop items.

MUSEUM MEMBERSHIPS

The benefits to be reaped by joining any of the city's myriad non-profit institutions are really quite amazing. There seem to be museums and societies for every possible interest, so if you're an aficionado of a particular discipline, seek out the institution which best reflects your avocation and join. You'll be inundated with free literature, offered perquisites of many kinds, and probably be invited to teas, cocktail parties, and even banquets if your contribution is big enough. For the generalist, membership in one or two of the city's established cultural citadels is a wonderful way of obtaining well-researched information on any number of subjects. As an indication of the kind of benefits memberships provide, we've noted below details for a few of New York's major institutions:

- **American Folk Art Museum**, 45 West 53rd Street, NYC 10019, 212-265-1040, www.folkartmuseum.org; a wide array of folk art from weathervanes to textiles is found depicting America's history from the 18th Century to the present. Membership ranges from $30 annually for an individual to $80 for a family and includes free admission to the museum, discounts on gift shop purchases, a subscription to the museum's newsletter, access to the museum's library and other perks.

- **American Museum of Natural History**, Central Park West at 79th Street, NYC 10024, 212-769-5100, www.amnh.org; an associate membership here entitles you to as many visits to the dinosaurs as you wish, to say nothing of the Rose Center for Earth and Space, a subscription to *Natural History* magazine and a 10% discount in the store. A family membership adds a monthly newsletter and calendar, 25% discount on Hayden Planetarium tickets and invitations to previews of the exhibitions. You also receive a 10% discount on most educational programs at the museum and a hefty discount at the IMAX Theater with its oversized retractable screen and a dizzying IMAX projector.
- **The Bronx Zoo** (its official name: **New York Zoological Society International Wildlife Conservation Park**), Fordham Road and Bronx River Parkway, Bronx, 718-367-1010, is the largest zoo in the five boroughs and, stretching over 265 acres, the largest urban zoo in the world. Membership includes admission to this zoo as well as to the **Central Park Zoo**, Central Park, East 64th Street and Fifth Avenue, 212-439-6500; the **New York Aquarium**, Surf Avenue and West 8th Street, Coney Island, Brooklyn, 718-265-3474; the **Queens Wildlife Center**, 718-271-1500, and **Children's Farm**, 111th Street at 54th Avenue, Corona Park, Flushing, Queens. Bronx Zoo membership also includes four free parking passes and discounts at gift shops, certain zoo restaurants, and on educational classes. These organizations are all part of the Wildlife Conservation Society, online at www.wcs.org.
- **Frick Collection**, 1 East 70th Street, NYC 10021, 212-288-0700, www.frick.org; membership in Friends of the Frick entitles you to unlimited admission to the collection, a subscription to the new *Frick Members' Magazine* with information on special exhibits, lectures, and concerts, and a 10% discount in the museum shop.
- **Guggenheim Museum**, 1071 Fifth Avenue, NYC 10128, downtown at 575 Broadway at Prince, NYC 10012, 212-423-3500, www.guggenheim.org; even the basic individual membership confers an architectural bonus, providing free admission to the justifiably famous Frank Lloyd Wright spiral uptown and the Peggy Guggenheim Collection in her palazzo on the Grand Canal in Venice. In addition, members get invitations to parties, private viewings, books signings, and discounts at Guggenheim stores and the Guggenheim café.
- **The Jewish Museum**, 1109 Fifth Avenue at 92nd Street, NYC 10128, 212-423-3200, www.jewishmuseum.org; Jewish culture is represented in 28,000 objects including fine arts, Judaica, and through the broadcast media. The permanent collection, Culture & Continuity: The Jewish Journey, depicts 4,000 years of Jewish history, including ancient times in Egypt, the Holocaust, and the formation of the State of Israel to the present. Membership includes unlimited admission, invitations to

special previews of new exhibitions, discounts in the museum store and the Weissman Café, guest passes, invitations to the Family Hanukkah Party and various other perks.

- **Metropolitan Museum of Art**, Fifth Avenue at 82nd Street, NYC 10028, 212-879-5500, www.metmuseum.org; the sumptuous *Bulletin* published quarterly by the Met, filled with high-quality color photographs and illuminating texts of catalog caliber, comes free with the museum's $85 individual membership. Other bonuses include the bi-monthly *Calendar News*, free admission to the museum and the Cloisters, invitations to previews and private viewings of two exhibitions a year, and copies of the Met's Christmas and spring catalogues illustrating the museum's publications and glamorous reproductions of everything from Chinese scarves to early American pewter pitchers, which, as a member, you can buy at a 10% discount. But probably the biggest bonus you'll receive is the program and exhibition information, which will impel you to get over to the Met more often than you might otherwise.
- **Museum for African Art**, 36-01 43rd Avenue, Long Island City, Queens 11101, 718-784-7700, www.africanart.org; the Queens-based museum is widely recognized as housing the pre-eminent exhibition of African art (completion of their permanent home on 110th Street in Manhattan is expected in 2006). Membership includes admission to public programs, a subscription to the newsletter, discounts in the museum store and on birthday party packages, plus invitations to holiday receptions and the annual gala dinner.
- **The Museum of Modern Art (MoMA)**, 11 West 53rd Street, NYC 10019, 212-708-9500, www.moma.org; in 2001, MoMA embarked on its most ambitious expansion to substantially increase space for its unparalleled collection of 20th century art. In the spring of 2002, museum operations moved to MoMA QNS, in a former Swingline factory at 33rd Street at Queens Boulevard, Long Island City, a half-block from the #7 train, where it remained until the museum re-opened in November 2004. Additions include a six-story gallery building and an eight-story Education and Research Center, with the top floors dedicated to the expanded library and archives; the renovated lobby offers views of the sculpture garden. Entry-level memberships receive a 10% discount at the museum store and on catalog and online merchandise, as well as admission to the galleries and daily film programs, and invitations to exhibition previews and special events.
- **South Street Seaport Museum**, 207 Front Street, NYC 10038, 212-748-8600, www.southstseaport.org; encompasses the new Fulton Market with its intriguing stores and jolly restaurants, restored Schermerhorn Row's handsome brick houses, and the Museum Block

with old shops and new walkways. Membership tends to be a youngish crowd, drawn as much by the ambiance and the idea of the museum as by the perks, which include free admission to the museums, galleries, and ships at the Seaport Gallery, invitations to gallery openings and educational programs, a subscription to *Seaport: New York's History Magazine*, plus discounts in several stores at the seaport.

- **Whitney Museum of American Art**, 945 Madison Avenue at 75th Street, NYC 10021, 212-570-3676, www.whitney.org; membership benefits its holder with museum admission for two, discounts on classes and lectures, discounts at the museum store, invitations to exhibition opening receptions, and a free museum publication, as well as a calendars of events. If American art or experimental film interests you particularly, it is worth belonging to the Whitney to have ready access to its excellent series of large and small exhibitions and also to the works presented by the museum's New American Filmmakers series in some 25 to 30 different programs every year.

CULTURE FOR KIDS

Perhaps the greatest asset in raising children in the city is the astonishing wealth of theater, film, museums, and programs designed for them. It goes without saying that all of the institutions and organizations above are accessible to and appropriate sooner or later for children: the New York City Ballet's exquisite "Nutcracker," the popular armor collection at the Metropolitan Museum, so much of the Museum of Natural History including the famed dinosaurs, the Bronx Zoo, children's museums in Manhattan and Brooklyn, to name just a few. Many of them design exhibits and programs specifically for children. And there are institutions and groups that exist specifically for the younger population.

How to find it all? You'll pick up a lot about what's going on where from school bulletin boards, from other parents, and from the parent magazines distributed free in school lobbies and libraries. Neighborhood weeklies such as *The Villager* often include events for children in their weekly listings. The comprehensive ***Kids Culture Catalog***, compiled and published by the **Alliance for the Arts**, 330 West 42nd Street, #1701, NYC 10036, 212-947-6340, www.allianceforarts.org, offers brief descriptions of and directions to scores of local institutions and attractions—from historic houses and botanical gardens to alternative art spaces and zoos. Their excellent *New York City Kids Arts Culture Calendar* is published twice yearly, and there is an annual **NYC Arts Calendar** available in June. Pick up either at the Alliance for the Arts office, New York's Visitor Center, or at area cultural institutions and libraries, or go online: www.kidsarts.org or www.nyc-arts.org.

Other resources include:

- *New York* **magazine** in the Cue section has a "Kids" page that carries listings of children's events and attractions, with free events marked and including times, prices, and telephone numbers.
- The *New York Times* in Friday's "Weekend" sections carries extensive descriptions of theater, museum, and zoo events for children in the "Spare Times for Children" column, further descriptions of special events under "Family Fare," and reviews of new movies from the perspective of their suitability for children.
- *Time Out New York*, www.timeoutny.com, is a good source of information for child-friendly events going on around town.

THEATER FOR CHILDREN

New Victory Theater, 209 West 42nd Street, 646-223-3020; revamped with a grand staircase rising to a jewel-box theater and family friendly. Engaging programming ranges from the pleasingly silly to the avant-garde but remains respectful of the audience's age and maturity.

Other venues offering theater for children include the following:

- **Asphalt Green's Mazur Theater**, 555 East 90th Street, Manhattan, 212-369-8890; puppet theater that runs during the school year.
- **Brooklyn Academy of Music**, 30 Lafayette Avenue, Brooklyn, 718-636-4100, www.bam.org
- **Brooklyn Arts Exchange**, 421 Fifth Avenue at 8th Street in Park Slope, 718-832-0018, also has classes for kids in theater, dance, and choreography.
- **Brooklyn YWCA**, The Shadow Box Theatre, 30 Third Avenue between State and Atlantic Avenue, Brooklyn, 212-724-0677, www.shadowboxtheatre.org
- **Henry Street Settlement, Abrams Art Center**, 466 Grand Street, Lower East Side, 212-598-0400, www.henrystreet.org
- **Theatreworks USA**, 2162 Broadway at 76th Street, 212-627-7373
- **South Street Seaport Museum and Marketplace**, South and Fulton streets, Lower Manhattan, 212-748-8600, www.southstseaport.org
- **Swedish Cottage Marionette Theater**, Central Park, 212-988-9093
- **Symphony Space**, 2537 Broadway at 95th Street, 212-864-5400
- **Thirteenth Street Repertory Company**, 50 West 13th Street, 212-675-6677

If you want to really inspire your kids, go to a performance of the **Broadway Kids**. Since 1994, this rotating troupe, comprised of children who have been in Broadway shows, has been wowing audiences at various venues around the city. For an upcoming schedule of performances, visit their web site at www.broadwaykids.com.

MUSEUMS AND LIBRARIES FOR CHILDREN

Many of the major museums and libraries host events and exhibitions specifically for children; others are dedicated entirely to kids.

- **American Museum of Natural History**, 79th Street and Central Park West, 212-769-5100, www.amnh.org; a must, naturally.
- **Brooklyn Children's Museum**, 145 Brooklyn Avenue at St. Mark's Place, Crown Heights, 718-735-4402, www.brooklynkids.org; wonderfully hands-on and inventive.
- **Brooklyn Museum of Art**, 200 Eastern Parkway at Prospect Park, 718-638-5000
- **Children's Museum of the Arts**, 182 Lafayette Street near Broome Street, 212-274-0986, www.cmany.org
- **Children's Museum of Manhattan**, 212 West 83rd Street, 212-721-1223, www.cmom.org; fun for adults too.
- **Historic Richmondtown**, Staten Island Historical Society, 441 Clarke Avenue, Richmondtown, Staten Island, 718-351-1611
- **Intrepid Sea Air Space Museum**, Pier 86, West 46th Street at 12th Avenue, 212-245-0072
- **Madame Tussaud's Wax Museum**, 234 West 42nd Street, 800-246-8872; pricey but fun.
- **Museum of the City of New York**, Fifth Avenue at 103rd Street, 212-534-1672
- **New York City Fire Museum**, 278 Spring Street, SoHo, 212-691-1303, little ones love this place.
- **New York Hall of Science**, 47-01 111th Street, Flushing, Queens, 718-699-0005, highly regarded and recently expanded, this hands-on technology center is popular with budding young scientists.
- **New York Public Library**, various branches, 212-340-0849, www.nypl.org
- **Queens Museum of Art**, Flushing Meadow Corona Park, 718-592-9700, home to the most amazing miniature panorama of the city with some 800,000 buildings capturing most every structure in the five boroughs—a must see to believe.
- **Queens Public Library**, various branches, 718-990-0700, www.queenslibrary.org
- **Staten Island Children's Museum** at Snug Harbor Cultural Center, 1000 Richmond Terrace, Livingston, Staten Island, 718-273-2060, www.silive.com

FILM FOR CHILDREN

The **Museum of Modern Art** (see above) screens movies for children, some of them about art, some artful, in their Roy and Niuta Titus Theater, 11 West 53rd Street, 212-708-9848 (will reopen in 2005). Children and their parents who attend the annual **New York International Children's Film Festival** at NYU's Cantor Film Center, 36 East 8th Street, 212-998-1212, in February choose the grand prize winners. Www.gkids.com describes the films and gives show times.

MUSIC AND DANCE FOR CHILDREN

Many of the major venues for music and dance in the city present special programs for children. Among them:

- **Alice Tully Hall, Jazz for Young People**, Lincoln Center, Broadway at 65th Street; for tickets call 212-721-6500.
- **Carnegie Hall**, family concerts, 57th Street and 7th Avenue, 212-247-7800, www.carnegiehall.org
- **Florence Gould Hall, Little Orchestra Society**, 55 East 59th Street, 212-971-9500
- **Brooklyn Arts Exchange**, 421 Fifth Avenue at 8th Street in Park Slope, Brooklyn, 718-832-0018, www.bax.org
- **Joyce Theater, Eliot Feld Kids Dance**, 175 Eighth Avenue at 19th Street, 212-242-0800
- **Symphony Space**, 2537 Broadway at 95th Street, 212-864-5400, www.symphonyspace.org
- **The Town Hall**, 123 West 43rd Street, 212-840-2824

PARKS

The city's parks and botanical gardens are hopping with children's programs and activities year-round. To name just several:

- **Central Park**, the park always has a variety of activities for children including the Swedish Marionette Theater, Belvedere Castle, and the Charles A. Dana Discovery Center, 110th Street near Fifth Avenue, 212-860-1370, www.centralparknyc.org, offers free activities and nature programs for children most weekends. Registration required. The Central Park Zoo, East 64th Street at Fifth Avenue, 212-861-6030, and Children's Zoo are perennial favorites and more accessible than the Bronx Zoo, although much smaller.

- **New York Botanical Garden**, 200th Street and Kazimiroff Boulevard in The Bronx, 718-817-8700, www.nybg.org; has a Children's Adventure Garden in addition to occasional programs for children, and the wonderful Christmastime miniature train extravaganza.
- **Prospect Park** on Flatbush Avenue in Brooklyn hosts a small zoo near Empire Avenue with sheep, chickens, rabbits, and a friendly snake, as well as activities for children, 718-399-7339, www.wcs.org. The Lefferts Homestead Children's Museum in the park along Flatbush Avenue near the zoo offers demonstrations and activities, 718-789-2822.

Not to be forgotten, of course, are the **Bronx Zoo**, the **New York Aquarium**, and the **Queens Wildlife Center and Children's Farm**, which sits adjacent to the Hall of Science.

LITERARY LIFE

Given that New York is home to many of the largest publishing houses in the world, it's no surprise that New Yorkers love to read. From breakfast over the Book Section of the Sunday *New York Times* to lunch hours spent browsing the pages of new best sellers at a Barnes & Noble superstore, New Yorkers enjoy their literature.

Just over 200 public libraries can be found in the five boroughs and several private membership libraries still survive, some dating back to the 18th century. In addition, several of the city's museums have libraries and nearly all have well-stocked book sections in their gift shops.

PUBLIC SPECIALTY LIBRARIES

Along with the neighborhood branches (see the list of resources following the neighborhood profiles at the beginning of the book), New York City is home to several public premier research libraries pertaining to specific areas of interest:

- **The New York Public Library: Center For the Humanities**, Fifth Avenue, between 40th and 42nd Streets, NYC 10018, 212-661-7220; exhibitions and programs, 212-869-8089; research, 212-930-0830; www.nypl.org/research/cyhss. Beyond the spectacular floor-to-ceiling marble entranceway you'll find an amazing collection of nearly 40 million items in the form of books, periodicals, newspapers, manuscripts, microfilm, maps, paintings, ephemera, and CDs. All are tucked away within this magnificent structure guarded by two larger than life stone lions flanking the grand Fifth Avenue entrance. Built over a ten-year period from 1901 through 1911, at a cost of nine million dollars, this world-famous library is home to the first five folios of Shakespeare's plays, ancient Torah scrolls, a Gutenberg Bible, and many other historic literary items. Free tours meet at the front entrance between 11 a.m. and 2 p.m. Monday-Saturdays. Note: this is not a lending library.

- **New York Public Library For The Performing Arts: Dorothy and Lewis B. Cullman Center**, 40 Lincoln Center Plaza, NYC 10023-7498, 212-870-1630, www.nypl.org/research/lpa; located in Lincoln Center, this newly renovated library features an extensive collection items related to the arts: posters, correspondence, sheet music, scripts, press clippings, periodicals, books, and recordings. Patrons include many budding performers, playwrights, choreographers, and musicians.

- **Science, Industry, and Business Library**, 188 Madison Avenue, NYC 10016, 212-592-7000, www.nypl.org/research/sibl; opened in 1996 at the price of $100 million dollars, this state-of-the-art facility is devoted to science, technology, economics, and business. Features over 60,000 volumes of reference materials, 50,000 circulating titles and over 100,000 periodicals. Membership includes discounts at the library shops and an informative newsletter/calendar.

- **Schomburg Center for Research in Black Culture**, 515 Malcolm X Boulevard, NYC 10037-1801, 212-491-2200, www.nypl.org/research/sc; featuring a vast array of resources collected by Arthur Schomburg, the library is part of the larger exhibit space, which displays African-American culture. The Jean Blackwell Hutson General Research and Reference Division includes rare books and writings available in text and electronic formats. Membership ranges from the $35 associate level to $1,000 conservator, and includes the newsletter, discounts to special programs, and other benefits.

MEMBERSHIP LIBRARIES

Before there were public libraries, there were private membership libraries, three of which survive in New York, a clubby step back in time and a haven for the book lover.

- **The New York Society Library**, 53 East 79th Street, 212-288-6900, www.nysoclib.org; the oldest library in the city, founded in 1754. Offers members the opportunity to search extensive holdings and even borrow some of the titles. Membership costs $175 per year or $125 for six months per household.

- **The Mercantile Library**, 17 East 47th Street, 212-755-6710, www.mercantilelibrary.org; formed in 1820 and houses only fiction. Is noted for its lively panel discussions. Individual membership is $60. Check their calendar for upcoming events.

- **The General Society Library**, 20 West 44th Street, 212-921-1767; founded in 1820, and seems little changed over the last century. More than 150,000 volumes can be found on its old wooden shelves, including a special collection of the works of Gilbert & Sullivan. Starting at $35 per year, general membership is a bargain.

BOOKSTORES

Bibliophiles are amply served in New York City, although Seattle, Minneapolis, and other cities take pride in housing more small, privately owned bookshops, which in Manhattan struggle to pay the high rents. The New York Yellow Pages lists nearly 20 chain outlets in Manhattan alone, with more opening up each year, including **Borders**, **B. Dalton**, and **Barnes & Noble**. Today's chains are more than just shelves of titles; they offer steaming lattés and scones in the far corner, as well as poetry readings and evening acoustical performances. But there are times when you don't know just what book you want, perhaps for your mother, or when you want Donald Westlake's latest and don't know what it is, or who was that Polish Nobel-Prize-winning poet you meant to read? At such times, a particular bookstore with a knowledgeable staff and the cozy feel of a traditional small bookshop is what you want. There are still some smaller bookstores left in Manhattan. You'll find descriptions of the best in *New York's 50 Best Bookstores for Book Lovers*, a paperback by Eve Claxton. We list a few of Manhattan's more notable ones:

- **Argosy Book Store**, 116 East 59th street, between Lexington and Park avenues, 212-753-4455, www.argosybooks.com; rare books, antique maps, photos, and documents.
- **Bank Street Bookstore**, 610 West 112th Street, at Broadway, Bank Street College, 212-678-1654, www.bankstreetbooks.com; offers books for and about children. www.bankstreetbookstores.com
- **Books of Wonder**, 16 West 18th Street, 212-989-3270, www.booksofwonder.net; offers a lovely selection of children's books, readings, and events.
- **Coliseum Books**, 11 West 42nd Street, NYC 10036, 212-803-5890, www.coliseumbooks.com; spacious long-time favorite has resurfaced in a midtown location, across from the New York City Public Library's main branch.
- **Corner Bookstore**, 1313 Madison Avenue, 212-831-3554; an established independent, offers everything from art and architecture to children's books. Will do special orders.
- **Creative Visions Bookstore**, 548 Hudson, NYC 10014, 800-434-7126, 212-648-7573, www.creativevisionsbookstores.com; features a vast collection of gay, lesbian, bi and transexual books and videos.
- **Gotham Book Mart**, 41 West 47th Street, 212-719-4448; 20th century literature, film and drama

- **Holland & Holland Limited**, 50 East 57th Street, 212-752-7755, www.hollandandholland.com; new and rare books on hunting, fishing, and travel.
- **Housing Works Used Book Cafe**, 126 Crosby Street, 212-334-3324, www.housingworks.org/usedbookcafe; sip espresso, browse books and pick up a used couch, proceeds go to house the homeless with HIV/AIDS.
- **Hue-Man Bookstore & Café**, 2319 Frederick Douglass Blvd., 212-665-7400, www.huemanbookstore.com; large selection of African-American literature and books.
- **Kitchen Arts & Letters**, 1435 Lexington Avenue at 93rd Street, 212-876-5550; new and hard-to-find books on food and wine.
- **Labyrinth Books**, 536 West 112th Street between Broadway and Amsterdam Avenue, 212-865-1588, www.labyrinthbooks.com; university press, and scholarly books and journals.
- **Murder Ink**, 2486 Broadway and West 92nd Street, 212-362-8905; 1465 Second Avenue, 212-517-3222; where you'll find that Donald Westlake title.
- **Oscar Wilde Bookshop**, 15 Christopher Street, 212-255-8097, www.oscarwildebooks.com; said to be the world's first gay and lesbian bookshop.
- **Posman Books**, 9 Grand Central Terminal, 212-983-1111, www.posman books.com; offers an eclectic selection of books and frequent author readings.
- **Rizzoli Bookstore**, 31 West 57th Street, 212-759-2424; great selection of exquisite art books. www.rizzoliusa.com
- **Ruby's Books Sale**, 119 Chambers Street, 212-732-8676; lots of dusty used titles at low prices.
- **Shakespeare & Co.**, 716 Broadway at Washington Place, 212-529-1330; 939 Lexington Avenue at 68th Street, 212-570-0201; 137 East 23rd Street at Lexington Avenue, 212-505-2021; and 1 Whitehall Street, south of Bowling Green, 212-742-7025, also two Brooklyn locations: The Brooklyn Academy of Music at 30 Lafayette Street 718-636-4136 and at 14 Hillel Place, 718-434-5326; www.shakeandco.com
- **Strand Bookstore Inc.**, 828 Broadway at 12th Street, main store, 212-473-1452, and 95 Fulton Street, 212-732-6070, www.strand books.com; the world's largest used bookstore, they say ("8 miles of books"), and mind-boggling.
- **Untitled on Prince Street**, 159 Prince Street, 212-982-2088, www.fineartinprint.com; art and design books, art prints
- **Urban Center Books**, 457 Madison Avenue, 212-935-3595, www.urbancenterbooks.com; urban history and architecture

COLLEGES AND UNIVERSITIES

You can visit some of these institutions on their web sites via links at www.ny.com/academia.

MANHATTAN AND THE BRONX

- **Bank Street College of Education**, 610 West 112th Street, NYC 10025, 212-875-4400, www.bnkst.edu
- **Barnard College**, 3009 Broadway, NYC 10027-6598, 212-854-5262, www.barnard.columbia.edu
- **Baruch College of Continuing and Professional Studies**, 17 Lexington Avenue, 10010, 212-802-5600, www.baruch.cuny.edu
- **City College**, CUNY, 138th Street and Convent Avenue, NYC 10031, 212-650-7000, www.ccny.cuny.edu
- **City University of NY Graduate School and University Center**, 365 Fifth Avenue, NYC 10016, 212-817-7000, www.gc.cuny.edu
- **Columbia University**, Broadway at 116th Street, NYC 10027, 212-854-1754, www.columbia.edu
- **Cooper Union**, 30 Cooper Square, NYC 10003, 212-353-4100, www.cooper.edu
- **Fordham University**, 113 West 60th Street, NYC 10023, 800-FORD-HAM or 212-636-6000, www.fordham.edu
- **Hebrew-Union College-Jewish Institute of Religion**, One West 4th Street, NYC 10012, 212-674-5300, www.huc.edu
- **Hunter College**, 695 Park Avenue at 68th Street, NYC 10021, 212-772-4000, www.hunter.cuny.edu
- **Jewish Theological Seminary**, 3080 Broadway, NYC 10027, 212-678-8000, www.jtsa.edu
- **Manhattan College**, Riverdale 10471, 718-862-8000, www.manhattan.edu
- **Marymount Manhattan College**, 221 East 71st Street, NYC 10021, 212-517-0400
- **New School University**, 66 West 12th Street, NYC 10011, 212-229-5600, www.newschool.edu
- **New York University**, 25 West 4th Street, NYC 10012, 800-771-4NYU, www.nyu.edu
- **Pace University**, 1 Pace Plaza, NYC 10038-1598 and 535 Fifth Avenue, NYC 10016, 800-874-PACE, www.pace.edu
- **Parsons School of Design**, 66 Fifth Avenue, NYC 10011, 212-229-8900, www.parsons.edu; part of NYU.
- **Pratt Manhattan**, 144 West 14th Street, NYC 100112, 212-647-7775, www.pratt.edu

- **Union Theological Seminary**, 3041 Broadway at 121st Street, NYC 10027, 212-662-7100, www.uts.columbia.edu
- **Yeshiva University**, 500 West 185th Street, NYC 10033, 212-960-5400, www.yu.edu

BROOKLYN

- **Brooklyn College**, 2900 Bedford Avenue, Brooklyn 11210, 718-951-5000, www.brooklyn.cuny.edu
- **Pratt Institute**, 200 Willoughby Avenue, Brooklyn 11205, 718-636-3600, www.pratt.edu
- **St. Joseph's College**, 245 Clinton Avenue, Brooklyn 11205, 718-636-6800, www.sjcny.edu

QUEENS

- **Queens College**, 65-30 Kissena Blvd., Flushing 11367, 718-997-5000, www.qc.edu
- **Queensborough Community College**, 222-05 56th Street, Bayside 11364, 718-631-6262, www.qcc.cuny.edu
- **St. John's University**, 8000 Utopia Parkway, Jamaica 11439, 888-9-STJOHNS, www.stjohns.edu

STATEN ISLAND

- **College of Staten Island**, CUNY, 2800 Victory Boulevard, Staten Island 10301, 718-982-2000, www.csi.cuny.edu
- **St. John's University**, 300 Howard Avenue, Staten Island 10301, 718-390-4500, www.stjohns.edu
- **Wagner College**, 631 Howard Avenue, Staten Island 10201, 718-390-3100, www.wagner.edu

N NEW YORK YOU CAN ROOT, ROOT, ROOT FOR THE HOME TEAM, canter along Central Park's cinder track, join a pickup basketball game, swim laps after work, or sit spellbound at the US Open Tennis Championships. The city hosts events for every season and activities for every appetite. To help you sort out the teams you wish to follow and the activities you wish to pursue, details about the area's major teams are listed below, followed by a section devoted to **Participant Sports**. For specifics about ticket sales see also **Tickets** in the **Cultural Life** chapter.

PROFESSIONAL SPORTS

For weekly specifics on leading amateur and professional sporting events check "This Week in Sports" in the "Sports" section of the Sunday *New York Times* and *Time Out New York's* "Sports" section.

BASEBALL

The season begins at the end of March and lasts until early October (or longer as is often the case for the Yankees). Tickets range from $8 for bleacher seats to $80 for boxes that are generally long sold out. There are also special $5 ticket nights: see the team schedule available at the box office or at www.yankees.com. Met tickets range from $8 to $53 depending on the location of the seats and which team they are playing. You can purchase tickets for Met or Yankee games through Ticketmaster, 212-307-7171 or www.ticketmaster.com; charge tickets to a credit card and have them sent or pick them up at one of 20 locations in Manhattan. Note: as with theater tickets, there is a service charge tacked on to the price of each ticket purchased through Ticketmaster, which can be costly. To save some money, you can purchase tickets at the stadium box office. Mets tickets are also available at the Mets Clubhouse shops: 143 East 54th Street and 11 West 42nd Street, both in Manhattan. For Yankee tickets, go to the Yankee Clubhouse stores at 110 East 59th Street, 393 Fifth Avenue, 8 Fulton Street, and 245 West 42nd Street in Manhattan. Schedules for upcoming Mets or Yankees games are always easy to find in the newspapers or at www.mlb.com, the official site of Major League Baseball.

- **New York Mets** (National League), Shea Stadium, 126th Street and Roosevelt Avenue, Flushing, NY 11368; 718-507-METS for information; box office: 718-507-8499, www.mets.com. Along with season tickets, the Mets have innumerable subscription plans, and buying single game tickets in advance is generally not difficult as they typically only sell out a few times a year. There are plenty of fun promotional days for kids with giveaway items. You can drive to Shea Stadium on the Grand Central Parkway and park for a fee in the stadium lot or take the #7 train, which takes about 50 minutes from midtown and brings you right to the stadium.
- **New York Yankees** (American League), Yankee Stadium, 161st Street and River Avenue, Bronx, NY 10451, 718-293-6000, www.yankees.com; the Yankees have several ticket subscription plans ranging from season tickets to several games. Games against top teams will sell out, but generally, tickets for weeknight games, and certainly weekday games are usually available on game day. Yankee Stadium (or the house that Ruth built) is a classic ballpark from the 1920s and a great place to watch a ballgame. Monument Park just over the centerfield fence pays tribute to classic Yankee teams and is a great place to explore prior to the game. There are also tours offered of the stadium, starting at $14 for adults and $6 for children and seniors. You can drive to Yankee Stadium, which is just off the Major Deagan Expressway, and park in one of several lots (for a fee) or take the #4 train from Manhattan—it's about 25 minutes from midtown and an easy trip as the subway stops right behind the bleachers.

BASKETBALL

The NBA basketball season begins when baseball leaves off, around late October, and continues through mid-April or into May or even June if the teams are in the playoffs. Knicks' home games are played in Madison Square Garden; the Nets play at the Meadowlands. Single seats for the Nets and the Knicks range between $25 and $1,500. Call Ticketmaster, 212-307-7171 to order tickets, or visit a Ticketmaster outlet to pick up your tickets.

- **New York Knickerbockers** (NBA), Madison Square Garden, 33rd Street between Seventh and Eighth avenues, NYC 10001, 212-465-5867 or 877-NYK-DUNK, www.nba.com/knicks; season plans cost several thousand dollars but there are some limited plans available. Individual tickets go on sale in early September and can be purchased at Ticketmaster outlets, 212-307-7171, as well as at the Garden Box Office. Seats are not easy to get so plan to purchase well in advance. To get to Madison Square Garden it's best to take the subway—1, 2, 3, 9, A, C, E trains—or the Long Island Railroad, which stops at Penn Station under the Garden. If you drive, your best bet is parking after 7 p.m. on side streets (24th through 29th streets), otherwise you'll end up in costly lots waiting for up to an hour to get your car after the game.
- **New Jersey Nets** (NBA) play in the Continental Airlines Arena in the Meadowlands Sports Complex in East Rutherford, NJ 07073, six miles west of the Lincoln Tunnel; call 800-7NJ-NETS or go to www.njnets.com for ticket information. Ticket plans range from season tickets for the 41-game home season, plus exhibition games, to short plans of six to ten games. You can always purchase single game tickets in advance and usually on game night. There is plenty of parking in the arena lot.
- **New York Liberty** (WNBA), Madison Square Garden, 33rd Street between Seventh and Eighth avenues, NYC 10001, 212-465-6250, www.nyliberty.com, is professional women's basketball at its best. Tickets can be purchased at the Madison Square Garden Box Office or at Ticketmaster outlets, 212-307-7171. Tickets are easy to get. The season runs from late May through August.

FOOTBALL

The popularity of Jets and Giants games during the pro football season, September-December, is clearly demonstrated by ticket scarcity.
- **Giants** (NFL), Giants Stadium, Meadowlands Sports Complex, East Rutherford, NJ 07073, 201-935-8111, www.giants.com; regular season tickets are sold out years in advance. Your best bet: become chums with a season ticket holder or buy through a ticket broker.
- **New York Jets** (NFL) also play at the Giants Stadium in the Meadowlands Sports Complex. Call 516-560-8200 for ticket information, www.newyorkjets.com. Renewals for season tickets to the eight home-game season are filled by May 15. New subscriptions are then issued from the fairly long waiting list on a first-come, first-served basis in early June. Good luck.

HOCKEY

The New York Rangers, Islanders, and New Jersey Devils play NHL hockey starting at the end of September and going into the spring.

- **New York Rangers** (NHL), Madison Square Garden, 33rd Street between Seventh and Eighth avenues, NYC 10001, 212-465-6486. Call Ticketmaster to order tickets by phone, 212-307-7171. Whether the Rangers are playing well or not, tickets are very hard to come by as most season ticket holders keep their seats for years. Be on line at the box office when tickets go on sale for the season or sign up in advance for a mini-plan if any are still available. Get ticket information at the team web site www.newyorkrangers.com. For information on Madison Square Garden see above.
- **New York Islanders** (NHL) Nassau Coliseum in Uniondale, Long Island, NY 11553, 516-501-6700, ticket hotline, 800-882-ISLES, www.newyorkislanders.com; tickets also available through Ticketmaster. Islander tickets are easier to get than Ranger tickets. In fact if you want to see a Rangers game, this is one way to do it—just don't let on that you're a Rangers fan while at the Coliseum—or for that matter if you're an Islander fan, be quiet at the Garden.
- **New Jersey Devils** (NHL) Continental Airlines Arena, Meadowlands Sports Complex, East Rutherford, NJ, six miles west of the Lincoln Tunnel, 800-NJ-DEVIL, www.newjerseydevils.com; they've won three Stanley Cups in recent years, making them the area's most successful hockey team and making tickets harder to get.

RACING: HARNESS AND THOROUGHBRED

All the local tracks are easily reached by public transportation. For those who enjoy betting but do not feel the need to be at the racetrack, the city features numerous off-track betting locations. More information can be found at the New York Racing Association's web site, www.nyra.com. Call the numbers listed below for directions.

- **Aqueduct**, Jamaica, Queens, 718-641-4700, www.nyra.com; the track is open from October until May for thoroughbred races starting at 12:30 p.m. daily except Mondays and Tuesdays.
- **Belmont Park**, Elmont, Long Island, 516-488-6000, www.nyra.com; thoroughbred races May-July and September-October.
- **Meadowlands Racetrack**, Meadowlands Sports Complex, East Rutherford, NJ, 201-935-8500, www.thebigm.com; open at 6 p.m. nightly Tuesday-Saturday. December-August harness racing; thoroughbreds run October-November.

- **Monmouth Park**, Oceanport, NJ, 732-222-5100, www.monmouth park.com, thoroughbred races daily Wednesday-Sunday at 12:55 p.m., late May-September.
- **Yonkers Raceway**, Yonkers, NY, 914-968-4200, www.yonkersrace way.com; the post time is 7:40 p.m. Daily schedule varies as the track is sometimes used for festivals and other events, so call in advance.

TENNIS

The biggest tournament held in the New York area is the US Open. The West Side Tennis Club at Forest Hills (once the site of the US Open) hosts the Tournament of Champions for men in May.

- **United States Open Tennis Championships**, United States Tennis Center, Flushing Meadow Park, Queens, NY 11365; for ticket information call 866-OPEN-TIX. The nation's premier tennis tournament, the US Open, consists of 13 days of afternoon and evening matches held in late August and early September. The finals take place the weekend after Labor Day. Individual tickets for the finals and semifinals are sold as soon as the first mailing goes out in late March or early April. Tickets for matches earlier in the tournament aren't as hard to come by and are sold at Ticketmaster outlets as well as the Tennis Center. If you drive, there is parking in lots for a fee. If the Mets are also playing that day, the area gets more congested, as Shea Stadium is practically across the street. You can also take the #7 train from Manhattan.

PARTICIPANT SPORTS

Swimming pools, tennis, squash and racquetball courts, bowling alleys, and billiard parlors, as well as roller and ice skating rinks dot the island for your sporting pleasure, and practically any outdoor recreation you want can be found in Central Park. It's not just a super place to ride bikes or listen to classical performances on summer evenings; you can also schedule football and softball games, play tennis, or row a boat around the Lake. Flanked by Central Park West and Fifth Avenue to the east, the park covers some 750 acres between 59th and 110th streets and is Manhattan's prime outdoor recreation area. So, before listing information about sports citywide, as well as multipurpose facilities such as health clubs and YMCAs, we've detailed opportunities to be found in the park, sport by sport. To learn more about the park itself, see the chapter on **Greenspace and Beaches**. For information about city parks you can call the **NYC Department of Parks & Recreation** at 212-360-3456 or visit their web site at www.nycparks.org. For information on **permits** call 212-408-0209.

CENTRAL PARK

The park's **Visitor Information Center** is located at the Dairy, 65th Street between the zoo and the carousel. The Arsenal, 830 Fifth Avenue at East 64th Street in front of the zoo, is the park's administrative hub. For event and park information, call the **Central Parks Conservancy**, which runs the park under contract from the city, 212-360-3444, or go to www.centralparknyc.org.

- **Ball**: **Baseball**, **Softball**, **Football**, **Rugby**, and **Soccer** fields are located in the North Meadow, at the Great Lawn and Heckscher Playground. Call 212-408-0209 for permits.
- **Bicycling** is popular when the park drives (but not the sunken crosstown transverses) are closed to motorized traffic on weekends from 7 p.m. Friday until 6 a.m. Monday (all day on holidays), and from 10 a.m. to 3 p.m. and 7 p.m. to 10 p.m. weekdays, from April through October. For rentals, see **Bicycling** below for names of bicycle shops near the park.
- **Boating**; the Loeb Boathouse, near East 74th Street, 212-517-2233, rents rowboats for outings on the Lake, from 10 a.m. until between 4 and 6 p.m. You can also glide beneath Bow Bridge in a black Venetian gondola, complete with a gondolier. Armchair sailors can enjoy the comfort and cuisine of lunch and brunch in the glass-enclosed Boathouse Café. Evening dining is offered from the end of March through the first of November.
- **Horseback Riding**; the Claremont Riding Academy, 175 West 89th Street, 212-724-5100, rents mounts to experienced riders for rides along the six miles of bridle paths that circle the park. You must reserve in advance.
- **Ice Skating**; the park boasts two beautiful rinks: Wollman Memorial on the East Side near 62nd Street, 212-439-6900, and Lasker Memorial at Lenox Avenue at 109th Street, 212-534-7639. Wollman is open September-April. Of the two, Lasker is less crowded. At both rinks, mornings and weekdays offer the best ice time: i.e., fewer skaters. Call for admission information.
- **Paddleball and Handball**; you can use the ten courts located near the North Meadow at West 97th Street and Transverse Road on a first-come, first-served basis.
- **Roller/In-line Skating**; in-line skaters and old-fashioned roller skaters can be found strutting their stuff (or falling down) throughout the park, but the road west of the Sheep Meadow near 69th Street is designated specifically for blading and skating. Skates can be rented for use at Wollman Memorial, 212-439-6900, April-November. Call for hours and admission.

- **Running**; joggers traditionally work out on the 1.58-mile cinder track girdling the Reservoir between East 85th and 96th streets, but running isn't limited to that patch. The **New York Road Runners Club**, 9 East 89th Street, 212-860-4455, www.nyrrc.org, sponsors races and clinics during the season. (See **A New York City Year** at the end of the book for specifics on New York Road Runners' New Year's Eve midnight run.) The 97th Street Field House contains lockers and showers for men and women.
- **Sledding**; the park has hills for all levels of experience. For children or timid sledders, a perfect spot is Pilgrim Hill by the 72nd Street and Fifth Avenue entrance closest to the pilgrim statue. For more of a challenge, try Cedar Hill close to the Belvedere Castle at the 77th Street entrance off Central Park West.
- **Tennis**; twenty-six clay and four all-weather courts, open from 7 a.m. to dusk, are located on the west side of the park near 95th Street. In season, play necessitates a seasonal tennis permit, which in turn requires a completed application, photo ID (service provided at the time of application), and $100 (no personal checks). Permits can be obtained by mail or in person at the Arsenal Building, Fifth Avenue and 64th Street, NYC 10021, between 9 a.m. and 4 p.m., weekdays. Permit holders can reserve a court by going to the Tennis House adjacent to the 95th Street Courts and paying a small fee. Call 212-360-8133 for permit information. You can also purchase single play tennis tickets at $7 for one hour of court time, which are issued at the courts on 93rd Street on a first-come, first-served basis. Tennis center daily information: 212-280-0206.

BEYOND CENTRAL PARK

BASEBALL

Most of Manhattan's more than two-dozen diamonds (seven of which are located in Central Park) are under the direction of the DPR. Call 212-408-0209 for information or visit www.nycparks.org. Fields can be difficult to get onto in the spring due to corporate softball leagues.

BASKETBALL

The **Department of Parks and Recreation (DPR)**, www.nycparks.org, maintains more than 1,000 courts throughout the city in gyms (see **Swimming** below) as well as in city parks, large and small. Some of the health clubs and YMCAs have basketball courts, and the **Chelsea Piers Sports and Entertainment** complex, 212-336-6000, www.chelsea

piers.com, includes two new courts with electronic scoreboards used in league basketball which is open to players of all skill levels for a fee.

NEW YORK CITY DEPARTMENT OF PARKS AND RECREATION:
- **Bronx**, 718-430-1858
- **Brooklyn**, 718-965-8941
- **Manhattan**, 212-408-0205
- **Queens**, 718-520-5936
- **Staten Island**, 718-816-6172

BICYCLING

- **Century Road Club Association**, P.O. Box 20412, Greeley Square Station, NYC 10001, 212-222-8062, www.crca.net, is a racing club, which provides coaching clinics for beginners and sponsors friendly competitions for kids of all ages.
- **Five Borough Bicycle Club**, 891 Amsterdam Avenue, 212-932-2300, www.bikenewyork.org, organizes bicycling events, rides, and courses.
- **Fast and Fabulous Cycling Club**, 212-567-7160, www.fastnfab. org, is a gay and lesbian bicycle club affiliated with Front Runners New York (see **Running** below). They organize training, morning rides in city parks, and road trips.
- **Hostelling International New York**, 891 Amsterdam Avenue, 212-932-2300, www.hinewyork.org; the city's largest cycling organization, sponsors Bike New York, the Great Five Borough Bicycle Race, which bumps and winds its way through all five boroughs each spring. Hostelling International New York also promotes a number of day rides as well as weekend trips for enthusiasts.
- **New York Cycle Club**, P.O. Box 20541, Columbus Circle Station, NYC 10023, 212-828-5711, www.nycc.org; sponsors rides in and around the city, offers training, and its members receive discounts from a handful of bike shops in the city.

If you don't own a bike, you may well want to rent one on a beautiful spring day. At least half of Manhattan's bike dealers rent bikes. Rates average $8 to $10 an hour and about $30 a day. You'll have to leave money, or a driver's license or major credit card behind as a deposit. A handful of the many bike rental outfits include:
- **Bicycles Plus**, 1400 Third Avenue, 212-794-2929, 1690 Second Avenue at 87th Street, 212-722-2201
- **Central Park Bicycle Tours and Rentals**, 310 West 55th Street, 212-541-8759, offer bike rentals, minimum two hours, and bike tours of Central Park.

- **Fourteenth Street Bicycle Discount House**, 332 East 14th Street at First Avenue, 212-228-4344
- **Gotham Bikes**, 112 West Broadway, 212-732-2453
- **Metro Bicycles**: 1311 Lexington Avenue at 88th Street, 212-427-4450; 360 West 47th Street, 212-581-4500; 231 West 96th Street, 212-663-7531; 332 East 14th Street, 212-228-4344; 417 Canal Street, 212-334-8000; and 546 Avenue of the Americas at 15th Street, 212-255-5100
- **Pedal Pusher Bike Shop**, 1306 Second Avenue at 69th Street, 212-288-5592
- **Toga Bikes**, 110 West End Avenue, 212-799-9625
- **Tread Bike Shop**, 225 Dykman Street, 212-544-7055

BILLIARDS

There are more than two-dozen pool halls in New York City, and no doubt, Minnesota Fats would still be comfortable at many of them. Others, with clubby ambiances that are different from the hustler hangouts of yore, have attracted women to the traditionally male pastime of pocket pool, billiards, and snooker, and have brightened the sport's image in the process.

- **Amsterdam Billiards & Bar**, 344 Amsterdam Avenue at 76th Street, 212-496-8180, and 210 East 86th Street, 212-570-4545, open noon to 3 a.m., 4 a.m. on weekends. Some 350 enthusiasts participate in league billiards here, where you can also throw a pool party (without water), or improve your skills in private or group instruction.
- **Brownstone Billiards**, 308 Flatbush Avenue at Seventh Avenue, Brooklyn, 718-857-5555; open noon to 1 a.m., to 4 a.m. Friday and Saturday. With 32 tables, six ping-pong tables, air hockey, and video games, Brownstone has positioned itself as a family entertainment center.
- **Corner Billiards**, 11th Street and 4th Avenue, 212-995-1314, www.cornerbilliards.com; some 28 tables at the ready and yearly locker rental available. Visit the café, book a party, or join one of several leagues available for players of all levels.
- **The Cue Lounge**, 220 West 19th Street between Seventh and Eighth avenues, 212-206-7665; on two floors of a converted warehouse with over 30 tables beneath brass chandeliers, two private rooms, and a snack bar with wait staff. You can rent the whole place for a party, or rack 'em up with the lunch crowd.
- **Eastside Amusements**, 163 East 86th Street between Lexington and Third avenues, 212-831-7665; features billiards, an arcade, and a party space for as many as 250 of your closest friends.
- **Slate Billiards**, 54 West 21st Street west of Fifth Avenue, 212-989-0096; a two-floor all-in-one restaurant/lounge/billiard parlor, complete

with 32 tables. Yet, you might have to wait for a table, Friday nights especially. Best times are mornings and Sunday daytime. There is a room with two tables for private parties.

BIRD WATCHING

"Oh! A winter wren," warbles naturalist Sarah Elliott as she leads a group of bird-watching enthusiasts through the Ramble in Central Park. Unlikely as it may seem, **Central Park** is a mecca for birders. Encircled in concrete, from the sky the park appears as an oasis in which to land, rest, and refuel. The city's outer parks also offer prime sites for dedicated birders. Below are a few organized groups and walks. For a greater selection, turn to *New York's 50 Best Places to Go Birding in and Around the Big Apple* by John Thaxton and Alan Messer.

- **The American Museum of Natural History**, 212-769-5700 (discovery tours), www.amnh.org; the **Brooklyn Botanical Garden**, 718-623-7200, www.bbg.org; and the **New York Botanical Garden** (Bronx Park), 718-817-8700, www.nybg.org, make the guidebooks as good bird-watching areas. **Rare Bird Alert**, 212-979-3070, provides recorded information on interesting sightings in the New York City area.
- **Brooklyn Bird Club**, www.brooklynbirdclub.org, founded in 1909, hosts lectures, monthly meetings, and weekly field trips, open to both non-members and members (membership $20) alike. Their attractive web site includes detailed maps and descriptions of some 15 excellent bird locations in Brooklyn and Queens, directions, some history, and lists of the species one is likely to find at each site.
- **Central Park Conservancy**, 212-310-6600, www.centralpark nyc.org, sponsors a Family Bird Watching Club, which meets every Saturday from 11 a.m. to 1 p.m., April-June and September-December at the Charles A. Dana Discovery Center, 110th Street near Fifth Avenue. Here Urban Park Rangers teach participants to identify birds by their song.
- **New York City Audubon Society**, 212-691-7483, www.nycas.org
- **Sarah Elliott** has become a noted fixture, a movable one, in Central Park, with her Wednesday and Sunday morning walks, spring and fall. She teaches bird-watching basics and leads her pack on their quest for the indigo bunting, the grackle, and the pileated woodpecker. The walks leave at 9 a.m. in spring and fall, Wednesdays from Fifth Avenue and 76th Street, and Sundays from the Loeb Boat House. The fee is $10; call 212-689-2763 for more information. For the bi-monthly "Elliott Newsletter: Nature Notes from Central Park," send a check for $20 to her at 333 East 34th Street, #4D, NYC 10016.

- **The Urban Park Rangers** sponsor a variety of bird walks, such as the fall hawk watch, in all five boroughs. For times and meeting places call 212-628-2345 for more information.

BOWLING

Check the Yellow Pages for the alley nearest you. Here are a couple:
- **AMF Chelsea Piers Bowling**, Pier 60, West Side Highway at 23rd Street, 212-835-2695, www.chelseapiers.com, 40 lanes, open seven-days. There's a bar and restaurant on site, a pro shop, and arcade with video games to keep the kids occupied. Thursday, Friday, and Saturday nights they offer "extreme bowling" (glow-in-the-dark bowling). League bowling and lessons are also available. Call for lane availability and/or to reserve. Be forewarned bowling here ain't cheap at $7.50 per game per person plus $4.50 for shoe rental, or $96 for a family of four (or two couples) to bowl just two games.
- **Gil Hodges Lanes**, 6161 Strickland Avenue, Brooklyn, 718-763-6800, is named after the famed Brooklyn Dodgers first baseman. This 68-lane alley is the biggest in the five boroughs.

BOXING

- **Church Street Boxing Gym**, 25 Park Place off Church Street, down-town, 212-571-1333, www.nyboxinggym.com; bills itself as "New York's last authentic boxing gym" (translate: Manhattan's). It's not a health club or fitness center; it's about boxing. The 8,000 square foot gym has two full-size rings and co-ed membership classes in boxing, kick-boxing, and Thai boxing. Membership is by the month, quarter, or year. It's probably also the best place in the city to watch boxing; enthusiastic crowds pack the occasional Friday night fights.
- **Gleason's Gym**, 75 Front Street at the foot of the Brooklyn Bridge in Brooklyn, 718-797-2872, www.gleasonsgym.com; going strong since 1937, it boasts seven world champions among its past or present membership, Riddick Bowe included. Women also work out here in this old-style boxing gym. Get lean and mean working up a sweat on the equipment or work with one of 62 trainers for an hourly fee. Closed Sunday.

CHESS

Though it's not a "sport," enthusiasts pursue chess with the intensity of an athletic competition. New York City, with its huge immigrant community, has a large and active chess community. If you're looking for information about where to play or compete, try the following leads (or head to Washington Square Park where "pick-up" games of speed chess are ongoing at the chess tables):

- **The Chess Forum**, 219 Thompson Street, NYC 10012, 212-475-2369, www.chessforum.com
- **The Chess Shop**, 230 Thompson Street, NYC 10012, 212-475-9580, www.chess-shop.com
- **Manhattan Chess Club**, New Yorker Hotel, Suite 1521, 481 Eighth Avenue, NYC 10001, www.manhattanchessclub.com
- **US Chess Federation**, 3054 NYS Route 9W, New Windsor, NY 12553, 914-562-8350; their web site, www.uschess.org, contains a great list of places to play.

FENCING

- **Blade Fencing**, 245 West 29th Street, 212-244-3090, www.blade-fencing.com, arms and dresses the duelist for competition with a full range of foils, épées and sabers, masks, gloves, knickers, fencing jackets, and shoes.
- **The Fencers Club**, 119 West 25th Street, 212-678-1108, www.fencersclub.com; in business since 1883, they offer classes, competitions, after school programs, and more for fencers of all skill levels.
- **Metropolis Fencing School**, 45 West 21st Street, second floor, 212-463-8044; there are private and group classes for children through adults, beginner through Olympian. Children's fencing birthday classes can be booked, and there is a seven-day foil fencing camp for children in August.

FOOTBALL

Most playing fields fall under the **Department of Parks and Recreation**, call 212-408-0209 for information and permits. Eighteen football fields, some of which are suitable also for soccer, are located in Manhattan.

GAMES

- **The Complete Strategist**, 11 East 33rd Street, 212-685-3880; selling war games, sci-fi, fantasy, and role-playing games, plus the classics, and offering games workshops.
- **Neutral Ground Gaming Room**, 122 West 26th Street, fourth floor, 212-633-1288, www.neutralground.net, offering role-playing games and games workshops daily.

GOLF

Manhattan boasts no 18-hole golf courses (a 17-acre course on Randall's Island has been in planning stages for years), but you'll find several city-owned public courses in the outer boroughs. A permit, which can be purchased at any of the New York City Courses or from the parks department, will get you onto the city courses where 18 holes will cost less than $20. There are also nine-hole rates and twilight rates plus discounts for juniors and seniors. Non-residents or city residents without a permit can also play for a few dollars more. Courses are popular during the spring and summer, so get there early and prepare to wait ... or go at 4 p.m. and take advantage of the longer daylight hours. Reservations can be made for several city courses by calling 718-225-4653. There are also plenty of even nicer public clubs on Long Island and in Westchester. Higher fees are the norm at suburban courses and you'll need to reserve tee times well in advance. Perhaps the nicest courses closest to NYC are those at Bethpage State Park at 99 Quaker Meeting House Road in Farmingdale, Long Island, 516-249-0700. These three award-winning courses have attracted top tournaments, top players, and garnered high ratings in the golf world.

New York City **public courses** include:

- **Mosholu Golf Course**, 3700 Jerome Avenue, The Bronx, 718-655-9164; also features a driving range.
- **Pelham/Split Rock Golf Course**, 870 Shore Road, north of Bartow Circle, The Bronx, near City Island, 718-885-1258
- **Van Cortlandt Park Golf Course**, Van Cortlandt Park at Bailey Avenue, The Bronx, 718-543-4595; a marvelous 100+ year old course that has seen everyone from Babe Ruth to the Three Stooges to presidents and diplomats tee off.
- **Dyker Beach Golf Course**, Seventh Avenue and 86th Street, Brooklyn, 718-836-9722
- **Marine Park Golf Course**, 2880 Flatbush Avenue, near the Belt Parkway, Brooklyn, 718-338-7149
- **Clearview Golf Course**, 202-12 Willets Point Boulevard, Queens, 718-229-2570
- **Douglaston Golf Course**, 6320 Marathon Parkway, Queens, 718-428-1617; if you like hills.
- **Forest Park Golf Course**, 101 Forest Park Drive off Woodhaven Boulevard, Queens, 718-296-0999; bring plenty of extra balls.
- **Kissena Park Golf Course**, 164-15 Booth Memorial Avenue, Queens, 718-939-4594
- **LaTourette Golf Course**, 1001 Richmond Hill road, Staten Island, 718-351-1889; also has a driving range.

- **Silver Lake Golf Course**, 915 Victory Boulevard, near Forest Avenue, Staten Island, 718-447-5686
- **South Shore Golf Course**, 200 Huguenot Avenue, Staten Island, 718-984-0101

Miniature golf courses can also be found in the outer boroughs, the best being **Turtle Grove Miniature Golf Course**, on the road to City Island in The Bronx: 1 City Island Road (off I-95), 718-885-2646. They also have a driving range.

Among the city's other **driving ranges** are:

- **The Golf Club at Chelsea Piers**, Hudson River at 17th Street, 212-336-6400, www.chelseapiers.com; this golf club, with its white shingled clubhouse entrance, pro shop, putting green, and golf academy has, as its *pièce de résistance*, 52 heated, weather-protected driving stalls with Japanese-designed, computerized automatic ball returns and tee-ups in four tiers fronting a 200-yard, net-enclosed artificial turf fairway with four target greens, overlooking the Hudson River ... No you can't aim at passing boats. Pay according to the number of balls used.
- **Randall's Island Driving Range**, Randall's Island, north of Downing Stadium, 212-427-5689

HANDBALL

A city sport, in which two or four players hit a rubber ball with their hands against a cement wall, volleying furiously for points, handball is played on outdoor courts all over the city. And at many sites it is also a spectator sport. Among the many handball courts in the city, two stand out as shrines:

- **Surf Avenue at West Fifth Street**, Coney Island, on whose six courts the Nationals are played. Attracts a colorful crowd of betting spectators.
- **"The Cage"** at West Fourth Street and Sixth Avenue, the Village; the action on the adjacent basketball court is equally spectacular.

To learn more about one of the world's oldest games go to www. ushandball.org.

HORSEBACK RIDING

Care to canter Central Park bridle trails or brush up on your dressage in the ring? Manhattan has one stable. In the outer boroughs and near New Jersey the trail rides meander woods and seaside, and you can practice your jumping outdoors.

- **Claremont Riding Academy**, 175 West 89th Street, corner Amsterdam Avenue; call 212-724-5100 for reservations, essential weekends. They stable about 100 horses here, some 70 for rental, English saddle only. You can ride either in Central Park or in the ring. Private and group lessons available.
- **Jamaica Bay Riding Academy**, Belt Parkway East between exits 11 (King's Plaza) and 13 (Rockaway Parkway), Marine Park, Brooklyn, 718-531-8949, www.horsebackride.com. Located on some 300 acres of prime real estate, they offer a riding shop, lessons, wooded trails, and can accommodate birthday parties. You need no appointment for a guided trail ride along Jamaica Bay beach, open year round. Bring your own helmet.
- **Kensington Stables**, 51 Caton Place at Coney Island Avenue, Brooklyn, 718-972-4588, www.kensingtonstables.com; operates guided trail rides, English or Western, in lovely Prospect Park. Private and group lessons offered. Call ahead. Take the F train to Ft. Hamilton Parkway.
- **Lynne's Riding School**, 88-03 70th Road, Forest Hills, 718-261-7679; you can take public transportation—the F train and then the Q23 bus—to Queens where Lynne's offers riders a choice between Eastern or Western tack. Private lessons are available, as are pony rides and boarding.
- **Overpeck Stables**, 40 Fort Lee Road, Leonia, NJ 07605, 201-242-0022; by #4 Red and Tan Lines or the #166 New Jersey Transit bus from the Port Authority Terminal, have the driver let you off at Overpeck Park. By car, take Route 80 off the George Washington Bridge, off at the first exit ("70 Leonia"). The stables are a quarter mile south on the right. Offers private lessons and group lessons. There are riding clinics, shows, and competitions in the indoor and outdoor rings. Boarding is also available. Bergen County residents are offered discounts.
- **Pelham Bay Riding**, 9 Shore Road, City Island/Orchard Beach, 718-885-0551, www.nychorse.com; open daily 8 a.m. until dusk, but call ahead for a guided trail ride, Western only, through woods by the Split Rock Golf Course and Pelham Bay. Lessons, English or Western, are offered individually or as a group. Reachable by car from the New England Thruway; or take the #6 train to the last stop and walk east or take the City Island Bus, number 29, which stops across the street from the stable.
- **Riverdale Riding Centre**, West 254th Street and Broadway, inside Van Cortlandt Park, 718-548-4848, www.riverdaleriding.com; four riding rings and an indoor Olympic-sized arena. Rabbits, raccoons, and other wildlife are a bonus on the guided trail rides in this large city park. Pony rides are available for children and pony parties can be arranged.

All rides by appointment. To get there by public transportation take the #1 train to 242nd Street (last stop) and the #9 bus (262nd Street); ask to get off at the stables. Or take the Liberty Line Bx-M3 bus, which goes up Madison Avenue, stopping every 10 blocks, and drops you at the stable door; 20 minutes from the Upper East Side.

ICE SKATING

In addition to the Wollman and Lasker rinks in Central Park (see above), and the Sailboat Pond at 73rd Street when it freezes, New York City boasts many fine places to skate.

- **Kate Wollman Rink**, sister to Central Park's Wollman Rink, is located on the east side of Prospect Park, off the Parkside and Ocean Avenue entrance, in Brooklyn, 718-287-6431. November-March
- **Riverbank State Park**, 145th Street and Riverside Drive, 212-694-3642; skate outdoors just above the Hudson River in this beautiful 28-acre park. Skate rentals available. Roller-skating here during the summer.
- **Rockefeller Center Rink**, 50th Street off Fifth Avenue, 212-332-7654; open daily and evenings in season. Skate rentals available. One of the country's most famous skating rinks sits adjacent to a lovely café and, in December, below the massive Rockefeller Center Christmas tree. Plenty of onlookers, so brush up on your skating skills. October-April
- **Skyrink at Chelsea Piers**, Pier 61 at Hudson River and 22nd Street, 212-336-6100, www.chelseapiers.com; with two indoor rinks in use some 20 hours a day, this facility offers public skating, figure skating, and hockey instruction for adults and children, league hockey, a skating club, and ice theater. Rentals and a skate shop are on site, as well as audience seating for 1,600, including two skyboxes for special events, and a snack bar. You can even hold a birthday party here. Year round
- **World's Fair Skating Rink** (sometimes referred to as Flushing Meadow Skate Rink), 111th Street, Corona, Queens, in Flushing Meadow Park, 718-271-1996. You can walk to this large, indoor rink from the Shea Stadium—111th Street subway stop on the #7 train. Skate rentals and weekend lessons available. Year round

LACROSSE

Chelsea Piers Field House, 23rd Street and the Hudson River, 212-336-6500, www.chelseapiers.com; offers lacrosse. Open to individuals and complete teams, men and women, for indoor, adult lacrosse league play on a variety of skill levels. Teams play one night a week for a season of 8 to

12 games and league playoffs. Games consist of two 25-minute halves.
For league information in New York and New Jersey, go to
www.eteamz.com/lacrosse.

RACQUETBALL

Devotees of this popular sport can burn calories at two of the Ys we men-
tion below—the West Side YMCA at 5 West 63rd Street and the 92nd Street
YMHA at Lexington Avenue (three practice courts only)—as well as:
*   **New York Health and Racquet Club**, 110 West 56th Street, 212-
    541-7200; 24 East 13th Street 212-924-4600; 132 East 45th Street,
    212-986-3100; 20 East 50th Street, 212-593-1500; 115 East 57th
    Street, 212-826-9650; 39 Whitehall Street, 212-269-9800; 1433 York
    Avenue, 212-737-6666, www.hrcbest.com; with eight locations in the
    city, one in Long Island, and still adding. They've taken charge of the
    racquetball scene in New York City.
*   **Printing House Fitness and Racquet Club**, 421 Hudson Street in
    Greenwich Village, 212-243-7600, is a membership club with five rac-
    quetball and four squash courts on the first floor. Membership rates
    depend on how much of the club the member intends to use. Call for
    specifics.

ROLLER/IN-LINE SKATING/SKATE BOARDING

For exhilarating outdoor fun, try **Central Park** for blade action. Roller
disco, though passé, also still has some followers. Other in-line skating hot-
spots: **Union Square**, **Battery Park City**, "the banks" under the
Manhattan side of the **Brooklyn Bridge**, and Brooklyn's **Prospect
Park**. In fact, now you can skate (walk or bike) along the Hudson River
from Gansevoort Street to Battery Park City. If you plan to rent, bring a
credit card for a deposit on the equipment.
*   **Blades Board and Skate**, 160 East 86th Street, 212-996-1644; 120
    West 72nd Street, 212-787-3911; 1414 Second Avenue, 212-249-
    3178; 901 Sixth Avenue, Lower Level II, 212-563-2448; Pier 61, Chelsea
    Piers, 212-336-6199; Pier 62, Chelsea Piers, 212-336-6299; 659
    Broadway in the Village, 212-477-7350; the outlet store is at 128
    Chambers Street downtown, 212-964-1944, www.blades.com. With
    the help of the friendly staffers at any of these locations, you too can
    join the fun. Rollerblades, the best-known brand, can be rented for the
    day with wrist guards and kneepads included. You can also buy skates,
    equipment, and gear.
*   **Chelsea Piers Skate Park and Roller Rinks**, 23rd Street and Hudson
    River, 212-336-6200, www.chelseapiers.com; besides general skating in

two outdoor, regulation-sized in-line and roller rinks, there are classes at various levels: from basic technique to hip-hop to aggressive, as well as league hockey games for adults and youths. Also, two half-pipes with 11- and 6-foot walls respectively. Or you can just watch. BLADES, 212-336-6299, operates a board and skate pro shop and rental outlet, and there's a snack bar. A credit card is required for security when renting equipment.

- **Empire Roller Skating Center**, 200 Empire Boulevard, Flatbush, Brooklyn, 718-462-1570; www.empirerollerskating.com; renovated in 2000, Empire offers skate rental, special teen nights, video games, roller skating sessions for all ages, birthday parties, and even a safe environment to skate while dancing to the latest in R&B and hip-hop. Call for directions and visit the web site for discounts.
- **Lezly Skate School**, 212-777-3232; offers skating instruction for every skill level in four week sessions, both indoor and out. Classes are at the Roxy at 515 West 18th Street or in Central Park and other locations. Skate rentals available for classes only.
- **Skate Key Roller Rink**, 220 East 138th street by Canal Street and Canal Place, The Bronx, 718-401-0700, www.keyskate.com; open for general skating Wednesday and Thursday. Special theme nights. Easy to reach by the 4, 5, or 6 train. Call for directions.

RUGBY

Gaelic Park, 718-548-9568, in The Bronx is the center of rugby play in New York City. The park is located at Broadway and West 240th Street.

RUNNING

- **Front Runners**, NY, 212-724-9700, www.frny.org, is the hyperactive local branch of Front Runners International, which organizes running, walking, cycling, and triathlon events for lesbians, gay men, and supportive non-gays. Their weekly "fun runs" take place in Central Park and Prospect Park in Brooklyn. Participants gather after the runs for a snack or a meal. The organization also offers coaching and training, events for cyclists and walkers, and competitions for runners and tri-athletes. Call, or visit their web site for a schedule of runs.
- **Hash House Harriers**, 212-427-4692, www.hashhouseharriers.com, is a group of not-totally-serious joggers who meet at various locations throughout the city and in Westchester to follow a flour-marked trail looping four to five miles and winding up at a bar for post-run analysis fueled by food and copious quantities of beer. Runners are called "hashers" and the trails are set by "hares." You need only running

shoes and about $15 in "hash cash" to join in. Some call it "the drinking club with a running problem." Hashing originated in 1938 in Kuala Lumpur and is now international, so you can hash away from home. Global information is on the web at www.gthhh.com.

- The **New York Road Runners Club**, with over 25,000 members "the world's largest running club," maintains an "International Running Center" at 9 East 89th Street, NYC 10128, 212-860-4455, www.nyrrc. org. The Road Runners Club sponsors the New York Marathon and more than 150 other races a year.

SAILING

If you want to bound over Long Island Sound, City Island in The Bronx is an accessible starting point. Take the #2 (Seventh Avenue) or #6 (Lexington Avenue) train to Pelham Parkway and transfer to The Bronx #12 City Island bus. This and some other watery options are listed here:

- **Manhattan Sailing School**, 393 South End Avenue in Battery Park City, NYC 10280-1003, 212-786-0400, www.sailmanhattan.com; sail out of classy North Cove Yacht Harbor in front of the World Financial Center. Beginners can take a 20-hour basic sailing course and continue on to basic coastal cruising, also 20 hours, in J-24 sailboats. Private lessons available.
- **New York City Downtown Boathouse**, 646-613-0375, 646-613-0740 (daily status line), www.downtownboathouse.org, is an "all-volunteer organization dedicated to providing access to the Hudson River." Boathouse locations in Tribeca, Chelsea, and Uptown. Contact them about sailing or kayaking lessons.
- **New York City Community Sailing Association**, 545 West 111th Street, NYC 10025, 212-222-1405, www.sailny.org; operating with nine 22- to 24-foot keel sloops, five of which are Solings, out of Lincoln Harbor Marina in Weehawken, NJ. This non-profit organization was founded in 1996 with the idea that sailing ought to be easy and affordable. An introduction to sailing seminar is available for $30, and their ASA Basic Keelboat 101 course is a bargain at $325. You must be a member to participate in recreational sailing and races. Call or check their web site for more information.
- **New York Sailing Center & Yacht Club**, 560 Minneford Avenue, City Island, The Bronx 10464, 718-885-0335, www.startsailing.com, is a sailing school, yacht club, instruction, boat rental, boat storage and more.
- **North Cove Sailing School & Club**, 393 South End Avenue, NYC 10280, 201-915-4398; shares the North Cove Yacht Harbor with the Manhattan Sailing School. $1,000 memberships for all individual crew members and $2,200 membership for families. Basic sailing courses

start at $545.

- **The New York Sailing School**, 22 Pelham Road, New Rochelle, Westchester 10801, 914-235-6052, www.nyss.com, offers sailing course, programs, boat rental and more.
- **Offshore Sailing School**, 62 Chelsea Piers, 646-638-2241, www. offshore-sailing.com; take the Learn to Sail course from this national sailing school, then stop back at Chelsea Piers for a relaxing dinner or to hit a bucket of balls.

SCUBA

While no one's suggesting dives to the murky depths of the Hudson, you can take certification courses in local pools preparatory to plunging into the Caribbean's turquoise waters.

- **PanAqua Diving**, 460 West 43rd Street between 9th and 10th avenues, 212-736-3483, www.panaquadiving.com; in addition to selling and repairing equipment, they organize group and individual diving travel and run certification courses evenings and weekends. Courses, held variously at the West Side Y, Vanderbilt Y, 92nd Street Y, and Manhattan Plaza, range from one weekend intensive to five weeks of evenings. The open water dive required for certification is extra.

SEA KAYAKING

That's right—sea kayaking. For those who seek watery adventure in and out of the city, the **Metropolitan Association of Sea Kayakers**, www.seacanoe.org, unites groups of paddlers who plan trips up and down the East Coast as well as to locations as far north as Greenland and Alaska. Two or three trips around the island of Manhattan each summer, light and currents permitting, start and end in Liberty State Park (New Jersey) and take about 11 hours. Membership includes a published schedule, a quarterly newsletter, and a guide to coastal launch sites along the East Coast. Contact Capt. Al Ysaguirre at the Metropolitan Association of Sea Kayakers, 195 Prince Street, basement, NYC 10012 or visit their web site. Also, check with the **New York City Downtown Boathouse** (see **Sailing** above) about kayaking lessons.

SKIING

You won't schuss downhill in New York City, but cross country skiers take to the gentle slopes of Central Park and, in the boroughs, Van Cortlandt Park, Split Rock Golf Course in Pelham Bay Park in The Bronx, Prospect Park in Brooklyn, and Flushing Meadow Park in Queens. No official trail grooming, so break your own, or follow trails carved out by fellow skiers.

Downhill skiers take to the slopes two-hours north of the city in the Catskills or at Bear Mountain, 909-866-5766, www.bearmtn.com, in northern Westchester. Lake Placid, www.lakeplacid.com, home of the 1980 Winter Olympics, is also a skiing destination. Vernon Valley/Great Gorge, 201-827-2000, www.skislopes.net, across the George Washington Bridge in New Jersey is another a popular ski destination for city dwellers. Check local sporting goods stores for day or weekend ski rental packages.

SOCCER

The **Cosmopolitan Soccer League**, 201-861-6606, www.newyork soccer.com, represents amateur and semi-pro clubs from New York, New Jersey, and Connecticut. The League has one semi-pro and two amateur divisions consisting of about 20 clubs each. You don't have to join a club to play on a team, but club facilities are limited to members. Coaches are available for training; all age groups are welcome.

Indoor league play is available now in the field house at **Chelsea Piers**, 23rd Street at the Hudson River, 212-336-6500, www.chelseapiers.com. Teams accommodating men and women at various skill levels play one night a week on an Astroturf indoor field. A season consists of eight or 12 games, consisting of two 25-minute halves, and league playoffs.

Some city parks also have soccer fields. For permit information in New York, contact the NYC Department of Parks and Recreation, 212-360-3456, www.nycparks.org.

SQUASH

When you consider that a tennis court takes up about ten times as much space as a squash court, it is easy to understand the great attraction squash holds for sports club operators as well as for a population determined to exercise, but at the lowest cost possible. See **Health Clubs** and **Ys** for other locations with courts.

- **New York Sports Clubs**, www.nysc.com; 61 West 62nd Street, 212-265-0995; 151 East 86th Street, 212-860-8630; 575 Lexington Avenue, 212-317-9400; and 110 Boerum Place (Cobble Hill), 718-643-4400
- **Printing House Fitness and Racquet Club**, 421 Hudson Street at Leroy Street in Greenwich Village, 212-243-7600, is a membership club with five international squash courts on the first floor. Membership rates depend on how much of the facility the member wishes to use. Call for specifics.

SWIMMING—POOLS

The Department of Parks and Recreation, www.nycparks.org, maintains a number of indoor and outdoor pools throughout the city with inexpensive admission. In the heat of summer, the outdoor pools are more for play and cooling off than serious lap swimming. The swimming is easier during off-hours in winter. Winter indoor pool hours are generally 3 p.m. to 10 p.m. weekdays, 10 a.m. to 5 p.m. Saturday, closed Sunday. Summer hours for the outdoor pools vary, and indoor pools are closed. Most of the pools require a membership or registration fee—pay by money order or credit card. In 2004, the permit fee was $75 for adults (annually), $10 for seniors (age 55 and older), and free for children 17 and under accompanied by an adult. Shower before and after using city pools. For saltwater swimming at city beaches see the chapter on **Greenspace and Beaches**. Check the DPR's web site for a complete list of public pools. Here are a few (with gyms attached) to get you started:

- **Asser Levy Pool**, 23rd Street, between First Avenue and FDR Drive, 212-447-2020; built in 1906 as a public bath modeled on the Roman baths, this granite gem with a marble lobby and 20-foot ceilings re-opened in 1990 after extensive renovations. The indoor pool is open until late June when it closes on behalf of the outdoor pool, which is open until around Labor Day.
- **Carmine Street Gymnasium and Pool**, Clarkson Street and Seventh Avenue South (Greenwich Village), 212-242-5228, offers a 20' by 70' indoor pool and a 50' by 100' outdoor pool. Two upstairs gyms and a running track. Annual membership.
- **East 54th Street Gymnasium and Pool**, 342 East 54th Street between First and Second avenues, 212-397-3159, offers a 50' by 54' indoor pool (open year round) and an upstairs gym and running track.
- **Hansborough Recreational Center**, 35 West 134th Street, 212-234-9603, in Harlem has an indoor pool and gym with dance and aerobic classes.
- **Metropolitan Pool and Fitness Center**, 261 Bedford Avenue, Greenpoint, Brooklyn, 718-599-5707, recently renovated, is probably the most beautiful of the pools operated by the city. Light pours through a copper-framed skylight into the somewhat Andalusian pool area, which is handicap-accessible. Best to avoid early evenings and Saturdays. Mornings from 7 to 9:30 are quiet.
- **West 59th Street Gymnasium and Pool**, West 59th Street and West End Avenue, 212-397-3166 or 3159, offers a 34' by 60' indoor pool and a 75' by 100' outdoor pool. The gym has basketball and paddleball courts.

Health clubs and Ys with pools are described at the end of this chapter. Dedicated swimmers might wish also to check out other swimming situations such as:

- **Coles Sports and Recreation Center**, Mercer and Houston streets, 212-998-2020; New York University's sports facility, with racquet ball and squash courts, a weight room, and a 25-meter pool with six lanes beneath frosted glass windows is available to residents from 14th to Canal streets, Fourth to Eleventh avenues, and students, faculty, and staff affiliated with NYU.
- **Manhattan Plaza Swim and Health Club**, 482 West 43rd Street at Tenth Avenue, 212-563-7001; the handsome, verdant, glass-enclosed 40' by 75' pool with four lap lanes is the main lure here, but there is also a gym and sauna. Of course, you'll need an annual membership and to get one, or to just get pricing information, you must first schedule an appointment for a personal consultation with one of the club's consultants.
- **Metropolitan Masters**, 914-260-3412, www.metroswim.org/clubs.html; call or visit their web site for a list of places where club members can swim in and around New York City. Options include several YMCAs, Chelsea Piers, and the New York Athletic Club.
- **Riverbank State Park**, 679 Riverside Drive at 145th Street, 212-694-3600; this glorious facility atop a waste treatment plant over the Hudson River is a treasure for Uptowners who pay a couple of dollars to go for a swim in its indoor Olympic-sized pool (50 meters)—no membership "or consultation" needed. There are a host of water classes and activities between sessions, and there is an outdoor pool open in the summer. Call for hours.
- **Trinity School Swim Club**, 91st Street, between Columbus and Amsterdam avenues, 212-873-1650; the 45' by 75' pool is available to members for swimming six nights a week. Membership is for a summer session and for a winter session that corresponds to the academic year (and therefore includes fall and spring). Currently, there's a long waiting list.

TENNIS

The Department of Parks Permit Office in each borough issues tennis permits for city courts. Manhattan permit particulars are detailed above under Central Park—Tennis. Of the city's 535 public courts, more than 100 are located in Manhattan at nine sites. The largest single concentration, 30 courts, is in Central Park off 96th Street. Seven of the other locations are north of 96th Street, and the eighth is at East River Park at Broome Street on the Lower East Side.

In Brooklyn, permits are sold at the Brooklyn Borough Parks Department office in Litchfield Mansion, 95 Prospect Park West off Fifth Street, 718-965-8900, Monday-Friday 9 a.m. to 4 p.m. Call for annual permit fees. The ten city courts located at the Parade Grounds, Coney Island, and Parkside avenues, open from April-November, are probably those most popular with tennis permit holders. The same courts are covered with a bubble and run as a concession in the winter.

Five private clubs with four or more courts in Manhattan, Roosevelt Island, and across the East River in Queens are listed below. Check the Yellow Pages for other facilities near you.

- **East River Tennis Club**, 44-02 Vernon Boulevard, Long Island City (located on the East River; courtesy minibus service leaves hourly on the half-hour from 57th Street and Third Avenue), 718-937-2381, under bubble in winter; membership.
- **Manhattan Plaza Racquet Club**, 450 West 43rd Street, 212-594-0554; membership, hourly and seasonal rates.
- **Midtown Tennis Club**, 341 Eighth Avenue at 27th Street, 212-989-8572, www.midtowntennis.com; hourly and seasonal rates.
- **Roosevelt Island Racquet Club**, 281 Main Street, Roosevelt Island, 212-935-0250, www.rirctennis.com; clay courts indoors, league play, a seniors' club, babysitting, membership, hourly rates.
- **West Side Tennis Club**, 1 Tennis Place, Forest Hills, Queens, 718-268-2300, has 43 outdoor courts, including grass, clay Deco-Turf, and four Har Tru courts under a bubble in cold weather. A membership club on the former site of the US Open and home to some 800 members, West Side hosts a variety of tennis programs and tournaments and includes on the premises a fitness room, platform tennis, basketball, and a new outdoor pool complex. Membership dues vary depending on age and family status. Lessons with a pro are available at extra charge.

Of course, if you really want to play where the pros play, you can rent a court at the **United States Tennis Center**, which is open to the public almost all year (closed for Thanksgiving, Christmas, and for two weeks in late August for a little tournament called the US Open). Located in Flushing Meadow Park, Queens—across from Shea Stadium (take the #7 train). For rates and information call 718-760-6200 or visit the USTA web site at www.usta.com. Junior and adult training programs plus junior summer camps are also available.

YOGA

Not a sport really, but since so many health and fitness clubs now include it along with aerobics, free weights, and Nautilus, we include yoga here. It's the unsport in sports. Listed below are just some of the many sites other than health clubs where yoga, in one form or another, is taught and practiced.

- **Be Zone**, 160 East 56th Street between Lexington and Third avenues, 12th floor, 212-935-9642, and 138 Fifth Avenue, 212-647-9642; classes in all levels of Ishta yoga. Orientation classes are offered monthly.
- **Dharma Yoga Center**, 297 Third Avenue at 23rd Street, 212-889-8160, www.dharmayogacenter.com, offers classical yoga, meditation, breathing classes, and posture classes for different levels.
- **Integral Yoga Institute**, 227 West 13th Street between 7th and 8th avenues, 212-929-0586, www.integralyogaofnewyork.org; classes on the Upper West Side and Lower East Side. The main location offers open classes in Hatha I, beginners, intermediate, and advanced Hatha, pre-natal and post-partum classes, Hatha in Spanish and for HIV participants. They operate an adjacent health food store and a vitamin store nearby. The Integral Yoga Teaching Center at 200 West 72nd Street and Broadway, 212-721-0400, offers a similar roster of classes as well as yoga for mobility and private lessons in yoga and meditation.
- **Om Yoga Center**, 826 Broadway, 6th floor, 212-254-9642, www.omyoga.com; with Hatha yoga classes at all levels, partner yoga, a breathing workshop, and meditation courses.
- **Prana Studio**, 5 West 19th Street between 5th and 6th avenues, 212-666-5816, www.thepranastudio.com, specializes in Ashtanga yoga.
- **Sivananda Yoga Vedanta Center**, 243 West 24th Street between 7th and 8th avenues, 212-255-4560, offering multi-level yoga for all ages, courses and one-day workshops on meditation, philosophy, and vegetarian cooking. They also offer yoga retreats at their ranch in the Catskills.
- **White Street Center**, 43 White Street between Broadway and Church Street downtown, 212-966-9005; yoga classes, personal trainers, body work, and massage therapy.
- **Yoga Studio**, 351 East 89th Street, 212-988-9474; private one-on-one classes by appointment only.

HEALTH CLUBS, YMCAs, YWCAs, AND YMHAs

Beyond offering personal trainers and customized fitness regimens most health clubs offer various classes, ranging from kick-boxing and spinning to yoga and fencing. Facilities go from bare bones weight rooms to ubiquitous all-purpose spas where you set your own pace using the most appealing facilities. These often include a pool (varying from postage stamp to Olympic in size), exercise equipment (aerobic and weight), steam-rooms, whirlpools, and saunas. Hospitals have gotten into the act as well by offering low-key but well-equipped exercise facilities for patients and others affiliated with the hospital; contact the hospital nearest you to find out what may be available. To indicate the amenities offered, a few of the dozens of health facilities located in the city are described here.

Get a tour, and if possible a free pass or two, before signing on the dotted line—you may decide that the reality of exercising to skull-pounding music is not so healthful after all. When you're told that the club you're visiting is having a "sale," take it with several grains of salt; with few fixed prices, words like "special" and "discount" are next to meaningless in the fitness business. The person on the treadmill next to you may have paid double or half what you paid. Ask at your place of work if they offer an employer-sponsored program. Finally, don't let yourself be pressured into signing up for a long-term commitment—unless you're *really* sure you want that multi-year membership.

- **Asphalt Green**, 1750 York Avenue at 90th Street, 212-369-8890; www.asphaltgreen.org; two gyms, indoor and outdoor running tracks, state-of-the-art cardiovascular and weight-training equipment at this community-oriented, not-for-profit 5.5-acre sports and fitness complex. But the centerpiece is its AquaCenter, a spectacular 50-meter Olympic-standard pool. Membership is on a monthly, semi-annual or annual basis. Non-members can purchase a day pass for full access to the facility.
- **Bally's Total Fitness Clubs**, www.ballyfitness.com; this nationwide club has a number of New York area locations including 1109 Second Avenue, 212-758-3434; 144-146 East 86th Street, 212-722-7371; 45 East 45th Street, 212-688-6630; 162 West 83rd Street, 212-875-1902; 335 Madison Avenue, 212-983-5320; 350 West 50th Street, Worldwide Plaza, 212-265-9400; 144 West 38th Street, 212-869-7788; and clubs in Queens, Riverdale, and New Jersey. Aqua fitness, step training, athletic training, dance fitness, conditioning, mind-body training, circuit training, yoga, spinning, and plenty of other classes are offered in the membership plans. Personal training is also available. Be sure to tour the club you will use most, as the clientele and facility vary greatly from place to place.
- **Battery Park Swim & Fitness Club**, 375 South End Avenue, 212-321-1117; swim in a glass-enclosed pool with a patio that opens out onto the Hudson River in summer. Swim classes and "aquacize" are offered, as well as free weights, Cybex and Nautilus, StairMasters, treadmills, and Lifecycles. A host of classes, whirlpool, saunas and steam rooms complete the facility. Membership.
- **Crunch Fitness**, www.crunch.com, is proliferating, with several locations in Manhattan: 25 Broadway, 212-269-1067; 404 Lafayette Street, 212-614-0120; 1109 Second Avenue between 58th and 59th streets,

212-758-3434, 54 East 13th Street near Fifth Avenue, 212-475-2018, 144 West 38th Street, 212-869-7788, 555 West 42nd Street, 212-594-8050, and 160 West 83rd Street, 212-875-1902. Crunch packs 'em in with catchy ads, an exercise program on ESPN2, and fairly outlandish exercise classes, which appeal to a mostly young crowd. Call it entertainment fitness. Amenities vary at the different clubs but include personal training, boxing, rock climbing walls, steam rooms, pools, saunas, and even tanning. Membership or day passes.

- **Dolphin Fitness Clubs**, www.dolphinfitness.com; in Manhattan at 242 East 14th Street between Second and Third avenues, 212-614-0390; 330 East 59th Street between First and Second avenues, 212-486-6966; 155 East Third Street at Avenue A, 212-533-0090; 94 East Fourth Street, 212-387-9500; 110 Greenwich Street, 212-233-0700. There are seven clubs total in The Bronx, Brooklyn, and Staten Island, plus some in Westchester and New Jersey. Provides all the basics including muscle toning and aerobic classes, Nautilus equipment, personal trainers, weight training, cardiovascular equipment and pools and racquetball courts at some locations. Membership or day passes.
- **Equinox Fitness Club**, www.equinoxnyc.com, several locations including 897 Broadway at 19th Street, 212-780-9300, 344 Amsterdam Avenue at West 76th Street, 212-721-4200, 2465 Broadway at 92nd Street, 212-799-1818, 140 East 63rd Street at Lexington Avenue, 212-750-4900, 205 East 85th Street, 212-439-8500, 54 Murray Street, 212-566-6555, 97 Greenwich Avenue, 212-620-0103, 14 Wall Street at Nassau, 212-964-6688, and at the Palladium at AOL-Time Warner Center, 212-871-0425. Certified personal trainers and some 200 classes, from high and low impact aerobics to Aerobox, pre- and post-natal exercise to yoga and meditation. Besides up-to-date equipment, the club boasts boxing circuit training, one-on-one boxing (for women too), and cardio/theater television with the cardiovascular workout equipment. In addition, you'll find childcare, a juice bar, shopping and more at these health emporiums. A nutritionist supervises personal weight-loss programs. At the Amsterdam Avenue location a physiology lab offers comprehensive metabolic testing for a fee to non-members as well as members. No boxing uptown. Membership.
- **Lucille Roberts**, 800-USA-LUCILLE, www.lucilleroberts.com, operates at several Manhattan locations: 143 Fulton Street, 212-267-3730, 300 West 40th Street, 212-268-4199, 505 West 125th Street, 212-222-2522, 80 Fifth Avenue at 14th Street, 212-255-3999, plus more gyms in Brooklyn, Queens, The Bronx, and New Jersey. Forget the sauna and the personal trainers, and bring your own towel. Classes are the draw, including one called "butt and gut." In some neighborhoods, there are classes in Spanish. The cost of membership, comparatively low, varies

by location, as do hours. Individual gyms have occasional sales promotions, when it's cheaper to join; they're worth checking out.

- **New York Health & Racquet Club**, www.hrcbest.com, 212-797-1500, has several locations (plus a yacht club on 23rd Street if you want to take a sea cruise). Rates go down considerably in the summer (watch for ads offering discounts, and ask about corporate discounts). Membership includes use (for a fee) of the club's tennis court in the Village and admission to any of its locations. Most locations have pools, saunas, and racquetball courts.
- **New York Sports Clubs**, www.nysc.com, over 20 locations, among them: 575 Lexington Avenue at 51st, 212-317-9400, 380 Madison Avenue at 46th, 212-983-0303, 1637 Third Avenue, 212-987-7200, 61 West 62nd Street, 212-265-0995, 1601 Broadway, 212-977-8880, 151 East 86th Street, 212-860-8630, and 110 Boerum Place, Brooklyn, 718-643-4400. Eagle and Nautilus circuits, Lifecycles, StairMasters, Gravitron, and other equipment available in all clubs. Most have one-on-one training, pools, squash courts, whirlpools, and saunas. Membership includes entrance to all clubs and access to tennis courts in Brooklyn (additional court fee). Fees vary by location. This is one of the few clubs that does not require payment for a full year up front but will bill you monthly.
- **The Printing House Fitness and Center**, 421 Hudson Street at Leroy, 212-243-7600; on the first floor are five squash courts, on the ninth floor are machines, treadmills, locker rooms, and a sauna, steam room, and whirlpool, as well as a cardiovascular fitness center, two dance studios and a full-service salon. On the roof above is a seasonal 20' by 30' heated outdoor pool. There are three different membership rates here, depending on whether you want to use just the squash courts, just the gym, or everything. Call for specifics.
- **Reebok Sports Club/NY**, 160 Columbus Avenue at 67th Street, 212-362-6800, www.reeboksportsclubny.com; is an upscale, landscaped urban country club. This state-of-the-art 140,000-square foot facility on six floors features a 45-foot climbing wall, a rooftop in-line skating and running track, full basketball and volleyball courts, swimming pool with underwater sound, sauna, a virtual reality sports simulator for skiing, wind-surfing, and golf, a bar, health food cafe, and a bistro. They even have a dry cleaning service.
- **Sports Center at Chelsea Piers**, 23rd Street and Hudson River, 212-336-6000, www.chelseapiers.com; this 150,000 square foot pier houses a four-lane, 1/4-mile running track, competition track, three basketball courts, a 100-foot climbing wall and a bouldering wall, a six-lane, 25-yard swimming pool, two outdoor sun decks, cardiovascular, circuit and strength training equipment, a boxing ring, aerobic studios,

and an infield for volleyball, sand volleyball, and touch football. Also training, sports medicine, spa facilities, and a physiology lab available. Members have the use of all the other Pier facilities at a 10% discount. Membership or day passes. Popular for kids' parties.

- **The Sports Club/LA**, 330 East 61st Street, 212-355-5100. www.the sportsclubla.com, is that glamorous seven-story building you see when entering Manhattan on the 59th Street Bridge from Queens: lots of tinted glass, gleaming chrome, and lithe-looking figures back-lit and working out. The big club accommodates a 20' by 40' pool, exercise machines, five international squash courts, sun deck, restaurant, and juice bar, among other amenities. The club also features classes in Tae Kwon Do, yoga, and boxing. Other location: 45 Rockefeller Plaza, 212-218-8600.

YMCAs, YWCAs, AND YMHAs

- **92nd Street YMHA (Young Men's and Women's Hebrew Association**), 1395 Lexington Avenue, 212-415-5500, www.92y.org; annual athletic membership entitles you to participate in many programs including indoor jogging, weight training, volleyball, and handball as well as fitness programs and use of the 50' by 75' pool.
- **Brooklyn YWCA**, 30 Third Avenue between State Street and Atlantic Avenue, Brooklyn, 718-875-1190; for a reasonably priced athletic membership plus a Y membership, both men and women can work out on the Universal machines, punching bags, the large basketball court, jogging track, and in the 20' by 60' swimming pool, and relax in the sauna.
- **Harlem YMCA**, 180-181 West 135th Street by Lenox Avenue, 212-281-4100, www.ymcanyc.org, offers two pools (for adults and children), Nautilus and weights, a track, basketball courts, table tennis, aerobics, yoga and karate classes, and personal trainers. Athletic membership (for men and women) plus initiation fee.
- **McBurney YMCA**, 225 West 14th Street, 212-741-9210, www.ymcanyc.org; this Y has a carefully developed children's after-school program as well as adult gymnastics, adult lap and recreational swimming, full-court basketball, indoor jogging track, fencing, handball, volleyball, and a weight lifting room. Annual adult membership plus joiner's fee for the first year.
- **Vanderbilt YMCA**, 224 East 47th Street, 212-756-9600, www.ymcanyc.org, has an after school program (with escorts from certain neighborhood schools) plus yoga, handball and paddleball, along with swimming, basketball, volleyball, indoor jogging, Nautilus and aerobics. Regular membership plus joiner's fee includes use of the

gym, 20' by 60' swimming pool, a 40' by 75' lap pool and other sports facilities. Annual dues for the Businessman's Club and the men's Athletic Club are higher.

- **The West Side YMCA**, 5 West 63rd Street, 212-875-4100, www.ymca nyc.org, is justifiably proud of its Sports Fitness Department, which keeps both men and women members in the very best of shape. The seven-story building houses two pools, a wrestling room, indoor running track, handball, squash, and racquetball courts, universal exercise machines, and numerous other facilities. Annual adult membership plus initiation fee.

A S THE RAINFOREST IS TO THE EARTH, PARKS ARE TO THIS RUSHED and hard-edged city. Each park provides a much-needed oasis of greenery from the city's densely packed apartments and skyscrapers and its nonstop hustle and bustle where New Yorkers can breathe, relax, play ... and smile. From the smallest community garden on a vacant lot in a dense neighborhood, where neighbors lovingly tend an iris bed and riotous morning glories, to green bands streaked with runners, bladers, and cyclists along watery borders, to Manhattan's great lush centerpiece, Central Park, and its sister, Prospect Park, in Brooklyn, New Yorkers use and cherish their parks. Beyond these groomed and cultivated parks familiar to most, there are almost 9,000 acres of urban wilderness in the domain of the city's parks department, where the nature lover can wander wooded paths, meadows, and marshlands alone and silent among swans, egrets, herons, turtles, muskrats, and rabbits. For the price of a subway ride, one can spend the day in a national park, Gateway National Recreation Area, a birder's paradise, parts of which are within the city. And the city's beaches, seaside parks of a sort, guarantee sandy access to the Atlantic Ocean and Long Island Sound.

There are some 1,650 parks and playgrounds throughout the 28,000 acres maintained by the Department of Parks and Recreation in the five boroughs. These range from vest-pocket neighborhood playgrounds to the 2,700-acre Pelham Bay Park in The Bronx. Suffice it to say we can't describe or even list them all. Rather, this chapter focuses on the major parks in each borough, with brief descriptive mention of some others and, finally, a look at the city's beaches. For further information about parks in general or a particular park call 800-201-PARK, or go online to www.nyc parks.org. A dandy book, *Nature Walks in and Around New York City* by Sheila Buff, leads the reader through a detailed stroll around Central Park and some 40 other parks and preserves in the metropolitan area.

Open from dawn to 1 a.m., all city parks are free and accessible by public transportation. Statistically speaking, the parks are very safe. That said, it is good to remember these are urban parks; common sense tells you it's not a good idea to stroll or jog through a wooded park area alone, day or night—there are plenty of trails in wide-open spaces. Unless you're watching one of the special concerts in the park, or visiting some other crowded park event, avoid the parks after dark. Dogs must be on leashes, and you are expected to clean up after your dog. It's the law.

PARKS

MANHATTAN

In 1858 Frederick Law Olmstead and Calvert Vaux won a design competition for the construction of the first public park to be built in America. It was to occupy swampy land inhabited by poor squatters, bone-boiling mills, and swill mills, an area described in one report as "a pestilential spot where miasmic odors taint every breath of air." The inhabitants were removed, buildings torn down, swamps drained, tons of earth moved and Manhattan schist blasted away. Following plans for a picturesque landscape of glades alternating with copses, water, and outcroppings, and threaded with drives, footpaths and bridle paths, over a period of 20 years the park emerged from wasteland. What Olmstead and Vaux had named Greensward became **Central Park**, 840 acres of man-made romantic landscape stretching rectangularly from 59th Street north to 110th Street, and from Fifth Avenue west to Central Park West (Eighth Avenue): the green jewel in the middle of Manhattan.

Today the park is managed, under contract with the city, by the **Central Park Conservancy**, a non-profit organization responsible for extensive restoration of the park. The most heavily visited area is the southern portion of the park, especially the area around the ever-popular **Central Park Zoo**, which includes the revamped Children's Zoo. The northern portion beyond the Reservoir, with its heavily used jogging track, contains the wildest terrain, including the Ravine area with its waterfall and the 1814 Blockhouse, as well as the only formal garden in the park, the elegant **Conservatory Garden** at 105th Street and Fifth Avenue. The **Charles A. Dana Discovery Center**, 212-860-1370, in the northeast corner of the park, features ecologically oriented exhibits and programs for all ages on a regular basis, and has fishing poles for use at the adjacent Harlem Meer. The Conservancy offers free seasonal events throughout the park, including birdwatching walks and ecological activities. Pick up the Conservancy's excellent *Central Park Map and Guide* at the Dairy, just north of Wollman Rink near the 65th Street Transverse, open Tuesday-Sunday, 11 a.m. to 5 p.m.

New Yorkers use Central Park: for sports, from croquet to horseback riding to league softball (see the chapter on **Sports and Recreation**); for cultural events such as Shakespeare in the Park, outdoor performances by the Metropolitan Opera and the New York Philharmonic; for children's recreation in its numerous playgrounds, for storytelling sessions, kite-flying and carousel riding, and organized nature activities; for sunbathing on its rocky outcroppings or on bucolic Sheep Meadow; for bird-watching in the Ramble, especially during the annual spring warbler migration; for boating in the Lake or floating beneath Bow Bridge in a Venetian gondola; for sailing toy boats in the Lake; for weddings; and even for films, many of which have been shot in or around the massive park—the musical "Hair," for example was primarily shot in Central Park. And it's used for daydreaming or reading a good book. In fact, sometimes just knowing it is there is enough.

Central Park is open from a half-hour before dawn to 1 a.m. As in the other large city parks, it is best visited in daylight or at night in the well-lighted areas along the edges and with companions. Check www.centralpark.org for an invigorating virtual visit and plenty of information. This excellent, non-official web site offers a colorful virtual tour, park history, sporting events, a listing of park events, and links to other park-related sites.

Having completed Central Park, Olmstead and Vaux focused their attention on the banks of the Hudson River and designed most of what is now **Riverside Park**. This elongated ribbon of green, stretching along the river from 72nd Street to 152nd Street and bisected lengthwise by the Henry Hudson Parkway, is particularly beautiful in the spring when daffodils dot the grassy banks and swarms of flowering trees create a haze of pink and white. Riverside Drive winds among great trees along the upper terrace, and the mighty Hudson, nearly a mile wide here, sweeps along past cyclists and joggers on the riverfront promenade. Sailboats and a few houseboats at the 79th Street boat basin bob at anchor, and in good weather reasonably priced sailing lessons are to be had here (see **Sports and Recreation**). Tennis, handball, soccer, and volleyball are played here, and a facility for bladers and boarders, with ramps and half-pipes at 108th Street, draws youthful enthusiasts. Soaring Riverside Church and Grant's Tomb add to the appeal of Riverside Park. For more information call the park administrator's office at 212-408-0264. Further along at 145th Street and Riverside Drive an iron-gate gives access to **Riverbank State Park**, 212-694-3600, built atop a waste treatment plant, where ice skating, swimming, and other athletic activities can be pursued at way-below-health-club rates.

Fort Tryon Park in Washington Heights stands atop a ridge of Manhattan schist at the island's highest natural point. The site of one of the earliest Revolutionary War battles (we lost), this land was purchased in 1917 by John D. Rockefeller Jr. He hired Frederick Law Olmstead, Jr. to design a park here, reserving four acres at the northern end of the 67 acres for a museum of medieval art, The Cloisters—a fortuitous pairing, those juniors. Taking advantage of the sweeping Hudson view at this 250-foot elevation, Olmstead designed a series of terraces with stone parapets and retaining walls, the whole threaded with eight miles of paths. The center-piece of the park is the three-acre Heather Garden, with heaths, brooms and thousands of bulbs, which bloom from January through autumn. Further along the Promenade are leafy Linden Terrace and The Cloisters, with its three medieval gardens. Bring a picnic lunch. For more information call Fort Tryon Park, 212-408-0100, or The Cloisters, 212-923-3700.

Just north of Fort Tryon Park at the very top of Manhattan, little-known **Inwood Hill Park** contains the last remaining natural woodland in Manhattan, not to mention arresting views of the Hudson River and the Jersey Palisades beyond. Interesting geology on the wooded ridge, which is criss-crossed with paved and graveled paths, includes glacial potholes and cliffs with a hodge-podge of blocky gray rocks, the Indian Rock Shelters, which once sheltered Algonquin Indians. From these rocky cliffs, paths descend to playing fields, grassy parkland, and marshland along swift Spuyten Duyvil Creek, across which the Henry Hudson Bridge soars to The Bronx. There is an excellent **Urban Ecology Center** here staffed by Urban Park Rangers. They lead occasional walks and canoe trips into the Hudson. For information call 212-304-2365.

South of Central Park, green space is measured out in much smaller portions. **Bryant Park** behind the Beaux Arts main branch of the New York Public Library at 42nd Street, between Fifth and Sixth avenues, for example, is too small to encourage sports much more strenuous than chess. But, having been recently reclaimed from drug dealers and revamped, it is now green space with a rather European feel, and those who work in the neighborhood are grateful for it. During the summer months it hosts concerts and private parties. Further downtown at the foot of Fifth Avenue, **Washington Square Park** is not much larger, but it is the green space for Greenwich Village and SoHo, where people-watching and attending the annual art show are the sports of choice. Nearly sur-rounded by New York University, which threatens to engulf it entirely, Washington Square Park has managed to retain a sense of its history, which has included being a potter's field, the site of the hangman's tree, a military parade ground, and an elegant park for the wealthy. Its Village location and the presence of college students keep it youthful and colorful. To the east, **Tompkins Square Park**, truly a people's park with an English provenance and great old trees that have always made it a shady haven in the summer for a working class population, is the front yard for the East Village. The population is changing as gentrification sets in, but the park is no less used. Dogs in the dog run there come in more exotic breeds now. Way downtown you'll find a series of small parks connected by a sinuous, elegant **Esplanade** spacious enough to accommodate joggers, cyclists, bladers, walkers, and baby strollers moving at their own pace within sight of the Statue of Liberty and Ellis Island. Students from nearby Stuyvesant High School toss frisbees in the offshore breeze and children romp and climb in a fanciful playground. The landscape at the south end was designed to resemble the original shoreline. Just to the south, at the very foot of the island is **Battery Park**, once part of New York Harbor with Castle Clinton surrounded by water rather than grass. This inviting, grassy stretch looks out on the harbor, the statue, Staten Island, and invites a hop onto the free Staten Island Ferry.

BROOKLYN

Who but Calvert Vaux and Frederick Law Olmstead could have designed **Prospect Park**, sister to Central Park and younger by just a few years? In fact, its designers considered it their masterpiece. Free of Manhattan's grid, it is irregularly shaped in a somewhat elongated ovoid, smaller at 526 acres, and unlike Central Park, it is undisturbed by criss-crossing traffic. Prospect Park was designed for strolling along a network of paths: on vast Long Meadow, the park's magnificent centerpiece, around Prospect Lake and the Lullwater, through The Ravine and the Midwood Forest, and by The Pools. Sounds English? It is. Olmstead and Vaux incorporated the natural terrain into their design, including water, magnificent old trees and geological features such as glacial kettle ponds, one of which became the charming Vale of Cashmere. To these features they added rustic bridges, a waterfall and lakes, the final effect of which is vistas, surprising nooks and glades, and hilltop prospects. There's even a Quaker cemetery, among whose residents is the actor Montgomery Clift, and an elegant, Palladian-style boathouse. This is not to say that strolling is the sole Prospect Park activity. **Wollman Rink** is here for ice-skating; birding is excellent in the park; jogging, tennis, softball, kite flying, and soccer flourish here; and on summer weekends the Bandshell at 9th Street and Prospect Park West features music, from calypso to jazz, klezmer, and new urban Latin grooves. For more information and for upcoming events in the park call the Prospect Park Administrator at Litchfield Villa, Prospect Park, 718-965-8999/8900, or 718-965-8951. The park is bounded by Ocean Avenue, Flatbush Avenue, Prospect Park SW, Prospect Park West, and Parkside Avenue.

Across Flatbush Avenue from Prospect Park, and behind the Brooklyn Central Library and the Brooklyn Museum, the **Brooklyn Botanic Garden**, 1000 Washington Blvd., 718-817-8700, www.bbg.org, has been an open invitation to Brooklynites and visitors since 1912. Within its compact 52 acres it contains an extraordinary variety of greenery and flora, beautifully landscaped so as never to seem crowded. The Cherry Esplanade, said to be the finest in America, draws crowds in May when the cherry trees are in exquisite bloom. Don't miss it, but come early and on a weekday if possible. There's a rock garden, water-lily ponds, and a lilac collection, offering intoxicating blooms each spring. An herb garden is arranged as an Elizabethan knot, and the stunning Japanese garden is a perennial favorite. Year-round, the gently undulating terrain invites wandering, beginning in February, when the witch hazel blooms and the snowdrops begin to come up. Call it mid-winter botanical balm. Before you bliss out, don't miss the original Palm House. You may decide to get married there, as many have.

Green-Wood Cemetery, with its main entrance on Fifth Avenue at 25th Street, is at once a cemetery and one of the most beautiful, not to mention unusual, parks in the city. You will not play soccer here, and jogging its winding, hilly drives would be a challenge. What you can do, if not on a cemetery-related mission, is walk, bird watch, identify exotic trees, of which there are many, and look for the graves of the once-famous, including Lola Montez, Boss Tweed, Peter Cooper, and Samuel F.B. Morse, to name but a few. Opened in 1840, before Prospect Park was conceived, on 478 acres of glacial terminal moraine, and overlooking New York Harbor from the highest point in Brooklyn, its developers promoted it as an idyllic spot for strolling among the hills, ponds, superb vistas, and plantings. It was, de facto, the city's first park. The extraordinary mausoleums, obelisks, temples, pyramids, and rustic grave markers make it something of a museum of Victoriana and a draw for occasional guided tours. The main gate building, designed by Richard Upjohn, is a Gothic Revival extravaganza, housing the office where you pick up a pass, brochure, and a map of the cemetery. The office is open Monday-Friday, 8 a.m. to 4 p.m., 718-768-7300. If you wish to roam the cemetery on the weekend you should pick up a pass in advance. Or join one of John Cashman's Sunday walking tours that last about two hours. Call 718-469-5277 for information.

Stepping out of the car at the **Marine Park** parking lot on Avenue U, just west of Flatbush Avenue, you'll find yourself in a landscape of salt marsh and meadow somewhat reminiscent of Holland. This 798-acre park, most of it saltwater wetlands surrounding Marine Park Creek, north of Sheepshead Bay, contains playing fields, tennis courts, a running track, and a golf course (718-338-7149), in addition to a watery urban wilderness. From the parking lot you can hike the Gerritson Creek Nature Trail for about a mile, through grasses, sedges, and reeds with glimpses, perhaps, of diamond-back terrapin, horseshoe crabs, cottontails, marsh hens, myrtle war-blers, cormorants, and peregrine falcons. It's hard to believe you're in New York City. For more information, call the Brooklyn Borough Office of the Department of Parks and Recreation at 718-965-8900. There's also the **Salt Marsh Nature Center** at 33rd Street and Avenue U, 718-421-2021.

Even more unbelievable, and not known to many New Yorkers, is the presence of a 26,000-acre national park, **Gateway National Recreation Area**, www.nps.gov/gate, which encompasses most of Jamaica Bay in Brooklyn and Queens, and part of the Rockaways in Queens, a long stretch of the southern shore of Staten Island, and parts of the Jersey shore. Besides Jacob Riis Park, an ocean beach with a boardwalk (see **Beaches**, below), the best known point of interest in the area is the **Jamaica Bay Wildlife Refuge**, 718-318-4340, a prime birding preserve with salt water marshes, upland fields, and woods, where land and shore birds stop dur-ing migration. After obtaining a permit at the visitor center on Crossbay Boulevard in Broad Channel, Queens, visitors can explore diverse habitats by hiking an extensive trail system. Insect repellent in summer is strongly advised. Rangers give interpretive talks and lead nature walks; evening walks, workshops, and other programs are offered on a seasonal basis. Fishing can also be done for the cost of a permit. **Floyd Bennett Field**, 718-338-3799, the city's first municipal airfield, contains the North 40 Nature Trail, miles of runways for cycling or blading, and Hangar Row, where outdoor concerts and special events are held. Across Flatbush Avenue from the Field, **Dead Horse Bay** is a popular fishing area with a nature trail. **Canarsie Pier** just off the Beltway in Brooklyn, 718-763-2202, is the site of summer concerts, excellent fishing, a children's play-ground, and a commercial restaurant. Fishing is also popular, along with bird watching, at **Breezy Point Tip** on the Rockaway Peninsula and at **Fort Tilden**, 718-318-4300, a 317-acre former Army base, where visitors can also hike and explore a military past, participate in organized athletics or attend special events. On the south shore of Staten Island, **Great Kills Park**, 718-987-6790, offers ocean beaches, nature trails, a model airplane field, and fishing areas. Ranger walks at Miller Field, 718-351-6970, a for-mer Army Air Corps defense station, and at Fort Wadsworth, 718-354-4500, dating from the 18th century, appeal to military buffs and children.

Admission to all portions of Gateway, except Sandy Point, NJ, is free. For the latest information on concerts, special programs and ranger-led activities visit Gateway on the web at www.nps.gov/gate. Or contact the National Park Service, Gateway National Recreation Area, Floyd Bennett Field, Building 69, Brooklyn 11234, 718-338-3799, for a seasonal program guide, which includes transportation directions to all parts of the area.

QUEENS

At long last **Flushing Meadows-Corona Park**, 718-760-6562, is coming into its own, becoming the grand park originally envisioned when the 1939 World's Fair was held there, and again at the time of the 1964 World's Fair. Built on what was once a garbage heap on Northern Boulevard, between Grand Central Parkway and the Van Wyck Expressway, both fairs were to pay for park construction, but neither made money and the great park limped along with World Fair leftovers and a neighboring baseball stadium, Shea. The Unisphere, the signature attraction of the 1,255-acre park, and its grassy surrounds have been renovated, and extensive landscaping and plantings have beautified the central portion of the park, which also hosts the New York Hall of Science, Science Playground, and the Queens Museum. It is expected that soon the park's entire waterfront along Flushing Bay will be distinguished by an elegant promenade with shade and orna-mental trees, shrubs, and flowers along a curved railing. From reproduction cast iron benches visitors will be able to view the crowds, gaze at the flowerbeds or the boats bobbing in the World's Fair Marina. Elsewhere in the park are the Queens Theater, the Queens Zoo, the US Tennis Association's Arthur Ashe Stadium and Tennis Center, an ice-skating rink, a par three pitch-and-putt golf course, running trails, and two large lakes lying to the south of the Long Island Expressway, one, Meadow Lake, with a boathouse.

Alley Pond Park sprawls and meanders south from Little Neck Bay to Union Turnpike. Despite being sliced by numerous parkways, it encompass-es forests, meadows, salt marshes, and wetlands, making it an ideal environ-ment for a network of nature trails from which one can observe muskrats, bullfrogs, salamanders, and hawks. Up on the northern end near Alley Creek, an environmental center offers a variety of educational classes and workshops: 718-229-4000.

Along Woodhaven Boulevard on route to the Rockaways, the beach, and JFK International Airport, you'll find **Forest Park**, 800-201-PARK or 718-235-4100. It offers a public golf course, playing fields, and a magnifi-cent 150-year old oak forest honeycombed with picturesque nature trails. Summer concerts and other events take place at the bandshell. Call for information.

In the heart of Flushing, within cheering distance of Shea Stadium and the US Tennis Center, **Kissena Park Corridor** contains the **Queens Botanical Gardens and Arboretum** and connects up with greater Kissena Park, 718-520-5359, a gracious green space surrounding a lake and meandering stream. There's also a bicycle track and a public golf course.

To the east, adjacent to Cross Island Parkway and Hempstead Tunpike, **Belmont Park** is famous for its exceedingly beautiful racetrack, where thoroughbreds compete annually for the Belmont Cup. But you don't have to be a horse-lover to enjoy the park.

Nearing Long Island, in the eastern part of Queens is **Cunningham Park**, 718-780-1999. The small park on Union Turnpike has several tennis courts, baseball fields, and even bocci courts. There are plenty of picnic locations in this small, but busy, park in Fresh Meadows. The Big Apple Circus pays an annual visit.

And finally, Queens is home to much of **Gateway National Park**, bordering Brooklyn and described above.

THE BRONX

Up in the northeast corner of The Bronx, sprawling alongside and into Long Island Sound, is the city's largest park, 2,700 acres of it. **Pelham Bay Park**, 718-430-1890, has it all: a city beach, a golf course, miniature golf and a driving range, a stable, tennis courts, baseball diamonds, picnic grounds, and a historic mansion-museum, not to mention a range of habitats—the most diverse of any of the city parks. Just offshore and connected to the park by a bridge, City Island dangles like a fish on a line. The largest portion of the park lies on the north side of the Hutchinson River and Eastchester Bay, with Split Rock Golf Course and Pelham Bay Golf Course (see **Sports and Recreation**) scenically occupying the northernmost part. Also on Shore Road are Pelham Bay Riding (again, see **Sports and Recreation**) and extensive bridle trails. Nearby is the **Thomas Pell Wildlife Refuge and Sanctuary**, home to a variety of owls, wild turkeys and deer. Just to the north and east, off Shore Road, is the Barton-Pell Mansion and Museum, dating from 1675 and with alterations done in the 19th century, it is the single manor house remaining of 28 country estates that once comprised the park area. It is well worth a visit. Orchard Beach (see **Beaches** below) cuts a great sandy arc on Long Island Sound. At its far end is the **Environmental Center**, where you can pick up literature and a guide booklet to the Kazimiroff Nature Trail, which winds through the adjoining Hunter Island Sanctuary, perhaps the most beautiful section of the park. Mature woodlands give way to salt marsh, where a profusion of water birds are to be spotted, year round, and in the fall, migrating hawks and ospreys. The great rounded boulders off-shore in the sound are glacial erratics, and the gray bedrock visible here is the southernmost extension of the ancient bedrock which forms most of the New England coast.

Directly to the west, abutting Riverdale and Yonkers, **Van Cortlandt Park**, 718-430-1890, also contains playing fields, two golf courses, a riding stable and trails, and a historic mansion museum. Heavily used for recreation and once the site of an extensive Native American village, the Parade Ground is also home to weekend cricket competitions by largely

West Indian teams. Nearby, you can visit the Van Cortlandt Mansion and Museum, 718-543-3344, the oldest house in The Bronx (1748) and a lovely example of vernacular Georgian architecture. To the north, where the Henry Hudson Parkway crosses Broadway and slices through the park, the **Riverdale Equestrian Centre** rents horses for trail rides and offers lessons (see **Sports and Recreation**). The **Van Cortlandt Golf Course**, the oldest municipal course in the country, surrounds much of long, narrow Van Cortlandt Lake, while the **Mosholu Golf Course** lies in the southeast corner of the park (see **Sports and Recreation** for both). Birders and nature lovers seek out two popular trails: the forested **Cass Gallagher Trail** with its dramatic rock outcroppings in the northwest portion of the park, and the **John Kieran Nature Trail** in the southern portion. The latter, which skirts freshwater wetlands and the Tibbetts Brook area, esteemed by bird watchers, follows a former rail corridor, where deer, wild turkeys, and coyotes are seen occasionally, and swings down along the lake, where egrets and great blue herons are to be found. The **Urban Forest Ecology Center**, 718-548-0912, offers restrooms and information at the southern end of the Parade Ground. Urban Park Rangers offer nature walks and programs out of this facility throughout the year.

Bronx Park in the center of the north Bronx is comprised entirely of the **New York Botanical Garden** and the **International Wildlife Conservation Park** (Bronx Zoo), neither of which, properly speaking, is a park. Separated by Fordham Road and each bisected by the scenic Bronx River, they bear mentioning here because of their natural beauty, their accessibility, and their popularity. The Botanical Garden, 718-817-8700, www.nybg.org, on the north, is at once an internationally recognized botanical research facility and an extraordinary Victorian Conservatory, with gardens and educational programs on 250 acres of geologically interesting virgin forest and a variety of landscaped gardens, all accessible by pathways and tram. Two cafes and picnic areas make it possible to spend the day here. Leave the dogs home and please don't pick the daisies. Note: the Botanical Garden operates a shuttle between it and the American Museum of Natural History and the Metropolitan Museum of Art in Manhattan weekends and Monday holidays, March-November. The **Bronx Zoo**, 718-367-1010, on similar wooded terrain with rock outcroppings and wonderfully varied flora, would be a great place to spend the day even without the animals. But it is, of course, a world-class zoo, where you can wander out of the northeast woods into a rainforest, a savanna, or a Himalayan mountain enclave. Avoid holiday weekends; during warm weather parking is easier on weekdays.

Another green space that bears mention, though it is not a park at all, is **Woodlawn Cemetery**, 718-920-0500, just east of Van Cortlandt Park, between the Bronx River and Jerome Avenue. Less spectacular in terrain than Green-Wood in Brooklyn, Woodlawn is nevertheless a splendiferous array of mausoleums, memorials, and tombstones, in a richly planted, peaceful setting. Stop by the office at the Webster Avenue entrance at 233rd Street for a map and brochure. You can drive or walk around the terminal mansions of Jay Gould, the Woolworths, Herman Melville, and Fiorello ("The Little Flower") LaGuardia, whose modest tombstone bears a simply carved little flower. The cemetery is open daily, 9 a.m. to 4:30 p.m.

STATEN ISLAND

Well into the middle of the 20th century, most of Staten Island remained something of a sleepy backwater of woods, meadows, and farms. Unbridled suburban sprawl threatened to sweep that away until community action resulted in the preservation of significant chunks of remaining natural lands in the center of the island—their designation: the **Staten Island Greenbelt**. Twelve individual parks strung together by narrow corridors form the 2,500-acre greenbelt, encompassing five distinct vegetative zones and an astonishing variety of terrain. The Wisconsin glacier stopped here some 10,000 years ago, which accounts for the rocky ridges and kettle ponds. Two trails traverse the area: the 8.5-mile **Blue Trail**, running roughly east-west, and the 4-mile **White Trail**, running roughly north-south—the two cross at Bucks Hollow in Latourette Park.

One of the parks in the Greenbelt, **High Rock Park** on Todt Hill, 718-667-2165, happens to be the highest coastal point in the East south of Acadia National Park in Maine. Trails crisscross the 90-acre park, which was once a Girl Scout campground, winding in and out of woods, along the **Richmond Country Club** golf course and freshwater wetlands, and down steep slopes to glacial kettle holes. It's a bird watcher's paradise, with woodcock, indigo buntings, northern orioles, and other birds, which generally shun urban areas. From the highest point on a clear day one can see the Atlantic Ocean.

Clay Pit Ponds State Park Preserve, 718-967-1976, near the southwest shore of the island, is the only state park preserve in the city, and its 260 acres preserve a remnant of Staten Island's rural past, its bogs, meadows, ponds, sand barrens, woodlands, and swamps. Some 160 acres are designated state freshwater wetlands and unique natural areas, and as such are closed to visitors. But the remainder has much to offer. Two interesting walking trails, with bridges and boardwalks through the wet areas, are easily hiked, even for children, who will marvel at the amphibians to be glimpsed along the way: black racer snakes, box turtles, frogs, lizards, and red-backed salamanders. One trail goes through part of one of the designated natural areas. A former pasture is now a meadow full of wildflowers and butterflies. An observation platform overlooks Abraham's Pond, a former clay pit abandoned in the 1920s. Look for muskrats, red-winged blackbirds, and painted turtles here. The park is free, open daily from dawn to dusk; the headquarters and restrooms are open weekdays, 9 a.m. to 5 p.m. No dogs allowed.

And, of course, there's **Miller Field** and **Great Kills Park**, Staten Island's share of Gateway National Recreation Area described above under **Brooklyn**; call 718-351-6970.

BEACHES

It's July. It's hot. You think, "gotta get in some saltwater, stretch out on the sand, smell a salt breeze, eat a hotdog." Grab your suit, your MetroCard, and hop on the subway. New York's got it. There are city-run saltwater beaches in every borough but Manhattan, all one fare away—except for Jones Beach on Long Island, which is not a city beach but is included here because it is wonderful and many prefer it to the more crowded city beaches. If you venture to Jones or any other city beach by car on those really hot summer weekends, prepare for a significant amount of beach traffic and make sure your a/c is working. City beaches are free and parking is usually in the $3 to $5 range, unless you get lucky and find street parking.

City strands traditionally open on Memorial Day and close the day after Labor Day. Managed by national, state, and city park departments, all the beaches mentioned below are staffed by lifeguards. For information on beaches open to the general public, as opposed to residents with permits in Nassau and Suffolk counties, call the Long Island Convention & Visitors Bureau, 631-951-3440, or visit www.licvb.com/beaches_and_parks.cfm for specific beach and park information. We begin with the northernmost beach, in The Bronx, and wind up on Long Island:

- **Orchard Beach**, 718-885-3273, on a long, sandy crescent on Long Island Sound in The Bronx with all of Pelham Bay Park at its back, is exceptionally popular, so much so you'll need to get there early on weekends if you're driving. Parking can be difficult.
- **Coney Island**, 718-946-1350, www.coneyislandusa.com, Coney Island Avenue and West 8th Street, is more than just a beach, it's a state of mind and an icon. The vast sandy beach and the long boardwalk reaching from near the tip of the "island" to the Esplanade at Manhattan Beach is a scene for sure on summer weekends. You've seen the pictures, now try the beach. While you're there, don't miss the New York Aquarium, which is excellent, the Cyclone roller-coaster, and Astroland, another scene. You might also catch a Cyclones game (the Mets class "A" minor league baseball team) at Keystone Park. If nothing else, you should certainly stop by the original Nathan's for one of their world famous hotdogs.

- **Brighton Beach**, 718-946-1350, at Brighton Court and Brighton Second Street, in the heart of heavily Russian Little Odessa, makes for exotic people watching along the long, broad boardwalk. Stock up on Russian gourmet specialties and incredibly cheap produce at the stands along Brighton Beach Avenue before taking the subway home. For more about the beach and the area you can go to www.brighton beach.com.
- **Manhattan Beach**, 718-946-1373, just east of Brighton Beach off Oriental Boulevard in Brooklyn, is a forty-acre public park and beach area with parking, a sandy beach, ball-field, and concession stand; a favorite with families. Best reached by car. After a day in the water you can eat at one of Sheepshead Bay's popular restaurants and perhaps catch an outdoor concert at nearby Kingsborough Community College.
- **Jacob Riis Park**, 718-318-4300, in the Gateway National Recreation Area on the Rockaway Peninsula in Queens, has a 13,000-car parking lot, a mile of wide, sandy beach with a boardwalk, and handsome, WPA-era buildings. It is perhaps the pre-eminent city beach. Until recent years, it was the only city beach where visitors could parade about in the all-together. Now, attire is required. Besides swimming and tanning, there's handball, paddle tennis, and shuffleboard. It is here that famous Polar Bear Club members take their winter water frolics in January. Lifeguards come on duty here in mid-June.
- **Great Kills Park**, 718-987-6790, in the Gateway National Recreation Area on Staten Island's south shore, boasts miles of trails for jogging and walking, a model airplane field, athletic fields, a fishing area and marina as well as the guarded beach.
- **Jones Beach State Park**, 516-785-2420, is six and a half miles long and beautiful, well worth the drive, the bus ride from the Port Authority Bus Terminal, or the train from Penn Station to Freeport, where there's a shuttle bus to the beach. Field six, the most popular, attracts a peaceful mix of seniors, families and gays, but on summer weekends the parking lot fills up early. Field five is sheltered from waves, good for kids. West End two allows fishing and surfing and is the most peaceful. Weekend traffic on the Long Island Expressway is daunting, to say the least. Easily accessible from all five boroughs, Jones is the most popular public beach. Also here, a pitch-putt golf course, a pool, and a summer concert series at the outdoor Marine Theater featuring familiar name acts.
- **Robert Moses State Park**, Babylon, Long Island, 631- 669-047; just beyond Jones Beach, over two bridges on the Robert Moses Causeway, you'll find five more miles of beach; less well known than Jones, but along the same Atlantic Ocean. There's a per car fee and you can enjoy the beach or visit the picnic area until the sun goes down. You'll also find a pitch-putt golf course, playgrounds, a day-use boat basin and

more ... just 48 miles from Manhattan, or about 90 minutes when you factor in traffic.

For information or travel directions to any of these beaches call your preferred beach directly or the Transit Authority, 718-330-1234, for directions.

I F YOU CAME FROM A SMALL TOWN, YOU MAY HAVE GONE TO *THE* Methodist church, *the* Catholic church, or *the* synagogue. No problem. But there are an estimated 2,300 churches (not counting storefront Pentecostals) and some 650 synagogues in New York City. You'll find some, but by no means all, of them listed by denomination in the Yellow Pages. Finding a suitable church or synagogue may be as simple as that or following the suggestion of an acquaintance. Or it may be as intensely personal and complex as choosing a spouse. The houses of worship listed below alphabetically were chosen specifically for their possible appeal to newcomers. It's a place to start.

BAHÁ'Í

- **Bahá'í Faith**, 53 East 11th Street, NYC 10003, 212-674-8998, www.bahainyc.org, conducts devotions and discussion Sunday at 11 a.m.

BUDDHIST

- **New York Buddhist Church**, 331-332 Riverside Drive at 105th Street, NYC 10025, 212-678-0305, www.newyorkbuddhistchurch.org; a stunning bronze statue of Shinran-Shonin in front of this landmarked building marks the presence of this Shin Buddhist Temple. Regular Dharma service in English at 11:30 a.m. Sunday is occasionally preceded by a service in Japanese. In addition, there are regularly scheduled Dharma study classes for adults and for children, meditation sessions, and other classes offered in various subjects.
- **Soka Gakkai International—USA**, 7 East 15th Street, NYC 10003, 212-727-7715, www.sgiusa.org; with lectures, discussions, and group chants for some 5,000 area members who practice the Buddhism of

Nichiren Daishonin. It's a warm and accepting community in a harmonious Romanesque Revival building.

CHRISTIAN

ROMAN CATHOLIC CHURCHES

Most Catholics attend Mass near their home or office. But there are a few churches, which, for one reason or another, attract worshipers from beyond the parish confines. One of these may suit you. Contact the **Archdiocese of New York**, 212-371-1000, or the **Archdiocese of Brooklyn** (also handles Queens), 718-399-5900, for your local parish. Or go to www.ny-archdiocese.org.

- **Cathedral-Basilica of St. James**, 230 Cathedral Place (at Jay Street near Tillary Street), Brooklyn Heights 11201, 718-852-4002, was built in 1822 and restored in recent years to a Georgian brick elegance befitting its prominence. St. James is Brooklyn's cathedral, a bishop's church, but it is also a non-territorial parish, and is especially popular among young professionals in the area, for whom the daily business communion at 12:10 is a special convenience. Mass here is traditional, and the music quite wonderful.
- **Church of the Epiphany**, 239 East 21st Street (Second Avenue and 22nd Street), NYC 10010, 212-475-1966, is at once striking and modest, an unusually successful modern structure of rounded verticals in brown brick. It's a family church, with a traditional Mass at 11:15 a.m. and a popular family mass to guitar accompaniment at 10 a.m. But there's a difference, for one thing, altar girls. Nuns are involved in work traditionally done by priests, and women's issues are addressed. The church is popular with young professionals in the community, and there is a social action group.
- **Church of St. Agnes**, 141 East 43rd Street at Lexington Avenue, NYC 10017, 212-682-5722, is convenient to Grand Central Station and offers multiple daily masses including a Latin Mass, Sundays at 11 a.m. (Latin Mass is also performed at St. Ann's Armenian Catholic Cathedral at 110 East 12th Street, 212-477-2030.)
- **Church of St. Thomas More**, 65 East 89th Street between Park and Lexington avenues, NYC 10028, 212-876-7718; stone Victorian Gothic, was built as an Episcopal Church and still feels a bit like one, with its intimately peaceful, fragrant interior beneath a timbered ceiling. Ever so decorous. You can linger for coffee after 10 o'clock Mass.
- **Holy Trinity Chapel**, 58 Washington Square South, NYC 10012, 212-674-7236, is the Catholic chapel at New York University, but its congre-

gants are by no means all students. A moderately liberal intellectual approach and active social life attract a committed band of Catholics from the surrounding Village and beyond to this modest but appealing modern brick structure. An active outreach program includes tutoring, a soup kitchen, and providing other neighborhood services. There are sessions of silent Christian meditation.

- **St. Francis Xavier**, 46 West 16th Street, NYC 10011, 212-627-2100; this hulking, gray stone Jesuit presence dominates the block between Fifth and Sixth avenues. The style here is rather less formal than you might expect, perhaps because the congregation covers such a broad social spectrum: Hispanics, knowledgeable Catholic activists, and young professionals. Actively involved in the community, the church shelters the homeless and serves 800 meals a week. It's equally busy on the spiritual front, with lay spirituality group retreats, healing Masses, and discussion groups for a fiercely devoted following.
- **St. Ignatius Loyola**, Park Avenue at 84th Street, NYC 10028, 212-288-3588; this solidly limestone Italian Baroque structure is definitely high church and upscale: incense, ornate vestments, and a fine professional choir at the traditionally sung morning High Mass. But the rigorous Jesuit approach is apparent in a strongly social and economic outlook from the pulpit. At 11 a.m. you can attend a folk Mass in the undercroft (Wallace Hall) and linger over coffee. The church is also known for its series of formal musical programs featuring the fine choir and organist as well as visiting musicians. Contemporary music Sundays at 7:30 p.m.
- **St. John the Baptist**, 210 West 31st Street, NYC 10001, 212-564-9070, as a distinct sideline to its normal parish activities, is host to the Catholic charismatic movement in Manhattan. There are seminars, prayer meetings, and a monthly charismatic Mass.
- **St. Joseph's**, 371 Avenue of the Americas at Washington Place, NYC 10014, 212-741-1274; in the heart of Greenwich Village, appeals to a variety of Catholics in the neighborhood and even outside the city. At once a bustling family church and an aesthetic experience, with professional musicians performing at traditional Masses and at evening concerts; distinctly high church. The lovely stone and stucco Greek Revival structure, resplendent inside with creamy plaster, crystal chandeliers and wide, carved balconies, is the oldest Catholic Church in the city (1833), and the first to open a shelter for homeless men.
- **St. Patrick's Cathedral**, 14 East 51st Street, NYC 10022, 212-753-2261, www.ny-archdiocese.org; this looming Gothic-style cathedral is the seat of the Archbishop of New York.

GREEK ORTHODOX CHURCHES

- **Cathedral of the Holy Trinity**, 319 East 74th Street, NYC 10021, 212-288-3215, www.thecathedral.goarch.org; tucked away between the modern buildings on the Upper East Side of Manhattan, this church has stood since the 1890s when it was originally built as a Protestant church. Today the church includes a full parochial school program, nursery through eighth grade, as well as afternoon language classes and Sunday school classes. Cultural and human services programs can also be found.
- **St. Demetrios' Cathedral**, 31st Street and 30th Drive, Astoria, Queens 11105, 718-728-1718; just over the Queensborough Bridge from Manhattan stand two expansive cathedrals that help serve the city's largest Greek Orthodox community, St. Demetrios' and St. Irene's. The more majestic of the two, St Demetrios' was built in 1927 and features the architectural stylings of the Byzantine cathedrals of Athens. Adult Greek language courses and Sunday school classes are offered.
- **St. Irene of Chrysovalantou**, 36-07 23rd Avenue, Astoria, Queens 11105, 718-626-6225; newer, and slightly larger than nearby St. Demetrios, St. Irene's is a large converted Protestant church with a grand and elaborate interior design. A full complement of elementary and junior high school programs is offered, plus many youth and teen activities. A day care center is also available weekdays from 9 a.m. to 5 p.m.

PROTESTANT CHURCHES

BAPTIST
- **Calvary Baptist Church**, 123 West 57th Street between Sixth and Seventh avenues, NYC 10019, 212-975-0170, www.cbcnyc.org, across from Carnegie Hall, is probably the largest Baptist Church in Manhattan. You might begin a typical Sunday at the 9:30 contemporary praise and worship service, followed by a Young Professionals' topical Bible study and fellowship at 11 a.m., and then coffee. Traditional worship service is at 11 a.m. Young Adult Ministries offers occasional weekend retreats, and there are outreach programs to the prison population, the poor, and welfare hotel children.

EPISCOPAL
- **Cathedral of St. John the Divine**, 1047 Amsterdam Avenue at 112th Street, NYC 10025, 212-316-7540, www.stjohndivine.org, dwarfs its surroundings even as it awaits the (hopeful) completion of its stone towers. One of the largest cathedrals in the world, at once

Byzantine, Romanesque, and Gothic, it is truly awesome, especially inside, where spectacular stained glass windows light the vast dark vaults and music echoes ethereally. It is also a bustling and exciting community church, a leader in the movement to feed and house the poor. And the performing arts flourish here almost around the clock. Don't miss the blessing of the animals on the first Sunday of October in honor of St. Francis.

- **Church of the Ascension**, 36 Fifth Avenue at 10th Street, NYC 10011, 212-254-8620; its communicants find this church especially pleasing aesthetically. A LaFarge altar fresco and a St. Gaudens altar relief enliven the quietly tasteful interior, and liturgical music of the highest quality in special evening concerts are a welcome treat.

- **Church of the Heavenly Rest**, 2 East 90th Street at Fifth Avenue, NYC 10128, 212-289-3400, sits confidently but un-ostentatiously—stripped contemporary Gothic in pale gray stone—facing Central Park. It's an upscale, neighborhood family church, where the congregants stay for coffee after the morning service while the children play decorously about the door.

- **Grace Church**, 802 Broadway at East 10th Street, NYC 10003, 212-254-2000, www.gracechurchnyc.org, despite its rather patrician, lacy English Gothic elegance, is relatively low church. Worship is traditional, however, with wonderful music, especially on holy days. The congregation runs to young families and a variety of students and artists. Pastoral counseling is available as well as adult classes on a variety of topics. Also: outreach groups to college students and victims of HIV/AIDS, programs for children and families, and a thrice-yearly Alpha Course, which is a 10-week introduction to Christianity.

- **St. Bartholomew's**, Park Avenue at 51st Street, NYC 10022, 212-378-0200, this landmarked Romanesque-Byzantine church houses a friendly, welcoming community numbering about 1,000 worshipers each Sunday. Lay participation in all aspects of church life is encouraged. Sundays feature a stimulating Rector's Forum and Sunday School, in addition to several services, and Bible studies are offered during the week. Several adult social clubs offer a variety of social, athletic and theatrical activities. Communicants and non-members alike volunteer at the homeless shelter and the feeding program operated by the church.

- **St. James'**, 865 Madison Avenue at 71st Street, NYC 10021, 212-774-4200; distinctly Upper East Side, this trim brownstone is a warm, neighborhood family church which is also decidedly activist in the community and beyond: feeding, mentoring, supporting, and sometimes even demonstrating. Despite its rather liberal bent, St. James' is moderately high church. Its education programs for adults and children are worthy of note.

- **Trinity Church**, 74 Trinity Place, NYC 10006, 212-602-0800, www. trinitywallstreet.org; this Neo-Gothic church dominated New York's skyline when it was finished in 1846. Now a bit more tucked away, it offers a peaceful respite to bustling lower Manhattan. Daily services, community outreach, and fellowship are all part of Trinity's ministry.

INTERDENOMINATIONAL

- **Judson Memorial** (Baptist-United Church of Christ), 55 Washington Square South, NYC 10012, 212-477-0351; worldly young adults and seminarians are attracted to this ornate Romanesque church designed by Stanford White and its fairly traditional Protestant liturgy with progressive elements, including a monthly Agape Meal. There is a consumer health library and support for AIDS victims.
- **Riverside**, 490 Riverside Drive at 120th Street, NYC 10027, 212-870-6700, www.theriversidechurchny.org; this towering Gothic gift of John D. Rockefeller, Jr. dominates the heights overlooking the Hudson River. Inspired by Chartres, it boasts spectacular stained glass and beautifully carved stone in the large but simple nave and chancel and about the entrance. Activist concerns under the leadership of the Rev. Dr. James A. Forbes, Jr. are dizzying, as are the opportunities for involvement in activities musical, intellectual and social, not to mention spiritual.
- **Chelsea Community Church**, 346 West 20th Street, NYC 10011, 212-886-5463, is a non-denominational Christian church welcoming "persons of all faiths and of uncertain faith" at its lay-led Sunday services at 11:45 a.m. in historic St. Peter's Church.

LATTER-DAY SAINTS/MORMON

- **The Church of Jesus Christ of Latter-Day Saints**; in Manhattan, the newly renovated Mormon temple is located at 125 Columbus Avenue at 65th Street (across from Lincoln Center), 917-441-8220, www.lds.org; several different congregations (called "wards" and "branches") conduct worship services every Sunday in three-hour blocks, beginning at 9 a.m. These include English-speaking "family" wards, an English-speaking ward for single adults, Spanish-speaking wards, and a deaf branch. Also, each congregation offers social and musical activities during the week.

LUTHERAN

- **Holy Trinity**, Central Park at 3 West 65th Street, NYC 10023, 212-877-6815, www.holytrinitynyc.org; offers challenging preaching at traditional, rigorously Lutheran services. But it is music, at the regular services and at the Sunday vespers, featuring Bach cantatas with professional musicians for which Holy Trinity is widely known (go to www.bachvespersnyc.org for more information). The sturdy Gothic Revival church is the setting for frequent evening concerts as well.

- **St. Peter's**, 619 Lexington Avenue at 54th Street, NYC 10022, 212-935-2200, www.stpeters.org, nestles, sleek and angular like a modern stone tent, beneath the towering Citicorp Center. A large Louise Nevelson sculpture punctuates the stark, light interior, scene of a sung Mass with traditional liturgy in the morning and Jazz Vespers with jazz as the sermon Sunday afternoons. Classical and jazz concerts, often free, theater, and provocative adult-forum lectures attract an ecumenical following, to say the least.

METHODIST

- **Christ Church**, 520 Park Avenue at 60th Street, NYC 10021, 212-838-3036, is sedately Byzantine outside, dazzlingly so inside, every inch covered with mosaics in blazing blues, greens and gold. It's a wonderful setting for the religious music-dramas occasionally performed here. The congregation, though relatively small, supports a weekly soup kitchen and excellent pastoral counseling.
- **John Street**, 44 John Street between Nassau and William Street, NYC 10038, 212-269-0014; to step into this landmarked little Italianate brownstone church (1841) among the towering monoliths of the financial district is to step out of place and time into a peaceful haven of creamy modest proportions and brass sconces. It's the oldest Methodist society in the US, and few know about it. Inquire about the occasional Wednesday noon hymn-sings.
- **Park Avenue**, 106 East 86th Street, NYC 10028, 212-427-5421, www.parkavemethodist.org; a mixed and growing congregation, mostly young families and singles, is attracted by the moderately liberal approach and active social scene at this smallish, restfully intimate, Moorish-looking church. Adult Bible study precedes and a coffee hour follows the traditional Sunday service with volunteer choir.

PRESBYTERIAN

- **Brick Church**, 62 East 92nd Street, between Park and Madison, NYC 10128, 212-289-4400, www.brickchurch.org; staid neo-Georgian with a rather ornate interior, is distinctly Park Avenue. But the welcome is friendly, including a popular coffee hour after the Sunday service. The church's day school is prestigious.
- **Fifth Avenue**, 7 West 55th Street, NYC 10019, 212-247-0490, www.fapc.org; the city's largest Presbyterian Church has a warm, woody interior behind its otherwise undistinguished brownstone facade. A variety of social fellowship groups attract large numbers to the traditional services. Activities of these groups may include Sunday

night church suppers, after-church brunch, movies, and ski retreats, as well as dinner meetings with outside speakers at the Women's Roundtable for business women and the Men's Fellowship. Also here, a Center for Christian Studies. Fees are minimal and non-members are welcome.

- **Madison Avenue**, 921 Madison Avenue at 73rd Street, NYC 10021, 212-288-8920, www.mapc.com, has a cozy, Scottish feel, with its Gothic-timbered white walls, carved pews and galleries. The music program is strong, including a volunteer choir and frequent Sunday afternoon concerts. You'll also find an adult education program and young adult fellowship group that meets for Bible study, discussion, and socializing.
- **Redeemer**, church office at 271 Madison Avenue, Suite 1600, NYC 10016, 212-808-4460; this recently organized and rapidly growing congregation holds three Sunday services in the Hunter College Auditorium, 69th Street between Park and Lexington avenues. The scripture-based emphasis is on preaching, which is intellectually engaging, and there is an array of spiritual, social, and outreach activities.

UNITARIAN

- **All Souls**, 1157 Lexington Avenue at 80th Street, NYC 10021, 212-535-5530, www.allsoulsnyc.org; New England simple and elegant, from 1891, this Federal-style brick church looks Unitarian. As might be expected here, the busy church calendar tends toward activism on a variety of fronts including running a soup kitchen and tutoring children. A fairly intellectual approach to adult education features book groups, films, and lectures. Music is stressed. Social activities are many and varied, including a Career Networking Group.

ETHICAL SOCIETIES

Ethical societies offer a meeting place and fellowship to members and visitors. Their "focus is on core ethical values that people have in common." Acknowledging that humans are both individualistic and social in nature, the society explores what it means to understand the inner workings of self and how to relate to each other in a respectful/ethical/moralistic way. For more information go to www.ethicalsociety.org.

- **Brooklyn Society for Ethical Culture**, 53 Prospect Park West, Brooklyn 11215, 718-768-2972, www.bsec.org
- **New York Society for Ethical Culture**, 2 West 64th Street, NYC 10023, 212-874-5210, www.nysec.org
- **Riverdale-Yonkers Society for Ethical Culture**, 4450 Fieldston Road, The Bronx 10471, 718-548-4445, www.ethicsny.org

HINDU

- **Ramakrishna Vivekananda Center**, 17 East 94th Street, NYC 10128, 212-534-9445, www.ramakrishna.org, is a Vedanta Hindu Temple of universal worship with a Sunday lecture service at 11 a.m. Tuesday evenings at 8 are devoted to the reading and discussion of the gospel of Sri Ramakrishna.
- **Vedanta Society**, 34 West 71st Street, NYC 10023, 212-877-9197, www.vedanta-newyork.org, is affiliated with the Ramakrishna Math and Mission in India. The shrine room is open for meditation daily from 9 a.m. to 6 p.m. There is a lecture Sunday at 11 a.m. and classes Tuesday and Friday evenings.

ISLAM

MOSQUES

- **The Mosque of New York**, in the Islamic Cultural Center, 1711 Third Avenue, NYC 10029, 212-722-5234; this imposing structure, the gift of a group of Islamic countries, houses the largest of some 80 mosques in the city. The design is modern, with numerous references to traditional elements of Muslim architecture. The effect is at once peaceful and spiritual. In addition to the weekly congregational prayer service, the Mosque is open for daily prayer at the five prescribed times. There are classes for children and adults, which cover a range of Islamic topics. There are Saturday classes for women only.
- **The Muslim Center of New York**, 137-58 Geranium Avenue off Kissena Boulevard, Flushing, NY 11355, 718-460-3000, serves the growing Muslim community in Queens and Long Island. In a modest neighborhood an octagonal minaret rises from the polished rose quartz structure. Congregational prayers Friday at 1:15 p.m. are followed by Koranic studies. There is a Sunday school and afternoon religious school for children weekdays. Call for hours.

JEWISH

REFORM SYNAGOGUES

- **Brooklyn Heights Synagogue**, 131 Remsen Street, Brooklyn 11201, 718-522-2070, www.bhsbrooklyn.org, moved up the street from its brownstone home of 20 years to the larger brownstone formerly housing the Brooklyn Club, in order to accommodate its after-school religious school for children and extensive adult education classes.

Preschool is also now available. Services here are characterized by a greater use of Hebrew and more congregational singing than is generally found in reform synagogues. The warmth and friendliness of this relatively small congregation and their purposeful inclusiveness makes this a particularly appealing synagogue for newcomers. Congregants come from all the boroughs; numbers swell sufficiently on the high holy days that these services are held in a church nearby.

- **Central**, 123 East 55th Street, NYC 10022, 212-838-5122, is the oldest Jewish house of worship (1872) in continuous use in New York. The Moorish brownstone structure with its interior richly stenciled in red, blue, and gold suffered extensive damage from a fire in 1998. While restoration proceeded, services were held across the street in the Community House Beir Chapel. Services resumed in the reconstructed synagogue in the fall of 2001. Traditional in orientation and ritual, the temple tends to the manifold interests, worldly as well as spiritual, of its 1,400-member congregation in groups and classes ranging from Hebrew and Yiddish to Bible to bridge, teens' and singles' groups. Hebrew school.
- **Temple Emanu-El**, 1 East 65th Street, corner of Fifth Avenue, NYC 10021, 212-744-1400, is perhaps a little less traditional, nevertheless classical Reform in approach, and it is the largest reform temple in the US, with over 3,000 members. The landmarked limestone Moorish-Romanesque temple facing Central Park seats 2,500 beneath a high, colorfully painted wood ceiling and stunning stained glass windows. The temple has a large staff to run its many facilities, classes and community outreach programs, as well as a large religious school. Services are broadcast every Friday evening at 5:30 over WQXR (96.3 FM).

CONSERVATIVE SYNAGOGUES

- **Ansche Chesed**, 251 West 100th Street at West End Avenue, NYC 10025, 212-865-9588, www.anschechesed.org, houses four separate congregations, each with a different approach to Conservative Judaism, in one medium-sized, squat, brick building. Alternatives within a framework of Jewish tradition are stressed at this much-talked-about West Side synagogue, which offers an adult beginners' service, courses on a wide range of Jewish topics, and social action projects.
- **Baith Israel Anschei Emes/Kane Street**, 236 Kane Street at Tompkins Place in Cobble Hill, Brooklyn 11231, 718-875-1550, has grown considerably in recent years, partly, perhaps, because of the emphasis on egalitarianism in its observances. Vibrant and involved, with challenging study groups, it is regularly packed with congregants, mainly young, from Cobble Hill and nearby Brooklyn Heights.

- **B'Nai Jeshurun**, 257 West 88th Street between Broadway and West End Avenue, NYC 10024, 212-787-7600; under the charismatic leadership of the late Rabbi Marshall Meyer, "BJ," as it is affectionately known, burst its ornately Byzantine/Romanesque seams. Emphasis is on study, with a variety of adult courses and lectures as well as a Hebrew school for children. And the diverse congregation thinks of itself as a community, with a strong commitment to social action, *Tikkun Olam*, in the wider Jewish and non-Jewish community beyond. Plan to come early for services, which tend to fill up fast; non-members will want to call about high holy days.
- **Brotherhood**, 28 Gramercy Park South, on East 20th Street, 10003, 212-674-5750, occupies a landmarked (1859) Friends' Meeting House, starkly beautiful in Italianate brownstone and overlooking lovely Gramercy Park. About its courtyards are housed a shelter for the homeless, a religious school, adult education and an educational program for the developmentally disabled.
- **Park Avenue**, 50 East 87th Street at Madison Avenue, NYC 10128, 212-369-2600, is the city's largest Conservative temple and an East Side Moorish landmark in carved golden stone. The rich interior boasts fine stained glass, sculpture, and paintings, and the traditional services are distinctly formal, with organ and choir. There are programs for children and a food pantry for the neighborhood's hungry.
- **Shaare Zedek**, 212 West 93rd Street between Broadway and Amsterdam Avenue, NYC 10025, 212-874-7005; this congregation, founded 160 years ago on the Lower East Side and housed now in a gray stone Greek Revival temple, has experienced a revival in the mid-1990s with an infusion of college students and young professionals. Friday evening services, usually downstairs in the social halls, can be especially busy. Special events fill out the social calendar.
- **Tifereth Israel/Town and Village**, 334 East 14th Street between First and Second avenues, NYC 10003, 212-677-8090, stresses sexual egalitarianism in its informally innovative, traditional services and attracts an involved family congregation, largely from the adjacent community, including Stuyvesant Town and Peter Cooper Village. Adult education and a young married group are both popular. The Sol Goldman YW-YMHA of the Educational Alliance next door, with whom it shares a Hebrew school, offers members the advantages of a social center with pool, gym, and classes.
- **United Synagogue of Hoboken**, 115 Park Avenue, Hoboken, NJ 07030, 201-659-4000, www.hobokensynagogue.org; Friday evening and Sabbath services are in the converted Victorian brownstone Hudson Street temple, the last of many serving the predominantly German Jewish community here at the turn of the century. The small

but growing egalitarian congregation is youngish and welcoming. Extensive adult education courses include Hebrew reading and Jewish history, a Hebrew discussion group, a book club, Jewish women's and men's discussion groups, karate, adult bar and bat mitzvah instruction. There is also a Hebrew School for children.

ORTHODOX SYNAGOGUES

- **Civic Center**, 49 White Street, west of Broadway, NYC 10013, 212-966-7141, occupies a small, award-winning, modern structure scrunched among cast iron manufacturing lofts and loading docks. Its flame-shaped interior houses a membership of about 100 families with about 1,000 supporters, including elderly members of long standing as well as artists and young professionals from surrounding Tribeca, Independence Plaza, and Battery Park. There are both Hebrew and adult education classes, as well as parenting sessions conducted by Educational Alliance West.
- **Kehilath Jeshurun**, 125 East 85th Street between Lexington and Park Avenues, NYC 10028, 212-774-8000; though old and rich and housed in classical Romanesque gray stone, this is probably the most progressive of the Orthodox congregations. Its size makes possible a host of activities for singles, couples, and children, recreational facilities, and an educational program including the Ramaz School. Emphasis is placed on outreach to beginners and singles, with classes, special services, and Friday night dinners for them.
- **Lincoln Square**, 200 Amsterdam Avenue at 69th Street, NYC 10023, 212-874-6100, www.lss.org, sometimes referred to as "the hip synagogue," might be described physically as synagogue-modern. Its nickname and popularity among the young professionals who pack four Saturday services is due in large part to the charm and zealous outreach efforts of Rabbi Ephraim Buchwald, who hosts the 9:15 "Learners' Minyan," which is followed by wine and cookies and, if you like, lunch with an experienced family. There are courses at all levels on Jewish law and thought as well as singles and youth groups.
- **Shearith Israel**, 8 West 70th Street at Central Park West, NYC 10023, 212-873-0300, known as the Spanish and Portuguese synagogue, is the oldest Jewish congregation in the US, dating from 1655, when a group of Sephardic Jews arrived from Brazil. In the formal sanctuary scholarly rabbis conduct formal services, which offer the best opportunity to observe Sephardic tradition and music. Excellent adult education explores Sephardic and Ashkenazic culture and tradition, with visiting scholars leading seminars. There are special educational and social events for young adults.

OTHER

- **Congregation Beth Simchat Torah**, 57 Bethune Street in the Westbeth complex, NYC 10014, 212-929-9498; with some 800 members the largest gay and lesbian Jewish congregation in the world, celebrated its 25th anniversary in 1999. The rabbi is Reconstructionist, the community liberal, and the services traditional, with egalitarian minyans rotating between traditional, liberal, tot shabbat, junior congregation, family minyan, and Hebrew egalitarian; Saturdays at 10 a.m. Friday evening services are so heavily attended the congregation moves to the Church of the Holy Apostles on Ninth Avenue at 28th Street.
- **Society for the Advancement of Judaism**, 15 West 86th Street off Central Park West, NYC 10024, 212-724-7000, www.thesaj.org; known as the SAJ, this is the original Reconstructionist synagogue. Reconstructionism, which attempts to reconcile traditional Conservatism with modern life, views Judaism as evolving rather than divinely inspired. The Torah is observed, and services are largely traditional but egalitarian. The approach here is distinctly intellectual, not social.
- **West End Synagogue**, 190 Amsterdam Avenue at 69th Street, NYC 10023, 212-579-0777, is a popular Reconstructionist congregation flourishing with a slightly more emotional, interpersonal emphasis and monthly Shabbat dinners as well as concerts, debates, and social action programs. Also a Hebrew school.
- **Young Israel of Fifth Avenue**, 3 West 16th Street at Fifth Avenue, NYC 10011, 212-255-4826, is one of three such temples in Manhattan. Young Israel can be defined as modern Orthodoxy, observing all the Orthodox forms, including separate seating of the sexes, but emphasizing programs serving the entire family. This includes communal singing and participation, youth and singles programs, outreach, adult education, and attention to community needs.

DESPITE THE CITY'S RAPID PACE AND ANONYMITY, OR PERHAPS because of it, New Yorkers by the thousands volunteer their services to hundreds of worthy causes. Motivations are as varied as the tasks. So are the rewards.

A mind-boggling array of public, private, and non-profit organizations will gladly put to use whatever talents or interests you have. Experience is not necessarily required; most institutions provide training. What kinds of jobs are available where? Read on. We've also listed the names of agencies that refer volunteers to other organizations and included a few alternative suggestions as well.

HOW YOU CAN HELP

THE HUNGRY AND THE HOMELESS

Scores of volunteers concern themselves with shelter for the city's homeless. Jobs include: monitoring and organizing the shelters, providing legal help, ministering to psychiatric, medical, and social needs, raising money, manning phones, and caring for children in the shelters. Many people solicit, organize, cook, and serve food to the destitute at sites throughout the city. Still others deliver meals to the homeless and the homebound.

CHILDREN

If involvement with children is especially appealing you can: tutor in and out of schools, be a big brother or sister, teach music and sports in shelters or at local community centers, run activities in the parks, entertain children in hospitals, and accompany kids on weekend outings. Schools, libraries, community associations, hospitals, and other facilities providing activities and guidance for children are all worth exploring.

HOSPITALS

The need for volunteers in both city-run and private hospitals is manifold: from interpreters to laboratory personnel to admitting and nursing aides, many volunteers are required. Assistants in crisis medical areas—emergency rooms, intensive care units, and the like—are wanted if you have the skills, as are volunteers to work with victims of sexual abuse. If you just want to be helpful, you might assist in food delivery or work in the gift shop. Most city hospitals are large and busy, and many are in need of help.

THE DISABLED AND THE ELDERLY

You can read to the blind, help teach the deaf, work to prevent birth defects, help the retarded and developmentally disabled, among others. You can also make regular visits to the homebound elderly, bring hot meals to their homes, and teach everything from nutrition to arts and crafts in senior centers and nursing homes.

EXTREME CARE SITUATIONS

Helping with suicide prevention, Alzheimer's and AIDS patients, rape victims, and abused children is a special category demanding a high level of commitment—not to mention emotional reserves and, in many cases, special skills.

THE CULTURE SCENE

There are museums all over the city in need of volunteers to lead tours or lend a hand in any number of ways. Libraries, theater groups, and ballet companies have plenty of tasks that need to be done. Fundraising efforts also require many volunteers to stuff envelopes and/or make phone calls. The Public Broadcasting Service (PBS) is a good example. Their large volunteer staff raises money for their stations through extensive on-air fundraising campaigns that include collecting pledges.

THE COMMUNITY

Work in your neighborhood. Block associations and community gardens are run strictly by volunteers. You can help out at the local school, nursing home, settlement house, or animal shelter.

WHERE YOU CAN HELP

SPECIFIC-NEED ORGANIZATIONS

The organizations in New York City that address a major disease, disability, or social problems are legion. For example, there's the Memorial Sloan-Kettering Cancer Center, The Coalition for the Homeless, Volunteer Services for Children, New York Association for the Blind (The Lighthouse), Literacy Volunteers of New York, Volunteers in the Schools, the Gay Men's Health Alliance, Women in Need, and City Harvest, which collects and distributes food to the hungry.

INSTITUTIONS

New York's health, education and, some would say, its very civilization rest upon the city's institutions. Hospitals, museums, libraries, schools, animal shelters, opera and ballet companies are mostly under-funded and rely on a veritable army of volunteers to survive.

THE RELIGIOUS CONNECTION

Individual churches and synagogues (in particular, those serving the homeless and the needy), and church federations such as the Federation of Protestant Welfare Agencies, the Catholic Charities, Lutheran Social Services, and the UJA-Federation of Jewish Philanthropies use volunteers for a variety of activities.

THE COMMUNITY

More than 5,000 block associations and neighborhood-wide organizations, such as Greenwich House in the Village and Yorkville's Civic Council, can use your talents. Citywide there is a need for volunteers in the schools, parks, shelters, and in consumer affairs. The Natural Resources Defense Council, located in New York, www.nrdc.org, is a national organization dedicated to improving city centers and deterring urban sprawl.

MULTI-SERVICE ORGANIZATIONS

Don't forget such well-known groups as the Salvation Army, American Red Cross, March of Dimes, United Way, and Visiting Nurse Service (you don't have to be a nurse).

THE CORPORATE CONNECTION

Corporations encourage employee voluntarism through company-supported projects such as literacy programs, pro-bono work, and management aid to non-profit groups. Check with the company personnel or public relations department to see if your firm is involved in any specific project. Many corporations have set up programs with the United Way.

REFERRAL SERVICES

If you don't know which way to turn, try one of several umbrella organizations that find volunteers for affiliated agencies. At these referral services, staff members will help you determine the tasks you would be interested in doing, where and when. Your interviewer will make specific suggestions and appointments at the places that sound appealing. Interview at several sites if you wish, and return to the referral agency until you find something you want to undertake.

- **Catholic Charities of New York**, 1011 First Avenue, 212-371-1000, www.archny.org; are affiliated with more than 100 different agencies dealing with shelters, food kitchens, and the homeless. An interview may be requested.
- **The Federation of Protestant Welfare Agencies**, 281 Park Avenue South, 212-777-4800, open 8:30 a.m. to 5 p.m., Monday-Friday; this ecumenical group, with connections to hundreds of agencies in the metropolitan area, finds jobs for volunteers of any religious persuasion.
- **The Mayor's Voluntary Action Center**, 1 Centre Street, NYC 10007, 12th floor, 212-788-7550, www.nyc.gov/volunteer; the center's mission: "to bridge individuals, corporations, government agencies, and non-profit organizations in order to connect people with meaningful volunteer opportunities that significantly improve the quality of life in New York City." This enormous clearing-house can place just about anyone in a useful job, especially in the human services, educational, and cultural areas.
- **New York Cares**, 214 West 29th Street, 5th floor Street, NYC 10001, 212-228-5000, www.ny.cares.org, is a favorite volunteer organization among busy young professionals who are discouraged by the time commitments required by other organizations. New York Cares lets its 8,000 volunteers choose from a monthly calendar of events set up with the more than fifty not-for-profit organizations they serve. These projects include reading with homeless children, serving brunch at soup kitchens, cleaning public parks, and visiting elderly homebound. Call to attend one of three weekly orientation meetings.

- **The United Jewish Appeal-Federation of Jewish Philanthropies**, 130 East 59th Street, NYC 10022, 212-980-1000, www.ujafedny.org; the Jewish Information Referral Service helps match volunteers with one of many volunteer projects. Programs include revitalizing old neighborhoods and synagogues as well as working with children, immigrants, the elderly, and the homeless.
- **The Volunteer Referral Center**, 161 Madison Avenue, NYC 10016, 212-889-4805, www.volunteer-referral.com; interviews by appointment. The center places adult and student volunteers at some 250 not-for-profit agencies throughout the city.

OTHER CONNECTIONS

- **Check bulletin boards** at your office, church, neighborhood grocery store, Laundromat, and school.
- Walk into local **churches**, **temples**, **community organizations,** and/or **libraries**.
- The **Yellow Pages**, under "Social and Human Services," contains more than five pages of organizations and institutions—in categories from "Abortion Alternatives Counseling" to "Youth Services"—many of which welcome volunteers. It's a great source of ideas, as well as a tool for follow-through.
- **www.volunteermatch.org**, offers a searchable database of volunteer options.

GETTING AROUND

BY SUBWAY

The subway is the quickest way to get around New York City. All city subway lines are administered by the Metropolitan Transit Authority (MTA), and the occasional scary story aside, subway crime is down, the graffiti plague has been all but eradicated, and many stations have been handsomely renovated. In 1999, commuters welcomed the opening of Grand Central North, an underground extension from Manhattan's Grand Central Terminal, which allows commuters to enter and exit as far north as 48th Street. In fact, Grand Central is once again an elegant destination in itself, with fine dining, boutique shopping, and gourmet food shops worth a detour.

The tragic events of September 11th, 2001 brought a major blow to the subway lines of lower Manhattan and to the PATH trains to New Jersey. It took nearly a year, but workers were able to remove the rubble and reconstruct the tunnel that services the number one and number nine subway trains. In 2002, sections of track between Chambers and Rector streets were reopened allowing the number two and number three trains to resume their normal downtown service, and the station at Ground Zero is now up and running.

For train information, call MTA at 718-330-1234 or stop by one of the Port Authority's information booths at Penn Station or Grand Central Station. Open from 7 a.m. to 11 p.m., the booths provide subway and bus maps for all five boroughs. The Metropolitan Transit Authority web site, www.mta.info, offers a complete subway map as well as information on local bridges, tunnels, fares, and service.

As of 2003, subway/bus tokens are no longer used for any public transit system. In their place is the **MetroCard**. The card, available at vending machines (accepting credit and debit cards) in subway stations, is to be used on all subway lines and on all city buses (though cash in the form of coins may still be used on buses). At press time, two MetroCard options were available at the following prices (recent news reports indicate a fare increase is likely). The pay per ride card works like a debit card, when the card is empty you deposit more money (putting $20 on your card gets you two free rides). A single ride is $2 ($4 for express buses). To use, swipe the card through the turnstile slot, and one fare is subtracted. The other option is the unlimited usage pass: one-day, weekly, or monthly. A one-day pass is $7, the seven-day pass is $21, and a 30-day MetroCard is $70—good if you ride the subway frequently. Because passes are sold in monthly increments, lines at the stations to buy MetroCards are long on the first and last days of the month. Seniors and people with disabilities are eligible for half-fare cards. Reduced fare information is available at 718-243-4999. Children under 44 inches in height travel free. School children are issued free passes if they attend a public or private school that is a specified distance from their home. Two-zone transfers means riders with the MetroCard can move from subway to a bus (and vice versa) without paying another fare, although this is only applicable in certain areas. For general MetroCard information call 212-METRO-CARD.

Subway trains operate 24-hours a day, but service slows appreciably after 11 p.m. At night, wait for trains near the subway booth or the turnstiles where transit cops seem to hang out. Be alert on subways or platforms and never leave personal items unattended.

For your immediate reference, we have provided a subway map at the back of this book. You can order a bus or subway map by calling the MTA customer assistance line at 718-330-3322, 9 a.m. to 5 p.m., weekdays.

BY PATH

The PATH (for Port Authority Trans-Hudson) tubes provide clean and efficient service connecting Manhattan with Hoboken, Jersey City, and Newark for $1.50 around the clock. Trains leaving 33rd Street at Avenue of the Americas (Sixth Avenue) go to Hoboken or Jersey City, with stops along the way at 23rd, 14th, 9th and Christopher streets. Schedules are available in most stations, or call 800-234-7284.

BY BUS

Independent bus lines found mainly in boroughs other than Manhattan co-exist with those run by the MTA. Call 718-330-1234 for Transit Authority information as well as telephone numbers for the independents. Also, you can now get up-to-date transit information on the MTA web site:

www.mta.info. Maps are sometimes available from drivers but are always stocked at the information booths mentioned under **Subways** above. Buses cost $2 (express buses are $4). Transfers to other buses are free. Use the MetroCard or exact change.

For bus service in Queens, contact **Queens Surface** at 28th Avenue, 718-445-3100, www.qsbus.com. **New Jersey Transit** can be reached at 973-762-5100 or 212-564-8484 (Port Authority) for bus routes and schedules, or pick up the same at the Port Authority Bus Terminal at Eighth Avenue and 41st Street in Manhattan. You can also go to www.njtransit.com. **Rideshare information** is available at 888-648-6007.

BY FERRY

There was, before the advent of the auto, a time when some 125 passenger-boats plied 50 different routes across the Hudson and East rivers. With the closing of the Hoboken Ferry in 1967, only the Staten Island Ferry remained, both a commuter necessity for Staten Islanders and an excursion delight for Manhattanites and tourists alike.

The water commute is once again a reality on more than a dozen privately operated routes connecting Manhattan with New Jersey, Brooklyn, and Queens. And the Hoboken Ferry is back, faster than ever, docking at a floating terminal with a canvas marquee in Battery Park City. These ferries cruise at 35 miles per hour, twice as fast as the Staten Island Ferry. In increasing numbers, commuters are choosing this alternative to traffic gridlock, exorbitant parking fees, and expressway dementia, especially during the oppressive heat of summer. As more passengers take to the water, increased service comes on line.

- **Staten Island Ferry**, free, and definitely New York's best deal in transportation (and entertainment). Taking 25 minutes, the ferry leaves the South Ferry Terminal at Whitehall in Lower Manhattan for St. George, Staten Island, every 20 to 30 minutes daily, less frequently at night. Car service is available. Call 212-NEW-YORK or 718-815-BOAT for information or go to www.statenislandferry.com.
- **NY Water Taxi**, 212-742-1969, www.nywatertaxi.com; service every 25 minutes from Brooklyn Army Terminal to Pier 11 in Manhattan during commuter hours and makes several other Brooklyn-Manhattan-Queens excursions daily from the Fulton Ferry Landing to Battery Park, Battery Park City, Chelsea, Midtown, and Queens. Fares vary.
- **New Jersey passenger ferries** are dominated by NY Waterway, 800-53-FERRY, www.nywaterway.com, which operates the **Hoboken Ferry**, running weekdays every six to ten minutes during rush hours between 6:15 a.m. and 10 p.m., and every 15 minutes off-peak. The fare is $3 each way. Service is every half-hour on weekends, 10 a.m. to 9

p.m.. The firm also operates service to Pier 11 from Liberty Harbor, Port Liberté, Newport, Harborside, Colgate, Weehawken, and Belford. Sightseeing cruises and special theater cruise packages are also offered. You can purchase monthly passes on the NY Waterway web site. Parking in New Jersey is extra; parking passes are available at the web site as well.

- **Seastreak**, 800-BOAT-RIDE, www.seastreak.com, operates commuter ferries from Highlands and Atlantic Highlands, NJ and from South Amboy in Middlesex County, NJ, to Pier 11 at the foot of Wall Street, and to 34th Street on the East River. Hours are weekdays between 5:30 a.m. and 9:30 p.m. Fares range from $15 to $18 one way and $25 to $33 for round trip depending on the hour. Call or visit the web site for schedules.

- **Yankee Clipper** and **Mets Express**, operated by NY Waterway, 800-53-FERRY, www.nywaterway.com; departs Weehawken, Pier 11, East 34th Street, and East 90th Street for night games and weekend day games at Yankee Stadium; service to Shea Stadium, weekends only. Round trip costs $16 from any point (except Belford) to either stadium.

BY BIKE

As street surfaces have improved and auto traffic has thickened to a near standstill, increasing numbers of New Yorkers are mounting bicycles as a means of city transportation. Just how many no one really knows because bicycles are not registered in the city. The virtues of the bicycle are obvious: speed and economy. The down side? Vulnerability in city traffic. Besides alert, defensive riding, many of the **city laws** governing bicyclists also contribute to their safety:

- Bicycles are allowed on all city streets, but not on highways unless signs permit.
- Always ride with traffic and never on sidewalks.
- Traffic rules apply to bicycles as well as to cars. Riders must use hand signals.
- Bicycles must use bike lanes where they are provided.
- Bicycles must be equipped with a bell or horn, brakes, a headlight, and tail light.
- Accidents resulting in injury must be reported to the police.
- A rider may not wear more than one earphone to an audio player.
- Common sense mandates the wearing of a bicycle helmet.

Bicycles are permitted on subways, but a few gates limit entry/exit. MetroNorth and the Long Island Railroad require a one-time purchase of a permit to carry a bike on a train, except during rush hours and on weekends, when they are not allowed. Call MTA/Metro North Railroad at 212-532-4900 and speak to a customer service representative or go to

Window 27 in Grand Central Station to purchase a permit. For the LIRR call 718-558-8228 or check www.mta.info. Jersey Transit requires no permit on its trains, but bicycles are not allowed during rush hours or on weekends. The same rules apply on the PATH tubes.

There are 107.5 miles of bike lanes in the city streets and 75 miles of greenway. **Cycling maps** for the five boroughs are available at the Department of City Planning, 22 Reade Street, NYC 10007-1216, 212-720-3300, and online at www.nyc.gov. City biking laws and safe riding tips are outlined on the city's Department of Transportation page: go to www.nyc.gov and click on "residents" and then "transportation."

Transportation Alternatives, 115 West 30th Street, 12th floor, 212-629-8080, is a member-supported non-profit citizens' group for the promotion of biking and public transportation. Their encyclopedic web site, www.transalt.org, provides up-to-date news of interest to bikers and hikers, links to biking organizations in the metropolitan area, lists of shops offering discounts to members and information on the annual September Bike Tour, as well as other tour rides which they sponsor.

For more concerning biking in the city, see **Bicycling** in the **Sports and Recreation** chapter.

BY CAR

For the most part, New Yorkers don't get around Manhattan by car, except when they're in a cab. Why? Because on-street parking is so limited and off-street parking so expensive. So what are all those cars causing the periodic gridlock? Cabs, car services, and we did say "for the most part." Those living in Manhattan may own a car or rent a car occasionally. Those in the other boroughs typically own at least one car, and many drive into Manhattan, adding to the major rush hour delays. We'll continue with a few things you need to know about driving in and out of the city. (See also **Parking** and **Parking Tickets and Towing** in the **Getting Settled** chapter and **Auto Services and Repair** in **Helpful Services**.) For those that don't want to deal with the fuss and muss of owning a car, but still want to have one readily available, you can join **Zipcar** (www.zipcar.com, 866-4ZIPCAR), an hourly car rental subscription service.

New York drivers are aggressive, cabbies especially. Get used to it. In an odd balance, almost like playing "chicken," New York pedestrians do not follow the rules either: they cross against the light and mid-block when they feel like it; watch out for them. Also, keep your eye out for bike messengers who defy all traffic rules as they weave in and out of traffic.

Gridlock is a way of life here, at least on weekdays. "Don't block the box," means don't enter the intersection unless you are sure you can cross it before the light changes. Failure to heed this command causes gridlock and can cost you points on your license. If you can, avoid entering or leaving the city during rush hour traffic (roughly 7 a.m. to 10 a.m. and 4 p.m. to 7 p.m.). Friday and Sunday evenings are especially bad. In New York, street signs are everywhere, so pay attention for bus lanes and turning only lanes. Unlike much of the country, right turns are NOT permitted on a red light in New York City, unless indicated by a rare sign.

Because of the logical street grid covering most of the island and because traffic is so slow, driving in Manhattan is easier than you might think. The north-south avenues for the most part are one-way, generally in an alternating pattern: hence, First Avenue runs uptown, and Second Avenue runs downtown. But Park Avenue is two-way. The east-west streets for the most part are one way, with the even-numbered streets running east (remember, even-east), and odd-numbered streets running west, the exceptions typically being major cross-town streets: Houston, 14th, 23rd, 34th, 42nd, and 57th streets, for example, which are two-way. Left turns are rarely permitted during the day, so watch signs closely. For driving in the other boroughs you'll need a map: AAA members get them free; Hagstrom maps are sold at bookstores and newspaper/magazine shops all over the city. A good selection of maps is available at www.first-books.com.

Manhattan is bracketed by two major north-south arteries, the **West Side Highway/Henry Hudson Parkway** (Rte. 9A) along the Hudson River on the west side, and **Harlem River/FDR Drive** along the East River on the east side. At the southernmost tip of the island the **Brooklyn Battery Tunnel** (toll) runs under the harbor to Brooklyn, where it connects to the **Brooklyn-Queens Expressway (BQE)**, Rte. 278, which arcs around the Brooklyn shoreline and into Queens on either end. The BQE also connects with the **Verrazano Bridge** (toll) to the **Staten Island Expressway** across the Goethals Bridge to New Jersey.

On the FDR Drive, three bridges cross the East River to Brooklyn: south to north, the **Brooklyn Bridge**, the **Manhattan Bridge**, and the **Williamsburg Bridge**. At 34th Street, the **Queens Midtown Tunnel** (toll) shoots under the river to Queens and the **Long Island Expressway** running east to Long Island. The **Queensborough Bridge** crosses from 59th Street into Long Island City for free (be prepared for construction, which seems continual on this stretch), and the **Triborough Bridge** (toll) at 125th Street crosses into either Queens or The Bronx (watch the signs carefully). The **Willis Avenue Bridge** also takes you across the East River from the FDR to the Bronx (no toll) and connects with the Major Deagan Expressway, a north/south highway that passes Yankee Stadium.

From the West Side Highway the **Holland Tunnel** (toll) at Canal Street goes under the Hudson to Jersey City, and the **Lincoln Tunnel** (toll) at 38th Street crosses to Weehawken, both connecting to the Jersey

Turnpike (I-95) and routes 78 and 22 west into New Jersey and the Garden State Parkway. Further north, the **George Washington Bridge** (toll) sweeps across the Hudson River on two levels to connect with the **Palisades Parkway** (I-9), which runs north along the west bank of the Hudson, the **New Jersey Turnpike** and **I-80**, which heads west straight across New Jersey. The **Cross Bronx Expressway**, which runs onto the bridge, also runs (crawls is sometimes more like it) east, connecting with I-95 north into Connecticut, I-87 north into Yonkers and Upstate New York, and the Bronx River Parkway north. From the northernmost tip of Manhattan the **Henry Hudson Bridge** (toll) soars into Riverdale north on the Henry Hudson Parkway to Rte. 87 and other routes north into Westchester and on to New England.

Tolls on the bridges and tunnels range from $3 to $7. But drivers with the **E-Z Pass** can save money. The pass also saves time, as it doesn't require counting money and more lanes are open for pass holders. To get the E-Z Pass, which also works on the New York State Thruway and in neighboring states, go to www.e-zpassny.com and apply online, or call 800-333-TOLL for an application. The pass works like a debit card, subtracting the toll from your balance with each use; you can pay to keep the pass filled by check or money order, but if you pay by credit card the pass is automatically filled as necessary. Your monthly statement will tally your toll spending.

TAXI AND CAR SERVICES

All car services in New York City, unlicensed as well as licensed, come under the jurisdiction of the **Taxi and Limousine Commission (TLC)**. Call the commission with questions, complaints, or for the lost and found, 212-227-0700, or go to www.nyc.gov/taxi.

Licensed cabs in New York City tend to be reliable and safe, although in 1994, for the first time, the TLC required licensed cabs to install plexiglas shields between driver and passenger. This is intended more for the driver's safety, however. The TLC licenses chauffeur-driven stretch limos as well as three types of cabs:

*   **Yellow cabs**, or "medallion" cabs—for the emblem affixed to the hood—are the only taxis authorized to pick up passengers on the street. A licensed cab (the ones you should get into) will have a photo license of the driver displayed on the right side of the dashboard. There are more than 12,000 of these charging $2.50 upon entry and 40¢ for each 1/5th of a mile, and 40¢ for each 120 seconds waiting time. A 50¢ surcharge is collected between 8 p.m. and 6 a.m. No legal surcharge for luggage. Tips in the 15% to 20% range are expected. If you are crossing a toll bridge or tunnel you are responsible for paying the tolls. If you're going cross-town, especially mid-day in the crush of midtown

traffic, it pays to take a cross-town bus. Better yet, walk; it's faster.

- **Black cars**, the trade term for those high-quality (somewhat limousine-like), radio-dispatched fleet cars you see around, aren't licensed to stop for street hails. Corporations and private charges account for most of the "black car" business. In theory, these meterless "voucher cabs" (which charge by zone or by mileage registered on the odometer) will respond to telephone requests from "charge-accountless" individuals. If a driver sees you hailing a cab and offers to pick you up, he's doing so illegally and you are taking a risk.

- **Car services** are licensed to work only from a telephone base and can't legally pick up passengers on the street. The vehicles, of which there are some 36,000 licensed, range from the less-than-lovely to the pristine-upscale, but they are never yellow. Each vehicle, as proof of licensing, must display the blue decal of the Taxi and Limousine Commission on the passenger side of the front windshield. Especially useful to residents of the outer boroughs, where cabs rarely cruise, and to baggage-laden wayfarers, these for-hire vehicles charge flat rates per trip, sometimes less than the cost of a metered cab. This is the way to go when you need to get home from the boroughs at night—share with a couple of people if possible.

It pays to shop around by phone. Some rides can be reserved 20 minutes before departure, others require a day's notice. Rates and features vary; you may wish to pay a few dollars extra for a mini van or for a Lincoln Town Car, and you may wish to arrange to have the car wait for you for the return trip, for which some services charge only half fare. In any case, be sure the service is licensed, and if you're shopping around, don't hesitate to ask how much liability insurance they carry for passenger injury; they should carry a minimum of $1 million.

The car lurching to your side looks a wreck, and there's no decal? Then it's probably an unlicensed **gypsy cab**, in which you'll ride at your own risk without recourse in case of bad service. Avoid them.

LIMOUSINE SERVICE

For those occasions when you wish to ride in style or have a car and driver at your beck and call, consider hiring a limousine. Many car services also operate limousines; rates are usually on a per hour basis, although some firms set flat rates for trips to airports or for dinner-and-theater evenings. White, 40-foot-long strrrretches, such as those operated by **Amex Limousine Service**, 800-804-7456, are the current ultimate. These block-long beauties carry 14 people, including two in the rumble seat; the garden-variety limos offer stereos, color TV, and a stocked bar with ice for five or six. One day's notice is usually required, though cars (but not necessarily your first choice) are sometimes available on short notice. Most firms accept major credit cards, but check when you call. Below are some representative rates. Add 15% to 20% gratuity for the driver. Several companies deal primarily with corporate accounts.

- **All-State Car and Limousine Service, Inc.**, 163 Eighth Avenue, 212-333-3333; this service requires a two-hour minimum plus gratuity when you rent a sedan or a stretch limo. All-State also offers good rates to LaGuardia, JFK and Newark airports. Rates vary depending on the neighborhood you are traveling to/from. Call for more information.
- **Carey International**, 62-07 Woodside Avenue, Woodside, Queens, 800-336-4646; call for rates.
- **Dav-El Livery**, 212-645-4242, www.davel.com; all trips are charged a two-hour minimum. Call for rates.
- **Fugazy International Corp.**, 212-661-0100; call for rates. Sedans and stretch limos available.
- **London Towne Cars**, Long Island City, 800-221-4009; call for rates, sedans and limousines available.
- **Tel Aviv Car and Limousine Service**, 139 First Avenue near Eighth Street, 212-777-7777, out of town, 800-222-9888, www.telaviv limo.com; *New York* magazine called Tel Aviv "the best ride in town."

CAR RENTALS

If you let your fingers do the walking through the 19 yellow pages of car rental firms in the Manhattan Telephone Directory, you will undoubtedly come up with the best rate for your particular needs. National and local companies rent everything from the latest model cars in all sizes to subcompacts, mini vans, and "oldies." Prices vary widely from firm to firm, and special rates (for a weekend or even midweek) are common; call around for cost comparisons. Keep in mind that companies located just outside the city may offer rates low enough to more than make up for the hassle of getting there. In White Plains, NY, for example, a half-hour by train from Grand Central, the Hertz office, across the street from the train station, offers rates lower than what can be found at Hertz offices in Manhattan.

Be sure to ask if there is a charge for leaving the car at another location, if that is your plan. Some other helpful hints: Manhattan car rental companies run out of availability quickly, especially on holiday weekends. Do not wait until the last minute to try to reserve a car, and calling early may also get you a better discount. Check with your employer as well, who may have a corporate account that can get you a reduced rate. When you book your reservation, ask for a confirmation number, which will help get the rate you were quoted when you reserved the car. It's also a good idea to arrive early to pick up your car.

Finally, becoming a member of New York City's **AAA**, 212-757-2000, even if you do not own a car, is a good idea. Benefits include discounts on car rentals, free travelers' checks, maps, travel guides, trip planning service, travel discounts, and travel agents. At $55 to join and $45 annually thereafter, it's a good deal.

Here are some of the largest car rental companies. All have several Manhattan locations and with the exception of Thrifty, all have locations at the three major area airports.

- **Avis**: in New York City call 212-308-2727 for information and reservations; elsewhere call 800-331-1212, www.avis.com.
- **Budget**, 800-527-0700, www.drivebudget.com
- **Dollar**, 800-800-4000, www.dollar.com
- **Hertz**, 800-654-3131, www.hertz.com
- **National**, 800-227-7368, www.nationalcar.com
- **Thrifty**, 800-THRIFTY, www.thrifty.com

COMMUTER AND NATIONAL RAIL SERVICE

Pennsylvania Station, between 31st and 33rd streets and Seventh and Eighth avenues, with the Long Island Railroad Station adjacent, between 33rd and 34th streets, and Grand Central Station at 42nd Street, between Vanderbilt and Lexington avenues at Park, are the railroad hubs in New York City. Grand Central has been restored to its former glory, its gray stone walls cleaned and the spectacular azure vaulted ceiling with gilded constellations uncovered. It is once again truly a destination worthy of its calling. The once dim and dirty passageways now house a spiffy mall: a seductive food court, fine restaurants, Godiva, Starbucks, and more. The Oyster Bar downstairs, unbelievably, is one of New York's best restaurants. Penn Station, on the other hand, remains a work in progress.

- **Amtrak** trains, 800-872-7245 for information and reservations, or go to www.amtrak.com. Leave Pennsylvania Station for the Northeast Corridor—between Washington and Boston—and for destinations throughout most of the country and to Canada. In 2000 Amtrak inaugurated high-speed Acela Express service with a sleek bullet train shooting along the Northeast Corridor between Boston and New York at speeds peaking at 150 mph, cutting travel time by a third. Recently the service has been extended to Washington D.C. Both Acela Express and the less expensive, and slower, Acela Regional come in two classes, first and business. Metroliner service between New York and Washington is also available. Look for "rail sale" entries online, where discounts on long-distance coach train tickets may be available.
- **Metro-North** trains, 212-532-4900, www.mta.info, leave from Grand

Central Station and include the Hudson Line to Poughkeepsie, NY; the Harlem Line to Brewster, NY; and the New Haven Line to New Haven, CT. Find up-to-date Metro-North information on the MTA web site.

- The **New Jersey Transit Information Center**, 973-762-5100 and 800-772-2222, is the place to call for Penn Station-New Jersey train schedules. Also, check www.njtransit.com.
- **Long Island Railroad (LIRR)** trains, 718-217-5477, TTY 718-558-3022, www.mta.info, leave from the LIRR station, right next to Penn Station. You'll find up-to-date LIRR information on the MTA web site.
- **Staten Island Rapid Transit**, 718-966-SIRT, www.mta.info, runs between St. George and Tottenville stations 24/7. At the St. George Station, riders can make connections with the Staten Island Ferry.

COMMUTER AND NATIONAL BUS SERVICE

- The **Port Authority Bus Terminal**, between 40th and 42nd streets and Eighth and Ninth avenues, 212-564-8484, www.panynj.gov; handsomely modernized and enlarged, is the center for almost all inter-city bus traffic. The exceptions are inter-borough expresses, which have designated pickup points at certain Manhattan intersections, and buses, mostly from New Jersey, that arrive and leave from the Port Authority Bus Station at the George Washington Bridge. Call the "Customer Connection" at 800-221-9903 for more specifics.
- **Greyhound Bus Lines**, 800-231-2222, www.greyhound.com, has its principal ticket offices in the Port Authority Terminal, and its buses arrive and depart from the Lower Level of the North Wing with entrances on both 41st and 42nd streets.
- **Peter Pan Trailways**, 800-343-9999, www.peterpanbus.com; uses Adirondack Trailways as its local ticket agent in the Port Authority Terminal. Its buses also arrive at and depart from the Lower Level of the North Wing.

AIRLINES

The Port Authority of New York and New Jersey manages John F. Kennedy, LaGuardia, and Newark airports, and strives mightily to upgrade airport transportation and services and to disseminate information to the public about the facilities. To this end, they distribute particularly helpful materials and staff several telephone information numbers.

Since deregulation, the 80-plus airlines serving the three airports seem to be perpetually changing flight schedules, destinations, and names, to say nothing of fares. To order this chaos, the Port Authority publishes the ***International and Domestic Consolidated Airline Schedule***, a pocket-sized quarterly useful for finding the flight to fit one's needs.

The Port Authority web site, airport section, www.panynj.gov/aviation.html, provides information on each of the three major New York City airports. For a menu of recorded information, including details about **ground transportation** and **parking information**, call 800-A-I-R-R-I-D-E.

AIRPORT TRANSPORTATION

The cheapest route (and one of the slowest) to JFK is the A train ($2, destination Rockaways, *not* Lefferts Blvd.) to the Howard Beach station; from there, connect with AirTrain ($5) for all stops at JFK. Allow an hour and a half or more. Call 800-247-7433 for Howard Beach Station departure times.

You can, of course, drive to the airport and park there for up to 30 days at Kennedy International, LaGuardia, or Newark (costly at $250+). Short-term parking is available at all airports. Day rates vary from $10 to nearly $50, depending on the airport and the proximity to the terminal. Also, keep in mind that on Fridays and during holiday periods the lots fill up quickly. Business travelers fill short-term lots on Wednesdays. Arrive at the lot before 3 p.m. most days to be sure of a parking spot, and don't expect to find a space at LaGuardia Sunday night.

For up-to-date information on transportation to any of the three airports go online to the Port Authority's web site, www.panynj.gov, or call the individual airport, below.

Every half-hour, between 6 a.m. and 10 p.m., **New York Airport Service Express**, 718-875-8200, www.nyairportservice.com, offers **Inter-Airport Service**, a shuttle bus that loops between the passenger terminals at Kennedy to LaGuardia, with service to Manhattan hotels, Penn Station, Grand Central Station, and the LIRR. Check the web site for schedules and rates—online discount rates may be available.

If you are traveling with a companion, or can find someone to share with, it is probably worth taking a taxi to and from any of the major airports. Get taxis only at taxi stands and do not follow someone who claims to be a driver to his "parked" cab somewhere in an airport lot, unless you're hoping to get mugged. More on airport transportation under each airport listing below.

JOHN F. KENNEDY INTERNATIONAL AIRPORT (JFK)

JFK, which has been shedding its various skins for a few years now, is expected to finish rebuilding itself handsomely by 2006. A new light rail system, **AirTrain**, is now in place, looping the eight terminals and linking up with the Long Island Railroad, subways, and buses at Jamaica

Station and at Howard Beach. Travelers can now zip from midtown to JFK in 45 minutes. For more information about AirTrain, call 877-535-2478 or go to www.panynj.com. Security at JFK is tight, so you need to give yourself additional time and be patient. It should go without saying, but do not leave your bags unattended. Call 718-244-4444 for **airport information**, 718-244-4225 for **lost and found**, and 718-244-4168 for **parking**; online, go to www.kennedyairport.com.

- **Taxis to Manhattan** cost a flat fee of $45, plus tolls and tip. If there is a second person going beyond the first stop in Manhattan, the meter is started after the first stop and this passenger pays the metered rate. From destinations in the other four boroughs, taxis will typically run from $20 (Queens) to $45 for Staten Island. Allow 45-90 minutes from Manhattan, depending on time of day, with rush hour being the longest commute. Remember, when leaving JFK *get taxis only at taxi stands*.

- **New York Airport Service Express Bus**, 718-875-8200, www. nyairportservice.com; buses leave from Jamaica Station, Queens, Grand Central, Penn Station, and the Port Authority Bus Terminal every 15 to 30 minutes. The trip takes 45 to 60 minutes or more, depending on time of day, and the one-way fare to or from most Manhattan destinations is $13 ($5 from Jamaica Station). See the web site for schedules and rates. Discounts may be available if you purchase tickets online.

- **SuperShuttle** (**Blue Van**), 212-315-3006, www.supershuttle.com; operates 24/7, shuttling passengers from all destinations in Manhattan to each of the three major airports. Call ahead and make reservations, which are required. You will be notified at the time of your reservation if delays of more than 15 minutes are expected. When arriving at JFK you can go to the ground transport desk located by the baggage claim area to reserve pick up. You can expect about a 15-minute wait. Fares range from $15 to $23, depending on your destination.

- **Bus or subway**; if you're looking to save money but not time, you can take the E or F train from Manhattan, or the Q60 bus from 60th Street and Second Avenue to the Union Square/Kew Gardens Station and transfer there to the Q10 to Kennedy, where it circles the airport, stopping at each airline terminal; one fare. The A train from 59th Street and Columbus Circle in Manhattan is the fastest route by subway. You will need to board either the Far Rockaway or Rockaway Park trains (not Lefferts Blvd.). At the final stop (Far Rockaway) are free shuttle buses to the airport. The A train cuts through lower Manhattan, Brooklyn and the Rockaway section of Queens.

LAGUARDIA AIRPORT

Call 718-533-3400 for airport information; 718-533-3988 for lost and found; and 718-533-3850 for parking. Online, you can visit www.laguardia airport.com.

- **Taxis** to and from midtown cost about $19 to $26, plus tolls and tip. If you can find a friendly fellow Manhattan (or wherever you are going) bound traveler you can split the fare.
- **New York Airport Service Express Bus**, 718-875-8200, www. nyairportservice.com; buses leave from Jamaica Station, Queens, Grand Central, Penn Station and the Port Authority Bus Terminal every 15 to 30 minutes. The trip takes about 30 minutes, more during rush hours, and costs $10 from most stops ($5 from Jamaica Station.). Discounts may be available if you purchase online.
- **SuperShuttle** (**Blue Van**), call 212-315-3006, www.super shuttle.com. They bought out Express Shuttle USA (Grey Line) and now operate 24/7 shuttling passengers from all destinations in Manhattan to each of the three major airports. You will be notified at the time of your reservation if van delays of more than 15 minutes are expected. Fares range from $13 to $23.
- **Public subway and bus**; call the Transit Authority, 718-330-1234, and Triborough Coast Line, 718-335-1000, for information. Take the E or F train to the Roosevelt Station in Queens and change to the Q33 bus, which runs to LaGuardia every 15 minutes 24 hours a day. Total cost: $2 one way using a MetroCard or a token. If you're leaving from the Upper West Side and have 45-60 minutes to spare, take the M60 bus from Broadway and 116th Street, or anywhere along Broadway north to 125th Street to Second Avenue before midnight. It goes to LaGuardia for one fare. The M60 connects with the 1, 2, 3, 4, 5, 6, 9, A, C, and E trains.
- **LaGuardia "QT"** (**Quick Trip**) leaves from all LaGuardia terminals and the Marine Air Terminal every 20 minutes from 6:35 a.m. to 11 p.m. The express bus leaves you at 21st Street and 41st Avenue in Long Island City, where you can catch the B or Q into Manhattan. Total cost is $5 in exact change or tokens.

NEWARK LIBERTY INTERNATIONAL AIRPORT

Call 973-961-6000 for airport information; 973-961-6230 for lost and found; and 800-AIRRIDE or 973-961-4751 for parking information. Online, visit www.newarkairport.com.

The Port Authority, which runs all three New York City area airports, supervises efficient, inexpensive transportation to and from Newark.

- **Taxis**, the trip from midtown to Newark Airport costs between $40 and $50 plus tolls. In addition, taxis can add a $15 surcharge. Returning to Manhattan, New Jersey cabs are limited to fixed fares determined by location. "Share and save" rates for groups of up to four passengers cut costs by almost half and are available between 8 a.m. and midnight. Check with the dispatcher at the terminal's hack stand.
- **Newark Airport Express by Coach USA**, 877-8-NEWARK, www.coachusa.com; round-trip service to Newark Airport from Manhattan (across 42nd Street from Grand Central Station) for $19 (round trip). Comfy ride. Other drop-off points available. Contact Coach USA for more specifics.
- **SuperShuttle (Blue Van)**, www.supershuttle.com: call 212-258-3826 on day of departure; from out of town or to reserve before day of departure, call 800-BLUEVAN. Operates 24-hours a day shuttling passengers from home, office or hotel to the three major airports. Call and make reservations, which are required. When arriving at Newark Airport, you can go to the ground transport desk in the baggage claim area and order a Blue Van pick up. There will typically be about a 15-minute wait until the van picks you up. The fare is $19.
- **Rail**: **NJ Transit**, 800-772-2222, www.njtransit.com; **PATH**, 800-234-PATH, www.pathrail.com; **Amtrak** 800-USA-RAIL, www.amtrak.com: trains operate from Penn Station in Manhattan to and from Newark Penn Station between 5 a.m. and 2 a.m. **AirTrain** is the new light rail system that whisks you between the train station and the airport terminals: 877-535-2478, www.panynj.com.

SATELLITE AIRPORTS

Three airports outside the city offer an attractive alternative to the JFK-LaGuardia-Newark axis: un-crowded access roads, easy parking, and fewer delays all around for domestic flights.

- **MacArthur Airport**, 100 Arrivals Avenue in Ronkonkomo, Long Island, 631-467-3210, www.macarthurairport.com. Served by several major airlines, including Delta Express, Continental Express, Southwest, and US Airways. One to two hours' drive from Manhattan, this is more of a boon to Long Islanders than to Manhattanites.
- **Stewart Airport**, 1180 Windsor, New Winston, New York; 845-564-2100, www.stewartintlairport.com; a former Air Force base 60 miles north of the city in Newburgh, NY, at the juncture of I-87 and I-84, opened for commercial service in 1990. Airlines include: Conair/Delta Connection, American Eagle, Southeast, and US Airways Express.
- **Westchester County Airport** on Airport Road in White Plains, 914-285-4860, www.westchestergov.com/airport, is served by Air Canada,

American, Continental Express, USAir, and United. The airport boasts a new terminal, completed in 1995, and ample parking in a three-story lot. Lacking a car, take the Harlem Line out of Grand Central to White Plains, and the Bee Line #12.

FLIGHT DELAYS

Information about flight delays can be checked online on your airline's web site, or at www.fly.faa.gov. Similarly, the site www.flightarrivals.com offers real-time arrival, departure, and delay details for commercial flights.

CONSUMER COMPLAINTS—AIRLINES

To register a complaint against an airline, the Department of Transportation is the place to call or write: 202-366-2220, Aviation Consumer Protection Division, C-75 Room 4107, 400 7th Street SW, Washington, D.C. 20590.

SUMMER ACCOMMODATIONS IN UNIVERSITY DORMS, Ys, CHURCH-run women's residences, hotels, and even B&Bs provide temporary shelter en route to a permanent living situation. Later, there may be the occasional visiting aunt and uncle whom you cannot squeeze into your cramped one bedroom. Descriptions of these varied lodgings are offered, together with a selection of hotels categorized by price and location.

A few generalizations: rates are often negotiable and vary depending on time of the year; weekends and the summer months offer the best opportunity for lodging bargains; holidays and the fall months are usually the priciest times to stay in the city. To avoid sticker shock at checkout, note that New York hotel rooms are subject to 15.25% tax.

SUMMER ONLY

Dorm accommodations and other special situations include:

- **International House New York** (near Columbia University), 500 Riverside Drive at 123rd Street, NYC 10027, 212-316-8400, www.ihouse-nyc.org; you don't have to matriculate at Columbia to be eligible for one of the approximately 700 dorm rooms and suites available to students, interns, and other visitors from late May to mid-August on a first-come, first-served basis. Rooms can be had at less than $50 per night if there is availability. Monthly stays are for students only. These bargain accommodations are sometimes available during the school year as well, but not often.
- **New York University Dormitories**, c/o New York University, Office of Summer Housing, 14A Washington Place, NYC 10003, 212-998-4621, www.nyu.edu/summer/housing; there is a three-week minimum stay requirement at the NYU dorms, which are open to other students, age 17 or older (and June graduates), from late May through

early August. Priority is given to enrolled summer students. Non-student rates start at around $280 per week for a single, more with meals included. Rates for shared rooms are less, and lower yet for enrolled students. You may apply for housing online; minimum three-weeks payment required upon application.

See also **Sublets and Sharing** in the **Finding a Place to Live** chapter.

TRANSIENT YMCAs

Two Ys in Manhattan, one in Brooklyn, and one in Queens offer accommodations for both men and women; all rent rooms on a daily basis only. To obtain reservations at the four YMCAs listed below, either contact each Y individually or go online to www.hostels.com. Rates vary ($67 for a single and $77 for a double at the Vanderbilt in Manhattan or $43 for a single and $80 for a double in Greenpoint, Brooklyn). In all cases the room rates include use of all athletic facilities on the premises (see **YMCAs** in **Sports and Recreation**).

- **Vanderbilt YMCA**, 224 East 47th Street, NYC 10017, 212-756-9600; 370 rooms
- **West Side YMCA**, 5 West 63rd Street, NYC 10023, 212-875-4100; 530 rooms
- **Flushing YMCA**, 138-46 Northern Boulevard, Flushing 11354, 718-961-6880; 130 rooms
- **Greenpoint YMCA**, 99 Meserole Avenue, Brooklyn 11222, 718-389-3700; 100 rooms

TEMPORARY RESIDENCES

Daily transients are not accepted by any of the residences noted below, which, with the exception of the 92nd Street YM-YWHA, are for women only. Weekly rates are the norm and many include two meals a day in the price. Full occupancy is the rule at most of these places, as is the requirement for a personal interview, and you should therefore make arrangements for a room well in advance of arrival. Some have special house rules, such as curfews, so inquire about these before booking.

- **92nd Street YM-YWHA**, 1395 Lexington Avenue, NYC 10128, 212-415-5500, www.92y.org; co-ed, for men and women ages 18 and older, with 400 rooms, minimum stay one month (by application only); rates start at $1,000. Must be working full time or going to school. Apply several months in advance.
- **Brandon Residence for Women**, 340 West 85th Street between Riverside Drive and West End Avenue, NYC 10024, 212-496-6901; with

120 single rooms, shared baths, a handsome lobby, and 24-hour security. Applicants who will be working or students must apply in advance, with approval pending an interview. Call for rates. Breakfast and dinner included.

- **Markle Residence** (Salvation Army), 123 West 13th Street, NYC 10014, 212-242-2400; private room and bath, includes two meals a day. Four-week minimum-stay. Call for rates.

- **St. Mary's Residence** (Daughters of the Divine Charity), 225 East 72nd Street, NYC 10021, 212-249-6850; $215 a week for private rooms with shared baths and facilities. Three-night minimum-stay; prefer a three-month commitment.

- **Webster Apartments**, 419 West 34th Street between Ninth and Tenth avenues, NYC 10001, 212-967-9000, www.websterapartments.org; call well in advance to reserve for a minimum of four weeks at this attractive establishment, which features gardens and a library. An interview is required of applicants in the area; out-of-towners write directly for an application. Current weekly rates range from $213 to $223. You must provide proof of enrollment in a school, a letter of proof of internship, or proof of employment. Many residents here stay for months at a time, so if you're moving to the city and your place isn't quite ready, or if you're looking for the right place, this is a good option for women.

BED AND BREAKFASTS

In Manhattan? Yes! Many a resourceful New Yorker has let out that extra room and thrown a Continental breakfast into the bargain. It's even possible to have the whole apartment, in a charming brownstone or a high-tech high rise, to yourself, which is to say un-hosted. In any case, it will be cheaper than comparable digs in a hotel, but the visitor may give up something in privacy, service, or convenience. However, don't look for hand lettered shingles advertising availability because owners require anonymity and an agency acts as intermediary.

This cottage industry is unregulated, though reputable agencies inspect the properties they represent and attempt to monitor the quality of service and accommodations on an ongoing basis through visitor critique cards. Shop around by phone; be as specific as you can be about preferred location, likes and dislikes, allergies, and other restrictions. There is usually a two-night minimum stay, but there may be exceptions off-season. For the best choice, book well in advance (reasonable B&Bs have gotten as scarce as affordable hotel rooms) and expect to pay a 25% deposit or more. The commission is included in the fee. Many accept credit cards. Unlike the hotel rooms, you'll pay a modest 8.65% sales tax above the given room price.

- **1871 House**, Upper East Side, Manhattan, 212-756-8823, www.1871house.com; want to stay in a historic brownstone on the fashionable Upper East side, just two blocks from Bloomingdale's? Now you can. High ceilings, oriental rugs, cozy sitting areas, fireplaces, and plenty of antiques (no, this isn't the place for the kids). Six spacious apartments, including a suite, with plenty of first-class amenities. Check availability and rates on the web site.
- **Abode Bed and Breakfast**, P.O. Box 20022, NYC 10021, 212-472-2000 (800-835-8880 for out-of-state callers only), www.abode nyc.com, represents about 50 un-hosted apartments, all in Manhattan, some long-term locations. They request business references from guests. Four-night minimum, rates vary.
- **Bed and Breakfast and Books**, 35 West 92nd Street, NYC 10025, 212-865-8740, e-mail bedbreakfastbook@aol.com; is a reservation service, so named because the owners also operate a book business. One of the more established agencies, it handles about 35 apartments, hosted and un-hosted, all in Manhattan. In telephone interviews, they attempt to match the visitor's background, age, and preferences to the location. Two or three-night minimum; some long-term stays available.
- **Bed and Breakfast Network of New York**, 130 Barrow Street, NYC 10014, 212-645-8134, lists 700 places, hosted and un-hosted, and suggests a few weeks' advance notice. There is a two-night minimum in most cases. Call to order a brochure.
- **City Lights Bed and Breakfast and Short Term Apartment Rental**, 212-737-7049, www.citylightsbandb.com, lists several hundred rooms and apartments, hosted and un-hosted, all in Manhattan. Rates vary depending on the accommodation; two-night minimum.
- **Manhattan Lodgings, Inc.**, 70 East 10th Street, NYC 10003, 212-677-7616, www.manhattanlodgings.com, offers a wide range of furnished, short-stay apartments in Manhattan. Five-night minimum; rates range from around $100 per night to $6,000 per month.
- **All Around the Town**, 270 Lafayette Street Suite 804, NYC 10012, 212-334-2655, (800-443-3800 from out of town), represents about 60 furnished apartments, all in Manhattan. Two-night minimum. Discounts for longer stays. Helpful and personalized attention a plus.

EXTENDED STAY HOTELS

A number of hotels, particularly smaller neighborhood properties equipped with kitchenettes, quote weekly and monthly as well as daily rates. You'll find several listed below under **Inexpensive Hotels**. The late 1990s saw the proliferation of high-end, all-suite hotels for extended stays only, sometimes in apartment buildings, sometimes within transient hotels, but all designed primarily for the business person, offering hotel services and amenities along with fax machines and multi-line telephones. Here are a few:

- **Affinia Hospitality**, 800-637-8483, www.affinia.com; formerly Manhattan East Suites Hotels, it represents 10 prime properties in Manhattan: The Shelburne (Murray Hill), Eastgate Tower (fringes of Murray Hill), Beekman Tower (near Sutton Place), Plaza 50, The Surrey and Lyden Gardens (Upper East Side), and Southgate Tower (Penn Station area). Expect to pay $7,000 a month or more for these luxury accommodations.
- **Marmara-Manhattan**, 301 East 94th Street, 212-427-3100, www.marmara-manhattan.com, has 108 apartments that were formerly condominiums. Amenities include an exercise room and a daily buffet breakfast (charged extra). From $4,500 to $13,000 monthly; studios, one-, two-, and three-bedroom units available.
- **The Phillips Club**, 155 West 66th Street, NYC 10023, 212-835-8800, www.phillipsclub.com; at the high end and designed for the corporate traveler, contemporary apartments in a sleek 32-floor building just north of Lincoln Center, a few short blocks from Central Park. From overnight stays to extended stays to owning a piece of Manhattan real estate, you can enjoy luxurious surroundings at this corporate minded hotel. Call for rates. Fully equipped kitchens.

HOTELS

There are over 63,000 hotel rooms in New York City. Prices and occupancy rates fluctuate seasonally depending on location. The friendly, and sometimes frenetic, first-class commercial establishments along Central Park West and Lexington and Park avenues in the East 40s and 50s are impossibly full on weekdays in the fall, winter, and spring, but both occupancy and prices languish during the dog days of summer. Typically, the in-season rates in New York City begin in the fall and extend through the holiday season. The most affordable deals can be had during the summer months when many New Yorkers head for the Hamptons and other beach locales. Additionally, there is significantly less business travel to the city during the summer and hotels are looking to fill their rooms, so many will offer amenities as part of a package.

Weekend rates are almost always lower than prices charged during the week. However, flossy "weekend packages" with champagne, flowers, and free brunches for two won't represent the best value. Ask about the no-frills prices available Friday, Saturday, and sometimes Sunday nights. Weekend rates are, in effect, contingency plans to fill the house as corporate weeknight visitors depart. If full occupancy looms, off they go.

One place to look for deals is at the web site of the **New York Convention and Visitors Bureau**, www.nycvisit.com. Visit it, or drop in to their Visitors Information Center at 810 Seventh Avenue at 53rd Street, 212-397-8200, for an extensive listing of discounted hotel rooms. This useful site includes pictures, hotel descriptions and ratings listed by date of availability, number of nights, number of beds, and online booking. There is also a listing of special summer rates for members of American Express, which sponsors the site.

Hotel discounters buy blocks of rooms from hotels at volume discounts and pass savings, some as high as 60%, on to consumers. Visit their web site or call for specifics. Generally, cancellations must be made 24 to 72 hours in advance; be sure to check in advance on their cancellation policy. Keep in mind, unless you know the city, you should inquire about the location of the hotel. A discounted room in a less desirable neighborhood may not be worth the savings. **Reservation services** include:

- **Central Reservation Services**, 800-548-3311; www.reservation-services.com; especially good at getting mid-to low-priced rooms in New York and in about a dozen other cities.
- **Express Reservations**, 800-356-1123, www.express-reservations.com, books into several hotels in mid-town Manhattan.
- **Quikbook**, 800-789-9887, www.quikbook.com; will connect you with a reservation agent who can reserve rooms at dozens of moderate to deluxe hotels all over Manhattan (and more than 30 other cities). Additionally, you can check with the following:
- **Expedia.com**, 800-397-3342, www.expedia.com
- **Hotels.com**, 800-964-6835, www.hotels.com
- **Hotwire.com**, 888-362-1234, www.hotwire.com
- **Priceline.com**, www.priceline.com

INEXPENSIVE HOTELS

Doubles for less than $200 a night, not including tax, may not seem cheap, but that's the range separating New York's hotel bargain category from the rest of the flock.

- **Best Western Seaport Inn**, 33 Peck Slip, NYC 10038, 212-766-6600; www.bestwestern.com/seaportinn; pleasingly restored 19th century building one block from the waterfront at the very lower tip of Manhattan. Rooms are a bargain, especially if you get one of the upper floor rooms with great views of the Brooklyn Bridge.
- **Chelsea Savoy Hotel**, 204 West 23rd Street, NYC 10011, 212-929-9353, www.chelseasavoynyc.com; good location in Chelsea, small (90 rooms), and reasonable prices.

- **Clarion Hotel on Fifth**, 3 East 40th Street between Fifth and Madison avenues, NYC 10016, 212-447-1500, www.clarionfifthavenue.com; reasonably priced and centrally located, this midtown newcomer offers spacious, no-frills comfort. You can walk to Grand Central Station and the glorious Morgan Library.
- **Excelsior**, 45 West 81st Street, NYC 10024, 212-362-9200, www. excelsiorhotelny.com; a landmarked building in a great location facing the Museum of Natural History and Central Park compensates for occasionally grungy rooms. Rates vary by season and range from very reasonably priced standard rooms to suites. Health club and concierge.
- **Gershwin Hotel**, 7 East 27th Street, 212-545-8000, www.gershwin hotel.com; east side hotel, within walking distance of Gramercy Park, the Village, and Chelsea.
- **Habitat Hotel**, 130 East 57th Street, NYC 10022, 212-753-8841, www. habitat-ny.com; recently renovated, the Habitat is well situated in a prime location. Despite no-frills and basic small rooms, the place is often full.
- **Hampton Inn**, 108 West 24th Street, NYC 10011, 212-414-1000, www.hamptoninn.com; in Chelsea. Prides itself on offering stylish contemporary rooms at reasonable rates.
- **Herald Square**, 19 West 31st Street, NYC 10001, 800-727-1888, 212-279-4017, www.heraldsquarehotel.com; with a handsome beaux-arts facade it's a favorite with European travelers looking for a good value. Good location, especially if you want to shop at Macy's.
- **Holiday Inn**, 138 Layfayette Street, 212-966-8898, www. hidowntown-nyc.com; near Chinatown and Little Italy.
- **Hotel Wolcott**, 4 West 31st Street, 212-268-2900, www.wolcott. com; near the Empire State Building and about 10 blocks from the theater district.
- **Hudson**, 356 West 58th Street, NYC 10019, 212-554-6000, www. ianschragerhotels.com, opened in 2000 with 1,000 small rooms behind a bland brick façade. Inside, however, hotelier Ian Schrager and designer Philippe Starck have fashioned a fascinating interior, which includes a public library with a pool table, a lobby-as-town-square, and a witty garden.
- **Off SoHo Suites**, 11 Rivington Street, off the Bowery, NYC 10002, 800-OFF-SOHO, www.offsoho.com, is technically on the edge of the old Lower East Side, a short walk from SoHo and Chinatown and a location which may not be for everybody. But the accommodations are clean and comfortable, and a bargain especially for a family or a group of four. There are 38 suites plus a café on site, and 24-hour parking (fee).
- **Paramount**, 235 West 46th Street, NYC 10036, 212-764-5500, www.ianschragerhotels.com; the designer of the avant-garde Royalton, Philippe Starck, turned his charms on a lower-priced venue.

This whimsical effort aimed at the young and hip includes an on-site restaurant and a fitness room. Ask about special weekend rates.

- **Pickwick Arms**, 230 East 51st Street between Second and Third avenues, NYC 10022, 212-355-0300, www.pickwickarms.com; 350 clean, randomly-sized rooms, some without baths, and a rooftop garden attracts fans to this East 50s location.
- **Radisson Empire**, 44 West 63rd Street, NYC 10023, 212-265-7400, www.radisson.com; the major selling point for the basic but cheerfully furnished 500+ room Empire is its location next to Lincoln Center and near Columbus Circle.
- **Washington Square Hotel**, 103 Waverly Place, 212-777-9515, www.washingtonsquarehotel.com; some rooms with views of the historic Washington Square Park.
- **Westpark Hotel**, 6 Columbus Circle on 58th Street, NYC 10019, 212-445-0200; with a grand and convenient location facing Columbus Circle and Central Park and tidily-renovated rooms—those 16 (out of 90) with park views are especially nice. Helpful staff, concierge, complimentary breakfast, and good rates.

WEST SIDE TOURIST HOTELS

The cheapest rates for reliable, if far from classy, rooms are found in the tourist hotels along Eighth Avenue and in the West 40s surrounding the theater district. Better deals are offered here in the winter than in the summer.

- **Hotel Edison**, 228 West 47th Street, NYC 10036, 212-840-5000, www.edisonhotelnyc.com; 770 rooms in this old standard from 1931, convenient to the theater and reasonably priced.
- **Howard Johnson's Plaza Hotel**, 851 Eighth Avenue and 51st Street, NYC 10019, 212-581-4100; a HoJo's is a HoJo's, even in New York: clean, decent and reasonably priced, with parking available for $24 per day.
- **Milford Plaza Hotel**, Eighth Avenue and 45th Street, NYC 10036, 212-536-2200, www.milfordplaza.com, is big, basic, and sometimes exceedingly reasonable. Call for rates.
- **Days Hotel**, 790 Eighth Avenue and 48th Street, NYC 10019, 212-581-7000; this hotel is the nicest motel in town—perhaps the only one too. Basic no-frills. Call for rates. Parking is $24 per day.

FIRST-CLASS COMMERCIAL OR DELUXE HOTELS

Manhattan is known for its grand and luxurious hotels, a handful of which are legendary: the Pierre, the Plaza, the Carlyle, the Plaza Athenée, the Waldorf Astoria. To these have recently been added I.M. Pei's marble Four Seasons, the Righa, and the Peninsula, to name but several—deluxe hotels all. We've chosen to list a few which are perhaps less well-known, on the basis of glamour and singularity, as well as fair prices, when they can be found. Discounts and good weekend values in these hotels are generally available only in the summertime. Typically rates in these hotels will be in the $300+ range, with occasional off-season discounts in the low $200s. Since rates change often and there are frequent special deals, you should call hotel reservations for rates or look online for special offers. The finer in-room amenities including cable television and mini-bars are typically offered and most hotels have a concierge and various services available including babysitting.

- **Omni Berkshire Place**, 21 East 52nd Street at Madison Avenue, NYC 10022, 212-753-5800, www.omnihotels.com; carefully created bouquets frame the elegant marble lobby and provide a backdrop for the classy tea and cocktail area on the far side of the flowers. An accommodating concierge caters to clients with dispatch in this bijou hotel, where the only major drawbacks are the smallish rooms. Fitness center on site.
- **Swisshotel**: The Drake, 440 Park Avenue at 56th Street, NYC 10022, 212-421-0900, www.swisshotel-newyork.com, glowingly updated in the continental manner complete with attractive lobby bar, the Drake is now owned by Swissair's hotel division. Restaurant and fitness center.
- **Grand Hyatt New York**, 42nd Street and Lexington Avenue at Grand Central Station, NYC 10017, 212-883-1234, www.grand newyork.hyatt.com; fast paced and glitzy with a terrific lobby, especially when the fountains are splashing, and a dramatic bar cantilevered over 42nd Street. Rooms and lobby recently renovated. The penthouse health club and other features appeal to business travelers. Weekend specials sometimes available. Commodore Grill, Sky Bar, and Lobby Café are all on the premises for dining.
- **The Mark**, 25 East 77th Street at Madison Avenue, NYC 10021, 212-744-4300 or 800-THE-MARK (out of town), www.mandarin oriental.com. Your Frette linens are tended to twice daily in this "most sophisticated" Upper East Side hotel. Dining is on a par with its "glorious" rooms. Health club on site.
- **Michelangelo**, at the Equitable Center, 152 West 51st Street at Seventh Avenue, NYC 10019, 212-765-1900, www.michelangelohotel.com; this is the old Taft Hotel resurrected in Eurostyle "neoclassical" elegance to which well-designed rooms and great baths attract a glitzy crowd. Bring the kids. Summer rates are particularly good, and weekend packages may be available.
- **Helmsley Middletowne**, 148 East 48th Street near Third Avenue, NYC 10017, 212-755-3000, www.helmsleyhotels.com; one-, two-, and three-room suites all with kitchenettes and cheerful flowered decor. A favorite of UN personnel when the General Assembly is in session.

- **The Millenium Hilton**, 55 Church Street, NYC 10007, 212-693-2001; www.hilton.com; classy and convenient (if you're visiting Wall Street), the Millenium offers stunning views as well as first-class amenities such as computers and a health club with an attractive pool. Service is also top-notch. Call for rates. Weekends all rooms are discounted.
- **Morgan's**, 237 Madison Avenue between 37th and 38th streets, NYC 10016, 212-686-0300; an upstart on New York's rather traditional hotel scene, this narrow, vertical little place around the corner from the Morgan Library has been redecorated and toned down from its original sleek look to a softer, earth-toned feel. Small but nicely appointed rooms.
- **Royalton**, 44 West 44th Street off Fifth Avenue, NYC 10036, 212-869-4400, www.ianschragerhotels.com; with mahogany beds, Danish faucets, French and Italian furniture, Ian Schrager has fashioned a swinging silk purse out of a sow's ear. Good location, especially if you love the theater.
- **SoHo Grand**, 310 West Broadway between Grand and Canal streets, NYC 10013, 212-965-3000; until recently the only hotel in SoHo, offers 369 rooms with amenities to suit the businessman as well as tourists. Located in the midst of the art galleries, boutiques, and cafés that fill the formerly industrial buildings of this landmarked cast-iron district. Check out the Grand Bar & Lounge. Rates vary almost daily.
- **San Carlos**, 150 East 50th Street, between Lexington and Third avenues, NYC 10022, 212-755-1800, www.sancarloshotel.com; quiet, small hotel with pleasantly spacious rooms and kitchenettes. Good location. Rooms renovated in 2003.
- **St. Regis**, 2 East 55th Street at Fifth Avenue, NYC 10022, 212-753-4500; www.starwood.com; this *grande dame* of Fifth Avenue reopened in all her Beaux Arts glory, and then some, after a multi-million dollar restoration in 1991. A continental hotel in the old style with no modern convenience overlooked. And, yes, you can still dance on the St. Regis Roof.
- **The Stanhope Park Hyatt**, 995 Fifth Avenue at 81st Street, NYC 10028, 212-774-1234, www.stanhopepark.hyatt.com; quiet, discreet, old-world luxury is what the Stanhope achieved with its $30-million facelift. It's all French antiques, crystal ashtrays, Egyptian cotton sheets, fresh flowers, not to mention unrivaled views of Central Park and the Metropolitan Museum. Superb food and impeccable service. Ask about special packages.
- **Millennium UN Plaza**, 44th Street and First Avenue, NYC 10017, 212-758-1234, www.unplazahotel.com; superior service and sensational views from every room because they begin on the 28th Floor. A good-sized pool, health club, tennis court, and free limousine rides to Wall Street make this classically modern hotel unique. Great location.

SOME FAVORITES

Small, charming, personal hotels are not the city's forte, but we list eight fairly priced, medium-sized hotels in other Manhattan areas that deserve special mention (the hotels mentioned here reflect a purely personal taste and are not meant to be an all-city catalog of lodgings):

- **Algonquin**, 59 West 44th Street, NYC 10036, 212-840-6800, 888-304-2047 www.algonquinhotel.com; completely refurbished in 2004, all muted rose, green, and burnished wood, the famous lobby bar combines with anachronistic elevators and smallish, genteel rooms to make you feel welcome, secure, and part of a pleasantly elite and talented group. Enjoy cocktails in the Blue Bar or dinner and cabaret in the Oak Room. Call for rates and ask about specials, particularly in the summer.
- **Doubletree Guest Suites**, 1568 Broadway, NYC, 212-719-1600, www.doubletree.com; overlooking Times Square, Doubletree rents suites (sitting room and bedroom) rather than single rooms, at reasonable rates. Trusted name in the hotel business.
- **Hotel Chelsea**, 222 West 23rd Street, 212-243-3700, www.hotel chelsea.com; where colorful eccentrics like to stay. In Chelsea. Great art. Affordable rooms.
- **Lowell**, 28 East 63rd Street, NYC 10021, 212-838-1400; is a small 65-room European style hotel, with plenty of amenities on a quiet Upper East Side street. The more-attractive-than-ever art deco hotel remains intimate and friendly. Great location. Ask about specials.
- **Salisbury**, 123 West 57th Street, NYC 10019, 212-246-1300, 888-692-5757 from out of town; pleasant, pastel rooms in a relatively intimate setting attract a high percentage of women travelers. Large rooms, good prices.
- **Sheraton Russell Park Avenue**, 45 Park Avenue at 37th Street, NYC 10016, 212-685-7676 or 866-233-9330, www.starwood.com; the wood-paneled, book-lined lobby and the agreeable welcome complement carefully decorated rooms. Fitness Center and concierge service.
- **Hotel Wales**, 1295 Madison Avenue corner of 92nd Street, NYC 10028, 212-876-6000, www.waleshotel.com; clean and cheerful little 86-room hotel, the Wales represents good value in tastefully renovated rooms. Terrific location for Museum Mile along Fifth Avenue.
- **Wyndham**, 42 West 58th Street, NYC 10019, 212-753-3500, www.hotelwyndham.com; small, attentively managed, and nicely furnished, the Wyndham is home to numerous theatrical luminaries whenever they're in town and is one of the best buys around. Not part of the larger chain, the hotel is well situated and provides comfortable rooms.

NEW YORK CITY FAIRLY CRACKLES WITH EVENTS: PARADES, FESTI-vals, celebrations, ethnic holidays, shows, feasts, and tournaments. Imperceptible at first, there is, in fact, a rhythm to this endless round of activity; many of these events occur annually at about the same time, and New Yorkers look forward to them. The calendar below lists them by month. Check out the *New York Times*, *New York* magazine, *Time Out New York*, or *The New Yorker* for specific dates and details. Or stop by the **New York Convention & Visitors Bureau** at 810 Seventh Avenue at 53rd Street, 212-484-1222, to pick up brochures and a complete seasonal calendar of events. Or go to www.nycvisit.com. For more information on the web, you can also check the following sites: www.nyclink.org, www.nytoday.com, or www.allianceforarts.org.

The following is just a fraction of what the Big Apple has to offer.

JANUARY

- **Big Apple Circus**, Lincoln Center
- **NY National Boat Show** at the Jacob Javits Center
- **Outsider Art Fair**, www.sanfordsmith.com/out/out
- **Three Kings Parade**, 5th Avenue, 104th to 116th streets
- **Winter Antiques Show** at the Seventh Regiment Armory
- **Winter Festival**, Central Park
- **Winter Restaurant Week**, various restaurants in Manhattan

FEBRUARY

- **Black History Month**, citywide events
- **Chinese New Year celebrations**, Chinatown and elsewhere
- **NY International Children's Film Festival**

- **Valentine's Day**, 24-hour Marriage Marathon at the Empire State Building
- **Westminster Kennel Club Dog Show**, Madison Square Garden

MARCH

- **Circus Animal Walk to Madison Square Garden**
- **Greek Independence Day Parade**, Fifth Avenue, 44th to 59th streets
- **International Cat Show**, Madison Square Garden
- **Israeli Day Parade**, Fifth Avenue
- **New York Flower Show** at the Jacob Javits Center
- **New York Underground Film Festival**, www.nyuff.com
- **Ringling Brothers & Barnum & Bailey Circus**, Madison Square Garden
- **St**. **Patrick's Day Parade**, Fifth Avenue, 44th to 86th streets

APRIL

- **Annual Egg Rolling contest**, Central Park
- **Cherry Blossom Festival**, Brooklyn International Botanic Garden
- **Easter Parade**, Fifth Avenue near 50th Street
- **Greater NY International Auto Show,** Jacob Javits Center
- **Mets and Yankees** baseball season begins
- **Spring Flower Show**, Brooklyn International Botanic Garden

MAY

- **9th Avenue International Food Festival**, 37th to 57th streets
- **Bike Week New York**: The Great Five Boroughs Bike Tour
- **Broadway Spring Festival**
- **Fleet Week**, Manhattan west side docks
- **Lower East Side Festival of the Arts**
- **Promenade Art Show**, Brooklyn Heights
- **Washington Square Outdoor Art Exhibit**
- **You Gotta Have Park celebration**, Central Park

JUNE

- **Annual Lesbian and Gay Pride March**
- **Brooklyn Pride Festival and Parade**
- **Feast of St**. **Anthony of Padua**, Sullivan Street below Houston

- **Hudson River Park** summer events, including the popular "Take Me to the River" film series on the pier. www.hudsonriverpark.org
- **Mermaid Parade**, Coney Island, Brooklyn
- **Midsummer Nights Swing at Lincoln Center**
- **Museum Mile Festival**, 5th Avenue, 82nd to 102nd streets
- **New York Jazz Festival**
- **Puerto Rican Day Parade**, 5th Avenue, 44th to 86th streets
- **Queens Festival**, Flushing Meadows-Corona Park
- **Restaurant Week**, various restaurants in Manhattan
- **Salute to Israel Parade**, Fifth Avenue, 52nd to 79th streets
- **Summer Stage concerts** begin, Central Park
- **Welcome Back to Brooklyn Festival**, Grand Army Plaza

JULY

- **Bryant Park Summer Film Festival**, Monday nights, Bryant Park
- **Free Shakespeare in Central Park**, Delacorte Theatre
- **Macy's 4th of July Fireworks**, Lower Hudson River

AUGUST

- **African-American and Hispanic Festival**, Harlem
- **Bronx Puerto Rican Day Parade**, East Tremont Avenue to East 161st Street
- **Brooklyn County Fair**, 718-689-8600
- **Brooklyn Puerto Rican Day Parade**, Lindsay Park in Williamsburg
- **Fringe Festival**, theater, music, dance and whatever from outside the mainstream, throughout the Lower East Side, www.fringenyc.org
- **Mostly Mozart Festival**, Lincoln Center
- **US Open Tennis Tournament**, Flushing, Queens

SEPTEMBER

- **African-American Day Parade**, Adam Clayton Powell Blvd., 111th to 142nd Street to Fifth Avenue
- **African-American/Caribbean Parade**, Bronx, Tremont Avenue to 161st Street
- **Feast of San Gennaro**, Mulberry Street, Little Italy
- **Greenwich Village Jazz Festival**, around the Village and in Washington Square Park
- **Labor Day Parade**, Fifth Avenue, 33rd to 72nd streets
- **Lincoln Center Out-of-Doors Festival**
- **Metropolitan Opera season** begins, Lincoln Center

- **NY Film Festival**, Lincoln Center
- **NY Giants** and **NY Jets Football Season** opens, Meadowlands, New Jersey
- **Van Steuben Day Parade**, Fifth Avenue, 61st to 86th streets
- **Washington Square Outdoor Art Show**
- **West Indian CarnivalWigstock**
- **Wigstock**, Pier 54, 13th Street and Hudson River

OCTOBER

- **Columbus Day Parade**, Fifth Avenue, 44th to 86th streets
- **Greenwich Village Halloween Parade**, 6th Avenue, Spring to 23rd streets
- **Hispanic Day Parade**, Fifth Avenue, 44th to 72nd streets
- **New York is Book Country**, Washington Square Park
- **New York Rangers hockey season** begins, Madison Square Garden
- **Next Wave Festival**, Brooklyn Academy of Music
- **Promenade Art Show**, Brooklyn Heights
- **Pulaski Day Parade**, Fifth Avenue, 26th to 52nd streets

NOVEMBER

- **Christmas Spectacular stage show**, Radio City Music Hall
- **New York City Marathon**, www.nycmarathon.org; all five boroughs
- **New York Knicks basketball season begins**, Madison Square Garden
- **NY City Ballet**, winter season, Lincoln Center
- **Macy's Thanksgiving Day Parade**, 77th Street to Herald Square
- **Veterans Day Parade**, Fifth Avenue, 39th to 24th streets
- **Virginia Slims Tennis Tournament**, Madison Square Garden

DECEMBER

- **Christmas Tree Lighting**, Rockefeller Center
- **Fireworks**, South Street Seaport; Grand Army Plaza, Brooklyn
- **First Night events throughout city**
- **New York Road Runners Club Midnight Run**, Central Park, 212-860-4455, www.nyrrc.org
- **New Year's Eve Celebration**, Times Square
- **New Year's Eve Concert**, NY Philharmonic, Lincoln Center

BELOW, WE LIST A FEW BOOKS THAT THE NEWCOMER MAY FIND helpful, enlightening, or just entertaining.

GUIDES

- ***AIA Guide to New York City*** edited by Elliot Willensky and Norval White (Three Rivers Press); *the* guide and reference book for anyone interested in New York City architecture. Includes maps, drawings, and directions to neighborhoods throughout the five boroughs. Encyclopedic and fascinating.
- ***The Cheap Bastard's Guide to New York City*** by Rob Grader (Globe Pequot Press); tips on leading the good life in the city ... for pennies.
- ***Living with Kids in Manhattan*** (Grownup's Guide Publishing) by Diane Chernoff-Rosen
- ***Nature Walks In and Around New York City*** by Sheila Buff (Appalachian Mountain Club Books); just the thing to get you out of the apartment for a walk in the woods, the fields, the wetlands—all in New York City.
- ***New York City for Free*** by Christopher C. Sulavik (Tatra Press); museums, lectures, concerts, festivals, tours, shows, and more, even in the outer boroughs, all free.
- ***New York Tenants' Rights*** by Mary Ann Hallenborg (Nolo Press)
- ***New York Times Guide to New York City Restaurants*** by William Grimes & Eric Asimov (*New York Times*); reviews some 1,000 of the city's restaurants.
- ***New York's 50 Best Places to Go Birding In and Around the Big Apple*** by John Thaxton and Alan Messer (now out of print, but if birding is your thing try to track down a copy).

- ***New York's Best 100 Best Little Places to Shop*** by Eve Claxton (City & Co.)
- ***Nosh New York: The Food Lover's Guide to New York City's Most Delicious Neighborhoods*** by Myra Alperson (St. Martin's Press)
- ***Queer New York City; The Annual Guide To Gay & Lesbian NYC*** edited by Martin J. Quinn (On Your Own Publications); from bars to bookstores.
- ***Retire in New York City—Even If You're Not Rich*** by Janet Hays (Bonus Books)
- ***Take Charge! The Complete Guide to Senior Living in New York City*** by John Vinton (New York University Press); encyclopedic how-to manual for seniors and gonna-bees.
- ***Where to Go: A Guide to Manhattan's Toilets*** by Vicki Rovere (published by Vicki Rovere); don't laugh! In a city with a dearth of public toilets this can be a life-saver. Now updated.

ZAGAT SURVEY GUIDES
- ***Zagat Survey: New York City Restaurants*** edited by Curt Gathje (Zagats)
- ***Zagat Survey: New York City Marketplace Survey*** by Eugene H. Zagat, et al (Zagats)
- ***Zagat Survey: New York City Theater Spring*** edited by Daniel Simmons (Zagats)

PETS

- ***The Dog Lover's Companion to New York City*** by Joanna Downey (Avalon Travel Publishing); offers the inside scoop on where to take your dog.
- ***The Great New York Dog Book; The Indispensable Canine Resource Guide for New York City Dogs and Their Owners*** by Deborah Loven (Harper Perennial Library); you can keep a dog here, and here's how.

NEW YORK CITY HISTORY

- ***Central Park, an American Masterpiece: a Comprehensive History of the Nation's First Urban Park*** by Sara Cedar Miller (Harry N. Abrams)
- ***The Encyclopedia of New York City*** edited by Kenneth T. Jackson (Yale University Press); from A&P to Zukofsky, this unwieldy literary monument will delight any Gotham-lover.
- ***Gotham: A History of New York City to 1898*** by Edwin G. Burrows and Mike Wallace (Oxford Press); the best and most comprehensive history, with volume two yet to come.

- *Literary Landmarks of New York City: The Book Lover's Guide to the Homes and Haunts of World Famous Writers* by Bill Morgan (Rizzoli); provides a unique look at the city through the city's great scribes from Poe to Mailer.
- *New York for New Yorkers: A Historical Treasury and Guide to the Buildings and Monuments of Manhattan* by Liza M. Greene (W.W. Norton & Co.)
- *New York Streetscapes: Tales of Manhattan's Significant Buildings and Landmarks* by S. Christopher and Braley Gray (Harry N. Abrams)
- *The WPA Guide to New York City: The Federal Writers' Project Guide to the 1930s New York* by William Whyte—Federal Writers Project (Pantheon Books); mapped, photographed, illustrated and described in this classic. Among the writers, the young John Cheever.

PARENTS/STUDENTS

- *City Baby: The Ultimate Guide for New York City Parents from Pregnancy to Preschool* by Kelly Ashton and Pamela Weinberg (Universal Books); everything from nannies to playgrounds.
- *Cool Parent's Guide to All of New York* by Alfred Gringold and Helen Rogan (Universal Books)
- *The Grownup's Guide to Living with Kids in Manhattan* by Diane Chernoff-Rosen and Lisa Levinson (Resource Marketing Group); comprehensive guide and resource book for parents of kids ages one to twelve.
- *How to Find the Best Doctors: New York Metropolitan Area* by John J. Connolly (Castle Connolly Medical Ltd.)
- *Manhattan Family Guide to Private Schools* by Victoria Goldman and Catherine Hausman (Soho Press)
- *New York City's Best Public Elementary Schools: A Parent's Guide* by Clara Hemphill and Pamela Wheaton (Teachers College Press); the last word on the city's public schools, how to choose and get into good ones.
- *New York City's Best Public Middle Schools: A Parent's Guide* by Clara Hemphill (Teachers College Press); the sequel to the above, with descriptions and ratings of middle schools, district by district. Dated (1999) but still helpful.
- *A Parent's Guide to New York City* by Judith Mahoney Pasternak (Mars Publishing); suggests child-friendly places to go and itineraries.

WHILE THERE IS CLEARLY NO SUBSTITUTE FOR CONDUCTING most newcomer business in person, a significant portion of preparatory work can be done by phone or online. Whether it is researching available apartment rentals, determining the nearest library in your neighborhood, or discovering which train to take from your friend's apartment in Brooklyn to your office on the first day on the job, much of the information you need may be gathered even before you arrive.

What follows is a partial listing of phone numbers and web sites that cover a variety of services. In addition, there are many others embedded throughout the book. Check in your section of interest for additional listings.

ALCOHOL AND DRUG DEPENDENCY

- **Alcoholics Anonymous**, 212-647-1680; **Alcoholics Anonymous General Services** 212-870-3400
- **Alcoholism Council of New York, Inc.**, 212-252-7001
- **Cocaine Anonymous**, 212-929-7300
- **Narcotics Anonymous, Inc.**, 212-929-6262
- **National Council on Alcoholism and Drug Dependency**, 212-206-6770, www.ncadd.org
- **The Watershed**, 212-431-4640, referral service for addiction to alcohol and drugs and 24-hour help line.

ANIMALS

- **ASPCA, American Society for the Prevention of Cruelty to Animals**, 212-876-7700, www.aspca.org
- **Animal Bites, Bureau of Veterinary Public Health Services**, 212-676-2483

- **Animal Medical Center**, 212-838-8100, www.amcny.org; open 24-hours; phone calls 9 a.m. to 11 p.m.
- **Center for Animal Care and Control (CACC)**, Manhattan Shelter and Adoption Center, 212-722-3620, www.nycacc.org; **Animal Rescue Service**, 718-649-8600

BIRTH/DEATH CERTIFICATES

- **New York City Department of Health Vital Records**, 212-788-4520, TTY 212-442-9038

CONSUMER COMPLAINTS AND SERVICES

- **Better Business Bureau**, 212-533-6200, www.newyork.bbb.org
- **Federal Trade Commission**, 212-607-2829, www.ftc.gov
- **NJ Governor's Consumer Protection Hotline**, 800-242-5846
- **NY State Attorney General's Consumer Help Line**, 800-771-7755, www.oag.state.ny.us
- **NY State Consumer Protection Board**, 518-474-3514, www.consumer.state.ny.us
- **NY State Department of Insurance**, Consumer Services Bureau, complaints and inquiries, 212-480-6400
- **New York State Department of Transportation**, 800-786-5368, www.dot.state.ny.us
- **New State Governor's Consumer Hotline**, 800-697-1220
- **Public Service Commission's Call Center**, 800-342-3330
- **New York City Department of Consumer Affairs**, 212-487-4444, TTY 212-487-4465, www.ci.nyc.ny.us/html/dca
- **US Consumer Product Safety Commission Hotline**, 800-638-2772, www.cpsc.gov

CRIME/CRISIS

- **Crime in Progress**, 911
- **Crime Victims**, 800-771-7755
- **Precinct Referrals** dial 311 or 212-NEW-YORK

CRISIS HOTLINES
- **Ambulance**, 911
- **Arson Hotline**, 718-403-1300
- **Girls & Boys Town National Hotline**, 800-448-3000, www.boys town.org
- **New Jersey School Safety Hotline**, 877-624-8082

- **Rape/Battered Persons Crisis Center Hotline**, 800-621-4673
- **Sex Crimes Unit**, Police Department, 212-267-7273, 24-hour service staffed by female NYPD detectives
- **Samaritans of New York Suicide Hotline**, 212-673-3000

CHILD ABUSE & FAMILY VIOLENCE
- **Abducted, Abused, and Exploited Children**, 800-248-8020
- **Battered Women Domestic Violence Program**, 800-621-4673, 24-hour
- **New York State Child Abuse and Maltreatment Register**, 800-342-3720, TTY 800-638-5163
- **Emergency Children's Services**, 212-966-8000

CULTURAL LIFE

- **Alliance for the Arts**, 212-947-6340, www.allianceforarts.org
- **Big Onion Walking Tours**, 212-439-1090, www.bigonion.com
- **City Search**, www.newyork.citysearch.com
- **City Web Site search**, www.nyclink.com
- **Curator's Choice**, www.NYMuseums.com
- **NYC/OnStage**, part of the Theatre Development Fund, 212-768-1818, www.tdf.org
- **New York City & Company**, Convention and Visitors Bureau, 212-484-1200, www.nycvisit.com
- *New York* **magazine and New York Metro**, www.newyork metro.com, customer service, 800-678-0900
- *New York Times*, www.nytimes.com or www.nytoday.com
- **Tele-Charge**, 212-239-6200, www.telecharge.com
- **Ticketmaster**, 212-307-7171, www.ticketmaster.com
- *Time Out New York*, 212-539-4444, www.timeoutny.com
- **Times Square Visitor's Center**, www.timessquarebid.org; business improvement district
- *Village Voice*, www.villagevoice.com

DISCRIMINATION

- **New Jersey Division of Civil Rights**, 609-292-4605, www.state.nj.us/lps/dcr/
- **New York City Commission on Human Rights**, 212-306-7450, TTY 212-306-7686
- **New York State Commission on Human Rights**, 212-961-8650, www.nysdhr.com

- **US Department of Fair Housing & Discrimination Hotline**, 800-424-8590

EDUCATION

- **New Jersey Department of Education**, 609-292-4469, www.state.nj.us/education
- **New York City Department of Education**, www.nycenet.edu

ELECTIONS

- **Board of Elections**, 212-868-3692, www.vote.nyc.ny.us

EMERGENCY

- **FEMA Disaster Assistance Information**, 800-525-0321
- **Fire, police, medical**, 911
- **Poison Control Center**, 212-764-7667, 24-hour service

GOVERNMENT

State and local government listings for all profiled communities are on the net at www.piperinfo.com/index.

NEW YORK CITY
- **Bronx Borough President**, 718-590-3500, www.bronx boropres.nyc.gov
- **Brooklyn Borough President**, 718-802-3900, www.brooklyn-usa.org
- **City Council**, 212-788-7100, www.council.nyc.ny.us
- **Manhattan Borough President**, 212-669-8300, www.cvfield smbp.org
- **New York Mayor's Office/City Hall**, 212-788-3000, www.nyc.gov
- **Official New York City Web Site**, www.nyc.gov
- **Public Advocate**, 212-669-7200, www.pubadvocate.nyc.gov
- **Queens Borough President**, 718-286-3000, www.queensbp.org
- **Staten Island Borough President**, 718-816-2200, www.staten islandusa.com

NEW YORK STATE
- **Attorney General**, 212-416-8000, TTY 800-780-9898, www. oag.state.ny.us
- **Governor's Office**, 212-681-4580, www.state.ny.us/governor

- **State Assembly,** www.assembly.state.ny.us
- **State Senate,** www.senate.state.ny.us

STATE OF NEW JERSEY

- **Governor's Office,** 609-292-6000, www.state.nj.us
- **Attorney General,** 609-292-8740, www.state.nj.us
- **New Jersey Legislature Office of Legislative Services,** 609-292-4840, www.njleg.state.nj.us

FEDERAL

- **Federal Citizen Information Center,** 800-688-9889, www.first gov.gov
- **Social Security Administration,** 800-772-1213, www.ssa.gov

HEALTH AND MEDICAL CARE

- **Ambulance Emergency Number,** 911
- **Dental Emergencies,** New York County Dental Society, 212-573-9502
- **Department of Health and Mental Hygiene Call Center,** Central Complaint Bureau, 212-442-9666, www.nyc.gov
- **Doctors on Call,** 212-737-2333, 718-238-2100
- **Doctors-on-Call** (private group), 718-745-5900; 24-hour house-call service
- **Lead Poisoning Prevention Program,** 212-676-6100, www.nyc.gov
- **National Health Information Center (NHIC),** US Department of Health and Human Services, 800-336-4797, www.health.gov/nhic
- **New York County Medical Society (AMA),** 212-684-4670, www.nycms.org
- **New York Public Advocate,** www.pubadvocate.nyc.gov
- **NJ State Board of Medical Examiners,** 609-826-7100, www.state.nj.us/lps/ca/medical.htm
- **NY State Department of Health, Office of Professional Medical Conduct,** 518-402-0855, www.health.state.ny.us
- **Poison Control Center,** 212-764-7667
- **US Department of Health and Human Services,** 202-619-0257, www.hhs.gov

HOSPITALS

- **Bayley-Seton Hospital,** Staten Island, 718-818-6000, www.svcmc ny.org
- **Bellevue Hospital Center,** 212-562-4141, www.med.nyu.edu/Bellevue

- **Beth Israel Medical Center**, 212-420-2000, www.bethisraelny.org
- **Calvary Hospital**, Bronx, 718-863-6900, www.calvaryhospital.org
- **Columbia-Presbyterian Medical Center**, 212-305-2500, www.cpmcnet.columbia.edu
- **Harlem Hospital Center**, 212-939-1000, www.harleminternal medicine.org
- **Jacoby Medical Center**, Bronx, 718-918-5000, www.nyc.gov
- **Jamaica Hospital and Medical Center**, Queens, 718-206-6000, www.jamaicahospital.org
- **Kings County Hospital Center**, Brooklyn, 718-245-3131, www.nyc.gov
- **Lenox Hill Hospital**, 212-434-2000, www.lenoxhillhospital.org
- **Mount Sinai Hospital**, 212-241-6500, www.mountsinai.org
- **New York Downtown Hospital**, 212-312-5000, www.nyudh.org
- **New York University Medical Center**, 212-263-7300, www.med.nyu.edu
- **St. Luke's Roosevelt Hospital Center**, 212-523-4000, www.slrhc.org
- **St. Vincent's Catholic Medical Center**, 212-604-7000, www.stvin.org
- **St. Vincent's Catholic Medical Center**, Staten Island, 718-876-1234, www.schsi.org
- **Woodhall Medical Center**, Brooklyn, 718-963-8000, www.nyc.gov

HOUSING RESOURCES

- **Department of Environmental Protection**, 212-639-9675, www.nyc.gov/dep
- **Division of Housing & Community Renewal**, 212-480-6732, rent information line 718-739-6400, www.dhcr.state.ny.us
- **Gas** or **Electric service shutoff hotline**, 800-342-3355
- **Housing Authority**, 212-306-3000, www.nyc.gov
- **Housing Discrimination** for New York (and New Jersey): Fair Housing Hub, US Department of Housing and Urban Development, 212-264-9610 or 800-496-4294; housing discrimination hotline, 800-669-9777, www.hud.gov/complaints/housediscrim.cfm
- **Landlord/Tenant Fact sheet** (NY State Attorney General), 212-416-2000, www.oag.state.ny.us
- **Metropolitan Council on Housing**, 212-979-0611, tenants union
- **New Jersey Landlord Tenant Information Service**, 609-292-4174, www.state.nj.us/dca
- **New Jersey Tenants Organization (NJTO)**, 201-342-3775
- **New York City Loft Board**, 212-788-7610, www.nyc.gov/html/loft

- **New York City Rent Guidelines Board**, 212-385-2934, www.housing nyc.com
- **New York State Rent Guidelines**, www.housingnyc.com
- **NYC Heat Hotline**, 311
- **NYC Urban League**, 212-926-8000, www.nyul.org
- **Office of Rent Administration, State Division of Housing and Community Renewal (DHCR)**, www.dhcr.state.ny.us
- **Rent Stabilization Association**, 212-214-9200, www.rsanyc.org
- **TenantNet**, www.tenantnet.net
- **Tenants & Neighbors**, 212-608-4320
- **US Department of Fair Housing and Anti-predatory Hotline**, 800-477-5977, www.fairhousing.com/fhsc

INFORMATION LINES

- New York's "311" line (212-NEW-YORK outside New York City) is a general information line for all city agencies and related services. Operators will transfer calls to appropriate agency departments based on your specific needs.
- 411, 212-555-1212, 718-555-1212, are general information lines that can be used for city agencies and for locating either commercial businesses or home phone numbers of anyone or any business listed in the New York City telephone directories. There is a charge of $1.25 to dial 411, and $.80 for the other numbers.

LIBRARIES

See **Literary Life** in the **Cultural Life** chapter for descriptions of area libraries.
- **Bronx Reference Service**, 718-579-4257, www.nypl.org
- **Brooklyn Central Library**, 718-230-2100, www.brooklynpublic library.org
- **New York Public Library Reference Service**, 212-340-0849, www.nypl.org
- **New York Public Library**, Staten Island, 718-442-8562, www. nypl.org
- **Queens Public Library**, 718-990-0700, www.queenslibrary.org
- **Branch libraries**: see listings following **Neighborhood Profiles**.

MARRIAGE LICENSES

- **NYC Marriage License Bureau**, 212-669-2400, www.nycmarriage bureau.com

MOTOR VEHICLES/PARKING

- **American Automobile Association**, 212-586-1166, www. aaany.com
- **Automobile Dealer** (used) **Complaints**, 212-487-4444
- **Licenses and Registration Information**, New York State Department of Motor Vehicles, 212-645-5550, 7:30 a.m. to 4 p.m., www.nysdmv.com
- **NYC Department of Transportation**, 212-442-7090, 24-hour service; calls tow trucks for highway (not street) breakdowns
- **Parking Violations Hotline**, NYC Department of Transportation automated help line, 718-422-7800, www.nyc.gov
- **State Department of Motor Vehicles**, 212- 645-5550, www.nysd mv.com
- **New Jersey Motor Vehicle Commission**, 609-292-6500, www.state.nj.us/mvc
- **NYPD Towing** (towed cars), 212-971-0773; 7 a.m. to 10 p.m. daily

PARKS AND RECREATION

- General information, including special events, 888-NY-PARKS, www.nyparks.org
- See **Sports and Recreation** and **Greenspace and Beaches** chapters.

POLICE

See **Neighborhoods** chapter for precinct stations.

- **Police Emergencies** dial 911
- **New Jersey State Police**, 609-882-2000, www.njsp.org
- **New York State Police Troop**, NYC, 718-319-5100, State Police Headquarters, 518-457-6721

POST OFFICE

- **US Postal Service**, 800-275-8777, www.usps.com

SANITATION AND GARBAGE

- **NYC Department of Sanitation**, dial 311 or 212-NEW-YORK, www.nyc.gov

SENIORS

- **NYC Department for the Aging**, 212-442-1000, www.nyc.gov
- **New York Foundation for Senior Citizens**, 212-962-7559
- **Social Security and Medicare Eligibility Information**, 800-772-1213, www.ssa.gov

SPORTS

Participant Sports and Activities
- **New York City Parks and Recreation**, www.nyc.gov/parks
- **Brooklyn**, 718-965-8941
- **Bronx**, 718-430-1858
- **Manhattan**, 212-408-0205
- **Queens**, 718-520-5936
- **Staten Island**, 718-816-6172
- **Central Park Conservancy**, 212-360-3444, www.central parknyc.org
- **Gateway National Recreation Area**, 718-338-3799, www. nps.gov/gate

PROFESSIONAL
- **New Jersey Devils**, 800-NJ-DEVILS, www.newjerseydevils.com
- **New Jersey Nets**, 800-7NJ-NETS, www.njnets.com
- **New York Giants**, 201-935-8111, www.nygiants.org
- **New York Islanders**, 800-882-ISLES, www.newyorkislanders.com
- **New York Jets**, 516-560-8200, www.newyorkjets.com
- **New York Knicks**, 212-465-5867, 877-NYK-DUNK, www.nba. com/knicks
- **New York Liberty**, 212-465-6250, www.wnba.com/liberty
- **New York Mets**, 718-507-METS, www.mets.com
- **New York Rangers**, 212-465-6486, www.newyorkrangers.com
- **New York Yankees**, 718-293-6000, www.yankees.com
- **Sports Phone scores and schedules**, 212-976-1313

STREET MAINTENANCE

- **Potholes, NYC Bureau of Highways**, 311 or 212-NEW-YORK; after 4:30 p.m. and weekends, 212-442-7090
- **Streetlights**, NYC Bureau of Electrical Control, 212-669-8353
- **Water mains and sewers**, NYC Department of Environmental Protection, 311 or 212-NEW-YORK

TAXES

CITY
- **NYC Department of Finance**, 718-935-6000, www.nyc.gov

FEDERAL
- **Internal Revenue Service**, 800-829-4477, www.irs.gov

STATE
- **NYS Department of Taxation and Revenue**, 800-225-5829, TTY 800-634-2110, www.state.ny.us
- **New Jersey Division of Taxation: Taxpayer Customer Service Center**, 609-292-6400, www.state.nj.us/treasury/taxation

TELEPHONE

- **AT&T**, 800-222-0300, www.att.com
- **MCI**, 800-444-3333, www.mci.com
- **RCN**, 800-891-7770, www.rcn.com
- **Sprint**, 800-877-7746, www.sprint.com
- **Verizon**, 212-890-2550, www.verizon.com

TIME/TEMPERATURE

- 212-976-1616

TRANSPORTATION

- **AirTrain**, 877-535-2478, www.panynj.gov
- **FMCSA**, 888-368-7238, www.fmcsa.dot.gov
- **NJ State Department of Transportation**, 609-530-2000, www.nj.gov/transportation
- **NY State Department of Transportation**, 718-482-4594, 800-786-5368, www.dot.state.ny.us
- **Port Authority of New York & New Jersey**, 212-435-7000, 800-221-9903, www.panynj.gov
- **US Department of Transportation**, 212-264-8701, www.dot.gov

AIRPORTS
- **John F. Kennedy International**, 718-244-4444, parking information, 718-244-4168, www.panynj.gov

- **LaGuardia International Airport**, 718-533-3400, parking information, 718-533-3850, www.panynj.gov
- **Newark Liberty International Airport**, 973-961-6000, parking information, 973-961-4751, www.newarkairport.com
- **Port Authority of New York & New Jersey**, 212-435-7000, 800-221-9903, www.panynj.gov

BUSES
- **Port Authority Bus Terminal Information**, 212-564-8484, 800-221-9903, www.panynj.gov
- **Greyhound Bus Lines**, 800-231-2222, www.greyhound.com
- **Peter Pan Trailways**, 800-343-9999, www.peterpanbus.com

FERRIES
- **NY Water Taxi**, 212-742-1969, www.nywatertaxi.com
- **New York Waterway**, 800-53-FERRY, www.nywaterway.com
- **Seastreak**, 800-BOAT-RIDE, www.seastreak.com
- **Staten Island Ferry**, 212-NEW-YORK, www.statenislandferry.com

RAIL
- **Amtrak** (Penn Station), 800-872-7245, www.amtrak.com
- **Long Island Railroad** (Penn Station), 718-217-5477, TTY 718-558-3022, www.mta.info
- **Metro-North** (Grand Central), 212-532-4900, TTY 800-724-3322, www.mta.info
- **New Jersey Transit** (Penn Station), 973-762-5100, 800-772-2222, www.njtransit.com
- **Staten Island Rapid Transit**, 718-966-7478, www.mta.info

SUBWAYS AND CITY BUSES
- **Lost and Found** (NYC Transit Authority), 212-712-4500, www.mta.info
- **MTA Customer Service**, 718-330-3322, www.mta.info
- **Metro Card**, 212-METRO-CARD
- **PATH service to New Jersey**, 800-234-7284, www.panynj.gov
- **Queens Surface Corp.**, 718-445-3100, www.qsbus.com.
- **Subway and Bus Schedules** (NYC Transit Authority automated system for fares, routes, schedules), 718-330-1234, www.mta.info

TAXIS, LIMOUSINES
- **Taxi and Limousine Commission**, 212-NYC-TAXI, www.nyc.gov/html/tlc/home.html

TOURISM AND TRAVEL

- **National Park Service**, www.nps.gov
- **New York & Company** (The Convention and Visitors Bureau), 212-397-8200, www.nycvisit.com
- **New York State Travel Information Center**, 800-CALL-NYS, www.iloveny.com
- **New Jersey Department of Travel & Tourism**, 800-537-7397, www.visitnj.org
- **New York Passport Agency**, Automated Appointment Number, 212-206-3500, www.travel.state.gov

UTILITY EMERGENCIES

- **Electrical emergencies or gas leaks**, Con Edison, 800-752-6633, www.conedison.com
- **Gas** or **Electric service shutoff hotline**, 800-342-3355

ZIP CODE INFORMATION

- **USPS zip codes request**, 800-275-8777, www.usps.com

MANHATTAN ZIP CODES

INDEX

We would appreciate your comments regarding this twentieth edition of the *Newcomer's Handbook® for Moving To and Living In New York City.* If you've found any mistakes or omissions or if you would just like to express your opinion about the guide, please let us know. We will consider any suggestions for possible inclusion in our next edition, and if we use your comments, we'll send you a *free* copy of our next edition. Please send this response form to:

Reader Response Department
First Books
6750 SW Franklin, Suite A
Portland, OR 97223-2542
USA

Comments:

_____

_____

_____

_____

_____

_____

Name: _____

Address _____

_____

_____

Telephone ( )_____

E-mail _____

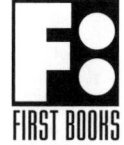

6750 SW Franklin, Suite A
Portland, OR 97223-2542
USA
503-968-6777
www.firstbooks.com

FIRST BOOKS

403

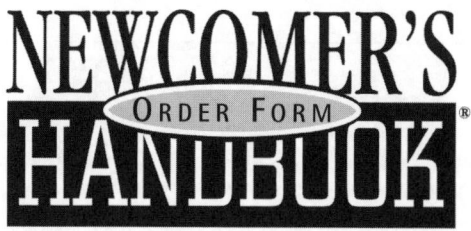

THE ORIGINAL, ALWAYS UPDATED, ABSOLUTELY INVALUABLE GUIDES FOR PEOPLE MOVING TO A CITY!

Find out about neighborhoods, apartment and house hunting, money matters, deposits/leases, getting settled, helpful services, shopping for the home, places of worship, cultural life, sports/recreation, volunteering, green space, schools and education, transportation, temporary lodgings and useful telephone numbers!

	# COPIES	TOTAL
Newcomer's Handbook· for Atlanta	_____ x $17.95	$_____
Newcomer's Handbook· for Boston	_____ x $23.95	$_____
Newcomer's Handbook· for Chicago	_____ x $21.95	$_____
Newcomer's Handbook· for London	_____ x $20.95	$_____
Newcomer's Handbook· for Los Angeles	_____ x $21.95	$_____
Newcomer's Handbook· for Minneapolis-St. Paul	_____ x $20.95	$_____
Newcomer's Handbook· for New York City	_____ x $22.95	$_____
Newcomer's Handbook· for San Francisco	_____ x $20.95	$_____
Newcomer's Handbook· for Seattle	_____ x $21.95	$_____
Newcomer's Handbook· for the USA	_____ x $23.95	$_____
Newcomer's Handbook· for Washington D.C.	_____ x $21.95	$_____
	SUBTOTAL	$_____
POSTAGE & HANDLING (*$7.00 first book, $1.00 each add'l.*)		$_____
	TOTAL	$_____

SHIP TO:

Name _____

Title _____

Company _____

Address _____

City _____ State_____ Zip _____

Phone Number (_____) _____

E-mail _____

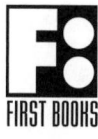

Send this order form and a check or money order payable to:
First Books
6750 SW Franklin, Suite A, Portland, OR 97223-2542

Allow 1-2 weeks for delivery

405

NYC SUBWAY MAP

Local Service Only

All Trains Stop
(local and express service)

Route Terminal

Free Subway Transfer

Normal service

Rush hour service

FLUSHING

Flushing Main St

CORONA

82 St-Jackson Heights

74 St-Broadway

111 St

Willets Point Shea Stadium

103 St Corona Plaza Junction Blvd 90 St-Elmhurst Av

FRESH MEADOWS

JAMAICA ESTATES

Jamaica 179 St

169 St

KEW GARDENS HILLS

HILLCREST

Parsons Blvd

Sutphin Blvd

Elmhurst Av

Woodhaven Blvd

67 Av

75 Av

Kew Gardens Union Tpk

Jamaica Center ParsonsArcher

Grand Av Newtown

63 Dr Rego Park

Forest Hills

KEW GARDENS

Jamaica Van Wyck

Sutphin Blvd Archer Av

FOREST HILLS

RICHMOND HILL

121 St

QUEENS

MIDDLE VILLAGE

111 St

104 St

Ozone Park Lefferts Blvd

Middle Village Metropolitan Av

Woodhaven Blvd

WOODHAVEN

111 St

GLENDALE

MASPETH

Fresh Pond Rd

Forest Av

85 St/Forest Pkwy

104 St

RIDGEWOOD

Myrtle Av

75 St

Rockaway Blvd

88 St

Morgan Av

DeKalb

Seneca Av

Cypress Hills

80 St

OZONE PARK

Jefferson St

Wyckoff Av

Halsey St

Crescent St

Norwood

Grant Av

Kinckerbocker Av

BUSHWICK

Wilson

Cleveland St

Aqueduct Racetrack

J.F.K. INT'L AIRPORT

Central Av

Gates

Bushwick Av Aberdeen St

Broadway Eastern Pkwy

Euclid Av

Shepherd Av

Aqueduct North Conduit Av

Flushing Av

Halsey

Alabama Av

Myrtle Av

Kosciusko St

Chauncey St

Broadway East New York

Liberty

Van Siclen Av

New Lots Av

HOWARD BEACH

Howard Beach JFK Airport

Myrtle-Willoughby Av

Ralph Av

Atlantic Av

Sutter Av

Van Siclen Av

BEDFORD-STUYVESANT

Rockaway Av

Pennsylvania Av

Bedford-Nostrand

Junius St

Livonia Av

Far Rockaway Mott Av

Classon Av

Nostrand Av

Saratoga Av

New Lots Av

Beach 25 St

Clinton-Washington

Kingston-Throop Av

Crown Heights Utica Av

East 105 St

Beach 36 St

Beach 44 St

Lafayette

CROWN HEIGHTS

Utica Av

Sutter Av-Rutland Rd

Broad Channel

Beach 60 St

Park Pl

Kingston Av

Canarsie Rockaway Pkwy

Beach 67 St

7 Av

Eastern Pkwy

Nostrand Av Franklin Av President St Sterling St

EAST FLATBUSH

CANARSIE

PARK SLOPE

Grand Army Plaza

Prospect Park

Winthrop St

BROOKLYN

Beach 90 St

7 Av

15 St Prospect Park

Church Av Beverly Rd Newkirk Av

Beach 98 St

Parkside Av

Beach 105 St

Ft Hamilton Pkwy

Church Av

Brooklyn College Flatbush Av

FLATLANDS

Rockaway Park Beach 116 St

Beverly Rd Cortelyou Rd Newkirk Av Avenue H

9 Av

Church Av

MIDWOOD

Ditmas Av 18 Av Avenue I

Avenue J

ROCKAWAY PARK

50 St

Avenue M

55 St

New Utrecht Av

Bay Pkwy

Kings Hwy

18 Av 20 Av

Avenue N

62 St

Avenue P

Avenue U

SHEEPSHEAD BAY

Ft Hamilton Pkwy

71 St

Bay Pkwy

Kings Hwy

Neck Rd

Sheepshead Bay

BRIGHTON BEACH

BAY RIDGE

79 St

BENSONHURST

20 Av

Avenue U

Avenue

Brighton Beach

18 Av

Bay Pkwy

25 Av

86 St

Ocean Pkwy

Bay 50 St

Neptune Av

Coney Island Stillwell Av

West 8 St NY Aquarium

CONEY ISLAND

407

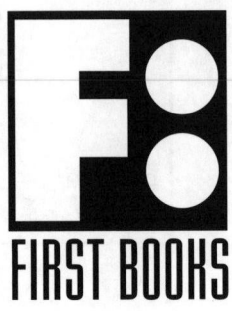

FIRST BOOKS

Visit our web site at

www.firstbooks.com

for a sample of all our books.